Luke Robinson

CCEA AS

PURE MATHEMATICS

2nd Edition

COLOURPOINT
EDUCATIONAL

© Luke Robinson and
Colourpoint Creative Ltd 2020

Second Edition
Third Impression 2023

ISBN: 978-1-78073-246-6

Layout and design: April Sky Design
Printed by: GPS Colour Graphics Ltd, Belfast

**COLOURPOINT
EDUCATIONAL**

Colourpoint Educational
An imprint of Colourpoint Creative Ltd
Colourpoint House
Jubilee Business Park
21 Jubilee Road
Newtownards
County Down
Northern Ireland
BT23 4YH

Tel: 028 9182 6339
E-mail: sales@colourpoint.co.uk
Web site: www.colourpointeducational.com

The Author
Luke Robinson took a mathematics degree, followed by
an MSc and PhD in meteorology. He taught at Northwood
College in London before becoming a freelance mathematics
tutor and writer. He now lives in County Down with his wife
and son.

Note: This book has been written to meet the AS
Mathematics specification from CCEA. While the
authors and Colourpoint Creative Limited have taken
all reasonable care in the preparation of this book, it is
the responsibility of each candidate to satisfy themselves
that they have covered all necessary material before
sitting an examination or attempting coursework based
on the CCEA specification. The publishers will therefore
accept no legal responsibility or liability for any errors or
omissions from this book or the consequences thereof.

Contents

Introduction

Why Study Mathematics?

Mathematics is all around us. It helps us to understand a complex and ever-changing world. It helps us to think analytically and, in turn with analytical thinking, we can investigate and know the truth about the world.

Many jobs require a high level of mathematical competence, such as engineering and various roles in the world of finance, statistics and computing. There are even data scientists who extract meaning from huge sets of data on population behaviour, such as voting patterns or internet usage. Even if you don't enter one of these fields of work, you will very likely use your AS and A2 Mathematics skills in your further studies and in your chosen career. Mathematics crops up in many surprising areas!

CCEA's AS and A2 Level Mathematics specifications are designed to prepare you for the mathematical content you will find in a wide range of different degree courses and occupations. Good luck!

Changes to the Specification

This book covers the revised specification for Unit AS 1: Pure Mathematics for CCEA, which was available for teaching from September 2018 onwards.

The following changes from the previous specification are worth paying particular attention to.

Problem solving

The new specification has a greater emphasis on **problem solving** and the final chapter of this book (Chapter 14: Problem Solving) has been included to address this. This chapter includes material explaining what a problem solving task will look like, as well as examples and an exercise of practice questions.

Problem solving questions may require techniques from any of the preceding chapters, and often more than one. They may also require understanding of the mathematics taught at GCSE level.

Straight line graphs in context

The new specification includes questions on straight line graphs set in context. In all questions set in a context, answers to problems should be expressed in terms of the context of the question. For more details see section 6.5 of Chapter 5: Straight Lines.

Proofs

Fewer proofs are required at AS Level in the new specification. The complete list of proofs required for AS Pure Mathematics is as follows.

- Addition law for logarithms:
  $\log_a x + \log_a y = \log_a(xy)$

- Subtraction law for logarithms:
  $\log_a x - \log_a y = \log_a\left(\dfrac{x}{y}\right)$

- Power law for logarithms:
  $n \log_a x = \log_a x^n$

These three proofs are detailed in Chapter 10: Exponentials and Logarithms.

Calculators

Calculators with new features, such as the Casio FX-991EX, are now available. These new features include:

- A quadratic and cubic equation solver.
- Evaluation of definite integrals.
- Evaluation of summations.

All of the functions on these calculators can be used in the AS and A2 examinations, but pay attention to the exact wording of the question. For example, if a question asks you to "show all the steps in your working", or states that "solutions relying on calculator technology will not be accepted", or "using algebra", then you will lose marks if you rely entirely on the calculator for a calculation. In these circumstances, you can still use any of these new features on your calculator to check your answer.

Calculator tips are given throughout this book.

Chapter 1
Indices and Surds

1.1 Introduction

Key words

- **Index (plural indices)**: A power, for example the power 3 in 5^3.
- **Index form**: A number or algebraic expression written using an index, for example 5^3 or x^2.
- **Surd**: A root (for example a square root or a cube root) of a number is called a surd if its value is an irrational number.

Before you start

You should know:

- How to recognise some common squares and cubes, e.g.
  $4^2 = 4 \times 4 = 16$
  $2^3 = 2 \times 2 \times 2 = 8$
- How to evaluate powers of 2, e.g.
  $2^5 = 2 \times 2 \times 2 \times 2 \times 2 = 32$
- How to use the difference of two squares:
  $a^2 - b^2 = (a - b)(a + b)$
- How to recognise rational and irrational numbers. Rational numbers are either integers, numbers with terminating decimals or recurring decimals. A rational number can be written as a fraction, with integers in both the numerator and denominator; irrational numbers cannot. Some examples are:
  Rational: $\frac{1}{2}$, $1.\dot{6}$, 3, -8, 2.888
  Irrational: π, 5π, $\sqrt{2}$, $\sqrt[3]{3}$, $\dfrac{5}{\sqrt{10}}$

Exercise 1A (Revision)

1. Evaluate:
   (a) The squares of 4, 12, 15 and 20
   (b) 3^3, 5^3, 10^3
   (c) $\sqrt{81}$, $\sqrt{6^2 + 8^2}$, $\sqrt{1.44}$, $\sqrt{169}$, $\left(\sqrt{17.2}\right)^2$
   (d) The cube roots of 64 and 8
   (e) 2^n where $n = 2, 3, 6, 9$

Exercise 1A...

2. Use the difference of two squares to rewrite the following:
   (a) $x^2 - 9$ (b) $a^2 - b^2$
   (c) $1 - c^2$ (d) $(d + 10)(d - 10)$
   (e) $e^2 f^2 - (gh)^2$

3. Are these numbers rational or irrational?
   (a) 1.15 (b) $1 + \pi$
   (c) $0.\dot{2}\dot{6}$ (d) $\sqrt{3} - 10$

What you will learn

In this chapter you will learn:

- How to understand and use **index notation**.
- More about using the **laws of indices**.

This chapter provides the basis for a lot of the pure mathematics used in AS and A2 Mathematics. You will use indices a lot in the chapters on differentiation and integration. You will learn how to simplify expressions and solve equations using the rules of indices (powers). Some of this section will be revision of the work you did at GCSE.

1.2 Index Notation

5^3 ('5 cubed') and 7^2 ('7 squared') are examples of numbers in index form.

The power 2 in 7^2 and the power 3 in 5^3 are known as **indices**. Indices are useful – for example, they allow us to represent numbers in standard form – and have a number of important properties. As a reminder:

$7^1 = 7$
$7^2 = 7 \times 7$
$7^3 = 7 \times 7 \times 7$ and so on.

Note: If you are asked to evaluate an expression, you should give your final answer as a number, e.g. 32 or $\dfrac{1}{5}$.

If you are asked to give an answer in index form, you will give an answer such as 2^5 or x^{-7}.

Exercise 1B

1. Evaluate:
   (a) 2^5 (b) 3^4 (c) 4^3

   (d) 14^2 (e) $2^3 + 3^2$ (f) $3^4 + 4^3$

   (g) $6^2 + 5^2$ (h) $(3^2)^2$ (i) $\left(\frac{2}{3}\right)^3$

   (j) $(0.2)^2$

2. Write the following in index form. There may be more than one way.
   (a) 49   (b) 100   (c) 0.01

   (d) 121   (e) 0.001   (f) $\frac{9}{49}$

   (g) 0.09   (h) $\frac{1}{100000}$ (i) 0.16

In the real world...

The population of the world is roughly 7.6 billion or 7 600 000 000 people. Doesn't it look much easier and neater to write 7.6×10^9?

How much storage space is on your USB pen drive? 16 GB is 1.6×10^{10} bytes.

1.3   The Laws of Indices

There are several rules for dividing and multiplying numbers written in index form. These properties only hold, however, when the same base is being used. For example, we cannot easily work out what $2^3 \times 5^2$ would be, but we can simplify $3^2 \times 3^3$.

Multiplication

When we multiply numbers with indices, we add the powers. So for example:

$z^a \times z^b = z^{a+b}$

Remember, this doesn't work if the base changes. For example, we cannot simplify:

$z^a \times w^b$

There is no easy way of simplifying:

$7^5 \times 2^{-3}$

because 7 and 2 are different bases. This is true for all our laws of indices.

Worked Example

1. Simplify:
   (a) $x^2 \times x^6$ (b) $5^5 \times 5^{-2}$ (c) $2y^2 \times 4y^5$

   (a) $x^2 \times x^6 = x^8$
   (b) $5^5 \times 5^{-2} = 5^3$ (because $5 + (-2) = 3$)
   (c) $2y^2 \times 4y^5$
   $= 2 \times 4 \times y^2 \times y^5$
   $= 8y^7$ (adding the powers of y)

Division

If we divide two numbers with indices, we subtract the powers. So for example:

$p^a \div p^b = p^{a-b}$

Worked Example

2. Simplify:
   (a) $\dfrac{r^2}{r^3}$ (b) $t^2 \div t^3$

   (c) $6^2 \div 6^{-5}$ (d) $6z^6 \div 2z^2$

   (a) $\dfrac{r^2}{r^3} = r^{-1}$
   (b) $t^2 \div t^3 = t^{-1}$
   (c) $6^2 \div 6^{-5} = 6^7$
   (d) $6z^6 \div 2z^2$
   $= (6 \div 2) \times (z^6 \div z^2)$
   $= 3z^4$

Brackets

If we have a number with an index, all raised to another power, this is the only time we multiply our indices:

$(x^a)^b = x^{ab}$

Worked Example

3. Simplify:
   (a) $(x^2)^3$ (b) $(5^3)^2$
   (c) $9^3 \times 3^4$ (d) $(3p^2)^3 \div p^4$

   (a) $(x^2)^3 = x^6$
   (b) $(5^3)^2 = 5^6$
   (c) As noted above, you cannot simplify an expression involving indices if the bases are different. However, sometimes it is possible to make the bases the same:
   $9^3 \times 3^4 = (3^2)^3 \times 3^4$
   $= 3^6 \times 3^4$
   $= 3^{10}$
   (d) $(3p^2)^3 \div p^4$
   $= 27p^6 \div p^4$
   $= 27p^2$

Exercise 1C

1. Simplify these expressions:
   (a) $x^2 \times x^4$ (b) $2x^2 \times 4x^{-3}$
   (c) $6p^3 \div 2p^2$ (d) $6r^3 \times 2r^{-2}$
   (e) $8s^3 \div 2s^{-2}$ (f) $(3a^3)^3 \div a^4$
   (g) $(3b^3)^2 \div b^2$ (h) $6c^3 \times 2c^2 \times c$
   (i) $6r^3 \times 2r^2 \div r^2$ (j) $(4d^3)^3 \div 2d^4$

Negative indices
A negative index denotes a **reciprocal**.

Worked Example
4. Simplify:

   (a) n^{-1} (b) n^{-a} (c) 3^{-2} (d) $\left(\dfrac{1}{2}\right)^{-3}$

   (a) $n^{-1} = \dfrac{1}{n}$

   (b) $n^{-a} = \dfrac{1}{n^a}$

   (c) $3^{-2} = \dfrac{1}{3^2} = \dfrac{1}{9}$

   (d) $\left(\dfrac{1}{2}\right)^{-3} = 2^3 = 8$

   (Remember: the reciprocal of $\dfrac{1}{2}$ is 2)

Note: A negative power does not make your answer negative!
$2^{-1} = \dfrac{1}{2}$, not $-\dfrac{1}{2}$

The power of zero
Anything to the power 0 is equal to 1. The table below may help you see why this is true. Looking at the sequence of numbers in the second row, try to fill in the missing number.

3^{-1}	3^0	3^1	3^2	3^3
$\dfrac{1}{3}$		3	9	27

Worked Example
5. Simplify:

   (a) 4^0 (b) $(-124)^0$ (c) x^0

   (a) $4^0 = 1$
   (b) $(-124)^0 = 1$
   (c) $x^0 = 1$

Fractional indices
If the index is a fraction, we must take a root of the number. For example, $4^{\frac{1}{2}}$ means take the square root of 4. Similarly, an index of ⅓ means take the cube root.

Usually we consider the square root sign $\sqrt{}$ and the power of ½ both to mean the positive square root.

Worked Example
6. Evaluate:

   (a) $\left(\dfrac{9}{64}\right)^{\frac{1}{2}}$ (b) $8^{\frac{1}{3}}$

   (c) $8^{-\frac{1}{3}}$ (d) $\left(\dfrac{1}{8}\right)^{-\frac{1}{3}}$

   (a) $\left(\dfrac{9}{64}\right)^{\frac{1}{2}} = \sqrt{\dfrac{9}{64}} = \dfrac{\sqrt{9}}{\sqrt{64}} = \dfrac{3}{8}$

   (b) $8^{\frac{1}{3}} = \sqrt[3]{8} = 2$ (the cube root of 8)

   (c) $8^{-\frac{1}{3}} = \left(\dfrac{1}{8}\right)^{\frac{1}{3}} = \dfrac{1}{2}$ (the cube root of $\dfrac{1}{8}$)

   (d) $\left(\dfrac{1}{8}\right)^{-\frac{1}{3}} = 8^{\frac{1}{3}}$ (take the reciprocal of the fraction while making the index positive) $= 2$

More complicated fractional indices
Sometimes the index is a more complicated fraction. For example, if it is ⅔ we must take the cube root of the number, then raise it to the power 2. For example, $8^{\frac{2}{3}}$ means take the cube root of 8, which is 2, then square it, which gives 4.

Note: The operations can be reversed: you can square first and then perform the cube root. However, performing the cube root first is often easier when working without a calculator.

In general:

$$a^{p/q} = \left(\sqrt[q]{a}\right)^p = \sqrt[q]{a^p}$$

You may be asked to write an index expression using surd notation. We will study surds in more detail in the next section.

Worked Examples

7. Rewrite using surd notation:

    (a) $a^{2/3}$ (b) $a^{5/2}$ (c) $2^{2/3}$

    (a) $a^{2/3} = \left(\sqrt[3]{a}\right)^2$

    (b) $a^{5/2} = \left(\sqrt{a}\right)^5$

    (c) $2^{2/3} = \left(\sqrt[3]{2}\right)^2$

8. Evaluate $8^{2/3}$

    Using the result from example 7(a):

    $8^{2/3} = \left(\sqrt[3]{8}\right)^2 = (2)^2 = 4$

9. Simplify $\dfrac{4x^{3/2}}{8x}$

    Cancel down the fraction ⁴⁄₈ and subtract the indices.

    $\dfrac{4x^{3/2}}{8x} = \dfrac{1}{2}x^{1/2}$

Exercise 1D

1. Evaluate the following:

    (a) $25^{1/2}$ (b) $8^{4/3}$ (c) $16^{-3/2}$

    (d) $16^{5/4}$ (e) $27^{-4/3}$ (f) 5^{-2}

    (g) $4^{-2} \times 4^{-3}$ (h) 64^0 (i) $\left(\dfrac{1}{16}\right)^{1/2}$

    (j) $\left(\dfrac{1}{64}\right)^{-1/2}$ (k) $64^{2/3}$ (l) $\left(1\dfrac{9}{16}\right)^{3/2}$

    (m) $(-4)^{-3}$

2. Simplify these expressions:

    (a) $g^{-3} \times g^{-3}$ (b) $\dfrac{1}{t^{-2}}$

    (c) $(q^3)^0$ (d) $(f^{3/2})^2$

    (e) $(b^{1/a})^a$ (f) $\dfrac{4x^{6/5}}{20x}$

    (g) $24x^{1\frac{1}{4}} \div 3x^{1/4}$ (h) $10x^{5/2} \div 5x$

    (i) $\dfrac{18x^{4/3}}{3x} \div \dfrac{45x^{4/3}}{5x}$ (j) $10x^{5/2} \times (4x^{3/4})^2$

    (k) $30x^{5/4} \times 3x$ (l) $(4x)^{5/2} \div 4x$

    (m) $-7x^{3/2} \div 14x^{5/2}$ (n) $(27x^2)^{2/3} \div 3x$

Solving equations

You may be asked to solve equations in which the unknown is in one or more of the indices.

Attempt to make the bases the same on both sides of the equation. Then you will use the fact that:

    If $a^b = a^c$

    then $b = c$

This is called equating the indices.

Worked Examples

10. Solve for y: $8^y = 64^4$

    $8^y = (8^2)^4$
    $8^y = 8^8$

    When the bases are the same, equate the indices:

    $y = 8$

11. Solve for x: $\dfrac{6^x}{36^{x-2}} = \sqrt{6}$

    $6^x = (\sqrt{6})(36^{x-2})$

    $6^x = (6^{1/2})(6^2)^{x-2}$

    $6^x = (6^{1/2})6^{2x-4}$

    $6^x = 6^{2x-7/2}$

    Equating indices:

    $x = 2x - 7/2$

    $x = 7/2$

Exercise 1E

1. Solve for the variable in the equation:

    (a) $\sqrt{2} = \dfrac{2^g}{4^2}$ (b) $\sqrt{3} \times 3^t = 9^4$

    (c) $\dfrac{\sqrt{3}}{3^{5f+2}} = 3^{-1/4}$ (d) $2^y = 4^5 \times \sqrt{2}$

    (e) $3^k = \dfrac{3^{2k+6}}{\sqrt{3}}$ (f) $\dfrac{\sqrt{2}}{4^2} = 2^d$

    (g) $\left(\sqrt{2}\right)^w = \dfrac{2^w}{4^3}$ (h) $\sqrt{3} = \dfrac{3^{4q+3}}{9^5}$

    (i) $\dfrac{4^2}{2^z} = \sqrt{2}$ (j) $4^3 \times 2^{6g+6} = 2^g$

1.4 Surds

Introduction

A root (for example a square root or a cube root) of a number is called a **surd** if its value is an irrational number.

Some examples of surds are $\sqrt{2}$, $\sqrt{3}$, $\sqrt{5}$, $\sqrt[3]{2}$, and $\sqrt[3]{3}$.

However, there are many roots that are **not surds**:

$\sqrt[3]{27}$ (this is equal to 3, which is a rational number)

$\sqrt{4}$ (this equals 2)

$\sqrt{\dfrac{9}{4}}$ (this equals $\dfrac{3}{2}$, which is rational)

Surds are often left in the solutions to equations, for example:

$$x = 1 + \sqrt{3} \qquad \text{or} \qquad z = \frac{\sqrt[3]{2}}{2}$$

In this way we can give more accurate answers to some problems. You will often use surds when you need to give an exact answer to a problem. For example, they are often used when solving quadratic equations.

Worked Example

12. What is the length of the diagonal of a square whose sides are 1 cm? Give your answer in surd form.

Using Pythagoras' Theorem:

$$x = \sqrt{1^2 + 1^2} = \sqrt{2} \text{ cm}$$

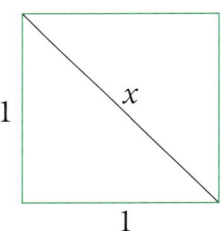

In the real world...

One very famous use of surds is in the Golden Ratio. The Golden Ratio appears frequently in art and nature, as well as in mathematics and science. It is sometimes given the Greek letter Φ and has the equation:

$$\Phi = \frac{1 + \sqrt{5}}{2} \approx 1.61$$

When it is used in art and architecture, the Golden Ratio is said to give the most beautiful results. The Acropolis in Greece was built over 2000 years ago. Some studies of this ancient building suggest that the Golden Ratio was used throughout, for example the width divided by the height of the front façade.

We also see the Golden Ratio in flower petals, pine cones, cauliflower florets, snails' shells, weather systems, etc.

Among mathematicians of the ancient world, the square root of 5 was controversial. It is an irrational number, so whenever you give its value to say 2 decimal places or 3 significant figures, you have introduced an error. Many mathematicians of the ancient world refused to believe irrational numbers even existed. We now know it is often best to leave an answer in surd form, e.g. $1 + \sqrt{5}$. This way it is exact, without any rounding error.

Use and manipulation of surds

In this section you will learn how to use and manipulate surds. There are some important rules when manipulating surds:

Rule 1: $\sqrt{a \times b} = \sqrt{a}\sqrt{b}$

Rule 2: $\sqrt{a} \times \sqrt{a} = a$

Rule 3: $\sqrt{\dfrac{a}{b}} = \dfrac{\sqrt{a}}{\sqrt{b}}$

Rule 4: $a\sqrt{b} \pm c\sqrt{b} = (a \pm c)\sqrt{b}$

Worked Example

13. Simplify the following expressions involving surds.

(a) $\sqrt{98}$ (b) $\sqrt{\dfrac{121}{100}}$ (c) $\sqrt{48} + \sqrt{108}$

(d) $\sqrt{30}$ (e) $\sqrt{5} \times \sqrt{5}$

(a) When simplifying a surd $\sqrt{a}$, find the biggest square number that is a factor of a. Then use Rule 1. In this case 49 is the biggest square number that is a factor of 98. So:

$$\sqrt{98} = \sqrt{49}\sqrt{2}$$
$$= 7\sqrt{2}$$

(b) Using Rule 3:

$$\sqrt{\frac{121}{100}} = \frac{\sqrt{121}}{\sqrt{100}}$$
$$= \frac{11}{10}$$

(c) Using Rule 1 for both surds:

$$\sqrt{48} + \sqrt{108} = \sqrt{16}\sqrt{3} + \sqrt{36}\sqrt{3}$$
$$= 4\sqrt{3} + 6\sqrt{3}$$
$$= 10\sqrt{3} \text{ (using Rule 4)}$$

(d) $\sqrt{30}$ – we leave this unchanged because there are

no square numbers that are factors of 30.

(e) Using Rule 2:

$$\sqrt{5} \times \sqrt{5} = 5$$

At the beginning of this chapter you revised the difference of two squares:

$$a^2 - b^2 = (a - b)(a + b)$$

This can be applied to some surd problems.

Worked Example

14. Simplify: $\left(7 - \sqrt{5}\right)\left(7 + \sqrt{5}\right)$

This is an expression of the form $(a - b)(a + b)$.

We can use the difference of two squares:

$$(a - b)(a + b) = a^2 - b^2$$

$$\left(7 - \sqrt{5}\right)\left(7 + \sqrt{5}\right) = 7^2 - \left(\sqrt{5}\right)^2$$

$$= 49 - 5$$

$$= 44$$

$7 + \sqrt{5}$ and $7 - \sqrt{5}$ are known as conjugate surds.

Rationalising the denominator

Usually, we do not leave a surd in the denominator of a fraction. For example, we would **not** give the answer to a question like this:

$$y = \frac{1}{\sqrt{3}}$$

or this:

$$x = \frac{4}{\sqrt{5} + 2}$$

Instead, we must multiply both numerator and denominator by something to make the surd appear only in the numerator.

Method 1: If the denominator is a simple surd, multiply top and bottom by this surd.

Method 2: If the denominator is of the form $a \pm \sqrt{b}$, multiply the top and bottom by the denominator's conjugate surd.

Worked Examples

15. Rationalise the denominator and simplify: $\frac{6}{\sqrt{3}}$

$$\frac{6}{\sqrt{3}} = \frac{6 \times \sqrt{3}}{\sqrt{3} \times \sqrt{3}}$$

$$= \frac{6\sqrt{3}}{3}$$

$$= 2\sqrt{3}$$

16. Simplify: $\frac{4 - \sqrt{5}}{\sqrt{5} - 2}$

giving your answer in the form $a\sqrt{5} + b$, where a and b are integers.

$$\frac{4 - \sqrt{5}}{\sqrt{5} - 2} = \frac{\left(4 - \sqrt{5}\right)\left(\sqrt{5} + 2\right)}{\left(\sqrt{5} - 2\right)\left(\sqrt{5} + 2\right)}$$

$$= \frac{4\sqrt{5} - 5 + 8 - 2\sqrt{5}}{5 - 2\sqrt{5} + 2\sqrt{5} - 4}$$

$$= \frac{2\sqrt{5} + 3}{1}$$

$$= 2\sqrt{5} + 3$$

Exercise 1F

1. Simplify:

   (a) $\sqrt{32}$

   (b) $\frac{\sqrt{27}}{3}$

   (c) $\sqrt{44} \div \sqrt{11}$

   (d) $\sqrt{1\frac{21}{100}}$

2. Express $\sqrt{450}$ in the form $a\sqrt{2}$ where a is an integer.

3. Express $\sqrt{180}$ in the form $a\sqrt{5}$ where a is an integer.

4. Express $\left(5 - \sqrt{2}\right)^2$ in the form $b + c\sqrt{2}$ where b and c are integers.

5. Express $\left(6 - \sqrt{5}\right)^2$ in the form $b + c\sqrt{5}$ where b and c are integers.

6. Express $\sqrt{18}$ in the form $a\sqrt{2}$ where a is an integer.

7. Express $\sqrt{245}$ in the form $a\sqrt{5}$ where a is an integer.

8. Express $\frac{3\left(2 + \sqrt{2}\right)}{2 - \sqrt{2}}$ in the form $b + c\sqrt{2}$ where b and c are integers.

Exercise 1F...

9. Express $\dfrac{2(3 + \sqrt{5})}{3 - \sqrt{5}}$ in the form $b + c\sqrt{5}$ where b and c are integers.

10. Rationalise the denominator and simplify:

    (a) $\dfrac{1}{\sqrt{5}}$ (b) $\dfrac{\sqrt{3}}{\sqrt{15}}$ (c) $\dfrac{1 + \sqrt{5}}{\sqrt{7}}$

11. Giving your answers in the form $a + b\sqrt{2}$, where a and b are rational numbers, find:

    (a) $\left(6 - \sqrt{8}\right)^2$ (b) $\left(1 + \sqrt{8}\right)^2$

    (c) $\dfrac{1}{5 - \sqrt{8}}$ (d) $\dfrac{1}{3 + \sqrt{8}}$

12. Giving your answers in the form $a + b\sqrt{3}$ where a and b are rational numbers, find:

    (a) $\left(7 - \sqrt{27}\right)^2$ (b) $\dfrac{1}{6 - \sqrt{27}}$

13. Expand and simplify:

    (a) $\left(4 + \sqrt{2}\right)\left(4 - \sqrt{2}\right)$

    (b) $\left(7 + \sqrt{2}\right)\left(7 - \sqrt{2}\right)$

    (c) $\left(4 + \sqrt{3}\right)\left(4 - \sqrt{3}\right)$

    (d) $\left(6 + \sqrt{3}\right)\left(6 - \sqrt{3}\right)$

14. Express in the form $a + b\sqrt{c}$ where a, b and c are integers.

    (a) $\dfrac{6}{3 + \sqrt{6}}$ (b) $\dfrac{20}{3 + \sqrt{5}}$

    (c) $\dfrac{24}{4 + \sqrt{8}}$ (d) $\dfrac{28}{2 + \sqrt{2}}$

15. Simplify:

    (a) $\sqrt{20} + \sqrt{80}$ (b) $\sqrt{12} + 3\sqrt{48}$

    (c) $\dfrac{\sqrt{125} + \sqrt{45}}{\sqrt{125} - \sqrt{45}}$ (d) $\dfrac{\sqrt{3} - \sqrt{7}}{\sqrt{3} + \sqrt{7}}$

1.5 Summary

The laws of indices are:

Rule 1 $a^p \times a^q = a^{p+q}$

Rule 2 $a^p \div a^q = a^{p-q}$

Rule 3 $(a^p)^q = a^{pq}$

Rule 4 $a^0 = 1$

Rule 5 $a^{-p} = \dfrac{1}{a^p}$

Rule 6 $a^{\frac{1}{p}} = \sqrt[p]{a}$

Rule 7 $a^{\frac{p}{q}} = \sqrt[q]{a^p} = \left(\sqrt[q]{a}\right)^p$

You can use the following rules to manipulate surds:

Rule 1 $\sqrt{a \times b} = \sqrt{a}\sqrt{b}$

Rule 2 $\sqrt{a} \times \sqrt{a} = a$

Rule 3 $\sqrt{\dfrac{a}{b}} = \dfrac{\sqrt{a}}{\sqrt{b}}$

Rule 4 $a\sqrt{b} \pm c\sqrt{b} = (a \pm c)\sqrt{b}$

If there is a surd in the denominator of a fraction, you can **rationalise the denominator** by multiplying top and bottom by a surd expression:

Method 1: If the denominator is a simple surd, multiply top and bottom by this surd.

Method 2: If the denominator is the sum of a surd and a number, $a + \sqrt{b}$, multiply top and bottom by $a - \sqrt{b}$.

Chapter 2
Quadratics

2.1 Introduction

Key words

- **Quadratic**: an expression or equation involving a term in x^2 and possibly a term in x and a number, for example $x^2 - 2x + 3$.
- **Parabola**: the shape of a quadratic curve when plotted on a graph.
- **Vertex**: The point at which a parabola is at its minimum or maximum.
- **Perfect square**: A quadratic expression that has two identical factors.
- **Root**: A solution to an equation.
- **Repeated root**: The solution to an equation if there are two solutions that are identical.
- **Discriminant**: In the quadratic expression $ax^2 + bx + c$, the value $b^2 - 4ac$.

Before you start
You should know:

- How to simplify surds, e.g. $\sqrt{98} = \sqrt{49}\sqrt{2} = 7\sqrt{2}$
- How to expand brackets, e.g. $(x + 3)(2x - 4)$ $= 2x^2 - 4x + 6x - 12 = 2x^2 + 2x - 12$

Exercise 2A (Revision)

1. Simplify:
   (a) $\sqrt{20}$ (b) $\sqrt{80}$
   (c) $\sqrt{72}$ (d) $(3 + \sqrt{5})(3 - \sqrt{5})$
   (e) $\dfrac{1}{2 - \sqrt{6}}$

2. Expand the brackets:
   (a) $(x + 1)(x - 2)$ (b) $(2x + 1)(2x - 3)$
   (c) $(1 - x)(1 - 3x)$ (d) $(1 - x)(1 + x)$
   (e) $(2p + 3)(3 - 5p)$

What you will learn
In this chapter you will learn how to:

- Solve quadratic equations by:
  - factorising,
  - completing the square;
  - using the Quadratic Formula;
- Solve quadratic equations in a function of the unknown.

2.2 Quadratic Functions and Their Graphs

Notation
You will see function notation, such as $f(x)$, throughout AS and A2 level mathematics.

For example, if $f(x) = 3x + 1$ we can find $f(4)$:

$f(4) = 3(4) + 1 = 13$

In this example, 4 is the input and 13 is the output.

General quadratic equation
The general quadratic equation is:

$y = ax^2 + bx + c$

or

$f(x) = ax^2 + bx + c$

If $a > 0$, the shape of the curve is like this:

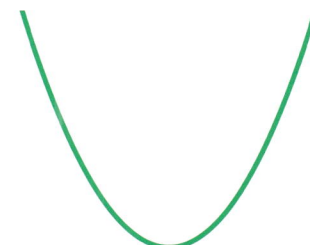

13

If $a < 0$, the shape of the curve is like this:

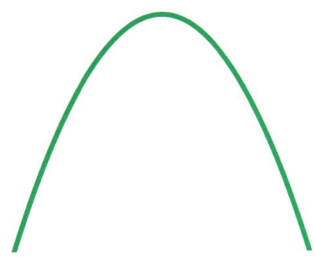

The shape of the quadratic curve is called a **parabola**.

An example of a quadratic is:

$f(x) = 3x^2 - 2x + 4$

Another would be:

$f(x) = x^2$

This is the simplest of all quadratic equations. It occurs when $a = 1, b = 0$ and $c = 0$.

If we want to find out where a quadratic curve cuts the x-axis, we must solve the equation:

$f(x) = 0$

Often, we can do this by factorising the quadratic. You learnt at GCSE that if $a = 1$, we must find two numbers that add up to b and multiply to make c.

Worked Example

1. Where does the curve defined by:
    $f(x) = x^2 - 3x + 2$
    intersect the x-axis?

    We must solve:
    $x^2 - 3x + 2 = 0$

    The two numbers that add up to –3 and multiply to make 2 are –1 and –2.

    So factorising gives:
    $(x - 1)(x - 2) = 0$

    Remember, if two terms multiplied make zero, one or both of them must equal zero.

    So either $(x - 1) = 0$ or $(x - 2) = 0$
    giving either $x = 1$ or $x = 2$.

Sometimes factorising and solving a quadratic equation leaves you with the same solution twice. This solution is known as a **repeated root**.

Worked Example

2. Where does the curve defined by:
    $y = x^2 + 6x + 9$
    meet the x-axis?

    We must solve:
    $x^2 + 6x + 9 = 0$

    Factorising gives:
    $(x + 3)(x + 3) = 0$
    $$x + 3 = 0$$
    $$x = -3$$

    So this curve meets the x-axis only once at the point $(-3, 0)$, as shown in the following diagram.

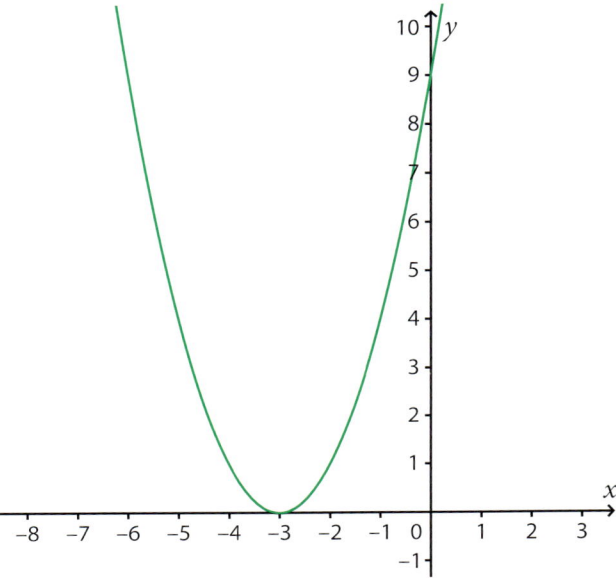

Note: Sometimes you will not be able to factorise and solve a quadratic equation.

Before solving a quadratic equation, you may need to re-arrange it to make the right-hand side zero.

Worked Example

3. Solve for x:
    $x(x - 1) = 2(x + 2)$

    $$x^2 - x = 2x + 4$$
    $$x^2 - 3x - 4 = 0$$
    $$(x - 4)(x + 1) = 0$$

    giving $x = 4$ or $x = -1$

However, you may not need to expand the brackets.

14

Worked Example

4. Solve for x:
$$3x(x - 1) = 2(x - 1)$$

Note that the brackets are the same on each side of the equation. So:

$$3x(x - 1) - 2(x - 1) = 0$$
$$(3x - 2)(x - 1) = 0$$

giving $x = \dfrac{2}{3}$ or $x = 1$

If the **coefficient** of the x^2 term is greater than one, factorising may be more difficult. The next example demonstrates one technique for solving this type of problem.

Worked Example

5. Factorise and solve:
$$2x^2 + 3x - 2 = 0$$

Looking at the coefficients of the three terms, $a = 2, b = 3, c = -2 \Rightarrow ac = -4, b = 3$.

So we attempt to find two numbers whose product is −4 and whose sum is 3.

These numbers are 4 and −1.

Now take the quadratic equation and split the term in x, using these numbers:
$$2x^2 + 3x - 2 = 0$$
$$2x^2 + 4x - x - 2 = 0$$

Factorise each pair of terms:
$$2x(x + 2) - 1(x + 2) = 0$$

Note that, in the line above, the terms inside the two sets of brackets will always be the same, $(x + 2)$ in this case. So:

$$(2x - 1)(x + 2) = 0$$

giving $x = \dfrac{1}{2}$ or $x = -2$

Watch out for the **difference of two squares**:
$$a^2 - b^2 = (a - b)(a + b)$$

Worked Example

6. Solve for x:
$$9x^2 - 64 = 0$$

$$(3x)^2 - 8^2 = 0$$

Using the difference of two squares formula gives:
$$(3x - 8)(3x + 8) = 0$$

So $x = \dfrac{8}{3}$ or $x = -\dfrac{8}{3}$

Exercise 2B

1. Solve the following quadratic equations:
   (a) $x^2 + 12x + 27 = 0$
   (b) $x^2 + 14x + 33 = 0$
   (c) $x^2 + 12x + 20 = 0$
   (d) $x^2 + 10x + 25 = 0$
   (e) $x^2 + 10x + 24 = 0$
   (f) $x^2 + 2x - 3 = 0$
   (g) $x^2 + 6x - 7 = 0$
   (h) $x^2 + x - 42 = 0$
   (i) $x^2 - 7x + 10 = 0$
   (j) $x^2 + 16x + 63 = 0$

2. Solve these equations for x:
   (a) $(x - 3)(x - 4) = 0$
   (b) $(2x - 5)(2x + 5) = 0$
   (c) $x(x - 4) = 0$
   (d) $3x(x - 1) = 0$
   (e) $2(x + 6)(x - 4) = 0$
   (f) $(x - 3)^2 = 0$
   (g) $7(1 - x)(x + 1) = 0$
   (h) $-5(1 - x)^2 = 0$
   (i) $(2x + 1)(2x - 7) = 0$
   (j) $x(x - 91) = 0$
   (k) $4(x + 6)(x + 8) = 0$
   (l) $(x + 1)^2 = 0$
   (m) $5(1 + x)(x - 1) = 0$
   (n) $-9(-1 - x)^2 = 0$
   (o) $(4x - 1)(8x + 1) = 0$

3. Expand the brackets to solve these quadratic equations for x:
   (a) $x(x - 6) = 2(x - 8)$
   (b) $x(x - 8) = 3(x - 6)$
   (c) $x(x - 9) = 3(x - 12)$
   (d) $x(x + 3) = 2(3x + 5)$
   (e) $x(x - 11) = 4(x - 14)$
   (f) $x(x - 8) = 4(15 - x)$
   (g) $x(x - 13) = 5(x - 16)$
   (h) $x(x - 7) = 3(x - 3)$
   (i) $x(x + 11) = -6(x + 12)$
   (j) $x(x - 7) = 6(x - 5)$
   (k) $x(x - 10) = 2(x - 18)$
   (l) $x^2 = 4(x - 1)$

Exercise 2B...

4. Factorise these equations and hence solve for x. Leave your answers as fractions where appropriate.
    (a) $2(x + 1) - x(x + 1) = 0$
    (b) $5(3x - 2) - 2x(3x - 2) = 0$
    (c) $6(x + 2) = x(x + 2)$
    (d) $4(6x + 3) = -9x(6x + 3)$
    (e) $8(2x + 1) = -5x(2x + 1)$
    (f) $7(7x + 3) = 3x(7x + 3)$
    (g) $-8(-x - 5) = 3x(-x - 5)$
    (h) $4(5x - 5) = 7x(5x - 5)$
    (i) $-3(7x - 5) = 8x(7x - 5)$
    (j) $2(-8x - 4) = 2x(-8x - 4)$
    (k) $6(-5x - 9) = 2x(-5x - 9)$
    (l) $2(6x - 7) = 6x(6x - 7)$
    (m) $6(-5x + 7) = 9x(-5x + 7)$
    (n) $-7(7x + 6) = -2x(7x + 6)$
    (o) $-6(8x - 3) = -4x(8x - 3)$

5. Factorise these equations and solve:
    (a) $2x^2 + 5x - 3 = 0$
    (b) $2n^2 - 11n + 12 = 0$
    (c) $2z^2 - 19z + 24 = 0$
    (d) $3p^2 - 4p + 1 = 0$

6. Use the difference of two squares to solve the following:
    (a) $x^2 - 49 = 0$ (b) $y^2 - 81 = 0$
    (c) $9z^2 - 49 = 0$ (d) $25b^2 - 9 = 0$
    (e) $25c^2 - 16 = 0$ (f) $64x^2 - 1 = 0$
    (g) $25m^2 - 49 = 0$ (h) $\dfrac{x^2}{36} - 1 = 0$
    (i) $\dfrac{y^2}{16} - 36 = 0$ (j) $\dfrac{z^2}{36} - 25 = 0$

7. In a right-angled triangle, the two shorter sides have lengths $2x$ and $x + 1$ cm. The length of the hypotenuse is $x + 3$ cm. Find the lengths of the sides of the triangle.

2.3 Completing the Square in a Quadratic Function

We referred earlier to quadratic expressions that contain two identical factors. Examples of expressions of this type are:

$(x - 6)^2$ $(x + 5)(x + 5)$ $x^2 - 6x + 9$

Such expressions are sometimes called **perfect squares**.

Worked Example

7. Solve the equation:
    $x^2 - 6x + 9 = 25$

    $x^2 - 6x + 9 = 25$
    $(x - 3)^2 = 25$
    $(x - 3) = \pm 5$
    So $x = -2$ or $x = 8$

You can use a technique called **completing the square** for any quadratic expression. It will give you a perfect square term and a single number. The next example demonstrates this technique.

Worked Example

8. Complete the square for the expression:
    $x^2 + 6x$

    The **coefficient** of x is 6. We take half of this coefficient and use it in our square term. We must also subtract the square of this number. So:

    $x^2 + 6x = (x + 3)^2 - 9$

    (You could expand the brackets to check that this is correct.)

You can solve any quadratic equation using the completing the square technique. We make the left side of the equation a perfect square.

Worked Example

9. Solve the equation:
    $x^2 + 14x + 10 = 7$

    Half the coefficient of x is +7. We use this in our square term. We must also subtract 7^2:

    $(x + 7)^2 - 49 + 10 = 7$

    (You could expand the brackets to check that the left-side has not changed.)

    Now collect all the number terms on the right side:

    $(x + 7)^2 = 46$
    $x + 7 = \pm\sqrt{46}$
    $x = -7 \pm \sqrt{46}$

You can also use **completing the square** when the coefficient of x is not 1.

Worked Example

10. Solve the equation:
$$2x^2 - 16x - 3 = 0$$

Take the number term to the right side.
Factorise the left side:

$$2(x^2 - 8x) = 3$$

$$x^2 - 8x = \frac{3}{2}$$

Complete the square for the left side.
The coefficient of x is -8.

$$(x - 4)^2 - 16 = \frac{3}{2}$$

$$(x - 4)^2 = \frac{35}{2}$$

$$(x - 4) = \pm\sqrt{\frac{35}{2}}$$

$$x = 4 \pm \sqrt{\frac{35}{2}}$$

Rationalise the denominator:

$$x = 4 \pm \frac{\sqrt{70}}{2}$$

Exercise 2C

1. Solve the following equations for x by taking square roots.
   (a) $(6x + 15)^2 = 9$ (b) $(5x - 3)^2 = 100$
   (c) $(7x - 12)^2 = 100$
   (d) $(8x + 8)^2 = 49$ (e) $(5x + 9)^2 = 1$
   (f) $(6x - 13)^2 = 16$ (g) $\left(\frac{x}{4} - 3\right)^2 = 4$
   (h) $\left(\frac{x}{5} - 13\right)^2 = 9$ (i) $\left(\frac{x}{6} + 10\right)^2 = 64$
   (j) $\left(\frac{x}{5} - 2\right)^2 = 4$ (k) $\left(\frac{x}{3} - 11\right)^2 = 1$
   (l) $\left(\frac{x}{6} + 12\right)^2 = 1$ (m) $\left(\frac{x}{5} - 9\right)^2 = 4$
   (n) $\left(\frac{x}{3} + 3\right)^2 = 64$ (o) $\left(\frac{x}{6} - 6\right)^2 = 36$

2. Solve these equations by completing the square. Give your answers in simplified surd form.
   (a) $x^2 + 6x - 4 = 0$
   (b) $2x^2 + 8x + \frac{3}{2} = 0$
   (c) $x^2 + 2x + 3 = 7$
   (d) $2x^2 + 12x + 9 = 11$
   (e) $4x^2 - 16x + 3 = 7$

(f) $2x^2 + 18x + 3 = 1 - 2x$
(g) $3x^2 + 6x + 3 = 11 - 2x - x^2$
(h) $-x^2 + 4x + 16 = 0$
(i) $-7x^2 - 28x - 2 = -9$

Using completing the square to sketch a graph

Completing the square is a powerful technique to help sketch a quadratic graph. You can quickly find the minimum or maximum value of the function and for which value of x it occurs.

Worked Example

11. Consider the quadratic:
$$y = x^2 + 6x + 2$$
   (a) Complete the square to write this in the form:
   $$y = (x + a)^2 + b$$
   (b) Find the minimum value of y.
   (c) What value of x gives this minimum value of y?
   (d) Find the points of intersection with both axes. Give **exact** answers.

(a) $y = x^2 + 6x + 2$
   $y = (x + 3)^2 - 9 + 2$
   $y = (x + 3)^2 - 7$

(b) The minimum value of y must be -7 because $(x + 3)^2$ will always be zero or more.

(c) $(x + 3)^2$ is zero when $x = -3$. So the coordinates of the minimum point are $(-3, -7)$.

(d) When $x = 0$, $y = 2$, so the curve crosses the y-axis at $(0, 2)$.
   When $y = 0$, $(x + 3)^2 = 7$, giving $x = -3 \pm \sqrt{7}$
   The curve crosses the x-axis at $\left(-3 + \sqrt{7}, 0\right)$ and $\left(-3 - \sqrt{7}, 0\right)$.
   These coordinates must be left as surds as the question requires exact answers.

Note: Remember that if the **coefficient** of x^2 is negative, there will be a maximum point, not a minimum point.

Worked Example

12. Consider the quadratic function:

$y = -x^2 + 4x + 12$

(a) Complete the square to write this in the form:
$y = -(x - a)^2 + b$

(b) Find the maximum value of y.

(c) What value of x gives this maximum value of y?

(d) Sketch the curve, showing the points of intersection with the axes and the maximum point.

(a) $y = -x^2 + 4x + 12$

$y = -[x^2 - 4x - 12]$

$y = -[(x - 2)^2 - 4 - 12]$

$y = -(x - 2)^2 + 16$

(b) The maximum value of y is 16, which occurs when $(x - 2)^2 = 0$.

(c) $(x - 2)^2 = 0$ when $x = 2$. So the coordinates of the maximum point are $(2, 16)$.

(d) When $x = 0$, $y = 12$, so the curve crosses the y-axis at $(0, 12)$.
When $y = 0$, $(x - 2)^2 = 16$, giving $x - 2 = \pm 4$
So $x = 6$ or $x = -2$. Therefore the curve crosses the x-axis at $(6, 0)$ and $(-2, 0)$.
We can now sketch the graph:

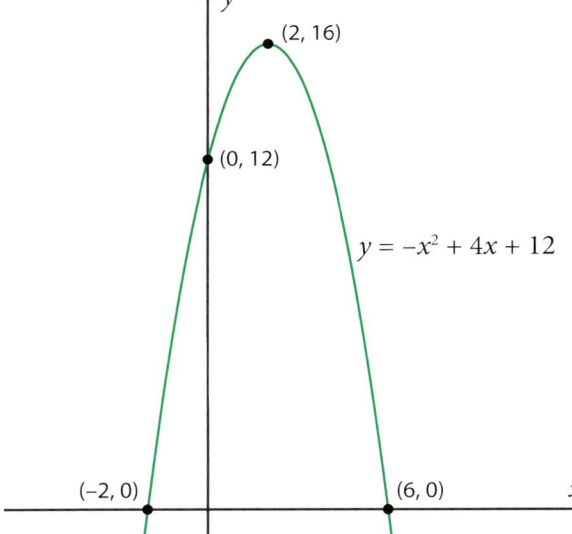

Exercise 2D

1. For each of the following quadratic curves, find the coordinates of:
   (i) the point of intersection with the y-axis;
   (ii) the points of intersection with the x-axis (if any);
   (iii) the minimum point.

   (a) $y = x^2 - 2x + 20$
   (b) $y = x^2 - 4x + 16$
   (c) $y = x^2 - 10x + 12$
   (d) $y = x^2 - 8x + 20$
   (e) $y = x^2 - 6x + 16$
   (f) $y = x^2 + 10x + 16$
   (g) $y = x^2 - 18x + 16$
   (h) $y = x^2 + 6x + 12$

2. For each of the following quadratic curves, find the coordinates of:
   (i) the point of intersection with the y-axis;
   (ii) the points of intersection with the x-axis (if any);
   (iii) the maximum point.

   (a) $y = -x^2 + 10x + 8$
   (b) $y = -x^2 - 6x + 16$
   (c) $y = -x^2 - 8x + 16$
   (d) $y = -x^2 + 10x + 16$
   (e) $y = -x^2 + 12x + 8$
   (f) $y = -x^2 - 14x + 12$
   (g) $y = -x^2 - 16x + 20$
   (h) $y = -x^2 + 18x + 20$

3. For each of the following quadratic curves:
   (i) find the coordinates of any points of intersection with the coordinate axes;
   (ii) find the coordinates of the maximum or minimum point;
   (iii) sketch each curve.

   (a) $y = x^2 - 14x + 20$
   (b) $y = x^2 + 16x + 16$
   (c) $y = x^2 + 12x + 16$
   (d) $y = -x^2 - 12x + 6$
   (e) $y = -x^2 + 14x + 8$
   (f) $y = -x^2 + 16x + 14$

2.4 Solving Quadratic Equations

The quadratic formula and the discriminant

Apart from completing the square, there is another way to solve a quadratic equation, which uses a formula:

$$x = \frac{-b \pm \sqrt{b^2 - 4ac}}{2a}$$

You have probably seen this formula, known as the **quadratic formula**, at GCSE. This formula is so frequently used it is sometimes simply referred to as "the formula"! Using the quadratic formula is a good idea if you cannot easily factorise a quadratic.

Worked Example

13. Solve:
$$x^2 + 2x - 7 = 0$$

We cannot factorise this, so we use the formula. We use $a = 1$, $b = 2$ and $c = -7$.

$$x = \frac{-b \pm \sqrt{b^2 - 4ac}}{2a}$$

$$x = \frac{-2 \pm \sqrt{2^2 - 4(1)(-7)}}{2}$$

$$x = \frac{-2 \pm \sqrt{32}}{2}$$

$$x = -1 \pm 2\sqrt{2}$$

So there are two solutions to this equation:

$$x = -1 + 2\sqrt{2} \text{ and } x = -1 - 2\sqrt{2}$$

Exercise 2E

1. Solve these equations using the quadratic formula. Give your answers in simplified surd form.
   (a) $x^2 + x - 1 = 0$ (b) $x^2 + 5x - 5 = 0$
   (c) $x^2 - x - 11 = 0$ (d) $x^2 + x - 31 = 0$
   (e) $2x^2 - 2x - 2 = 0$ (f) $2x^2 - 4x + 1 = 0$
   (g) $x^2 + 3x - 9 = 0$ (h) $3x^2 + 4x - 1 = 0$
   (i) $x^2 + 2x - 6 = 0$ (j) $2x^2 + 4x + 1 = 0$

2. Re-arrange these equations into the form $ax^2 + bx + c = 0$. Using the quadratic formula, find solutions to each equation, giving your answers in surd form.
   (a) $x^2 + 1 + 4x = 0$
   (b) $2x^2 - 1 + 5x = 0$
   (c) $-x + 3x^2 - 1 = 0$
   (d) $4x + 5 - 2x^2 = 0$

Exercise 2E...

  (e) $4x - 1 + 4x^2 = 0$
  (f) $-2 + 3x^2 + 4x = 0$
  (g) $-2x - 1 + 2x^2 = 0$
  (h) $3x + 4 - 3x^2 = 0$
  (i) $-4x - 4 + x^2 = 0$
  (j) $-4x + 3 - 3x^2 = 0$

The discriminant

Some quadratic equations do not have a real solution. This occurs when $b^2 - 4ac < 0$. In the quadratic formula we take the square root of $b^2 - 4ac$. You cannot find the square root of a negative number.

Because $b^2 - 4ac$ is so important, we give it a special name: the **discriminant**.

In summary:

Discriminant $b^2 - 4ac$	Meaning
< 0	No real solutions
$= 0$	Two solutions that are the same (a **repeated root**)
> 0	Two distinct solutions

Worked Examples

14. Find the number of solutions to the equation:
$$x^2 = 1 - 4x$$

Re-arranging gives:
$$x^2 + 4x - 1 = 0$$

So we let $a = 1$, $b = 4$, $c = -1$.

Therefore $b^2 - 4ac = 4^2 - 4(1)(-1) = 20$

The value of $b^2 - 4ac > 0$, so there are two distinct solutions to this quadratic equation. **Note** that the question does not ask us to find these solutions.

15. Find the values of k for which the equation $x^2 + kx + 1 = 0$ would have only one real solution (a repeated root).

We let $a = 1$, $b = k$, $c = 1$.

Therefore $b^2 - 4ac = k^2 - 4(1)(1) = k^2 - 4$

For the equation to have only one solution, $b^2 - 4ac = 0$.

$$\therefore k^2 - 4 = 0$$
$$k^2 = 4$$

So $k = 2$ or $k = -2$

(You could check the answers by setting $k = \pm 2$ in the original equation and factorising.)

Exercise 2F

1. For each of the following equations, calculate the value of the discriminant. From this, decide whether the equation has two solutions, only one, or none. If there are solutions, calculate them, leaving your answers in surd form where appropriate.
   (a) $x^2 + 2x - 2 = 0$ (b) $x^2 - 3x + 39 = 0$
   (c) $4x^2 + 2x - 1 = 0$ (d) $x^2 - x + 19 = 0$
   (e) $3x^2 + 2x + 1 = 0$ (f) $4x^2 + x + 2 = 0$
   (g) $4x^2 + x - 2 = 0$ (h) $x^2 - x + 3 = 0$
   (i) $x^2 - 4x + 4 = 0$ (j) $3x^2 - 3x - 3 = 0$
   (k) $x^2 + 2x - 4 = 0$ (l) $3x^2 - 3x + 4 = 0$
   (m) $2x^2 - x + 4 = 0$ (n) $5x^2 - 2x - 1 = 0$

2. The equation $x^2 + px + (p + 8) = 0$, where p is a constant, has two different real roots. Show that $p^2 - 4p - 32 > 0$.

3. Given that the equation $kx^2 + 8x + k = 0$, where k is a positive constant, has a repeated root, find the value of k.

4. The equation $4x^2 - 3x - (q + 2) = 0$, where q is a constant, has no real roots. Find the set of possible values of q.

5. The equation $x^2 + 5tx + 2t = 0$, where t is a constant, has real roots. Prove that $t(25t - 8) \geq 0$.

2.5 Quadratic Equations in a Function of the Unknown

You may be asked to solve a quadratic equation in some function of the unknown.

Worked Examples

16. Solve the equation:
$$x^4 - 2x^2 + 1 = 0$$

The equation can be rewritten:
$$(x^2)^2 - 2x^2 + 1 = 0$$

This is a quadratic equation in the variable x^2.
Let $y = x^2$. The equation becomes:
$$y^2 - 2y + 1 = 0$$

Factorise:
$$(y - 1)^2 = 0$$
$$y = 1$$

But $y = x^2$, so $x^2 = 1$
So $x = \pm 1$

Note: If you use a substitution, remember to give your answer in terms of the original variable.

17. Solve the equation:
$$\frac{2}{x^2} + \frac{3}{x} - 1 = 0$$

The equation can be rewritten:
$$2\left(\frac{1}{x}\right)^2 + 3\left(\frac{1}{x}\right) - 1 = 0$$

This is a quadratic equation in the variable $\frac{1}{x}$.
Let $y = \frac{1}{x}$. The equation becomes:
$$2y^2 + 3y - 1 = 0$$

This cannot be factorised, so use the quadratic formula:
$$y = \frac{-3 \pm \sqrt{3^2 - 4(2)(-1)}}{2 \times 2}$$
$$y = \frac{-3 + \sqrt{17}}{4} \text{ or } y = \frac{-3 - \sqrt{17}}{4}$$

But $y = \frac{1}{x}$. So:
$$x = \frac{4}{-3 + \sqrt{17}} \text{ or } x = \frac{4}{-3 - \sqrt{17}}$$

Rationalising the denominator gives:
$$x = \frac{3 + \sqrt{17}}{2} \text{ or } x = \frac{3 - \sqrt{17}}{2}$$

Note: You could also solve this equation by multiplying both sides by x^2.

18. Solve the equation:
$$2^{2x+3} - 6(2^x) + 1 = 0$$

The first term can be rewritten:
$$2^{2x+3} = 2^{2x} \times 2^3 = 8(2^{2x}) = 8(2^x)^2$$

Therefore the equation can be rewritten:
$$8(2^x)^2 - 6(2^x) + 1 = 0$$

This is a quadratic equation in the variable 2^x.
Let $y = 2^x$. The equation becomes:
$$8y^2 - 6y + 1 = 0$$

Factorise:
$$(4y - 1)(2y - 1) = 0$$

$y = ¼$ or $y = ½$

But $y = 2^x$, so:
$2^x = ¼$ or $2^x = ½$
So $x = -2$ or $x = -1$

Note: You can check your solutions to any equation by substituting them back into the original equation. You can do this fairly quickly on the calculator.

Exercise 2G

1. Solve the following equations by using a substitution to form a quadratic equation. Some of the quadratics may factorise, others may not.
   (a) $x^4 - 3x^2 + 2 = 0$
   (b) $2x + 3\sqrt{x} - 5 = 0$
   (c) $\dfrac{2}{x^2} - \dfrac{3}{x} - 2 = 0$
   (d) $3(x + 1)^2 - (x + 1) - 4 = 0$
   (e) $\dfrac{x^2}{25} - \dfrac{x}{5} - 2 = 0$
   (f) $x^6 + 7x^3 - 8 = 0$
   (g) $2^{2x+2} - 9(2^x) + 2 = 0$

2. Use the difference of two squares to solve the following equation, giving your answers as simplified surds: $9x^4 - 64 = 0$

Note: In Chapter 9 (Trigonometry), you will learn how to solve quadratic equations in one of the trigonometric functions, e.g. $\sin^2 x + 2 \sin x + 1 = 0$.

Note: In Chapter 10 (Exponentials and Logs) there will be further examples and questions on solving a quadratic equation in a function such as a^x.

2.6 Summary

You have now seen three techniques for solving a quadratic equation:

- Factorising. Use this whenever possible.
- Completing the square.
- The quadratic formula.

The second and third techniques can both be used in all cases, so unless you are specifically asked to use a particular technique, you can choose. However, it is good to be familiar with both methods.

The **discriminant** $b^2 - 4ac$ of a quadratic equation tells you how many real solutions there are:

- $b^2 - 4ac < 0$: no real solutions,
- $b^2 - 4ac = 0$: one real solution (a repeated root),
- $b^2 - 4ac > 0$: two distinct solutions.

Sometimes a substitution should be used to transform an equation into a quadratic equation.

Chapter 3 Simultaneous Equations and Inequalities

3.1 Introduction

Before you start

You should know:

- How to re-arrange and solve linear equations.

Worked Examples

1. Make p the subject of the equation: $n = 4p - 3$

   First isolate the term in p:

   $4p = n + 3$

   Then, divide both sides by 4:

   $p = \dfrac{n + 3}{4}$

2. Solve the following equation: $2(x + 6) = 15$

   Expand brackets:

   $2x + 12 = 15$

   $2x = 3$

   $x = \frac{3}{2}$

- How to factorise a quadratic expression.

Worked Example

3. Factorise the quadratic expression: $x^2 - x - 12$

   The two numbers that have a product of –12 and sum –1 are: –4 and +3.

   So: $x^2 - x - 12 = (x + 3)(x - 4)$

- How to solve simultaneous linear equations.

Worked Example

4. Solve the simultaneous equations:

   $3x + y = 1 \qquad (1)$

   $2x + 4y = 7 \qquad (2)$

   Multiply one or both of the equations so that the x or the y terms are the same in both.

   Multiply equation (1) by 4: $\quad 12x + 4y = 4$

   Rewrite equation (2): $\qquad 2x + 4y = 7$

The y terms are now equal. Subtract the equations:

$10x = -3$

$x = -\dfrac{3}{10}$

Substitute into equation (1):

$-\dfrac{9}{10} + y = 1$

$y = \dfrac{19}{10}$

Therefore this system of simultaneous equations has the solution:

$x = -\dfrac{3}{10}, y = \dfrac{19}{10}$

Exercise 3A (Revision)

1. Make y the subject of these equations.
   - (a) $4x - 2y = 1$
   - (b) $2x - 5 - y = 0$
   - (c) $4(x + 3y) = 3$
   - (d) $5(x + 1) - 3(x + y) = 12$

2. For each linear equation, solve to find the unknown.
   - (a) $2(a + 3) = 6$
   - (b) $15 - 2(b + 1) = 3$
   - (c) $7 + c = 8 - c$
   - (d) $6d = 5(3d + 18)$
   - (e) $\dfrac{3}{2 + e} = 4$

3. Factorise the following quadratic expressions.
   - (a) $x^2 + 11x + 18$ (b) $x^2 - 10x + 24$
   - (c) $x^2 - 6x + 5$ (d) $x^2 + x - 12$
   - (e) $x^2 - x - 42$

4. Solve each pair of simultaneous equations:
   - (a) $6y + 6x = 6$ $3y + 5x = 5$
   - (b) $6x + 7y = 3$ $2x + 4y = 6$
   - (c) $6x + 2y = 42$ $-3x + 6y = -21$
   - (d) $8x + 6y = 62$ $-4x + 4y = 4$

What you will learn

In this chapter, you will learn:

- How to solve three simultaneous linear equations in

three variables.

- How to solve simultaneous equations in two variables including one linear and one quadratic equation.
- How to solve quadratic inequalities.
- How to solve simultaneous inequalities.

In the real world...

Simultaneous equations are used in industry for the manufacture of many different products. For example, it may be important to maximise the profits on a particular type of a breakfast cereal by reducing the amount of an expensive ingredient. But at the same time, it is important not to affect the flavour. There may be other important variables to consider too, such as legal limits on particular ingredients. If each of these factors can be modelled by an equation, then we must solve them simultaneously to find a solution.

3.2 Simultaneous Equations in Two Variables

In GCSE mathematics you learnt two techniques for solving simultaneous equations: elimination and substitution. In this section you will again use both methods.

Simultaneous quadratic and linear equations

At GCSE you learnt that you could think about simultaneous equations graphically. For example, if you were trying to solve the simultaneous equations:

$x + y = 5$

$3x + 5y = 19$

you could draw a graph of the two lines:

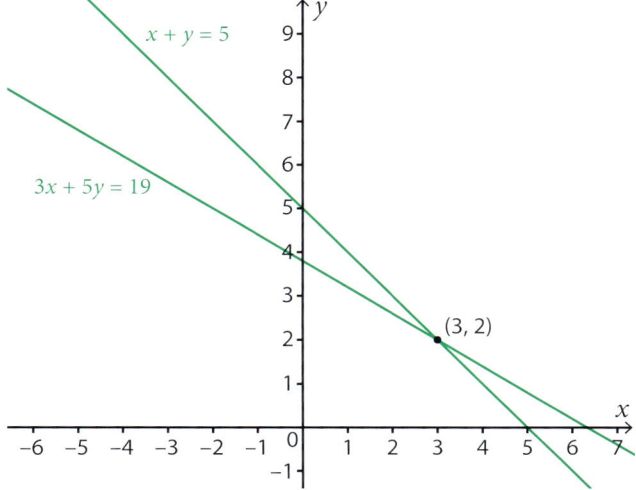

Because the lines intersect at the point (3, 2), the solution to the simultaneous equations is $x = 3, y = 2$. If the lines

are parallel, there will not be a solution.

> **Note:** If the question relates to the intersection of lines or curves, the solutions should always be given as a coordinate pair, e.g. (3, 2).

You can do a similar thing if one of the equations is a quadratic. Sometimes there are two solutions, sometimes one and sometimes none:

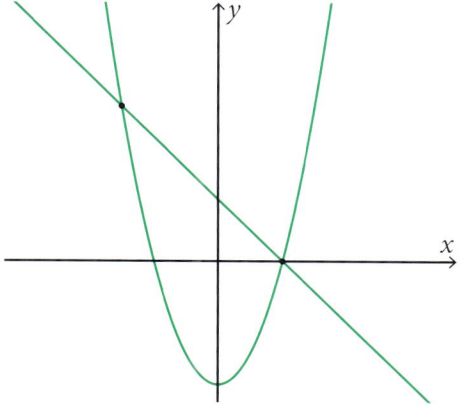

Two solutions.

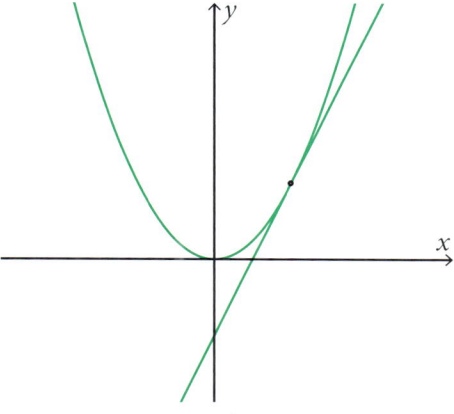

One solution.

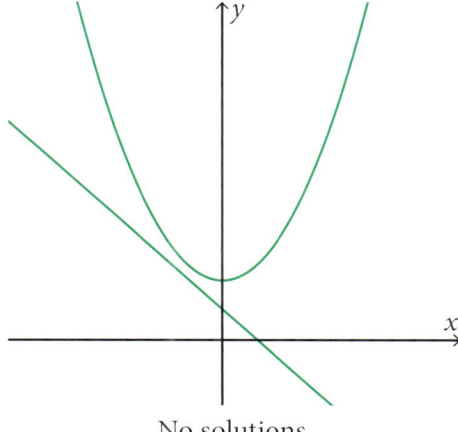

No solutions.

The best way to solve simultaneous quadratic and linear equations is the **substitution method**.

23

Worked Examples

5. Solve the simultaneous equations:
   $$y = x^2 - 4 \qquad (1)$$
   $$y = 2 - x \qquad (2)$$

   Wherever y occurs in (1), substitute from equation (2):
   $$2 - x = x^2 - 4$$
   Simplify: $\qquad x^2 + x - 6 = 0$
   Factorise: $\quad (x + 3)(x - 2) = 0$

   So: $\qquad x = -3$ or $x = 2$
   When: $\quad x = -3, y = 5$
   When: $\quad x = 2, y = 0$

   Hint: when finding the final variable, substitute the variables you have found into the equation that looks simplest.

6. Solve the simultaneous equations:
   $$x - 5y + 1 = 0 \qquad (1)$$
   $$x^2 - 5xy + y^2 = 15 \qquad (2)$$

   This time, we substitute for x. We could use y, but it is simpler to make x the subject of equation (1). Wherever x occurs in (2), we substitute from equation (1):

   From (1): $\quad x = 5y - 1 \quad (3)$

   Substituting into (2) gives:
   $$(5y - 1)^2 - 5(5y - 1)y + y^2 = 15$$

   Expand brackets:
   $$25y^2 - 10y + 1 - 25y^2 + 5y + y^2 = 15$$

   Simplify: $\quad y^2 - 5y - 14 = 0$

   Factorise: $\quad (y - 7)(y + 2) = 0$

   So: $\qquad y = 7$ or $y = -2$
   Using (3):
   When: $\quad y = 7, x = 34$
   When: $\quad y = -2, x = -11$

You can also use this method to work out where a quadratic curve intersects a straight line on a graph.

Worked Example

7. By solving simultaneous equations, work out the intersection points of the straight line given by:
   $$y + 8x = 0 \qquad (1)$$
   and the parabola given by:
   $$y = x^2 - 9 \qquad (2)$$

Substituting for y gives:
$$x^2 - 9 + 8x = 0$$
$$x^2 + 8x - 9 = 0$$

Factorising gives:
$$(x - 1)(x + 9) = 0$$

So $x = 1$ or $x = -9$

Intersection points: $(1, -8)$, $(-9, 72)$

> **Note:** If there are two solutions, always remember to pair your x and y values together correctly!

Sometimes a set of equations needs some work before you obtain the set of simultaneous equations to solve.

Worked Example

8. Solve the simultaneous equations:
   $$4^x \times 8^y = 4\sqrt{2} \quad (1)$$
   $$8x - 3y = \frac{5}{2} \qquad (2)$$

   We must manipulate equation (1) to obtain a linear equation. Rewrite everything as a power of two:
   $$(2^2)^x \times (2^3)^y = (2^2)(2^{1/2})$$

   Using the laws of indices:
   $$2^{2x} \times 2^{3y} = 2^{5/2}$$

   Add the powers on the left side:
   $$2^{2x+3y} = 2^{5/2}$$

   Because the bases are equal, the powers must be equal, so we have:
   $$2x + 3y = \frac{5}{2} \qquad (3)$$

   Now we have two linear equations, (2) and (3):
   $$8x - 3y = \frac{5}{2} \qquad (2)$$
   $$2x + 3y = \frac{5}{2} \qquad (3)$$

   Adding them gives:
   $$10x = 5$$
   So $x = \frac{1}{2}$

   Substituting x into (3):
   $$2\left(\frac{1}{2}\right) + 3y = \frac{5}{2}$$
   $$3y = \frac{5}{2} - 1$$
   $$y = \frac{1}{2}$$

Exercise 3B

1. Solve each pair of simultaneous equations.
   (a) $x + y = 6$ $\qquad$ $x^2 + 8y = 81$
   (b) $x + y = 4$ $\qquad$ $x^2 + 4y = 48$
   (c) $x + y = 4$ $\qquad$ $x^2 + 6y = 51$
   (d) $x + y = 2$ $\qquad$ $x^2 + 4y = 29$
   (e) $x + y = 5$ $\qquad$ $x^2 + 6y = 46$
   (f) $x + y = 5$ $\qquad$ $x^2 + 4y = 32$

2. Solve the following pairs of simultaneous equations to find x and y.
   (a) $x - 3y + 1 = 0$ $\qquad$ $x^2 - 3xy + y^2 = 11$
   (b) $x - 4y + 1 = 0$ $\qquad$ $x^2 - 4xy + y^2 = 6$
   (c) $x - 3y + 1 = 0$ $\qquad$ $x^2 - 3xy + y^2 = 19$
   (d) $x - 2y + 1 = 0$ $\qquad$ $x^2 - 2xy + y^2 = 9$
   (e) $x - 4y + 1 = 0$ $\qquad$ $x^2 - 4xy + y^2 = 22$
   (f) $x - 6y + 1 = 0$ $\qquad$ $x^2 - 6xy + y^2 = 8$

3. Work out the intersection points of the following pairs of curves and straight lines.
   (a) $y = x^2 - 16$ $\qquad$ $y + 6x = 0$
   (b) $y = x^2 - 25$ $\qquad$ $y + 24x = 0$

4. Solve the simultaneous equations, giving your answers in the form $a \pm b\sqrt{3}$.
   (a) $y = x - 4$ $\qquad$ $2x^2 - xy = 8$
   (b) $y = x - 8$ $\qquad$ $2x^2 - xy = 11$

5. Solve the simultaneous equations.
   (a) $\dfrac{4^p}{2^q} = 16$ $\qquad$ $5p - 3q = 9$
   (b) $\dfrac{1}{\sqrt{x+6}} = \dfrac{3}{\sqrt{y}}$ $\qquad$ $2y + 3x = 3$
   (c) $5^{2a}\sqrt{5} = 125^{b+1} \times 5^{\frac{3}{2}}$ $\qquad$ $a + 3b = 11$
   (d) $9^{1-x} \times 27^{1-x} = 3^y\sqrt{3}$ $\qquad$ $1 - 10x = y$
   (e) $10^{2m-5}\left(\dfrac{1}{100^n}\right) = \dfrac{1}{10^{m+n}}$ $\qquad$ $4m - 3n = 0$

3.3 Solving Simultaneous Equations in Three Variables

Until now, you have solved simultaneous equations involving **two** variables. You will also encounter systems of linear equations involving **three** variables.

Essentially, the same methods are used as for two variables: substitution and elimination. We usually eliminate one variable using two of the equations, then eliminate the same variable from a different pair of equations. This leaves two equations in two unknowns, which can be solved.

Worked Example

9. At a toll booth on a motorway, different prices are charged for cars, trucks and motorbikes.

   During one hour, 48 cars, 12 trucks and 4 motorbikes passed through the toll. The amount of money collected was £132.

   During the second hour, 36 cars, 24 trucks and 6 motorbikes passed through. The amount of money collected was £141.

   During the third hour, £141 was collected from 54 cars, 6 trucks and 12 motorbikes.

   Find the cost for a car, a truck and a motorbike to pass through the toll booth.

Let us say it costs £x for a car at the toll, £y for a truck and £z for a motorbike. Then:

$48x + 12y + 4z = 132$ $\qquad$ (1)
$36x + 24y + 6z = 141$ $\qquad$ (2)
$54x + 6y + 12z = 141$ $\qquad$ (3)

Dividing equation (1) by 4 gives:
$12x + 3y + z = 33$ $\qquad$ (4)

Dividing equation (2) by 3 gives:
$12x + 8y + 2z = 47$ $\qquad$ (5)

Dividing equation (3) by 3 gives:
$18x + 2y + 4z = 47$ $\qquad$ (6)

Subtracting (4) from (5) eliminates x to give:
$5y + z = 14$ $\qquad$ (7)

We can also eliminate x from (5) and (6):
$3 \times$ (5) gives: $\quad 36x + 24y + 6z = 141$ $\quad$ (8)
$2 \times$ (6) gives: $\quad 36x + 4y + 8z = 94$ $\quad$ (9)

Subtracting (9) from (8) gives:
$20y - 2z = 47$ $\qquad$ (10)

Now we have two equations (7) and (10) involving the two variables, y and z.
$4 \times$ (7) gives: $\qquad 20y + 4z = 56$
Subtract (10): $\qquad 6z = 9$
So: $\qquad z = 1.5$

Substituting z into (7) gives: $\quad 5y = 12.5$
So: $\qquad y = 2.5$

Substituting y and z into (4) gives:
$12x + 7.5 + 1.5 = 33$
$12x = 24$
So: $x = 2$

Therefore the prices are: cars £2, trucks £2.50, motorbikes £1.50.

Exercise 3C

1. Solve each pair of simultaneous equations.
   (a) $3x - 2y + z = 1$
   $2x + 2y + z = 15$
   $x + 4y + z = 21$
   (b) $3x + y + 2z = 0$
   $6x - z = 11$
   $x + 2y + z = -13$
   (c) $x + y + 2z = 4$
   $2y - z = 4$
   $5x + 2y - 5z = 80$
   (d) $-x - y + 2z = -2$
   $12x + 2y - 10z = 9$
   $2x + 3y + 4z = -18$

2. At *Frugal Supermarket* it costs me £1.22 to buy 6 apples, 2 bananas and 1 carrot. The person behind me in the queue buys 2 apples, 1 banana and 4 carrots. His bill is 93p. The person following him buys 1 apple, 6 bananas and 3 carrots. She is charged £1.96. What do apples, bananas and carrots cost?

3. At the local cinema, a packet of popcorn, a cola and a ticket for a film costs £9. Last week, I went with some friends. We bought 3 cinema tickets, 3 packets of popcorn and two colas. The cost was £25.50. Today I bought 2 tickets, 1 box of popcorn to share and no drinks, which came to £13. Assuming the prices have not changed, how much are the ticket, the popcorn and the cola?

3.4 Solution of Linear and Quadratic Inequalities

Revision
Solving an equation involves finding a particular value, or values, that satisfy that equation. Solving an **inequality** is different: you will find a set of values. You did some work on solving linear inequalities in GCSE mathematics.

Worked Example
10. Solve the following inequality and plot the set of values on a number line:
    $-3x - 3(x + 14) > 0$

    Expand brackets: $\quad -3x - 3x - 42 > 0$
    $-6x - 42 > 0$
    $-6x > 42$
    $x < -7$

    > **Note:** Remember that when you multiply or divide an inequality by a negative number, you reverse the inequality sign.

    Plot these answers on a number line:

At the ends of these inequality lines, we use an open circle (as above) to indicate that the value is not included in the set (corresponding to a < or > sign), or a full (filled) circle to indicate that the value is included (e.g. if we were displaying the inequality $x \leq -7$). An arrow indicates that the set goes on indefinitely in that direction.

Solving quadratic inequalities
To solve a quadratic **inequality**, you will need to remember how to sketch a quadratic graph.

Worked Example
11. Solve the following inequality and plot the set of values on a number line:
    $x^2 + 2x > 8$

    Rearrange: $\qquad x^2 + 2x - 8 > 0$
    Factorise: $\qquad (x - 2)(x + 4) > 0 \qquad$ (1)

    Now sketch the graph of: $y = (x - 2)(x + 4)$

    To find the points where the curve crosses the x-axis, set $y = 0$.
    So: $\qquad (x - 2)(x + 4) = 0$
    This has solutions: $x = 2$ or $x = -4$

    We also know that the quadratic has a minimum point (not a maximum) because we have a positive x^2 term. So the graph looks like this:

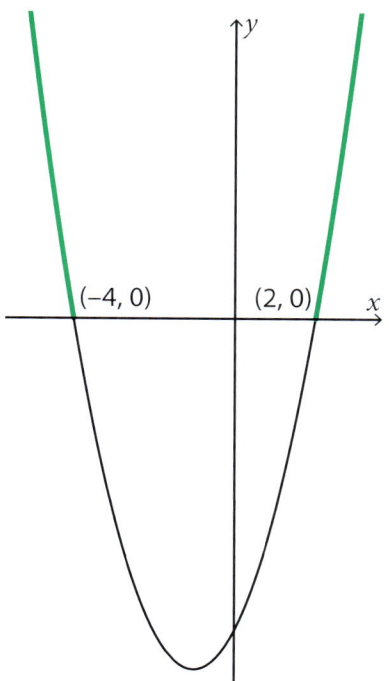

Now we can see that $(x - 2)(x + 4) > 0$ is satisfied in the green regions of the curve.

The values of x that correspond to these parts of the curve are: $x < -4$ or $x > 2$.

This composite set of values is shown as below:

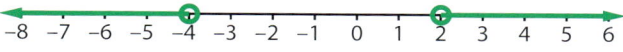

Sometimes you will be faced with simultaneous inequalities.

Worked Examples

12. Find the values of x that satisfy both the following inequalities:

$$x^2 + 2x > 8 \qquad (1)$$
$$2x + 1 < 3 \qquad (2)$$

From Example 11 we know that inequality (1) is satisfied when $x < -4$ or $x > 2$.

Equation (2) gives us: $x < 1$

For both to be true, we must find where the two sets overlap.

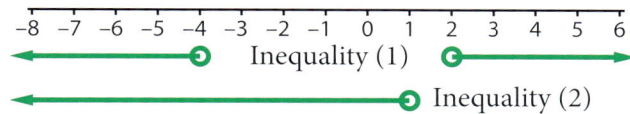

The set of values satisfying both inequalities is $x < -4$.

13. Find the values of x that satisfy the following inequality:
$$-x^2 - 5x + 6 \geq 0$$

Consider the graph of $y = -x^2 - 5x + 6$. We must determine where the curve lies above the x-axis.
$$y = -x^2 - 5x + 6$$
$$y = -(x^2 + 5x - 6)$$
$$y = -(x + 6)(x - 1)$$

So the curve crosses the x-axis at $x = -6$ and $x = 1$. It has a maximum point, since the coefficient of x^2 is negative. Hence, a sketch of the curve is as below.

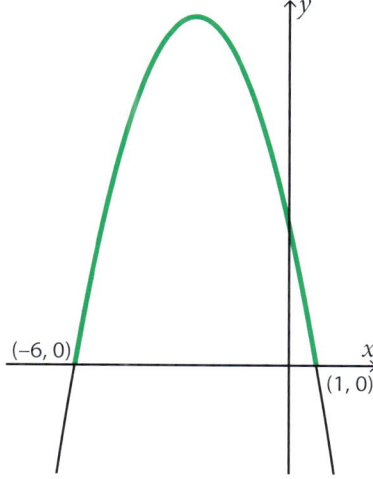

The curve is above the x-axis in the green region, i.e. $-6 \leq x \leq 1$.

> **Note:** We must use $\leq$ signs here, as specified in the original inequality. (Check it: the values $x = -6$ and $x = 1$ do satisfy the inequality.)

Exercise 3D

1. Solve:
   (a) $7 + x \leq 14$ (b) $x - 9 \leq 12$
   (c) $4x - 7 < x$ (d) $1 - x \leq 6$
   (e) $\dfrac{3x}{2} - 1 \geq 1 - \dfrac{3x}{2}$ (f) $6x - 1 < 65$
   (g) $12x + 7 > 8x + 3$ (h) $6x - 1 < x$
   (i) $1 - x \leq x - 1$ (j) $7x + 8 > 3x + 2$
   (k) $\dfrac{x}{2} > x + 3$ (l) $6 - \dfrac{4x}{3} \leq \dfrac{21x}{5} + 2$

2. Find the set of values satisfying the following inequalities.
   (a) $2(t + 1) \geq 4(t - 1)$
   (b) $w - 4(3 - 2w) > 6$

Exercise 3D...

   (c) $4p + 2(1 - p) \geq 2(2p + 1)$
   (d) $3v > 2(2v + 5)$
   (e) $z - 1 - 3(1 - z) < 0$
   (f) $3(u + 6) - 4u \leq 4(u - 1)$

3. By sketching an appropriate quadratic curve, find the set of values that satisfies each of the following inequalities.
   (a) $(x + 4)(x - 1) > 0$
   (b) $(x + 5)(x - 4) > 0$
   (c) $(x - 3)(x + 3) < 0$
   (d) $(2x - 3)(x - 4) > 0$
   (e) $-(x - 2)(x + 5) > 0$
   (f) $-(x - 1)(x + 4) < 0$
   (g) $(x - 2)(x + 5) < 0$
   (h) $-(x - 3)(x + 7) < 0$

4. Find the set of values that satisfy the following inequalities.
   (a) $x^2 - 2x - 24 \geq 0$ (b) $x^2 - 3x - 10 > 0$
   (c) $x^2 + 2x - 3 < 0$ (d) $x^2 - 5x - 24 > 0$
   (e) $x^2 + 3x - 88 < 0$ (f) $x^2 + 2x - 99 > 0$
   (g) $x^2 - 3x - 10 > 0$ (h) $x^2 - 6x - 16 \geq 0$
   (i) $x^2 + 3x - 4 < 0$ (j) $x^2 + 2x - 8 > 0$
   (k) $x^2 - 4x - 12 > 0$ (l) $x^2 + 6x - 16 < 0$
   (m) $x^2 + 3x - 154 < 0$ (n) $x^2 - 5x - 36 \geq 0$

5. Find the values of x that satisfy the following inequalities:
   (a) $x^2 + 5x - 1 \geq 2x + 3$
   (b) $x^2 + 8x - 2 \leq 5x + 2$
   (c) $x^2 - 5x - 33 > -7x + 2$
   (d) $x^2 + 8x - 50 \geq 5x + 4$
   (e) $x^2 + 6x - 98 < 4x + 1$
   (f) $x^2 - 4x - 126 \geq -7x + 4$
   (g) $x^2 + 6x - 74 > 2x + 3$
   (h) $x^2 + 7x - 103 < 4x + 5$
   (i) $-x^2 + 6x + 2 > 2x - 3$
   (j) $-x^2 - x < -10x + 14$
   (k) $-2x^2 + 30 > -x^2 + 7x$

6. Using a number line to help, if necessary, find the set of values of x satisfying both inequalities:
   (a) $5x - 5 < 2x + 4$
       $3x^2 - 15x + 12 < 0$
   (b) $7x - 10 < 3x + 4$
       $-2x^2 + 12x - 10 > 0$
   (c) $8x - 9 \leq 3x + 4$
       $2x^2 - 14x + 20 \leq 0$
   (d) $3x - 3 > x + 2$
       $3x^2 - 18x + 15 > 0$

Exercise 3D...

   (e) $5x - 5 \geq 3x + 3$
       $-2x^2 + 11x - 5 < 0$
   (f) $9x - 7 > 4x + 2$
       $x^2 - 5x + 4 \geq 0$
   (g) $5x - 8 \leq 3x + 4$
       $3x^2 - 25x + 28 < 0$
   (h) $6x - 5 \geq 3x + 1$
       $3x^2 - 17x + 10 > 0$
   (i) $5x - 7 \leq 3x + 3$
       $-3x^2 + 20x - 12 \geq 0$
   (j) $6x - 7 < 4x + 4$
       $3x^2 - 24x + 21 < 0$
   (k) $5x - 4 > 3x + 4$
       $-3x^2 + 19x - 20 < 0$
   (l) $6x - 9 > 2x + 5$
       $-3x^2 + 24x - 21 \leq 0$

3.5 Summary

To solve three **simultaneous equations** in three variables, eliminate one of the variables from two different pairs of equations. Then solve the remaining two equations in the remaining two variables.

To solve simultaneous equations where one is a quadratic, use the method of substitution.

When you solve any **inequality**, the solution is a range or set of values, not a single value.

Use the normal rules of algebra to re-arrange an inequality, but if you divide or multiply by a negative number, the inequality sign reverses.

To solve a quadratic inequality, sketch a graph of the corresponding quadratic equation.

When solving simultaneous quadratic and linear inequalities, a number line is often useful to see where the two sets overlap.

Chapter 4
Algebraic Manipulation

4.1 Introduction

> **In the real world...**
>
> The word algebra comes from the Arabic *al-jabr*, meaning restoration. The idea has been studied for thousands of years. The ancient Babylonians used algebra to calculate the square root of two, about 3000 years ago!

Key words

- **Expanding:** The process of removing the brackets.
- **Factorising:** Rewriting an expression as a product of its factors; the opposite of expanding brackets.
- **Terms:** Each part of an algebraic expression, separated by + or – signs.
- **Like terms:** Terms that contain the same variables, e.g. $4x$ and $2x$. However $4x$ and $4xy$ are not like terms.
- **Polynomial:** A function of x, whose terms are ax^n for any values a and non-negative n, e.g. $4x^2 + 2x + 1$. (The last term has $a = 1$ and $n = 0$).
- **Coefficient:** The number multiplying a power of x. For example, in $3x^2 + 1$, the coefficient of x^2 is 3.
- **Degree**: The highest power a polynomial contains. We say a polynomial has degree n if the highest power of x is n. For example, a quadratic has degree 2.

Before you start

You should know:

- How to simplify algebraic expressions by collecting like terms.

Worked Example

1. Simplify: $q + 5p - 4q - (-3p) - pq$

   Remember that $-(-3p)$ is $+3p$.

   Remember that you cannot mix your p or q terms with your pq term.

   So: $q + 5p - 4q - (-3p) - pq = 8p - 3q - pq$

- How to evaluate algebraic expressions.

Worked Example

2. Find the value of $x^2 + 3x$ given that $x = 5$.

   When $x = 5$: $x^2 + 3x = 5^2 + 3(5)$
   $$= 40$$

- How to expand brackets.

Worked Example

3. Expand:
   (a) $-3x(2x + 4)$
   (b) $(4x - 1)(2x + 3)$

   (a) Remember that the minus sign affects all the terms inside the brackets. So:
   $-3x(2x + 4) = -6x^2 - 12x$

   (b) Remember all four combinations and be careful with signs. So:
   $(4x - 1)(2x + 3) = 8x^2 + 12x - 2x - 3$
   $$= 8x^2 + 10x - 3$$

- How to factorise linear expressions.

Worked Example

4. Factorise: $-18x + 48y$

   Note that each term has a factor of 6. So:
   $-18x + 48y = 6(8y - 3x)$

   Remember: you can always check your factorisation by expanding the brackets.

- How to factorise quadratic expressions.

Worked Example

5. Factorise: $x^2 - x - 6$

   The coefficient of x^2 is 1.
   The coefficient of x is –1.
   The units term is –6.

We must find two numbers that add up to –1 and multiply to make –6:

$$x^2 - x - 6 = (x - 3)(x + 2)$$

Again, you can check your factorisation by expanding brackets.

....

- How to recognise and use the difference of two squares.

> **Note:** The general rule for the difference of two squares is: $a^2 - b^2 = (a - b)(a + b)$.

....

Worked Example

6. Solve: $9x^2 - 64 = 0$

$$(3x)^2 - 8^2 = 0$$
$$(3x - 8)(3x + 8) = 0$$
So: $\qquad x = \dfrac{8}{3} \text{ or } x = -\dfrac{8}{3}$

....

- How to perform long division without a calculator.

....

Worked Example

7. Calculate $702 \div 26$.

We will demonstrate this calculation using the 'bus stop' method, since this will be used later with polynomials:

$$
\begin{array}{r}
27 \\
26\overline{)702} \\
520 \\
\hline
182 \\
182 \\
\hline
0
\end{array}
$$

The answer is 27 with no remainder.

....

Exercise 4A (Revision)

1. Simplify:
(a) $a + 3a - b - 3b$
(b) $2c - (-d) + c$
(c) $2e - f + ef + f$
(d) $a^2 + b^2 - 5a + 6b - 2ab$
(e) $a + 6b - 4b - 2a$
(f) $d - (-7c) + (-2d) - c$
(g) $7e - 2f + 3f + ef$
(h) $2g^2 + 3h^2 - 4g - 3h + 2gh$

Exercise 4A (Revision)

2. Evaluate these expressions using the value of x given.
(a) If $x = 1$, find $3x - 7$
(b) If $x = 2$, find $x^3 - 2x^2$
(c) If $x = 3$, find $3(1 - x)$
(d) If $x = 4$, find $(x - 5)(x + 5)(x - 4)$
(e) $f(x) = x^2 - 2x - 7$. Find $f(1)$
(f) If $x = 5$, find $x^2 - 2x + 1$
(g) If $x = 2$, find $2 + 2x^2$
(h) If $x = 3$, find $3(1 - x)(2 - x)$
(i) If $x = 4$, find $(x - 4)(x^3 - 3x^2 + 21x - 17)$
(j) $f(x) = 3x^2 + 2x - 7$. Find $f(1)$.

3. Expand the brackets in the following expressions.
(a) $2v(1 + v)$ $\qquad$ (b) $-4(w^2 - 2)$
(c) $y(3y + 1)$ $\qquad$ (d) $(4x + 3)(4x - 3)$
(e) $4v(2 + 3v)$ $\qquad$ (f) $-3(2w^2 - 1)$
(g) $y(-2y + 6)$ $\qquad$ (h) $(4x + 4)(4x - 4)$

4. Factorise the following expressions.
(a) $-5y^2 - 25y$ $\qquad$ (b) $36p - 6p^3$
(c) $26qr - 13r$ $\qquad$ (d) $-4s^5 + 5s^4$
(e) $-9y^2 - 24y$ $\qquad$ (f) $6p - p^2$
(g) $16q - 8qr$ $\qquad$ (h) $3s^4 - 4s^3$

5. Factorise the following quadratic expressions.
(a) $x^2 + 5x + 4$ $\qquad$ (b) $x^2 + 20x + 100$
(c) $x^2 - 12x + 27$ $\qquad$ (d) $x^2 - 15x + 54$
(e) $x^2 + 10x + 16$ $\qquad$ (f) $x^2 - 5x + 4$
(g) $x^2 + 14x + 48$ $\qquad$ (h) $x^2 - 2x - 24$

6. Use the difference of two squares to factorise the following.
(a) $x^2 - 4$ $\qquad$ (b) $16x^3 - 36x$
(c) $x^2 - 9$ $\qquad$ (d) $9x^3 - 16x$

7. Calculate by long division.
(a) $1248 \div 24$ $\qquad$ (b) $9999 \div 99$
(c) $2088 \div 32$ $\qquad$ (d) $2920 \div 71$
(e) $2208 \div 23$ $\qquad$ (f) $975 \div 39$
(g) $5466 \div 65$ $\qquad$ (h) $3840 \div 85$

What you will learn

In this chapter, you will learn how to:

- Divide by an algebraic fraction.
- Cancel algebraic terms.
- Put an algebraic expression over a common denominator.
- Perform algebraic division (similar to the long division above).

All of the skills you have revised (expanding brackets, collecting like terms and factorisation) will be put to use in this chapter. In addition, we will introduce further techniques, which you may or may not have met before.

4.2 Algebraic Fractions

Dividing by an algebraic fraction
Remember that dividing by a fraction is achieved easily, by turning the fraction upside down (finding the **reciprocal**) and multiplying instead of dividing.

Worked Example

8. Work out $16 \div \dfrac{2}{3}$.

$$16 \div \frac{2}{3} = 16 \times \frac{3}{2}$$
$$= \frac{48}{2}$$
$$= 24$$

You can perform division by an algebraic fraction in the same way.

Worked Example

9. Simplify: $\dfrac{1}{x} \div \dfrac{a+b}{c}$

Multiply by the reciprocal of the second fraction:

$$\frac{1}{x} \div \frac{a+b}{c} = \frac{1}{x} \times \frac{c}{a+b}$$
$$= \frac{c}{x(a+b)}$$

Cancelling algebraic terms
You can also cancel algebraic terms in the same way you can cancel the terms in numerical fractions.

Worked Example

10. Simplify: $\dfrac{a^2 - b^2}{2} \times \dfrac{1}{a+b}$

Using the difference of two squares:

$$\frac{a^2 - b^2}{2} \times \frac{1}{a+b} = \frac{(a+b)(a-b)}{2} \times \frac{1}{a+b}$$

Cancelling the two $(a+b)$ terms:

$$= \frac{a-b}{2} \times \frac{1}{1}$$
$$= \frac{a-b}{2}$$

Putting an algebraic expression over a common denominator
When algebra is involved, the common denominator can usually be found by multiplying the two denominators together.

Worked Example

11. Use a common denominator to simplify the following: $\dfrac{1}{x-1} + \dfrac{x}{x+3}$

We use $(x-1)(x+3)$ as the common denominator. Multiply the top and bottom of the first fraction by $(x+3)$. Multiply the top and bottom of the second fraction by $(x-1)$. Putting the two terms over the common denominator gives:

$$\frac{x+3}{(x-1)(x+3)} + \frac{x(x-1)}{(x-1)(x+3)}$$
$$= \frac{(x+3) + x(x-1)}{(x-1)(x+3)}$$
$$= \frac{x^2 + 3}{(x-1)(x+3)}$$

Beware of factors that are repeated in the denominators of both fractions.

Worked Example

12. Simplify: $\dfrac{x-1}{(x+1)(x+2)} - \dfrac{x-3}{(x+1)(x+3)}$

Because the factor $(x+1)$ is repeated in both denominators, we need to include it only once in the common denominator.

Therefore we use $(x+1)(x+2)(x+3)$ as the common denominator.

$$\frac{x-1}{(x+1)(x+2)} - \frac{x-3}{(x+1)(x+3)}$$
$$= \frac{(x-1)(x+3) - (x-3)(x+2)}{(x+1)(x+2)(x+3)}$$
$$= \frac{(x^2 + 2x - 3) - (x^2 - x - 6)}{(x+1)(x+2)(x+3)}$$

$$= \frac{3x + 3}{(x + 1)(x + 2)(x + 3)}$$

$$= \frac{3(x + 1)}{(x + 1)(x + 2)(x + 3)}$$

$$= \frac{3}{(x + 2)(x + 3)}$$

Exercise 4B

1. Factorise each expression, where possible, and simplify the fractions.

   (a) $\dfrac{x^2 - 14x + 45}{x - 9}$ (b) $\dfrac{x^2 + 12x + 35}{x + 7}$

   (c) $\dfrac{x^2 + 6x - 7}{x - 1}$ (d) $\dfrac{x^2 - 3x - 28}{x + 4}$

   (e) $\dfrac{x^2 + 5x + 6}{x + 3}$

2. Factorise and simplify the following.

   (a) $\dfrac{x^2 + 8x + 16}{x^2 + 5x + 4}$ (b) $\dfrac{x^2 - 9x + 14}{x^2 - 8x + 7}$

   (c) $\dfrac{x^2 - 2x - 15}{x^2 + 4x + 3}$ (d) $\dfrac{x^2 - 8x + 12}{x^2 - 3x - 18}$

   (e) $\dfrac{x^2 + 4x - 32}{x^2 + 6x - 16}$

3. Simplify:

   (a) $(x^2 + 3x - 4) \div \dfrac{x + 4}{x + 6}$

   (b) $(x^2 - 6x + 5) \div \dfrac{x - 1}{x - 8}$

   (c) $(x^2 - 4x + 3) \div \dfrac{x - 3}{x + 7}$

   (d) $(x^2 - 12x + 36) \div \dfrac{x - 6}{x + 9}$

   (e) $(x^2 + 3x - 54) \div \dfrac{x - 6}{x - 8}$

4. Put the following expressions over a common denominator and simplify as far as possible.

   (a) $\dfrac{x}{x + 1} + \dfrac{1}{x - 1}$

   (b) $\dfrac{2}{3x - 2} - \dfrac{4}{2x - 3}$

   (c) $\dfrac{1}{(x^2 + 5x + 6)} - \dfrac{2}{x + 2}$

   (d) $\dfrac{4 + 2x}{(x - 1)(x + 2)} + \dfrac{3 - x}{(x - 1)(x - 3)}$

Simple algebraic division

The following technique is also known as **polynomial long division**. It is very similar to the numerical long division you have already practised. You should be familiar with the following key words when carrying out algebraic division:

- **Dividend:** The polynomial being divided. The numerator.
- **Divisor:** The polynomial being used to divide the dividend. The denominator.
- **Quotient:** The answer.
- **Remainder:** What is left over after division.

Worked Example

13. Work out: $\dfrac{x^3 + 3x^2 - 10x - 24}{x + 4}$

Because this is a division, we set it out like this:

Quotient

$$x + 4 \,)\overline{x^3 + 3x^2 - 10x - 24}$$

Divisor   Dividend

In the **divisor** $(x + 4)$, the **lead term** is x. What must we multiply x by to get x^3? The answer is x^2. This becomes the first term in the quotient:

$$\begin{array}{r} x^2 \\ x + 4 \,)\overline{x^3 + 3x^2 - 10x - 24} \end{array}$$

Now, multiply the divisor by this part of the answer, write the result on the next line down and subtract:

$$\begin{array}{r} x^2 \\ x + 4 \,)\overline{x^3 + 3x^2 - 10x - 24} \\ \underline{x^3 + 4x^2} \\ -x^2 \end{array}$$

At this point, we must bring down the term in the next column, $-10x$:

$$\begin{array}{r} x^2 \\ x + 4 \,)\overline{x^3 + 3x^2 - 10x - 24} \\ \underline{x^3 + 4x^2} \downarrow \\ -x^2 - 10x \end{array}$$

Repeat the operation: what must we multiply the lead term x by, in order to get $-x^2$?

The answer is $-x$, so this becomes the second term in the quotient. Then multiply the divisor by the $-x$, write the result in the next line down, subtract and bring down the next term, -24:

$$x + 4 \overline{)\begin{array}{c} x^2 - x \\ x^3 + 3x^2 - 10x - 24 \end{array}}$$
$$\begin{array}{c} \underline{x^3 + 4x^2} \\ -x^2 - 10x \\ \underline{-x^2 - 4x} \\ -6x - 24 \end{array}$$

We perform the division for a third time: the lead term x goes into $-6x$ a total of -6 times.

So -6 is the third term of the quotient. Again, multiply the divisor by this and write the result, $-6x - 24$, in the next line down. Performing the subtraction again gives 0:

$$x + 4 \overline{)\begin{array}{c} x^2 - x - 6 \\ x^3 + 3x^2 - 10x - 24 \end{array}}$$
$$\begin{array}{c} \underline{x^3 + 4x^2} \\ -x^2 - 10x \\ \underline{-x^2 - 4x} \\ -6x - 24 \\ \underline{-6x - 24} \\ 0 \end{array}$$

The zero indicates that there is no remainder. So from this we can write down:

$$\frac{x^3 + 3x^2 - 10x - 24}{x + 4} = x^2 - x - 6$$

Because there is no remainder, we know that $(x + 4)$ is a factor of $x^3 + 3x^2 - 10x - 24$.

From the previous example, you can see that polynomial long division has a lot in common with numerical long division. Here are some rules to follow, to help you organise your work:

- You can use polynomial long division if the **degree** of the divisor is less than or equal to the degree of the dividend. In the previous example, the divisor has degree 1; the dividend has degree 2.
- Sometimes, the dividend will not have a term in (for example) x^2. If any terms are missing from the dividend, fill them in with zero terms, as shown in the next example.

Worked Example

14. Work out: $(x^3 - x + 5) \div (x - 1)$

Remember to include the $0x^2$ term in the dividend. Then proceed as before:

$$x - 1 \overline{)\begin{array}{c} x^2 + x + 0 \\ x^3 + 0x^2 - x + 5 \end{array}}$$
$$\begin{array}{c} \underline{x^3 - x^2} \\ x^2 - x \\ \underline{x^2 - x} \\ 0x + 5 \\ \underline{0x - 0} \\ 5 \end{array}$$

The remainder is 5. From this we can say:

$$(x^3 - x + 5) \div (x - 1) = x^2 + x + \frac{5}{x - 1}$$

When writing out your answer like this, remember to put the remainder over the divisor. This is similar to saying:

$$11 \div 2 = 5\frac{1}{2}$$

Exercise 4C

1. Use long division to rewrite these expressions.
   (a) $(x^3 - x^2 - 2x) \div (x + 1)$
   (b) $(x^3 + 2x + 3) \div (x + 1)$
   (c) $(3x^3 + 2x^2 + 3x + 2) \div (3x + 2)$
   (d) $(x^3 - x^2 - x + 1) \div (x + 1)$

2. Rewrite these expressions with a remainder.
   (a) $(3x^3 + 4x^2 + 4x) \div (x + 1)$
   (b) $(3x^3 - 2x + 2) \div (x + 2)$
   (c) $(x^3 + 2x^2 - 3x + 1) \div (x + 2)$
   (d) $(2x^3 + 3x^2 - 2x + 1) \div (x + 3)$
   (e) $x^3 \div (x + 3)$
   (f) $(3x^3 - 3x^2 - x - 4) \div (x + 3)$

3. Use long division to rewrite these expressions.
   (a) $(x^4 + x^3 - x^2 + 1) \div (x + 1)$
   (b) $(x^4 + x^3 + 3x^2 + 4x + 1) \div (x + 1)$
   (c) $(2x^4 + 4x^3 - 4x^2 - 3x + 3) \div (x + 1)$
   (d) $(2x^4 - 3x^3 + 3x + 1) \div (2x + 1)$
   (e) $(2x^4 + 3x^3 - 4x^2 - 3x + 2) \div (x + 2)$
   (f) $(3x^4 + 4x^3 - 3x^2 - 2x + 2) \div (x + 1)$

4. Using long division, rewrite these expressions with a remainder.
   (a) $(x^4 + x^3 - 4x^2 - x + 1) \div (x + 2)$
   (b) $(x^4 + x^3 + 3x^2 - 4x + 2) \div (x + 1)$
   (c) $(x^4 + 3x^3 + 3x^2 + x + 2) \div (x + 3)$
   (d) $(2x^4 - x^3 - 3x + 1) \div (x + 1)$
   (e) $(3x^4 - 4x^3 - x^2 + 2) \div (x + 1)$

4.3 The Remainder Theorem

The remainder theorem is a quick method to find the remainder following a polynomial division.

> **The remainder theorem states that:**
>
> When any polynomial $f(x)$ is divided by $(ax - b)$, where a and b are real numbers, the remainder is $f\left(\dfrac{b}{a}\right)$.
>
> (Similarly, when $f(x)$ is divided by $(ax + b)$, the remainder is $f\left(-\dfrac{b}{a}\right)$.)

Proof of the remainder theorem

> **Note:** The CCEA specification (at the time of publication) does not require you to know this proof.

Consider the polynomial $f(x)$ and divide by $(ax - b)$.

We are left with some function $Q(x)$ (the quotient) and a remainder r:

$$\frac{f(x)}{ax - b} = Q(x) + \frac{r}{ax - b}$$

Multiplying throughout by $(ax - b)$ gives:

$$f(x) = (ax - b)Q(x) + r$$

When $x = \dfrac{b}{a}$, substituting for x gives:

$$f\left(\frac{b}{a}\right) = \left[a\left(\frac{b}{a}\right) - b\right]Q(x) + r$$

$$\Rightarrow f\left(\frac{b}{a}\right) = r$$

Examples of the remainder theorem

Worked Examples

15. Find the remainder when $(x^2 + 7x + 4)$ is divided by $(x - 2)$.

    Let $f(x) = x^2 + 7x + 4$

    As we are dividing by $(x - 2)$, we must evaluate $f(2)$:
    $$f(2) = 2^2 + 7(2) + 4$$
    $$= 22$$

    So dividing $(x^2 + 7x + 4)$ by $(x - 2)$ gives a remainder of 22.

    Note: This method doesn't tell us anything about the quotient. It is, of course, possible to check your answer using long division.

16. Find the remainder when $f(x) = 8x^3 + 7x^2 - 3x - 4$ is divided by $(3x + 1)$.

    According to the remainder theorem, we must evaluate $f\left(-\dfrac{1}{3}\right)$.
    $$f\left(-\frac{1}{3}\right) = 8\left(-\frac{1}{3}\right)^3 + 7\left(-\frac{1}{3}\right)^2 - 3\left(-\frac{1}{3}\right) - 4$$
    $$= -\frac{8}{27} + \frac{21}{27} + 1 - 4$$
    $$= \frac{13}{27} - 3$$
    $$= -\frac{68}{27}$$

You will also find the remainder theorem useful when finding a missing constant in a polynomial function.

Worked Example

17. The function $f(x) = x^3 + ax^2 + 6x - 7$ has remainder –3 when divided by $(x - 2)$. Find the value of a.

    According to the remainder theorem, $f(2) = -3$
    $$\therefore (2)^3 + a(2)^2 + 6(2) - 7 = -3$$
    $$8 + 4a + 12 - 7 = -3$$
    $$13 + 4a = -3$$
    $$4a = -16$$
    $$a = -4$$

Sometimes you will combine these techniques. You will find an unknown constant, then use it to evaluate a remainder.

Worked Example

18. Given that $f(x) = 4x^3 + 3x^2 - 49x + c$ and that $f(x)$ has a factor $(x - 3)$:
    (a) Evaluate the constant c.
    (b) Factorise $f(x)$ completely.
    (c) Find the remainder when $f(x)$ is divided by $(2x - 3)$.

    (a) $f(x)$ has a factor $(x - 3)$. By the remainder theorem, this means that $f(3) = 0$.
    $$f(3) = 4(3)^3 + 3(3)^2 - 49(3) + c$$
    $$= 108 + 27 - 147 + c$$

    Because $f(x)$ has a factor $(x - 3)$:
    $$108 + 27 - 147 + c = 0$$
    $$c = 12$$

(b) "Factorise completely" means factorise as fully as possible. Firstly, take out the factor of $(x - 3)$ we have already found:

$f(x) = (x - 3)(4x^2 + 15x - 4)$

The quadratic factor can be found using long division, which is left as an exercise for the reader. In this case, the function can now be written as the product of three linear terms:

$f(x) = (x - 3)(4x - 1)(x + 4)$

(c) When $f(x)$ is divided by $(2x - 3)$, the remainder is given by $f\left(\dfrac{3}{2}\right)$:

$f\left(\dfrac{3}{2}\right) = \left(\dfrac{3}{2} - 3\right)\left(4\left(\dfrac{3}{2}\right) - 1\right)\left(\dfrac{3}{2} + 4\right)$

$= -41.25$

Exercise 4D

1. In each case, find the remainder when $f(x)$ is divided by the given linear function of x.
   (a) $f(x) = 4x^3 + 4x^2 - 7x - 2$
       divided by $(x + 2)$
   (b) $f(x) = 3x^3 + 3x^2 - 6x - 2$
       divided by $(x - 2)$
   (c) $f(x) = 6x^3 + 5x^2 - 3x - 5$
       divided by $(x + 1)$
   (d) $f(x) = 7x^3 + 7x^2 - 4x - 1$
       divided by $(x - 1)$
   (e) $f(x) = 4x^3 + 2x^2 - 8x - 3$
       divided by $(2x + 3)$
   (f) $f(x) = 3x^3 + 5x^2 - 7x - 6$
       divided by $(x + 2)$
   (g) $f(x) = x^4 - 3x^3 - 2x^2 + 2x + 3$
       divided by $(x + 1)$
   (h) $f(x) = 2x^4 - 4x^3 - 5x^2 - 4$
       divided by $(x - 2)$
   (i) $f(x) = 3x^4 - 5x^2 - 5x - 4$
       divided by $(x + 2)$
   (j) $f(x) = 4x^4 - 4$ divided by $(x + 2)$
   (k) $f(x) = 2 + x^4$ divided by $(x - 2)$
   (l) $f(x) = -x + 3x^2 + 3x^3 + 4x^4$
       divided by $(x + 1)$
   (m) $f(x) = 5x^4 - 3x^2 - 1$ divided by $(x - 1)$
   (n) $f(x) = -2 - x^2 + x^4$ divided by $(x - 2)$

2. Find the value of a given that:
   $f(x) = x^3 + ax^2 + 10x - 11$
   has remainder -3 when divided by $x - 4$.

Exercise 4D...

3. Given: $f(x) = 4x^3 - 12x^2 - 4x + 12$,
   (a) find the remainder when $f(x)$ is divided by $(x - 2)$.
   (b) Given that $(x + 1)$ is a factor of $f(x)$, factorise $f(x)$ completely.

4. $f(x) = 3x^3 + 4x^2 - 13x + c$
   (a) Given that $f(1) = 0$, find the value of c.
   (b) Factorise $f(x)$ completely.
   (c) Find the remainder when $f(x)$ is divided by $(4x - 2)$.

5. Given: $f(x) = px^3 + 5x^2 + 11x + q$, and given that the remainder when $f(x)$ is divided by $(x - 1)$ is equal to the remainder when $f(x)$ is divided by $(2x + 1)$,
   (a) find the value of p.
   (b) Given also that $q = 3$, and p has the value found in part (a), find the value of the remainder.

6. Given: $f(x) = 12x^3 + px^2 + qx + 6$, and given that $f(x)$ is exactly divisible by $(3x - 1)$, and also that when $f(x)$ is divided by $(x - 1)$ the remainder is -24,
   (a) find the value of p and the value of q.
   (b) Hence factorise $f(x)$ completely.

7. The function f is defined such that:
   $f(x) = (x^2 + p)(5x + 74) + 222$,
   where p is a constant.
   (a) Write down the remainder when $f(x)$ is divided by $(5x + 74)$.
   (b) Given that the remainder when $f(x)$ is divided by $(x - 6)$ is 3654, prove that $p = -3$;
   (c) factorise $f(x)$ completely.

8. The function f is defined such that:
   $f(n) = n^3 + pn^2 + 15n + 14$
   where p is a constant.
   (a) Given that $f(n)$ has a remainder of 5 when it is divided by $(n + 3)$, prove that $p = 7$.
   (b) Show that $f(n)$ can be written in the form:
       $f(n) = (n + 3)(n + s)(n + t) + 5$
       where s and t are integers to be found.

4.4 The Factor Theorem

The factor theorem is a special case of the remainder theorem. It is a quick method for deciding whether $(x - a)$ is a factor of $f(x)$.

> **The factor theorem states that:**
>
> If $(ax - b)$ is a factor of the polynomial $f(x)$,
>
> then $f\left(\dfrac{b}{a}\right) = 0$.

Proof of the factor theorem

> **Note:** The CCEA specification (at the time of publication) does not require you to know this proof.

The factor theorem follows from the remainder theorem:

If $(ax - b)$ is a factor of the polynomial $f(x)$, then $(ax - b)$ divides $f(x)$ exactly and the remainder is zero.

Hence, by the remainder theorem, $f\left(\dfrac{b}{a}\right) = 0$.

Examples of the factor theorem

Worked Example

19. Show that $(x - 8)$ is a factor of:
$$f(x) = x^3 - 5x^2 - 18x - 48$$

$f(8) = (8)^3 - 5(8)^2 - 18(8) - 48$
$\qquad = 512 - 320 - 144 - 48$
$\qquad = 0$

Hence, $(x - 8)$ is a factor of $f(x)$.

Note: Be careful with your signs!
If $f(a) = 0$, then $(x - a)$ is a factor.
If $f(-a) = 0$, then $(x + a)$ is a factor.

Sometimes, as in the remainder theorem, you will need to find a missing constant in the polynomial.

Worked Examples

20. Find the value of a, given that $(x - 2)$ is a factor of $f(x)$, where: $f(x) = x^3 + ax^2 + 9x - 10$

By the factor theorem, $f(2) = 0$

So: $(2)^3 + a(2)^2 + 9(2) - 10 = 0$
$\qquad\quad 8 + 4a + 18 - 10 = 0$
$\qquad\qquad\quad 16 + 4a = 0$
$\qquad\qquad\qquad\quad a = -4$

21. (a) Show that $(x - 4)$ and $(x - 5)$ are factors of:
$$f(x) = x^3 - 8x^2 + 11x + 20$$
(b) Factorise $f(x)$ completely.

(a) $f(4) = (4)^3 - 8(4)^2 + 11(4) + 20$
$\qquad\quad = 0$
Hence $(x - 4)$ is a factor of $f(x)$.

$f(5) = (5)^3 - 8(5)^2 + 11(5) + 20$
$\qquad = 0$
Hence $(x - 5)$ is a factor of $f(x)$.

(b) $f(x) = (x - 4)(x - 5)(\ldots)$
$f(x) = (x - 4)(x - 5)(x + 1)$

This last step can be done by inspection to complete the final set of brackets:
- we must have $1x$ to give x^3 when multiplied out;
- we must have $+1$ to make the units $+20$ when multiplied out.

Alternatively, use long division to find the final linear factor.

If you know one linear factor of a cubic, there will be a quadratic factor that you can also find using long division. When you have found the quadratic, you might be able to factorise it to end up with three linear factors for the cubic. Of course, not all quadratics will factorise.

Worked Example

22. (a) Show that $(x - 7)$ is a factor of:
$$f(x) = x^3 - 10x^2 + 11x + 70$$
(b) Using long division, factorise $f(x)$ completely.

(a) $f(7) = (7)^3 - 10(7)^2 + 11(7) + 70$
$\qquad\quad = 0$
Hence $(x - 7)$ is a factor of $f(x)$.

(b) Use long division to find the quadratic factor:

$$
\require{enclose}
\begin{array}{r}
x^2 - 3x - 10 \\[-2pt]
x - 7 \enclose{longdiv}{x^3 - 10x^2 + 11x + 70} \\
\underline{x^3 - 7x^2} \\
-3x^2 + 11x \\
\underline{-3x^2 + 21x} \\
-10x + 70 \\
\underline{-10x + 70} \\
0
\end{array}
$$

Note: The remainder is zero because, as we have already discovered, $(x - 7)$ is a factor. Hence:
$$f(x) = (x - 7)(x^2 - 3x - 10)$$

Now, factorise the quadratic:
$$f(x) = (x - 7)(x - 5)(x + 2)$$

Sometimes you may need to use trial and improvement to find one of the factors of a cubic, before going on to factorise it completely.

Worked Example

23. Factorise $f(x)$ completely, where:
$$f(x) = x^3 - 5x^2 - 4x + 20$$

Trial and improvement:

Guess $(x + 1)$ is a factor:
$$f(-1) = (-1)^3 - 5(-1)^2 - 4(-1) + 20$$
$$= -1 - 5 + 4 + 20$$
$$= 18$$
Hence $(x + 1)$ is not a factor.

Guess $(x + 2)$ is a factor:
$$f(-2) = (-2)^3 - 5(-2)^2 - 4(-2) + 20$$
$$= -8 - 20 + 8 + 20$$
$$= 0$$
Hence $(x + 2)$ is a factor.

Find the quadratic factor using long division:

$$
\begin{array}{r}
x^2 - 7x + 10 \\
x + 2 \overline{)x^3 - 5x^2 - 4x + 20} \\
\underline{x^3 + 2x^2} \\
-7x^2 - 4x \\
\underline{-7x^2 - 14x} \\
10x + 20 \\
\underline{10x + 20} \\
0
\end{array}
$$

Hence: $f(x) = (x + 2)(x^2 - 7x + 10)$
$$ = (x + 2)(x - 5)(x - 2)$$

Exercise 4E

1. For each of the following functions $f(x)$, decide whether the given linear expression is a factor. If not, give the remainder when $f(x)$ is divided by the linear expression.
   (a) $f(x) = x^3 + 5x^2 - 62x - 22$ $\qquad(x - 2)$
   (b) $f(x) = x^3 + 3x^2 - x - 18$ $\qquad(x - 2)$
   (c) $f(x) = x^3 - 2x^2 - 33x - 14$ $\qquad(x - 1)$
   (d) $f(x) = x^3 + 12x^2 + 39x - 59$ $\qquad(x + 1)$
   (e) $f(x) = x^3 + 4x^2 - 17x - 12$ $\qquad(x - 3)$
   (f) $f(x) = x^3 - 3x^2 - 6x - 20$ $\qquad(x - 5)$
   (g) $f(x) = x^3 + 11x^2 + 33x - 19$ $\qquad(x - 1)$
   (h) $f(x) = x^3 + 5x^2 - 35x - 4$ $\qquad(x - 4)$
   (i) $f(x) = x^3 - 6x^2 - 5x - 17$ $\qquad(x + 1)$
   (j) $f(x) = x^3 + 13x^2 + 44x - 14$ $\qquad(x - 2)$
   (k) $f(x) = x^3 + 5x^2 - 46x - 20$ $\qquad(x - 5)$
   (l) $f(x) = x^3 - 4x^2 - 14x - 49$ $\qquad(x - 3)$

Exercise 4E...

2. Show that $(x - 8)$ and $(x - 9)$ are factors of $f(x) = x^3 - 13x^2 + 4x + 288$ and factorise $f(x)$ completely.

3. **(a)** Using the factor theorem, show that $(x + 3)$ is a factor of: $f(x) = x^3 - 2x^2 - 11x + 12$
   (b) Factorise $f(x)$ completely.

4. Given that $f(x) = 2x^3 + x^2 - 166x + 240$:
   (a) Use the factor theorem to show that $(x + 10)$ is a factor of $f(x)$.
   (b) Factorise $f(x)$ completely.
   (c) Write down all the solutions to the equation: $2x^3 + x^2 - 166x + 240 = 0$

5. Find the value of a given that $(x - 2)$ is a factor of $f(x)$, where $f(x) = x^3 + ax^2 + 8x - 4$

6. Given that $(x - 3)$ is a factor of $f(x)$, where $f(x) = x^3 + px^2 + 9x - 9$, find the value of p.

7. Use the factor theorem to factorise $f(x)$ completely:
   (a) $f(x) = x^3 - x^2 - 16x + 16$
   (b) $f(x) = x^3 - 4x^2 - 3x + 18$
   (c) $f(x) = x^3 - 3x^2 - 9x + 27$
   (d) $f(x) = x^3 - 2x^2 - 9x + 18$

4.5 Summary

There are many ways in which an algebraic expression can be manipulated:

- You can divide an algebraic fraction by another by finding the reciprocal of the second fraction and multiplying.
- You can cancel algebraic terms if the same expression appears in numerator and denominator.
- You can use a common denominator when adding or subtracting expressions.

You can use **polynomial long division** to divide one polynomial by another, providing the degree of the divisor is less than or equal to the degree of the dividend.

If only the remainder is required, the **remainder theorem** is quicker than long division.

If you need to know whether a linear expression is a factor of a polynomial (i.e. the remainder is 0), the **factor theorem** can be used.

Chapter 5
Graphs and Transformations

5.1 Introduction

At GCSE you learnt how to draw an accurate **plot** of a curve or straight line, usually from its equation and a table of (x, y) values.

At A level, you will often be asked to draw a **sketch** of a curve. A sketch does not have to be as accurate as a plot. But you will need to highlight certain key points, for example the general shape of the curve and where it crosses the axes.

Key words

- **Cubic**: An equation linking x and y, in which there is a term in x^3.
- **Reciprocal**: One over. For example, the reciprocal of 2 is ½; the reciprocal of x is $\dfrac{1}{x}$.
- **Root**: A solution to $f(x) = 0$. One way to find a root is to sketch a graph.
- **Asymptote**: On a graph, a straight line that a curve approaches, but never touches.

Before you start

You should know:

- How to factorise an expression.
- How to sketch the graph of a quadratic function.

Worked Examples

1. Factorise $x^3 + 3x^2 - 4x$

   $x^3 + 3x^2 - 4x = x(x^2 + 3x - 4)$
   $= x(x + 4)(x - 1)$

2. Sketch the curve $y = x^2 - 6x + 8$

   Firstly, because we have a positive coefficient of x^2, this curve has a minimum point.

   Factorising gives:
   $y = (x - 4)(x - 2)$

   To find out where the graph intersects the x-axis, we set $y = 0$: $(x - 4)(x - 2) = 0$
   so: $(x - 4) = 0$ or $(x - 2) = 0$
   giving: $x = 4$ or $x = 2$

To find out where the graph intersects the y-axis, we set $x = 0$. When $x = 0$, $y = 8$.

We now have enough information to sketch the curve:

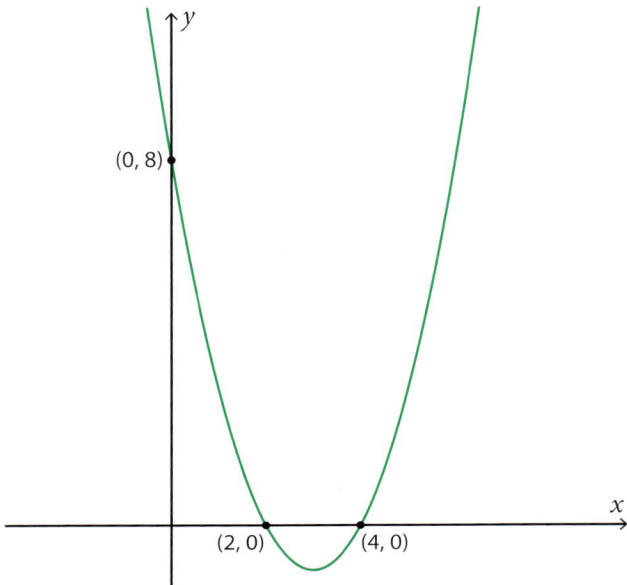

Remember that a sketch is exactly that! You do not need to draw a table of values or plot any (x, y) points exactly. You are not plotting a graph. Instead, you will need to show the shape of the curve, and where it crosses the axes.

Exercise 5A (Revision)

1. Factorise the following expressions.
   (a) $x^3 + 5x^2 + 6x$ (b) $9x^3 - 16x$
   (c) $9x^3 - 25x$ (d) $x^3 - 4x^2 + 3x$
   (e) $x^3 - 3x^2 + 2x$

2. Sketch the following quadratic curves, indicating all important points, such as where the curves cross the axes.
   (a) $y = (x - 1)(x + 1)$
   (b) $y = x(x + 3)$
   (c) $y = x^2 - 2x - 3$
   (d) $y = -x^2 - 5x - 6$
   (e) $y = x^2 - 16$

What you will learn

In this chapter you will learn how to:

- Sketch a cubic curve.
- Sketch a reciprocal curve.
- Solve equations using these graphs.
- Perform simple transformations on these graphs.

In chapter 2, you learnt that **completing the square** is a useful technique for finding the maximum or minimum point of a parabola (a quadratic curve).

In chapter 11, you will learn how to find the coordinates of the maximum or minimum points for all the curves you are sketching. These points are also known as the **turning points** or **stationary points**.

In this chapter, you will not mark these points on your sketches, but you will need to do so if you are asked to sketch a curve in an exam.

In the real world...

Modern architecture is all about mathematics. A highly geometrically-shaped building, like **the Gherkin** in London, is often defined using a set of equations. A sketch of the building using these equations is a starting point for all modern architecture.

Many Computer Assisted Design software packages are available to help in the task of designing a building. These assist the architect not just with the physical appearance, but also with the airflow inside and around the building, the strength of the structure, ensuring there is enough light in and around the building, the location of doors and windows, etc.

5.2 Sketching Cubic Curves

The general cubic equation is:
$$y = ax^3 + bx^2 + cx + d$$
where a, b, c and d are constants, usually integers.

The shape of a cubic curve is typically one of these:

If a > 0:

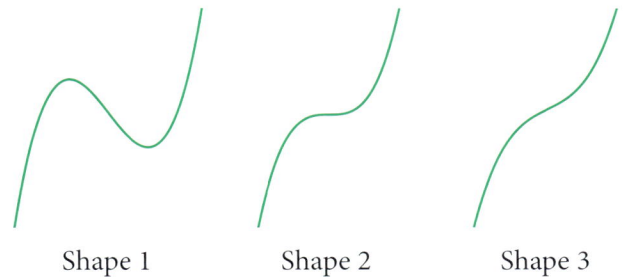

Shape 1   Shape 2   Shape 3

If a < 0:

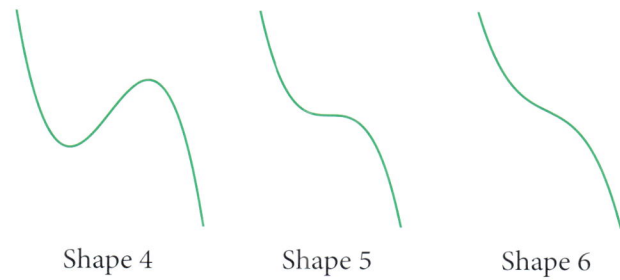

Shape 4   Shape 5   Shape 6

As with quadratic curves, it is possible to sketch a cubic curve without plotting exact points.

Worked Example

3. Sketch the graph of the cubic:
$$y = (x + 1)(x - 1)(x - 2)$$

Expanding the brackets would give a positive x^3 term. This indicates that the curve takes one of the curve shapes 1 – 3 above. Note that we do not need to expand the brackets fully.

Secondly, work out where the curve crosses the x-axis. When $y = 0$:
$$(x + 1)(x - 1)(x - 2) = 0$$
So either $x = -1$, $x = 1$ or $x = 2$.

This curve crosses the x-axis in three places: $(-1, 0)$, $(1, 0)$ and $(2, 0)$. Because there are three crossing points, the curve must be similar to shape 1 above.

Finally, work out where the curve crosses the y-axis:
When $x = 0$:
$$y = (0 + 1)(0 - 1)(0 - 2)$$
$$= 2$$
So this curve crosses the y-axis at the point $(0, 2)$.

We now have enough information to sketch the curve:

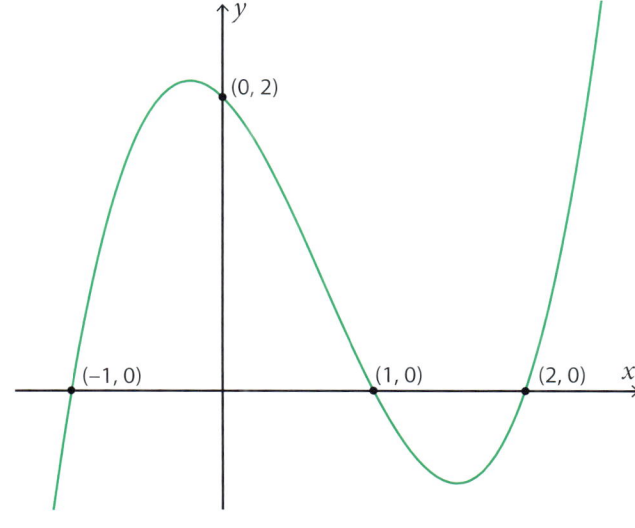

As we have already discussed, later in this book you will learn how to find the coordinates of the stationary points of a curve (one maximum and one minimum point in this case).

Worked Example

4. Sketch the graph defined by the equation:
$y = -x(x - 1)(x - 2)$

Expanding brackets would give a negative x^3 term:
$y = -x^3 + \cdots$
You don't need to expand the brackets fully. So this time the curve is one of the curve shapes 4 – 6 above, since $a = -1$.

First, find out where the curve crosses the y-axis.
When $x = 0$: $y = -(0)(-1)(-2)$
$= 0$.
So the curve passes through $(0, 0)$.

Next, find out where the curve crosses the x-axis.
When $y = 0$, $x = 0$, $x = 1$ or $x = 2$. So the curve passes through $(0, 0)$, $(1, 0)$ and $(2, 0)$.

Because there are three crossing points, the curve must be similar to shape 4 above.

We now have enough information to sketch the curve:

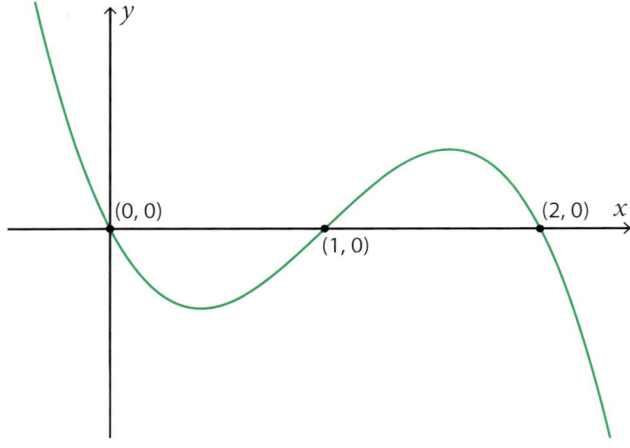

In the two examples above, we have looked at two cubic curves that both intersect the x-axis three times. This indicates that the solution to the equation $y = 0$ has three roots. Here are some of the possibilities for the number of roots.

- Three **unique roots**. Given in its factorised form, the curve shown below is $y = -x(x - 1)(x - 2)$ with roots at $x = 0$, $x = 1$ and $x = 2$.

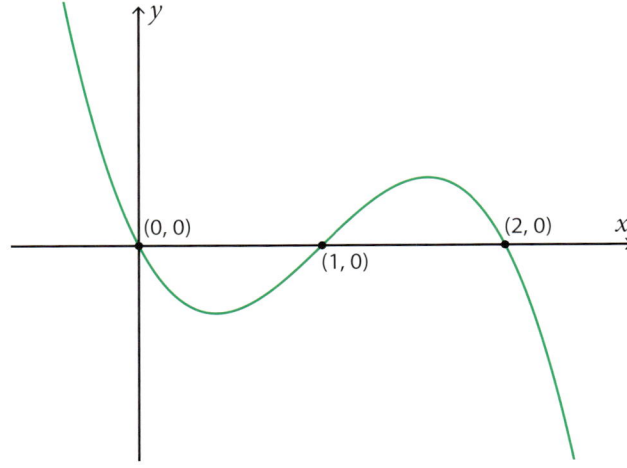

- One **unique root** and one **repeated root**. The example shown below is $y = (x - 1)(x - 2)^2$. In this case the repeated root is $x = 2$. The curve touches the x-axis at this point, but does not pass through it.

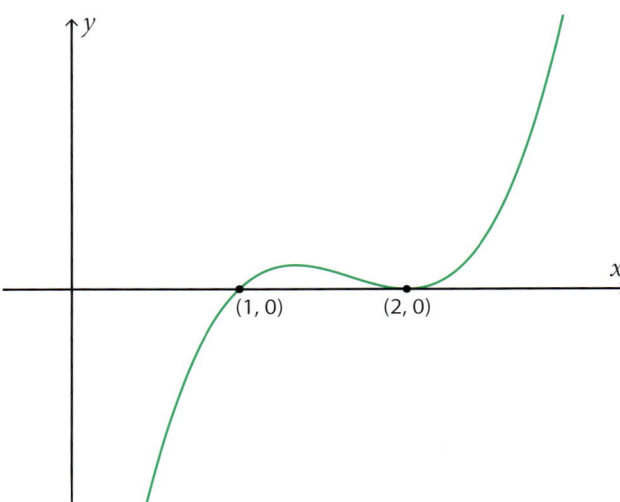

- One **triple root**. The curve becomes flat on the x-axis. The example shown below is $y = (x + 1)^3$.

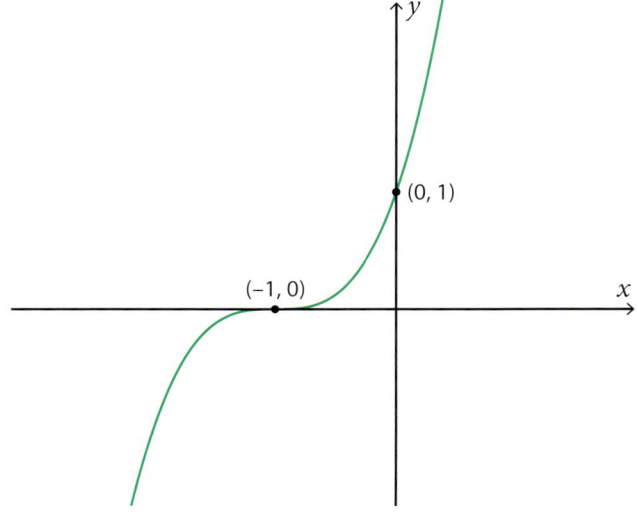

- One **unique root**. The example shown below is $y = x^3 - 3x^2 + 4x - 2$.

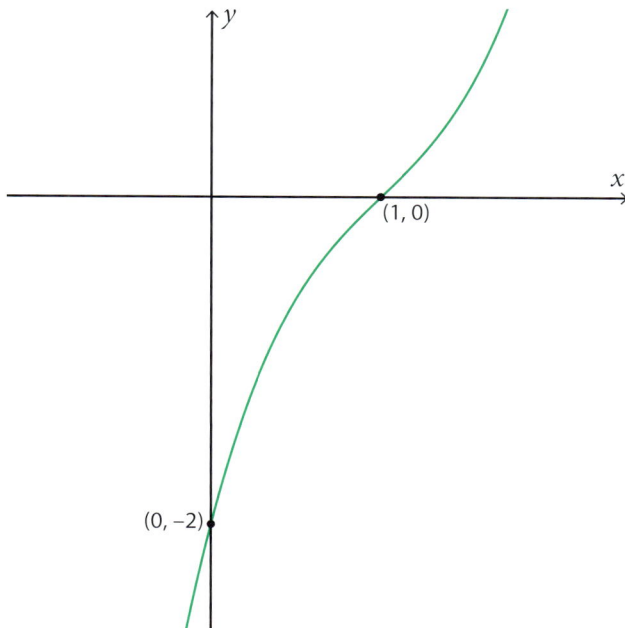

In the case of the **triple root**, notice that the curve is flat when it intersects the x-axis. This is a new type of stationary point, which is neither a maximum nor a minimum. We call it a **point of inflection**.

As with quadratics, it can be difficult or impossible to factorise some cubics (factorising cubic equations using the factor theorem was covered in chapter 4.) In the next example, you will learn a technique that can be used to estimate the number of roots of a cubic.

Worked Example

5. By sketching two suitable curves on the same diagram, estimate the number of roots of:
$y = x^3 - x - 3$

Finding the roots means finding where the curve crosses the x-axis or, in other words, solving:
$x^3 - x - 3 = 0$

First, note that it is not possible to factorise our function of x. But it is equivalent to solving:
$x^3 = x + 3$

So now we can sketch the two curves, $y = x^3$ and $y = x + 3$. Any intersection points will be the roots of our original equation:

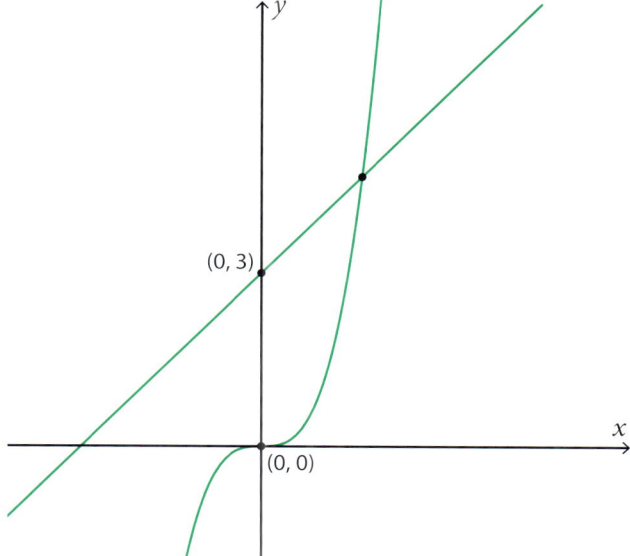

We can see that the two curves intersect once. This means that there is **one** root to the original equation, $y = x^3 - x - 3$.

Note: the question does not ask us to find or estimate the solution(s). It only asks how many there are.

> **Note** the use of the word **curve** in the previous example. Two **curves** were sketched, even though one is a straight line. It may seem odd, but straight lines are all curves.

Exercise 5B

1. State where each curve intersects both the y-axis and the x-axis.
   (a) $f(x) = (x + 4)(x - 3)(x + 1)$
   (b) $f(x) = -(x - 3)(x - 9)(x + 1)$
   (c) $f(x) = x(x - 3)(x + 2)$
   (d) $f(x) = -x(x - 9)(8 - x)$
   (e) $f(x) = (2x - 1)(x - 3)^2$
   (f) $f(x) = (2x + 1)x^2$
   (g) $f(x) = -x(x^2 - 25)$
   (h) $f(x) = (x + 3)^3$
   (i) $f(x) = (2x - 1)^3$
   (j) $f(x) = x^3 - 12x^2 + 36x$

2. Factorise and find the roots of each equation. Hence sketch the curves.
   (a) $y = x^3 - 18x^2 + 81x$
   (b $y = x^3 - 30x^2 + 225x$

3. Factorise and find solutions to $f(x) = 0$. Hence sketch the curve $y = f(x)$.
   (a) $f(x) = x^3 + 5x^2 + 6x$
   (b) $f(x) = x^3 + 18x^2 + 80x$

Exercise 5B...

(c) $f(x) = -x^3 - 11x^2 - 10x$
(d) $f(x) = x^3 + 13x^2 + 40x$
(e) $f(x) = x^3 + 17x^2 + 70x$
(f) $f(x) = 16x^3 - 25x$
(g) $f(x) = 9x^3 - 16x$
(h) $f(x) = -x^3 + 3x^2 - 2x$
(i) $f(x) = x^3 - 5x^2 + 4x$
(j) $f(x) = -x^3 + 12x^2 - 35x$

4. Given each function $f(x)$ below:
   (i) Express $f(x)$ in the form
      $x(ax^2 + bx + c)$
      where a, b and c are constants.
   (ii) Hence factorise $f(x)$ completely.
   (iii) Sketch the curve $y = f(x)$.
   (iv) State the roots of the equation $f(x) = 0$.
   (a) $f(x) = (x^2 - 8x)(x - 4) + 3x$
   (b) $f(x) = (x^2 - 8x)(x - 3) + 4x$
   (c) $f(x) = -(x^2 - 9x)(x - 5) - 3x$

5.3 Sketching Reciprocal Curves

In this section you will learn how to sketch curves with equations in the form:

$$y = \frac{k}{x} \text{ or } y = \frac{k}{x^2}$$

where k is an integer. These curves are known as reciprocal curves.

A sketch of a reciprocal graph of the form $y = \frac{k}{x}$ takes one of these two shapes:

Curve shape 1, if $k > 0$:   **Curve shape 2, if $k < 0$:**

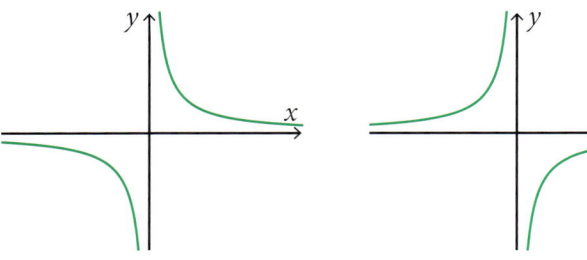

Reciprocal graphs have two distinct branches. Both branches of the curve approach the x-axis (the line $y = 0$), but never touch it. They also approach the y-axis (the line $x = 0$), but never touch it. We call the lines $x = 0$ and $y = 0$ the **asymptotes** of these curves. We say:

y approaches 0 as x approaches infinity

And we write:

$y \to 0$ as $x \to \infty$

You can also see in both sketches:

$y \to 0$ as $x \to -\infty$

You can also find the position of a horizontal asymptote using the equation of a curve, in this case $y = \frac{k}{x}$.

You can see that, as x gets larger, y gets closer to zero, but never becomes zero. So $y = 0$ is the horizontal asymptote.

To find the position of the vertical asymptote, look at the denominator. x can never take the value 0, because you cannot divide by 0. So the line $x = 0$ is the equation of the vertical asymptote.

If you are asked to sketch a reciprocal curve, you will use these techniques to discover where the asymptotes lie.

For the curve $y = \frac{k}{x}$, the lines $x = 0$ and $y = 0$ are therefore **asymptotes** of the curve (both when $k > 0$ and when $k < 0$). The curve approaches these asymptotes, but never touches them.

....

Worked Examples

6. Sketch the graph of $y = \frac{2}{x}$

A table of values gives these points:

x	-4	-2	-1	-0.5	0.5	1	2	4
y	-0.5	-1	-2	-4	4	2	1	0.5

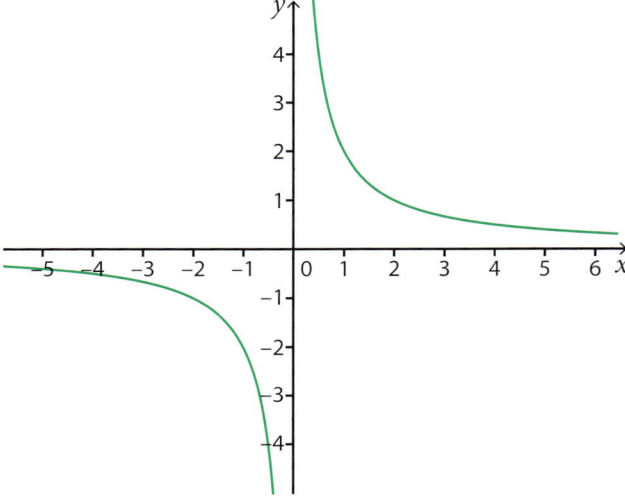

The lines $x = 0$ and $y = 0$ are asymptotes to the curve.

7. Sketch the graph of $y = \frac{4}{x^2}$

A table of values gives these points:

x	-4	-2	-1	-0.5	0.5	1	2	4
y	0.25	1	4	16	16	4	1	0.25

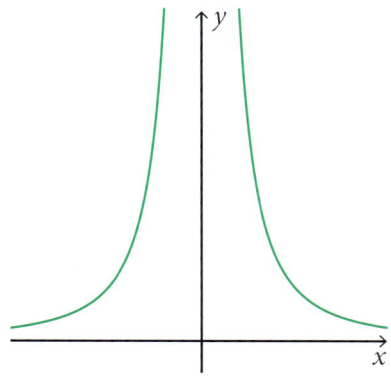

The lines $x = 0$ and $y = 0$ are asymptotes to the curve.

....

For curves whose equations are of the form $y = \dfrac{k}{x^2}$, both branches of the curve lie above the x-axis because y cannot take a negative value. As with curves of the form $y = \dfrac{k}{x}$, a larger value of k gives a curve that lies further from the axes.

Now that you know the general shape of the reciprocal curves, you do not need to draw a table of values for every sketch.

....

Worked Example

8. Sketch the curves $y = -\dfrac{2}{x}$ and $y = -\dfrac{4}{x}$ on the same diagram.

Recall that this type of reciprocal curve has asymptotes along $x = 0$ and $y = 0$.

We can also see that the second curve will always have y-values double those of the first curve.

Using this information, the sketch looks like this:

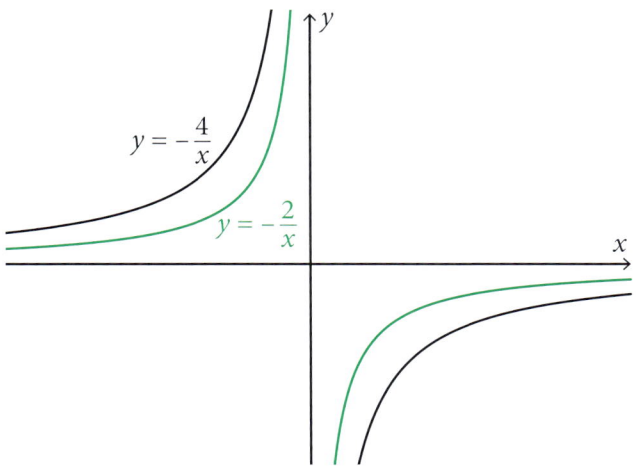

In general, the further k is from 0 (positive or negative), the further the curve lies from its asymptotes.

....

1. Sketch each pair of curves on the same diagram.
   (a) $y = \dfrac{1}{x}$ and $y = \dfrac{3}{x}$
   (b) $y = -\dfrac{2}{x}$ and $y = -\dfrac{6}{x}$
   (c) $y = \dfrac{1}{2x}$ and $y = \dfrac{1}{4x}$
   (d) $y = -\dfrac{1}{2x}$ and $y = -\dfrac{1}{6x}$

2. (a) Sketch the curve given by $y = \dfrac{1}{x}$
   (b) Sketch, on the same diagram, the curve given by $y = \dfrac{1}{x^2}$

3. Consider the curve $y = \dfrac{x}{(x - 1)}$
   (a) Considering the denominator, what value can x not take? What is the equation of the vertical asymptote?
   (b) Where does the curve cross the y-axis?
   (c) What happens to y as x approaches infinity and minus infinity?
   (d) Sketch the curve.

5.4 Simultaneous Equations and Intersection Points

Using intersection points of graphs to solve equations

In chapter 3, you learnt how to solve simultaneous **quadratic** and **linear** equations algebraically. You also learnt that if you plot the curves of the two equations, the solution to the simultaneous equations is given by the intersection points.

This technique can be taken further. In general, any two simultaneous equations can be solved graphically by finding the intersection points of two curves.

You will rarely be asked to plot an accurate graph to find the intersection points. Instead, a sketch can be used. In this way the number of solutions can be estimated.

Worked Example

9. A sketch of the graph of $y = \dfrac{1}{x} + 1$ is shown.

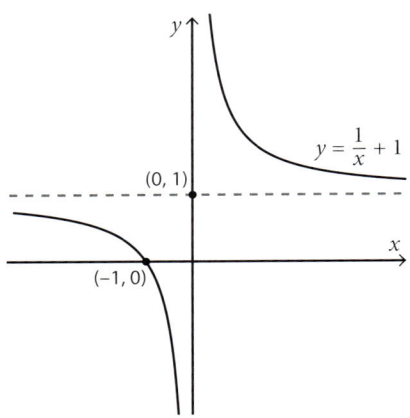

(a) On the same diagram, sketch the curve $y = x^2(x - 2)$.

(b) Hence find the number of solutions to the equation $x^2(x - 2) = \dfrac{1}{x} + 1$.

(a) The graph of $y = x^2(x - 2)$ is a cubic curve. It passes through the x-axis when $x = 2$ and has a repeated root (touches the x-axis) at $x = 0$. Because of the positive x^3 term, it starts low and finishes high. So we can sketch:

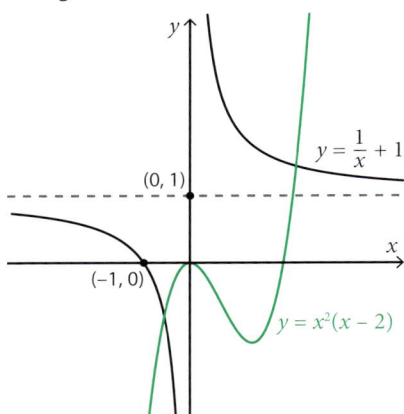

(b) From the sketch we can see that there are two points of intersection. Hence there are two solutions to the equation $x^2(x - 2) = \dfrac{1}{x} + 1$

Interpreting the algebraic solution of equations graphically

You will also be asked to use this technique in reverse. Solving two simultaneous equations algebraically can then give you information about the intersection points of two curves you are sketching.

Worked Example

10. (a) Solve these simultaneous equations:
$$y = \frac{5}{x} \text{ and } y = 2x + 3$$

(b) Sketch the graph of the curve $y = \dfrac{5}{x}$.
On the same diagram, sketch the line $y = 2x + 3$.

(c) Find the range of values of x for which
$$2x + 3 > \frac{5}{x}.$$

(a) Using the substitution method to eliminate y:
$$\frac{5}{x} = 2x + 3$$

Multiplying throughout by x gives:
$5 = 2x^2 + 3x$

Re-arranging leaves a quadratic equation:
$2x^2 + 3x - 5 = 0$

Factorising:
$(2x + 5)(x - 1) = 0$
Giving: $2x = -5$ or $x = 1$
So: $x = -\dfrac{5}{2}$ or $x = 1$

To find y, substitute both values into one of our equations. Choose the simplest one, $y = 2x + 3$:
When $x = -\dfrac{5}{2}, y = -2$
When $x = 1, y = 5$
Be careful to pair the x and y values together correctly!

(b) Using the reciprocal curve sketching techniques learnt in the previous section, we can sketch the curve $y = \dfrac{5}{x}$.

We can also sketch the straight line $y = 2x + 3$, knowing that the y-intercept is 3 and the gradient is 2.

We can mark the intersection points of the curves A(-2.5, -2) and B(1, 5) using the answers from part (a):

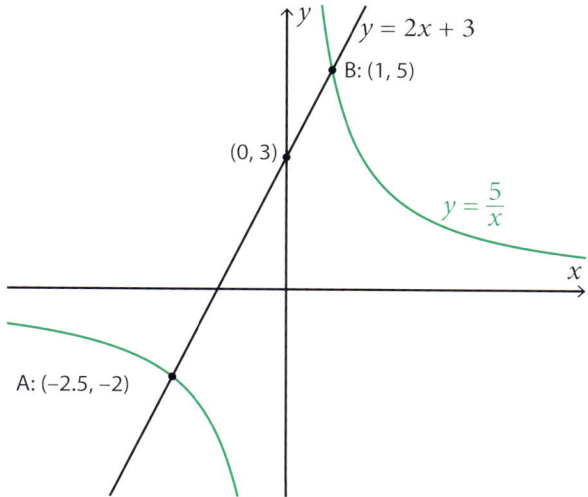

Note that, in this case, the straight line intersects the curve once on each branch of the curve. It is possible in some cases for a straight line to intersect the same branch twice.

(c) From the sketch we can see that the straight line $y = 2x + 3$ lies above the curve $y = \dfrac{5}{x}$ between point A and the y-axis, then again to the right of point B.

Hence $2x + 3 > \dfrac{5}{x}$ when $-2.5 < x < 0$ or $x > 1$.

....

If you are asked only to calculate the number of points of intersection, not their coordinates, try to re-arrange the equations into a single quadratic equation. As discussed in chapter 2, calculating the **discriminant** $b^2 - 4ac$ will then give information about the number of solutions:

- $b^2 - 4ac > 0 \Rightarrow$ two real roots,
- $b^2 - 4ac = 0 \Rightarrow$ one real root,
- $b^2 - 4ac < 0 \Rightarrow$ no real roots.

....

Worked Example

11. Determine the number of intersection points of the curve $y = x^2 - 3x + 5$ and the straight line $y = -4x$.

Consider the simultaneous equations:
$y = x^2 - 3x + 5$ and $y = -4x$

To find points of intersection, we would solve:
$x^2 - 3x + 5 = -4x$
$\Rightarrow x^2 + x + 5 = 0$

To find the number of points of intersection, we do not need to solve the equation, but only calculate the discriminant:
$b^2 - 4ac = 1^2 - 4(1)(5) = -19$

A negative discriminant means that there are no solutions to this quadratic. Hence there are no points of intersection.

....

Exercise 5D

1. Draw a sketch of each pair of curves on the same diagram, showing that there are two intersection points. Find the solutions to each pair of simultaneous equations.
   (a) $y = -\dfrac{1}{x}$, $y = 2x - 3$
   (b) $y = -\dfrac{3}{x}$, $y = 2x + 7$
   (c) $y = -\dfrac{4}{x}$, $y = 2x + 9$
   (d) $y = \dfrac{24}{x}$, $y = 4x + 10$
   (e) $y = -\dfrac{15}{x}$, $y = 2x - 11$
   (f) $y = -\dfrac{52}{x}$, $y = 4x - 34$

2. Sketch the following pairs of curves on the same diagram. Find all the solutions to the simultaneous equations.
   (a) $y = x^2 - 2x + 5$, $y = 7x - 15$
   (b) $y = x^2 - 4x + 8$, $y = 13x - 62$

3. (a) Solve the simultaneous equations:
   $y + 4x = 6$, $4x^2 - 2x - y = 6$
   (b) On the same diagram, sketch the two curves.
   (c) Using your sketch, or otherwise, find the set of values of x for which:
   $4x^2 - 2x - 6 > 6 - 4x$

4. In each part below, two quadratic curves have equations given. In each case:
   (i) Eliminate y to obtain a single quadratic equation.
   (ii) By calculating the **discriminant**, decide whether the curves have 0, 1 or 2 points of intersection.
   (iii) Sketch the two curves on the same diagram, marking any points of intersection.
   (a) $y = 2x^2 + 3$, $y = x^2 + 4$
   (b) $y = 2x^2$, $y = 4x^2 + 4x + 2$
   (c) $y = x^2 + 2x + 1$, $y = 2x^2 + 4$
   (d) $y = -x^2$, $y = x^2 + 5x + 2$
   (e) $y = -x^2 + 2x - 4$, $y = 2x^2 - 4x - 1$
   (f) $y = -x^2 - 4x - 4$, $y = 4x^2$

45

Exercise 5D...

5. Eliminate y to obtain a single equation and find any points of intersection of the two curves:
$$y = x^2 + 6x + 3, \qquad y = x^2 + 4x + 3$$
Sketch the two curves, marking any points of intersection.

6. Consider the two equations:
$$y = (x - 1)(x - 2)(x - 3), \qquad y = 2x - 6$$
(a) Solve the simultaneous equations. (Hint: eliminate y and then factorise the cubic.)
(b) Sketch the two curves on the same diagram. (Using your solution to part (a) you will be able to mark on the points of intersection.)

7. For each pair of equations:
(i) On the same axes sketch the two curves and give the coordinates of all the points where the curves cross the x-axis.
(ii) Use algebra to find the coordinates of the points where the curves intersect.
(a) $y = x^2(x - 2), \qquad y = x(12 - x)$
(b) $y = x^2(x - 3), \qquad y = x(24 - x)$

8. (a) Sketch, on the same diagram, the two curves:
$$y = x(4 - x), \qquad y = x^2(5 - x)$$
(b) Mark on your diagram where each curve crosses the coordinate axes.
(c) Using your sketch, estimate the number of solutions to the equation
$$x(x^2 - 6x + 4) = 0$$

5.5 Transformations of Curves

You will need to know the effects of transformations on the shapes of curves. These transformations are: translations parallel to the x- and y-axes, stretches parallel to the x- and y-axes and reflections in the x- and y-axes.

Given the sketch of a function, you may be asked to draw the sketch after a transformation. To do this, note the important features of the given function, e.g. where the curve crosses the axes and the positions of any turning points. Work out where the corresponding features will be on the new curve.

Translations

To **translate** an object on the x-y plane means to move it without changing its shape or orientation.

Suppose you know the shape of the curve $y = f(x)$. Then, the curve:

- $y = f(x) + a$ will be a **translation** by a units in the positive y-direction;
- $y = f(x - a)$ will be a **translation** by a units in the positive x-direction.

Worked Example

12. The diagram shows the curve $y = f(x)$.

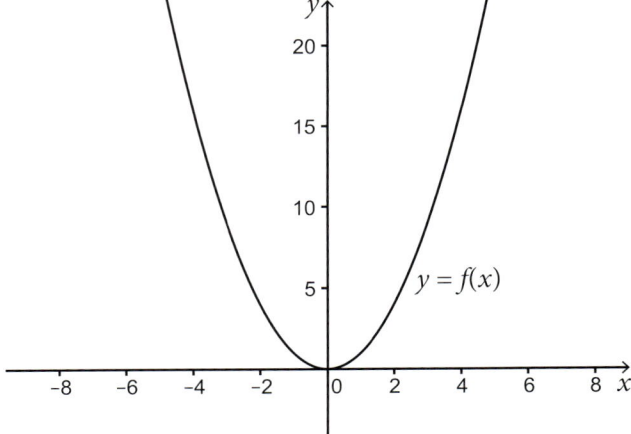

(a) On the same diagram, sketch the graphs of:
(i) $y = f(x) + 4$
(ii) $y = f(x) - 5$
(b) On the same diagram, sketch the graphs of:
(i) $y = f(x - 2)$
(ii) $y = f(x + 3)$

(a) (i) The transformation $y = f(x) + 4$ represents a translation by 4 units upwards.
(ii) The transformation $y = f(x) - 5$ represents a translation by 5 units downwards. So:

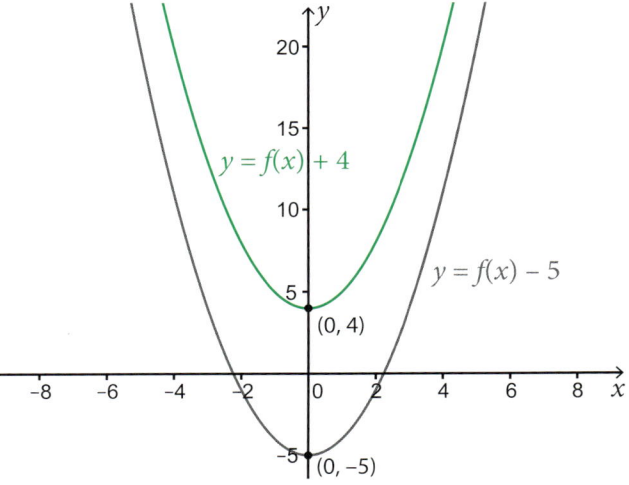

(b) (i) The transformation $y = f(x - 2)$ represents a translation by 2 units in the positive x-direction.

(ii) The transformation $y = f(x + 3)$ represents a translation by 3 units in the negative x-direction. So:

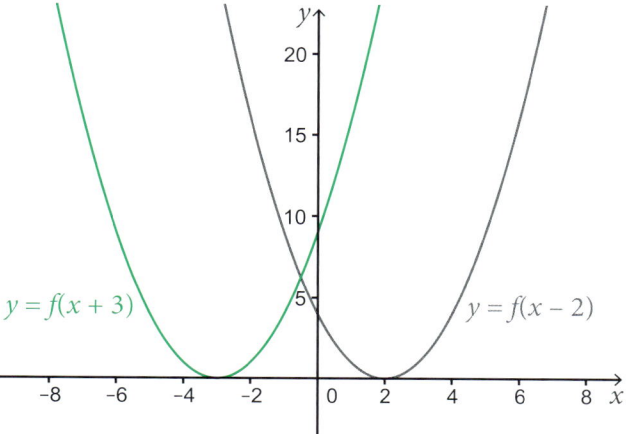

Note again that $f(x + a)$ causes a translation in the **negative** x-direction, whereas $f(x - a)$ causes a translation in the **positive** x-direction.

> **Note:** You do not need to know the equation of the original function to perform these transformations. However, in this example, the function given was actually $f(x) = x^2$. If you had been asked for the equations of the four transformations, you would have stated:
> - $f(x) + 4 = x^2 + 4$
> - $f(x) - 5 = x^2 - 5$
> - $f(x - 2) = (x - 2)^2$
> - $f(x + 3) = (x + 3)^2$

....

You may have to describe a transformation in words.

....

Worked Example

13. $f(x) = \dfrac{3}{x}$

(a) Describe the transformation that has taken place from f to each of the following functions:

(i) $g(x) = \dfrac{3}{x} + 3$

(ii) $h(x) = \dfrac{3}{x + 4}$

(b) (i) Sketch the curves $y = f(x)$ and $y = g(x)$ on the same diagram.

(ii) Sketch the curves $y = f(x)$ and $y = h(x)$ on the same diagram.

(a) (i) Here, we have added a constant to $f(x)$:
$g(x) = f(x) + 3$
So this is a translation of 3 units in the positive y-direction (3 units upwards).

(ii) Here, we have replaced x by $x + 4$, so:
$h(x) = f(x + 4)$
This is a translation of 4 units in the negative x-direction (4 units to the left).

(b) (i) $g(x)$ is a translation of $f(x)$, three units in the positive y-direction. Note the horizontal asymptote lies at $y = 3$. So:

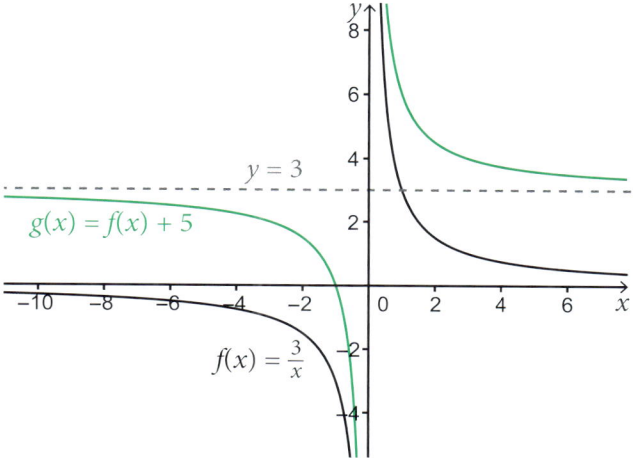

(b) (ii) $h(x)$ is a translation of $f(x)$, four units in the negative x-direction. Note the vertical asymptote lies at $x = -4$. So:

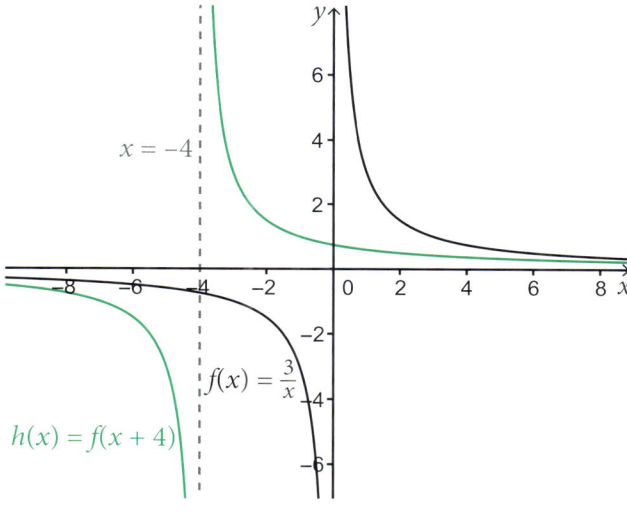

....

You may be asked to perform a transformation on a given function (one whose equation is known).

Worked Examples

14. Given $f(x) = x^3$, write down the equation of the function $g(x)$ that represents
   (a) a translation of $f(x)$ by 3 units in the positive x-direction;
   (b) a translation of $f(x)$ by 3 units in the positive y-direction.

(a) $g(x) = f(x - 3)$
$$= (x - 3)^3$$
(b) $g(x) = f(x) + 3$
$$= x^3 + 3$$

15. The graph of the function $y = f(x)$ is shown below.

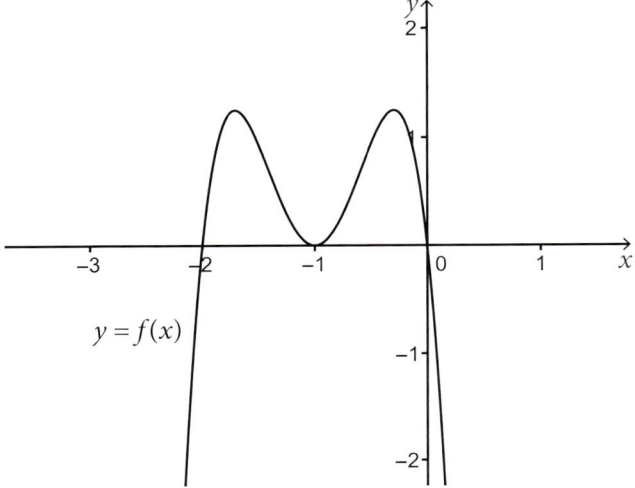

Draw sketches of the graphs of:
(a) $y = f(x) + 2$
(b) $y = f(x + 2)$

First note the key features of the graph of $y = f(x)$:
- It crosses the x-axis when $x = -2$ and 0.
- It also touches the x-axis when $x = -1$ at a minimum point.
- There are two maximum points.

(a) $y = f(x) + 2$ is a translation by 2 units in the positive y-direction. All points on the curve have 2 added to their y-coordinates. Their x-coordinates remain unchanged. The curve cuts the y-axis at $y = 2$. So:

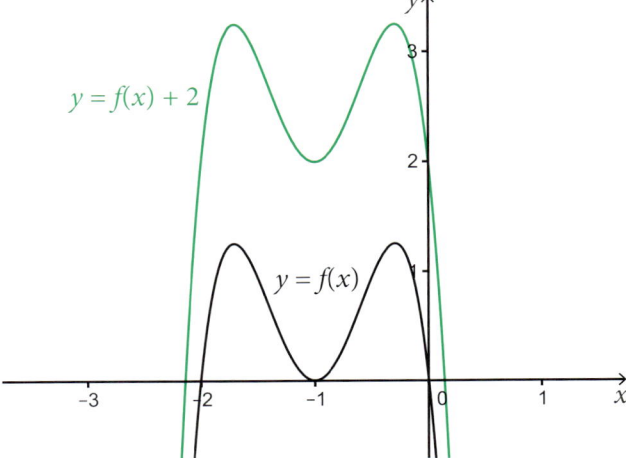

(b) $y = f(x + 2)$ is a translation by 2 units in the negative x-direction. All points on the curve have had 2 subtracted from their x-coordinates. The curve crosses the x-axis when $x = -4$ and -2. It also touches the x-axis when $x = -3$ at a minimum point. So:

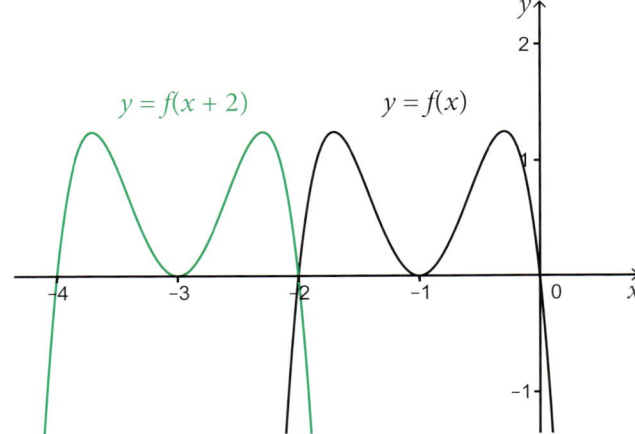

Note: In both parts of this example, the original curve $y = f(x)$ was drawn, as well as the translated curve. This has been done to illustrate each translation more clearly. In examination questions you will not usually be asked to draw the original curve.

To summarise, the curve $y = f(x)$ can be translated (moved) in these two ways:

- $y = f(x) + a$ performs a translation by a units in the **positive** y direction;
- $y = f(x + a)$ performs a translation by a units in the **negative** x direction.

Exercise 5E

1. Describe in words the following transformations on the graph $y = f(x)$.
   (a) $y = f(x) - 3$
   (b) $y = f(x - 3)$

2. The diagram below shows the curve with equation $y = f(x)$. Sketch the following curves, taking care to mark the coordinates of the turning point in each case.
   (a) $y = f(x) - 3$
   (b) $y = f(x - 3)$

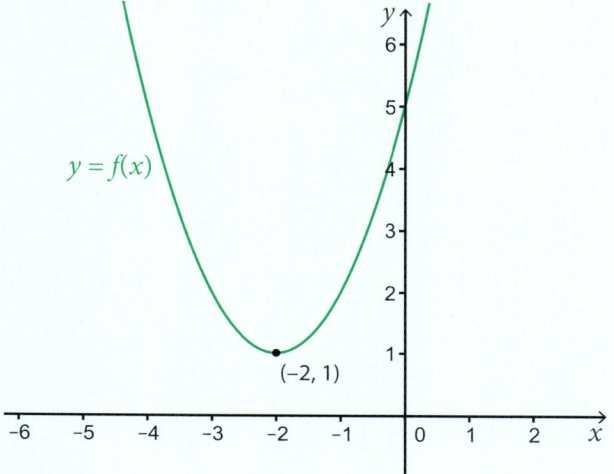

3. In each case, describe the translation that has taken place from f to g.
   (a) $f(x) = x^2$; $g(x) = (x + 1)^2$
   (b) $f(x) = x^2$; $g(x) = x^2 - 20$
   (c) $f(x) = \dfrac{5}{x}$; $g(x) = \dfrac{5}{x + 2}$
   (d) $f(x) = \dfrac{5}{x}$; $g(x) = \dfrac{5}{x} - 10$

4. Write down an equation for $f(x) + a$ for the given function $f(x)$ and constant a.
   (a) $f(x) = 3x$; $a = 2$
   (b) $f(x) = x - 1$; $a = 1$
   (c) $f(x) = x^2 - 2x + 2$; $a = -4$
   (d) $f(x) = x^3$; $a = -1$

5. For each function $f(x)$ that follows:
   (i) Sketch the graph of $f(x)$.
   (ii) Given $g(x) = f(x) - 2$ and $h(x) = f(x + 2)$, write down the equations for the functions $g(x)$ and $h(x)$.
   (iii) On the same diagram sketch the graphs of $g(x)$ and $h(x)$. Label each curve carefully.

Exercise 5E...

   (iv) For each curve on your diagram, describe what transformation has taken place.
   (a) $f(x) = x^2$
   (b) $f(x) = 3x$
   (c) $f(x) = \dfrac{1}{x}$
   (d) $f(x) = (x - 2)^3$

6. Sketch the graph of $y = f(x) = x(x - 1)(x + 2)$. On the same diagram, sketch the graph of $y = f(x) + 3$. Describe this transformation in words.

7. (a) Sketch the graph of $y = f(x)$ where $f(x) = -x(x - 1)(x + 1)$. On the same diagram, sketch the graph of $y = f(x + 2)$. Mark clearly all the points where the two curves intersect the x-axis.
   (b) Where do the two curves intersect each other?

Reflections and stretches

To sketch the graph of $y = -f(x)$, the graph of $y = f(x)$ is reflected in the x-axis.

....

Worked Example

16. Given $f(x) = x^2$, write down the function $-f(x)$ and sketch its graph.

   _____

   $-f(x) = -x^2$

   The graph of $y = -f(x)$ is a reflection in the x-axis of the graph of $y = f(x)$. So:

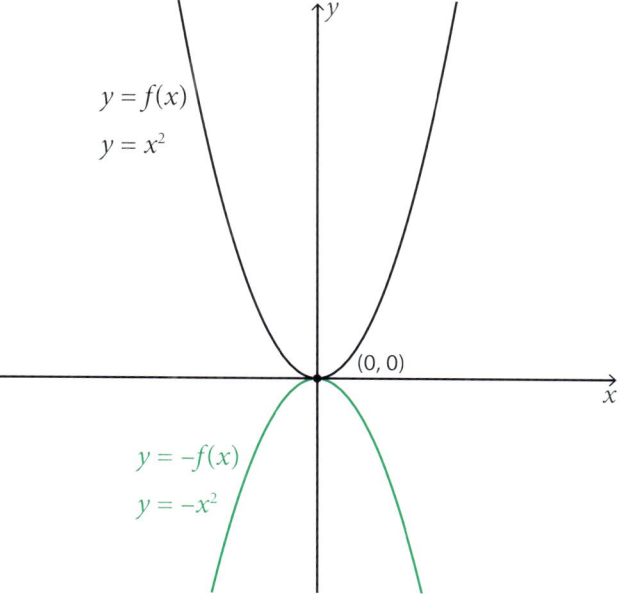

To sketch the graph of $y = f(-x)$, the graph of $y = f(x)$ is reflected in the y-axis.

Worked Example

17. The function $y = f(x)$ is shown in the diagram below. Sketch the graph of $y = f(-x)$.

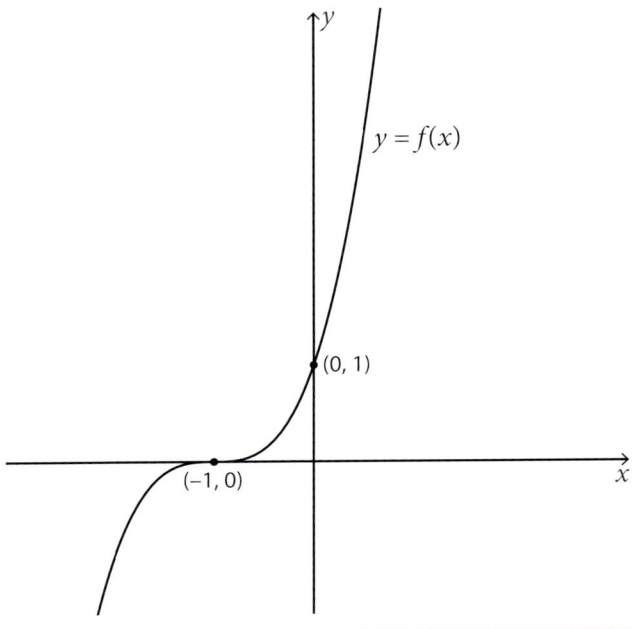

To sketch the curve, reflect the graph of $y = f(x)$ in the y-axis. So:

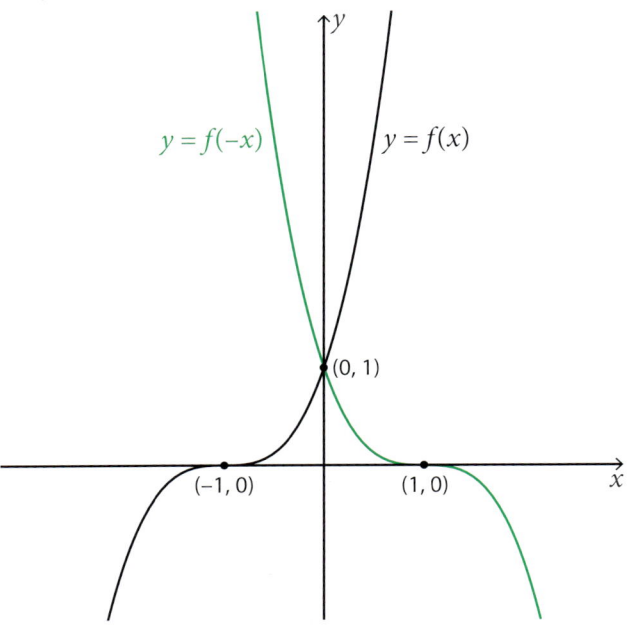

Multiplying a function by a constant represents a **stretch** of its graph parallel to the y-axis.

Worked Example

18. Given $f(x) = \dfrac{1}{x}$, sketch the graph of $y = 3f(x)$.

The graph of $af(x) = \dfrac{3}{x}$ is a stretch, scale factor 3, parallel to the y-axis, of the graph of $y = f(x)$. So:

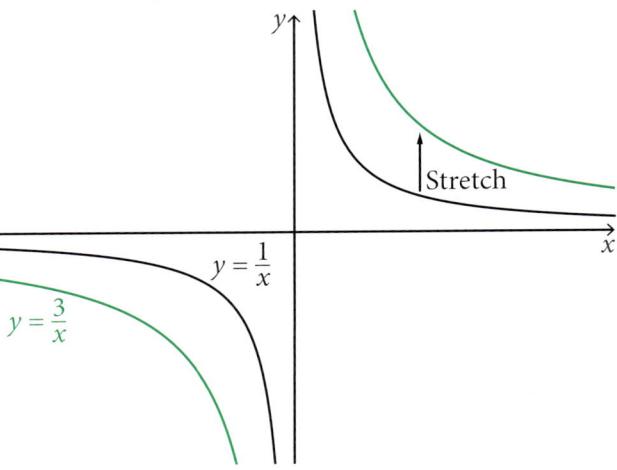

The graph of the function $f(ax)$ can be obtained by **stretching** the graph of $f(x)$ parallel to the x-axis, with a stretch factor of $\dfrac{1}{a}$.

Worked Example

19. Given $f(x) = x^2$, sketch the graph of the function $y = f(2x)$.

The graph of $y = f(ax)$ is a stretch, scale factor ½, parallel to the x-axis. So:

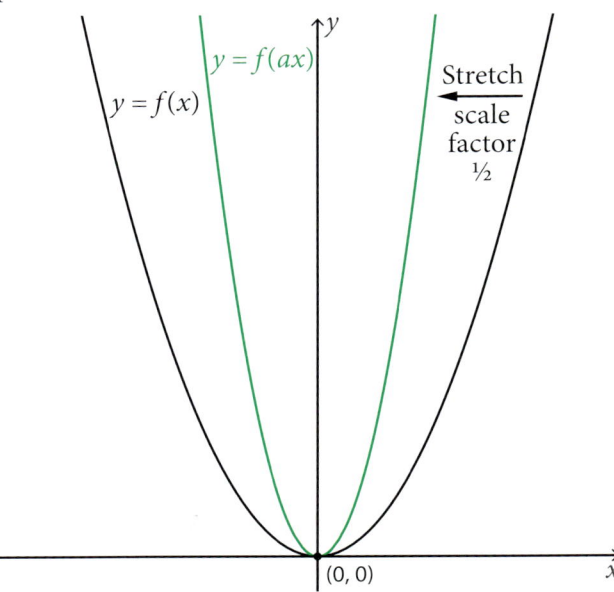

The next example shows a stretch in both the x- and y-directions.

Worked Examples

20. Given $f(x) = x(x-1)^2$, sketch the graphs of the following functions on the same diagram.
(a) $y = f(x)$
(b) $y = f(2x)$
(c) $y = 2f(x)$

(a) We can sketch the graph of $y = f(x)$, using the techniques discussed for sketching cubic curves earlier in this chapter.
(b) The graph of $y = f(2x)$ is a stretch, scale factor ½ in the x-direction.
(c) The graph of $y = 2f(x)$ is a stretch, scale factor 2 in the y-direction.

So we can draw the sketch:

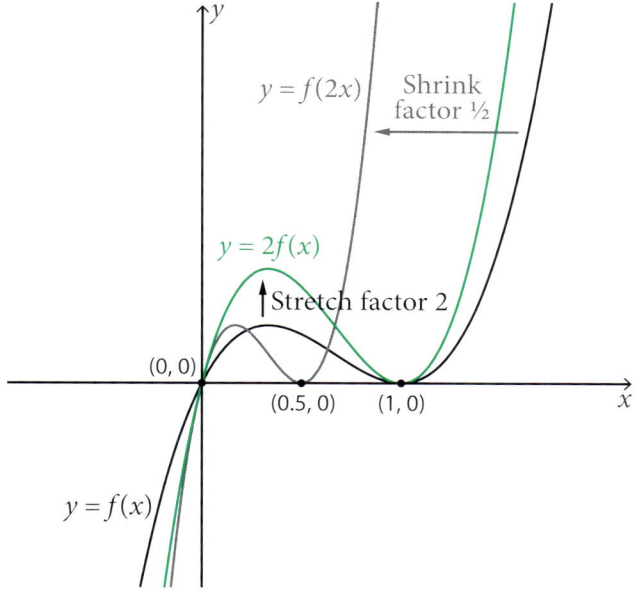

21. Consider the graph of the function $y = f(x)$ shown below.

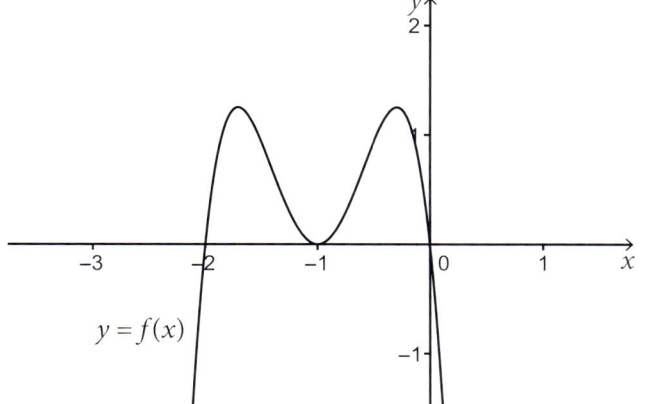

Draw sketches of the graphs of:
(a) $y = 2f(x)$
(b) $y = f(2x)$
(c) $y = -f(x)$
(d) $y = f(-x)$

(a) $y = 2f(x)$ is a stretch with scale factor 2 in the y-direction. All points on the curve have their y-coordinates multiplied by 2. The x-coordinates remain unchanged. The curve meets the x-axis in the same places as $y = f(x)$. So:

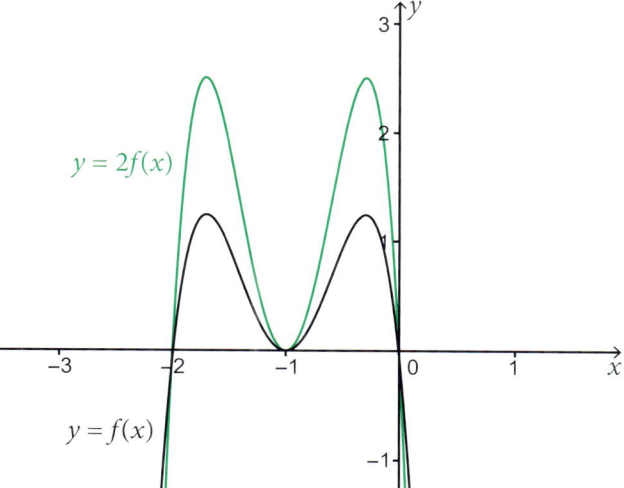

(b) $y = f(2x)$ is a stretch, scale factor ½ in the x-direction. All points on the curve have their x-coordinates halved, while the y-coordinates remain unchanged. The curve meets the x-axis at $x = -1, -0.5$ and 0. So:

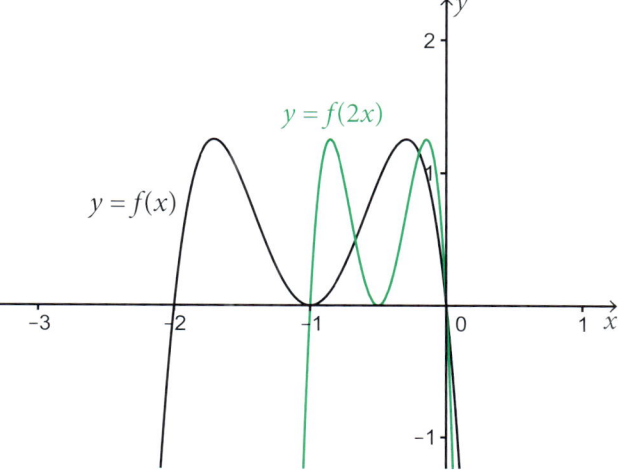

(c) $y = -f(x)$ is a reflection in the x-axis. All points on the curve have their y-coordinates multiplied by –1, while the x-coordinates remain unchanged. The curve meets the x-axis at the same points as $y = f(x)$. So:

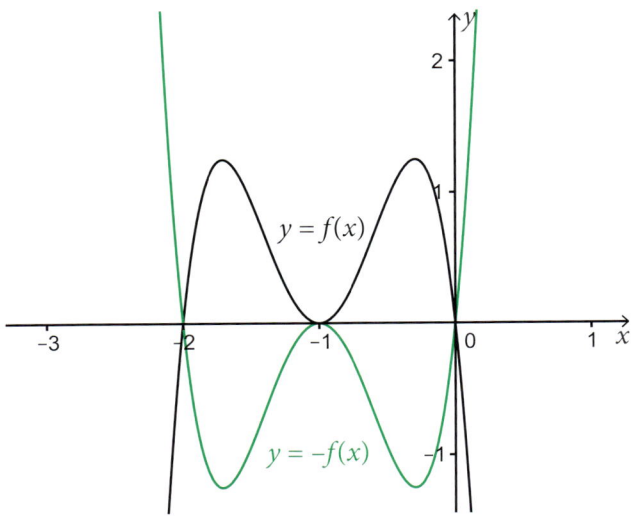

(d) $y = f(-x)$ is a reflection in the y-axis. It meets the x-axis when $x = 0$, 1 and 2. The x-coordinates of the points on the curve have been multiplied by -1, while the y-coordinates remain unchanged. So:

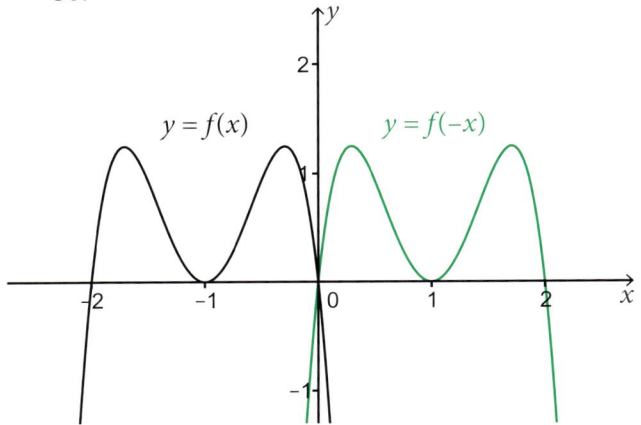

Exercise 5F

1. Describe in words the following transformations on the graph $y = f(x)$.
   (a) $y = -f(x)$
   (b) $y = 2f(x)$
   (c) $y = f(2x)$
   (d) $y = f(-x)$

2. The diagram that follows shows the curve with equation $y = f(x)$. On separate diagrams, sketch the following curves, taking care to mark the coordinates of point A in each case.
   (a) $y = -f(x)$
   (b) $y = 2f(x)$
   (c) $y = f(2x)$
   (d) $y = f(-x)$

Exercise 5F...

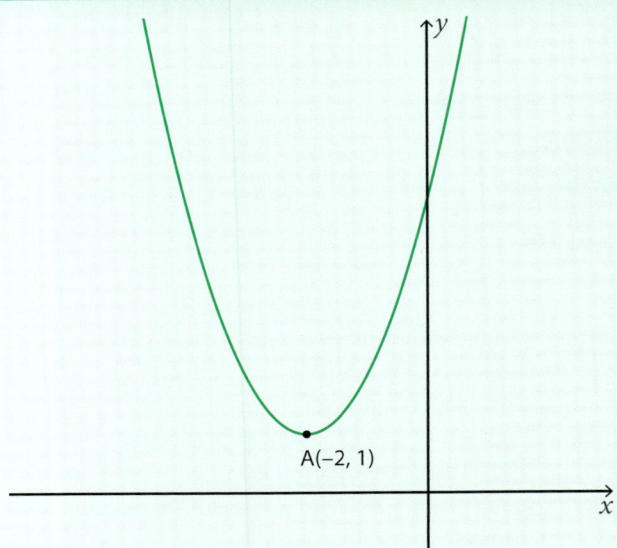

3. For each of the following functions $f(x)$, find the corresponding functions $af(x)$ and $f(ax)$, where a is given.
   (a) $f(x) = x^2$; $a = 2$
   (b) $f(x) = x^3 + 1$; $a = 2$
   (c) $f(x) = 2x$; $a = 3$
   (d) $f(x) = \dfrac{2}{x}$; $a = 5$
   (e) $f(x) = x^2$; $a = -1$
   (f) $f(x) = \dfrac{1}{x^2}$; $a = -1$
   (g) $f(x) = 3x^3$; $a = -1$
   (h) $f(x) = 1 - x$; $a = -2$
   (i) $f(x) = x(x - 1)(x - 2)$; $a = 2$
   (j) $f(x) = x^2(x - 1)$; $a = -2$

4. For each of the following functions $f(x)$, sketch the graphs of $y = f(x)$ and $y = af(x)$ on the same diagram. From your graphs, state the value of x where $f(x) = af(x)$.
   (a) $f(x) = x^3 + 1$; $a = -1$
   (b) $f(x) = 2x + 1$; $a = 2$
   (c) $f(x) = (x - 1)(x + 1)$; $a = 2$

5. For each of the following functions $f(x)$, sketch the graphs of $y = f(x)$ and $y = f(ax)$ on the same diagram. From your graphs, state the value of x where $f(x) = f(ax)$.
   (a) $f(x) = x^2 + 1$; $a = 2$
   (b) $f(x) = x^2 - 1$; $a = \dfrac{1}{2}$
   (c) $f(x) = 2x^3$; $a = \dfrac{1}{2}$
   (d) $f(x) = x(x - 1)$; $a = -1$

The following exercise contains mixed questions on the six different types of transformation you have learnt about: translations and stretches in both x- and y-directions and reflections in the x- and y-axes. These questions are similar in style to those found on the AS Mathematics exam paper.

Exercise 5G (Mixed Questions)

1. The diagram below shows the curve with equation $y = f(x)$. On separate diagrams, sketch the following curves, taking care to mark the asymptotes in each case.
   (a) $y = -f(x)$ (b) $y = 2f(x)$
   (c) $y = f(x) - 3$ (d) $y = f(2x)$
   (e) $y = f(x - 3)$ (f) $y = f(-x)$

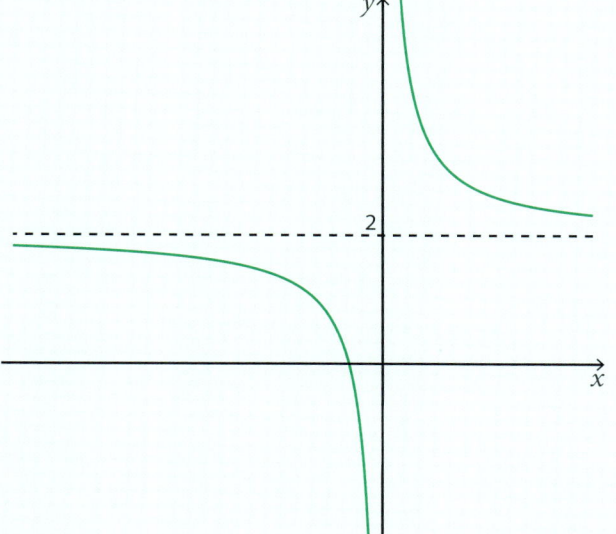

2. The sketch below shows the function with equation $y = f(x)$. On separate diagrams, sketch the graphs of the following. In each case clearly label the images of points A and B.
   (a) $y = -f(x)$ (b) $y = 2f(x)$
   (c) $y = f(x) - 2$ (d) $y = f(2x)$
   (e) $y = f(x - 2)$ (f) $y = f(-x)$

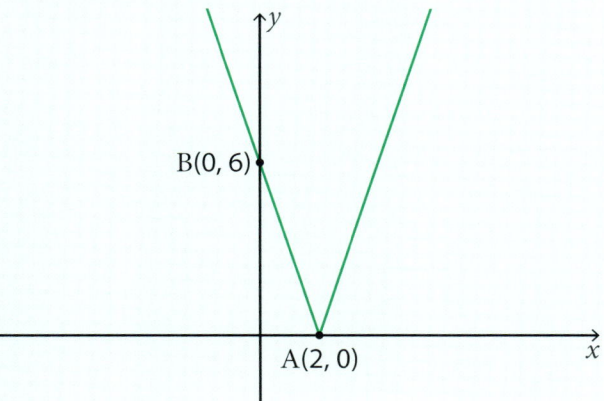

Exercise 5G...

3. The diagram below shows a sketch of the function $y = f(x)$. On separate diagrams, sketch the following graphs. In each case clearly label the images of points A and B.
   (a) $y = -f(x)$ (b) $y = 2f(x)$
   (c) $y = f(x) + 2$ (d) $y = f(2x)$
   (e) $y = f(x + 2)$ (f) $y = f(-x)$

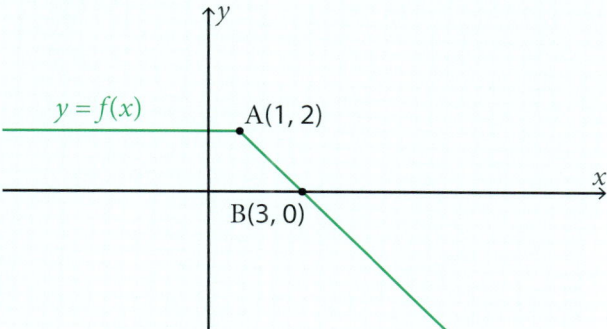

4. The diagram below shows a part of a curve with equation $y = f(x)$. On separate diagrams, sketch the curves of the following. In each case clearly label the images of points A and B.
   (a) $y = -f(x)$ (b) $y = 2f(x)$
   (c) $y = f(x) + 2$ (d) $y = f(2x)$
   (e) $y = f(x + 2)$ (f) $y = f(-x)$

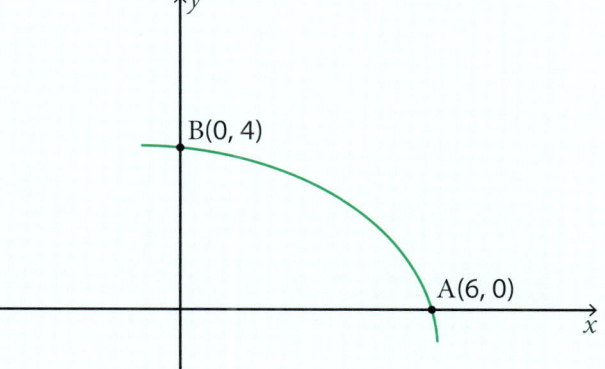

5.6 Summary

In this chapter you have learnt the shape of cubic curves and reciprocal curves.

The general equation for a cubic curve is:
$$y = ax^3 + bx^2 + cx + d$$

The shape of a cubic curve is typically one of these:

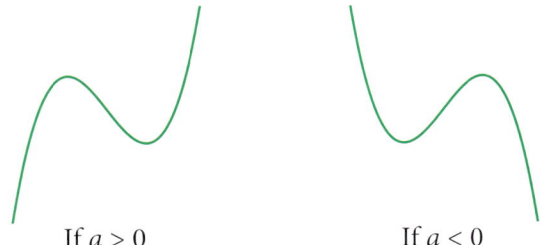

If $a > 0$ If $a < 0$

The general equation of a reciprocal function is: $y = \dfrac{k}{x}$ (where k is an integer). Reciprocal curves have two branches. A sketch of a reciprocal curve looks like one of these two:

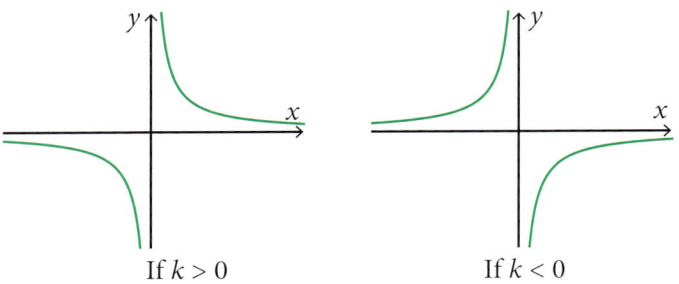

If $k > 0$ If $k < 0$

Reciprocal curves of the form $y = \dfrac{k}{x^2}$ (where k is an integer) also have two branches. A sketch of this type of reciprocal curve takes this shape:

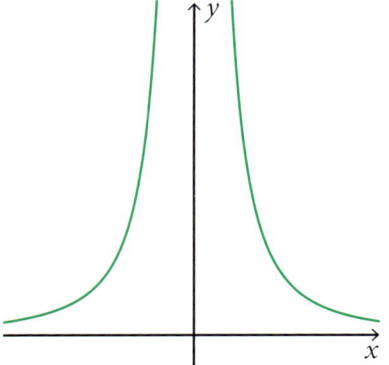

For each of these reciprocal curves, the closer k is to zero (positive or negative), the closer the curve lies to the asymptotes.

For all reciprocal curves you can find the asymptotes as follows:

- Vertical asymptote: Inspect the equation to see which values x cannot take (you cannot divide by 0).

- Horizontal asymptote: Consider the value y approaches as x approaches plus and minus infinity.

You have also learnt that simultaneous equations can be solved by plotting two curves on the same graph. The intersection points are the solutions.

You can use this method in reverse: solving simultaneous equations tells you the intersection points of two curves.

There are various useful techniques when sketching the graph of any curve:

- Remember the general shape.
- Identify the points where the curve crosses the axes.
- With quadratic curves, you can identify **turning points** by **completing the square**. Later you will learn a method to find the turning points of any curve.

The graph of $y = f(x)$ is transformed according to the following rules:

- $y = f(x) + a$ Translation by a units in **positive** y-direction.
- $y = f(x + a)$ Translation by a units in **negative** x-direction.
- $y = af(x)$ Stretch in y-direction, scale factor a.
- $y = f(ax)$ Stretch in x-direction, scale factor $\dfrac{1}{a}$.
- $y = -f(x)$ Reflection in x-axis.
- $y = f(-x)$ Reflection in y-axis.

Chapter 6
Straight Lines

6.1 Introduction

At GCSE you learnt how to draw a **plot** of a straight line, usually by writing up a table of (x, y) values from the equation of the line. In this chapter you will learn more about the equations of straight lines. You will also learn some properties of parallel and perpendicular lines.

Key words

- **Linear**: Any relationship that can be plotted on a graph as a straight line is said to be **linear**, for example conversion graphs to change miles to kilometres, or for currency exchange rates.
- **Gradient**: The steepness of a line on a graph.
- **y-intercept**: Where a straight line crosses the y-axis.
- **Parallel**: Parallel lines do not cross. They have the same **gradient**.
- **Perpendicular**: Perpendicular lines cross each other at right angles.

Before you start
You should know:

- How to recognise a linear equation.
- How to plot a straight line graph.
- How to identify the gradient and y-intercept from the equation of a straight line.

Worked Examples

1. State whether the following are linear equations:
   - (a) $y = 3x + 4$
   - (b) $y = 3x^2$
   - (c) $\dfrac{x - 1}{2y + 3} = 5$
   - (d) $3 - xy = x + y$

   - (a) This **is** a linear equation. The powers of x and y are 1.
   - (b) This is **not** a linear equation. It contains a term in x^2.
   - (c) This **is** a linear equation. Re-arranging gives:
     $x - 1 = 10y + 15$
     The powers of x and y are 1.
   - (d) This is **not** a linear equation. It contains a term in xy.

2. Plot the straight line given by the equation $y = 2x - 3$.

   First use a table of values to find some of the points on the line. Choose any x-values and work out the y-values from the equation:

x	0	1	2	3
y	−3	−1	1	3

   Then draw the straight line.

   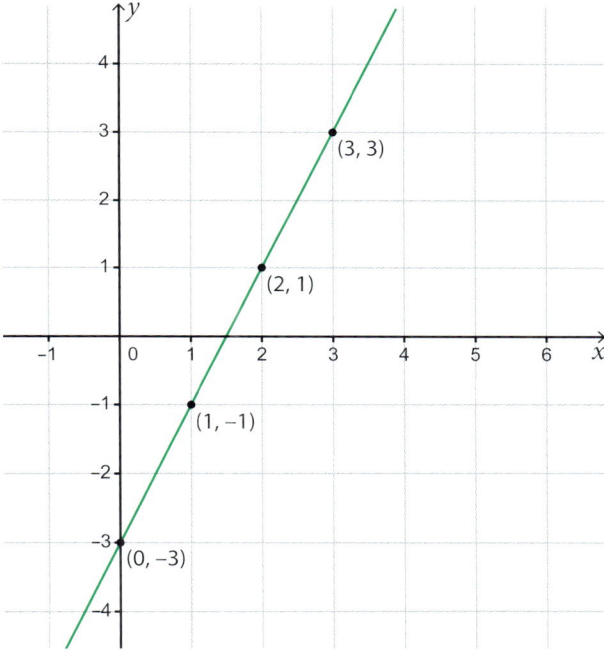

3. State the gradient and y-intercept of the line $y = 2x - 3$.

   The gradient is 2 and the y-intercept is −3.

   The gradient tells us that the y-coordinate increases by 2 units every time the x-coordinate increases by 1.

   The y-intercept tells us that the line crosses the y-axis at the point $(0, -3)$.

What you will learn
In this chapter you will learn:

- How to find the gradient of a line between two points.
- How to recognise a linear equation in various forms.
- How to find the equation of a straight line.
- How to identify the gradient and y-intercept from the equation of a straight line.
- Some of the properties of parallel and perpendicular lines.

In the real world...

In 2005, scientists studying the amount of ice in the Arctic Ocean discovered an alarming trend: the ice was disappearing. When they plotted a graph of the total surface area of the ice measured each summer from 1997 to 2005, they spotted a linear trend. This meant that the total surface area of the ice was decreasing by roughly the same amount each year. Using this straight line graph, the scientists predicted that there would be no ice left in the Arctic Ocean by about 2040.

Since then, the trend has become even more worrying. The latest measurements show that the decrease in ice cover is speeding up. A straight line graph may no longer be the best way to model the sea ice data.

The latest predictions suggest that the Arctic Ocean could be ice-free during the summer very soon.

Exercise 6A (Revision)

1. Which of these equations are linear equations?
   (a) $4y + 3x = 1$
   (b) $y = 7x^2$
   (c) $2(x - 1) + 4(y + 1) = 0$
   (d) $x + y + xy = 3$
   (e) $\dfrac{y - 1}{x + 1} = 1$
   (f) $x = 1$

2. By drawing up a suitable table of values, plot the following straight line graphs. State the gradient and the y-intercept for each.

   (a) $y = x + 1$ (b) $y = \dfrac{x}{2} + 1$

   (c) $y = 2x + 1$ (d) $y = -x - 1$

3. Without plotting the graphs, state the gradient and the y-intercept of the following straight lines.
   (a) $y = 5x + 3$ (b) $y = -2x - 3$
   (c) $2y = 4x + 7$ (d) $y + 1 = x$

6.2 The Equation of a Straight Line

The gradient
The gradient is a measure of the steepness of a straight line. As shown in the following diagram, the gradient of a straight line connecting the points (x_1, y_1) and (x_2, y_2) is:

$$m = \frac{y_2 - y_1}{x_2 - x_1}$$

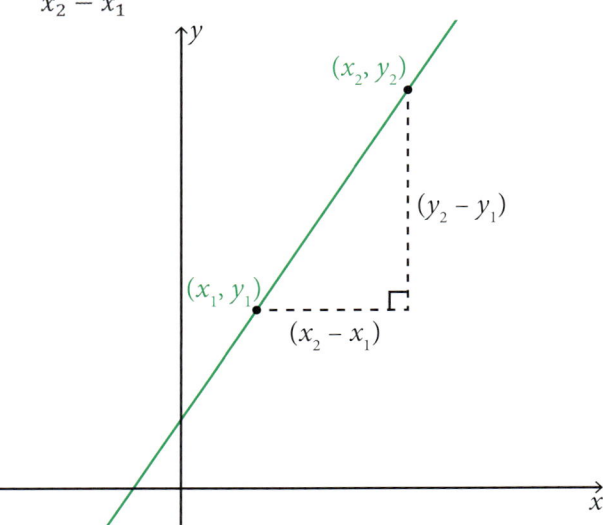

Some people find it helpful to remember $m = \dfrac{rise}{run}$.

In other words, the gradient is how much the straight line rises between the two points divided by the horizontal distance it runs across.

Worked Example

4. Find the gradient of the straight line connecting the points (2, 1) and (−4, −3).

$$m = \frac{y_2 - y_1}{x_2 - x_1}$$

$$m = \frac{-3 - 1}{-4 - 2}$$

$$m = \frac{2}{3}$$

At GCSE, you learnt that a straight line is often written in the form $y = mx + c$.

In this section you will learn about two other forms for the equation of a straight line.

The form $y - y_1 = m(x - x_1)$
If you know the coordinates of any point on the line, (x_1, y_1), and the gradient, m, of the line, you can use the form $y - y_1 = m(x - x_1)$ to find the equation of the straight line.

Worked Example

5. Find the equation of the line that passes through the point $(2, 0)$ with gradient 3. State where the line crosses the y-axis.

We use $(x_1, y_1) = (2, 0)$ and $m = 3$:
$y - y_1 = m(x - x_1)$
$\therefore y - 0 = 3(x - 2)$
$\Rightarrow y = 3x - 6$

The y-intercept is -6.

You can also find the equation of the line by using two points on the line. Firstly, use the two points to find the gradient of the line. The gradient is given by:

$$m = \frac{rise}{run} = \frac{y_2 - y_1}{x_2 - x_1}$$

Then find the equation of the line as before.

Worked Example

6. Find the equation of the line passing through the points $(2, 3)$ and $(4, 10)$.

We use $(x_1, y_1) = (2, 3)$ and $(x_2, y_2) = (4, 10)$:
$$m = \frac{y_2 - y_1}{x_2 - x_1}$$
$$= \frac{10 - 3}{4 - 2}$$
$$= \frac{7}{2}$$

Then, use $y - y_1 = m(x - x_1)$. We can use any point on the line for (x_1, y_1), so let us use $(x_1, y_1) = (2, 3)$:
$$y - 3 = \frac{7}{2}(x - 2)$$
$$y = \frac{7}{2}x - 4$$

Note: Use improper fractions in the equations of straight lines, not mixed numbers.

Exercise 6B

1. Find the gradient of the straight line passing through the following pairs of points.
   (a) $(-4, 0)$ and $(-2, 2)$
   (b) $(1, -2)$ and $(-1, -1)$
   (c) $(0, 2)$ and $(5, -2)$
   (d) $(-5, -4)$ and $(1, 4)$
   (e) $(0, -1)$ and $(4, 0)$

Exercise 6B...

2. Find the equation of the straight line with the given gradient, passing through the given point.
   (a) Gradient 2, point $(2, 1)$
   (b) Gradient 1, point $(-2, 2)$
   (c) Gradient 3, point $(-1, -1)$
   (d) Gradient ½ , point $(5, 0)$
   (e) Gradient -2, point $(0, 0)$
   (f) Gradient -1, point $(-1, -1)$

3. Find the equation of the straight line passing through the two points given.
   (a) A$(0, 0)$, B$(3, 3)$ (b) A$(2, 0)$, B$(3, 3)$
   (c) A$(0, 2)$, B$(3, 5)$ (d) A$(-2, 2)$, B$(6, 6)$
   (e) A$(0, 0)$, B$(-2, 6)$ (f) A$(-2, 3)$, B$(1, -3)$

4. The points A and B have coordinates $(4, 3)$ and $(5, 12)$ respectively. Find, in the form $y = mx + c$, an equation for the straight line through A and B.

5. Write down the equation of a straight line that has gradient 4 and passes through the point $(0, 3)$.

6. Write down the equation of a straight line that has gradient -1 and passes through the point $(0, -1)$.

7. The line $y = mx + 2$ passes through the point A$(1, 3)$. Find the value of m, the gradient of the line.

8. A straight line l has gradient 5 and passes through the point $(11, 7)$. Find its equation.

9. A straight line l has gradient 7 and passes through the point $(8, 3)$. Find its equation.

10. Find an equation for the straight line passing through A$(6, 5)$ and B$(5, 3)$. Give your answer in the form $y = mx + c$.

11. Find an equation for the straight line passing through A$(-3, 4)$ and B$(-6, -5)$. Give your answer in the form $y = mx + c$.

12. Find an equation for the straight line passing through A$(7, 1)$ and B$(7, -4)$.

13. The points A and B have coordinates $(3, 1)$ and $(5, 11)$ respectively. Find, in the form $y = mx + c$, an equation for the straight line through A and B.

14. The straight line $y = 5x - 1$ intersects the x-axis at the point C and the y-axis at the point D. Write down the coordinates of C and D.

The general form for the equation of a straight line

The form $ax + by + c = 0$ is known as the **general form** for the equation of a straight line, where a, b and c are integer constants.

Worked Examples

7. A straight line is described by the equation $y = 5x + 3$. Write this equation in the form $ax + by + c = 0$.

Rearrange: $5x - y + 3 = 0$

8. Write the following equation in the form $ax + by + c = 0$:

$$\frac{1}{x + 1} = \frac{2}{2y - 3}$$

Rearrange: $2y - 3 = 2(x + 1)$
$2x - 2y + 5 = 0$

Exercise 6C

1. Write the following equations in the form $ax + by + c = 0$.
   (a) $2y = 3x + 3$ (b) $3y = 5$

   (c) $x - 1 = 0$ (d) $2y = \dfrac{3}{2}(x - 1)$

   (e) $\dfrac{x}{5} = \dfrac{y}{4}$ (f) $\dfrac{2x}{5y} = \dfrac{5}{2}$

   (g) $7(1 + y) = 2(2 - x)$

   (h) $\dfrac{1 + x}{1 + y} = \dfrac{3}{4}$

   (i) $\dfrac{2 + 3x}{3} = \dfrac{3 + 2y}{4}$

   (j) $\dfrac{2}{1 + 3x + 2y} = \dfrac{4}{3 - x - 2y}$

2. Find where the line $4x + 3y - 12 = 0$ crosses
   (a) the x-axis (b) the y-axis

3. Find where the line $5x + 12y = 0$ crosses
   (a) the x-axis (b) the y-axis

4. Find the equation of the line with gradient -2 and y-intercept 3. Give your answer in the general form $ax + by + c = 0$.

5. Find the equation of the line with gradient ⅔ and y-intercept $-½$. Give your answer in the general form $ax + by + c = 0$.

Exercise 6C...

6. The point $(1, 3)$ lies on the line with equation $ax + by - 6 = 0$. The line has a gradient of -3. What are the values of the integers a and b? Write down the equation of the line in its general form.

7. The following two straight lines intersect each other at the point A:
   $x + 2y - 12 = 0$
   $-2x + y - 1 = 0$
   (a) Find the coordinates of A. (Hint: you will need to use simultaneous equations.)
   (b) Sketch the two lines.

6.3 The Midpoint of a Line Segment

A straight line is infinitely long in both directions. A **line segment** is a part of a straight line and has a finite length, as shown in the following diagram.

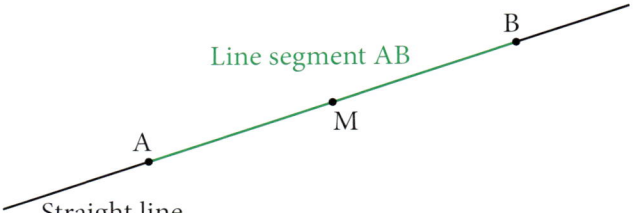

Line segment AB

Straight line

You may be asked to find the **midpoint** of a line segment, shown as point M in the diagram above.

The x-coordinate of the midpoint of a line segment is the average of the x-coordinates of the end points. The y-coordinate is the average of the two y-coordinates.

> **Midpoint of a line segment**
>
> The midpoint of line segment $A(x_1, y_1)$ and $B(x_2, y_2)$ is $M(x_3, y_3)$, given by:
>
> $$x_3 = \frac{x_1 + x_2}{2} \quad \text{and} \quad y_3 = \frac{y_1 + y_2}{2}$$

Worked Examples

9. Find the midpoint M of the line segment between the points $A(1, 8)$ and $B(7, 10)$.

For the midpoint, $M(x_3, y_3)$:

$$x_3 = \frac{x_1 + x_2}{2} = \frac{1 + 7}{2} = 4$$

$$y_3 = \frac{y_1 + y_2}{2} = \frac{8 + 10}{2} = 9$$

Therefore, M has coordinates $(4, 9)$.

10. Point M(3, 4) is the midpoint of the line segment AB. Given the coordinates of point A are (5, 7), find the coordinates of B.

To find $B(x_2, y_2)$:

$$x_3 = \frac{x_1 + x_2}{2}$$

$$\Rightarrow x_2 = 2x_3 - x_1$$

$$x_2 = 2 \times 3 - 5 = 1$$

$$y_3 = \frac{y_1 + y_2}{2}$$

$$\Rightarrow y_2 = 2y_3 - y_1$$

$$y_2 = 2 \times 4 - 7 = 1$$

Therefore B has coordinates (1, 1).

Exercise 6D

1. Find the midpoints of the line segments joining points A and B.
   (a) A(1, 3), B(9, 7)
   (b) A(−1, 3), B(11, 5)
   (c) A(−3, 3), B(1, −13)
   (d) A(4, 2), B(19, 6)
   (e) A(6, 1), B(−1, −10)
   (f) $A(1 + \sqrt{2}, 0), B(3 - \sqrt{2}, 2)$
   (g) $A\left(\frac{\sqrt{3} - 1}{2}, 4\right), B\left(\frac{1 - \sqrt{3}}{2}, 6\right)$

2. Find the **exact** coordinates of the midpoints of the following line segments.
   (a) $A(1, 16), B(\pi, 6)$
   (b) $A(3, 2\sqrt{2}), B(2, 2)$

3. M is the midpoint of the line segment AB. Given the coordinates of A and M, find the coordinates of B.
   (a) A(2, 10), M(0, 8)
   (b) A(0, 7), M(2, 7)
   (c) A(8, −3), M(−9, 7)
   (d) A(1, 10), M(−10, −7)
   (e) A(2π, −π), M(1 + π, π)

4. The endpoints of a line segment are A(4k + 1, −7) and B(2k² + 1, 1), where k is an integer. The midpoint of the line segment is M.
   (a) Find the y-coordinate of M.
   (b) Show that the x-coordinate of M is $(k + 1)^2$.
   (c) Given that the x-coordinate of M is 4, find the two possible values of k.

6.4 Parallel and Perpendicular Lines

Conditions for two straight lines to be parallel or perpendicular to each other

Consider the two straight lines:

$$y = 3x + 4$$

$$y = 3x - 10$$

These lines both have gradient 3, so they are **parallel** and do not intersect.

> **Two lines with the same gradient are parallel.**

Now consider the two straight lines:

$$y = 2x + 4$$

$$y = -\frac{1}{2}x - 5$$

If these lines were plotted on a graph, you would see that they are at right angles to each other (**perpendicular**).

These two straight lines have gradients 2 and −½ respectively. Notice that $2 \times -\frac{1}{2} = -1$.

> **Two straight lines are perpendicular if the product of their gradients is −1.**

Using these two rules, it is possible to determine whether any two straight lines are parallel, perpendicular or neither, without plotting or sketching the lines.

Worked Examples

11. Re-arrange the equations of these two straight lines to find out whether they are parallel, perpendicular or neither.

    $$y + 3x - 6 = 0 \qquad (1)$$
    $$3y - x + 4 = 0 \qquad (2)$$

    From (1), $y = -3x + 6$
    So this line has gradient −3 and y-intercept 6.

    From (2), $3y = x - 4$, giving $y = \frac{1}{3}x - \frac{4}{3}$

    So this line has gradient $\frac{1}{3}$ and y-intercept $-\frac{4}{3}$.

    Now compare the gradients: −3 and $\frac{1}{3}$. They are not the same, so the lines are not parallel.

    However, $-3 \times \frac{1}{3} = -1$. So the lines are perpendicular.

12. These two straight lines are perpendicular:

$px + 4y + r = 0$ (1)

$-4x + y + 3 = 0$ (2)

Find the value of p.

From (1), $4y = -px - r$, giving $y = -\dfrac{p}{4}x - \dfrac{r}{4}$

So the gradient of this line is $-\dfrac{p}{4}$.

From (2), $y = 4x - 3$.

The gradient of this line is 4.

We have been told the two lines are perpendicular.
Therefore:

$\left(-\dfrac{p}{4}\right) \times 4 = -1$

$-p = -1$

$p = 1$

13. Consider the straight line $y = \dfrac{1}{2}x - 4$

This line runs parallel to another straight line, which passes through the points $(3, a)$ and $(a, 27)$. Find the value of a.

For the first straight line, the gradient is ½. Because the two lines are parallel, the gradient of the second line must also be ½.

We learnt earlier that, if we know two points on a straight line (x_1, y_1) and (x_2, y_2), the gradient can be found using: $m = \dfrac{y_2 - y_1}{x_2 - x_1}$

Two points on the second line are:

$(x_1, y_1) = (3, a)$

$(x_2, y_2) = (a, 27)$

Therefore, the gradient of the second line is $\dfrac{27 - a}{a - 3}$.

Therefore:

$\dfrac{27 - a}{a - 3} = \dfrac{1}{2}$

$54 - 2a = a - 3$

$3a = 57$

$a = 19$

··

Exercise 6E

1. By re-arranging both equations into the form $y = mx + c$, determine whether each pair of equations represents parallel lines, perpendicular lines or neither.

(a) $y = 2x$; $y = 2x + 3$

(b) $y = 3x + 4$; $y = \dfrac{1}{3}x - 2$

Exercise 6E

(c) $2y + 3x + 4 = 0$; $4y + 6x - 1 = 0$

(d) $6y + 3x + 1 = 0$; $y = 2x$

(e) $2(3 - y) = 3(2 - x)$; $y = \dfrac{2}{3}x + 1$

(f) $y = -x - 4$; $x = -y - 4$

(g) $2(1 - x) - 3(1 - 2y) = 2(1 + x) + 5(2 + 2y)$; $4x - y + 3 = 0$

2. Put these equations into pairs. There is one pair of parallel lines, one pair of perpendicular lines and one pair which are neither:

(a) $y = 3x + 4$

(b) $2y + 2x = 1$

(c) $y = -\dfrac{1}{3}x - 5$

(d) $y - 2x - 3 = 0$

(e) $x = -y$

(f) $y = \dfrac{1}{2}x + 3$

3. A straight line has the equation $y - px + 14 = 0$. It is parallel to a line with the equation $2y + 14x - p = 0$. Find the value of p.

4. A line, L, has the equation $7x + 2y + 5 = 0$.

(a) Write the equation in the form $y = mx + c$.

(b) Find the gradient of a line perpendicular to L.

5. The line with equation $6x + 2y - 9 = 0$ is parallel to the line with equation $y = ax - 8$. Find the value of a.

6. The line with equation $2x + 4y - 1 = 0$ is perpendicular to the line with equation $y = ax + 13$. Find the value of a.

7. The straight line L is parallel to the line $2y + 3x - 4 = 0$. L passes through the point $(1, 3)$. Find the equation of the line L in its general form.

8. The straight line M is perpendicular to the line N, which has equation $3y + x - c = 0$. M and N both pass through the point $(3, 10)$.

(a) Find the equation of the line M in its general form.

(b) Find the value of c.

9. Find the equation of the straight line passing through the point $(3, -1)$, which is perpendicular to the line with equation $3x - 2y - 7 = 0$.

Exercise 6E...

10. The line L_1 passes through the point $A(a, 2a)$. It is parallel to another line L_2, which passes through the point $B(0, a)$. A third line L_3 passes through both A and B and is perpendicular to both L_1 and L_2.
    (a) Find the gradient of L_3.
    (b) Find the equation of L_1 in its general form, leaving the constant a in your answer.

6.5 Straight Line Models in Context

When the equation of a straight line is written as $y = mx + c$, m is the gradient (or steepness) of the line, and c is the y-intercept (where the line crosses the y-axis). Plotting a graph using this form of the equation can be quite straightforward, using a table of values, particularly if m and c are integers. In relationships of this type, x is sometimes called the **input variable** and y the **output variable**.

In this section, we will discuss real world meanings that the gradient and y-intercept can have.

The slope of a line measures how much the value of y changes for one unit of change in x. For example, in the line $y = \frac{2}{3}x - 2$, the gradient is $\frac{2}{3}$. This means that, starting at any point on the line, you can get to another point on the line by going 1 unit to the right, and up by two thirds of a unit. This can be a useful idea when considering real-life situations.

Word problems involving linear (straight-line) equations often relate to how much something changes as time passes.

When $x = 0$, the corresponding y-value is the y-intercept. In the context of word problems, the y-intercept is the starting value; i.e. the value when the first reading was taken.

You may see different variables being used, instead of x and y, for example $P = 10t + 40$. This equation would give a straight line graph, with P on the y-axis and t on the x-axis. The gradient would be 10 and the y-intercept would be 40.

Worked Example

14. A town planner models the population growth in a small town. She uses a linear equation model.
    (a) Plot a graph of the town's population from the year 1970 to 2015 according to this model. Use

time t on the x-axis, where x is the number of years after 1970. Use a gradient of 200 and a y-intercept of 2000.
    (b) In terms of the town's population, what is the meaning of (i) the gradient (ii) the y-intercept?

(a)

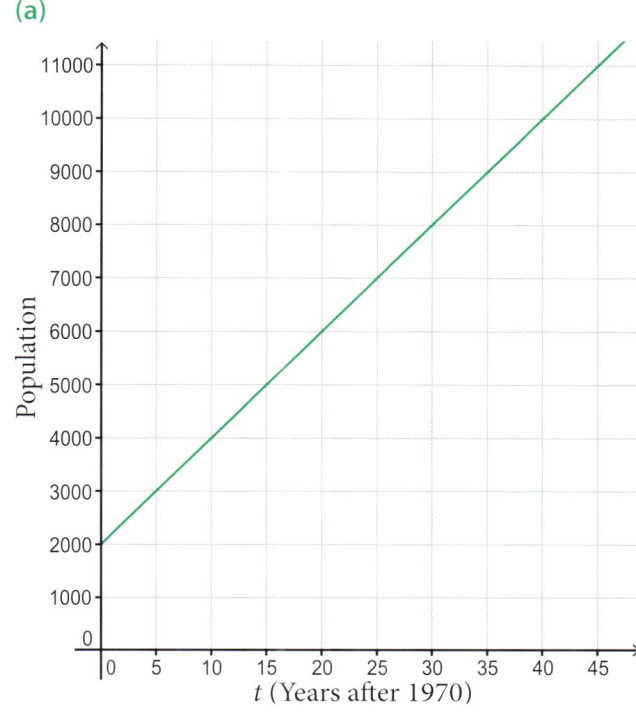

t (Years after 1970)

(b) (i) The gradient of 200 means that the population increases by a fixed amount 200 every year.
    (ii) The y-intercept of 2000 corresponds to the population when the first measurement was taken in 1970.

Word problems involving linear equations almost always work in this way:

- The y-intercept is the starting value.
- The gradient is the amount of change in y for each unit of change in x. (In other words, the gradient is the **rate of change**.)

Exercise 6F

1. The average lifespan of British men has been recorded. The model for the data is $y = 0.2t + 73$ where $t = 0$ corresponds to the year 1960. This relationship between y and t forms a straight line when plotted on a graph.
   (a) What are the gradient and y-intercept?
   (b) By how much does y increase every time t increases by 1?

Exercise 6F

(c) In the context of the question, explain the meaning of the gradient and the y-intercept.

2. A ball is thrown straight up in the air. The equation for the velocity of the ball is $v = 40 - 10t$ where v is the velocity (in m s^{-1}) and t is the number of seconds after the ball is thrown.
   (a) With what initial velocity was the ball thrown?
   (b) Sketch the graph of v against t for values of t from 0 to 8.
   (c) In relation to the graph, what is the significance of the number 40?
   (d) In the context of the question, what is the significance of the number 40 and the gradient of the graph?

3. Fishermen on the River Nagal have been recording the number of dead fish they find. Scientists at the Department for the Environment monitor the pollution index for the river. They find that a model for the annual number of fish deaths D for a given pollution index p is $D = 5.6p + 221.7$. When plotted on a graph, D against p, a straight line is formed.
   (a) What is the gradient of the line?
   (b) What is the meaning of the gradient?
   (c) Where does the straight line graph pass through the D-axis and what is the significance of this number?

6.6 Summary

You can find the gradient of a line between two points (x_1, y_1) and (x_2, y_2) using the formula:
$$m = \frac{y_2 - y_1}{x_2 - x_1} \qquad (1)$$

A linear equation can appear in various forms including:
$$y = mx + c$$
$$ax + by + c = 0$$

If the gradient m and a point (x_1, y_1) on a straight line are known, you can find the equation of the line using:
$$y - y_1 = m(x - x_1) \qquad (2)$$

If two points on a straight line are known, first calculate the gradient using equation (1), then use equation (2) to find the equation of the line.

The form $ax + by + c = 0$ is known as the **general equation** of a straight line.

To identify the gradient and y-intercept of a straight line, first re-arrange the equation into the form $y = mx + c$.

Parallel lines have equal gradients. **Perpendicular** lines have gradients that multiply to make -1.

Chapter 7
Circles

7.1 Introduction

In this chapter you will learn about the coordinate geometry of a circle. You will revise some of the circle theorems you learnt in GCSE Mathematics. You will also learn about the equation of a circle, how to find the intersection points between a circle and a straight line and how to find the equation of a tangent to a circle.

Key words
- **Circumference**: The distance around a circle.
- **Chord**: A line segment between two points on a circle.
- **Diameter**: A chord passing through the centre of a circle.
- **Radius**: Half a diameter, from centre to circumference.
- **Tangent**: A line touching a circle at only one point.
- **Bisect**: To cut in half.
- **Perpendicular**: At 90°.
- **Perpendicular bisector:** A line that cuts another line exactly in half at 90°.

Before you start
You should know:

- How to find the equation of a line joining two points.
- How to complete the square for a quadratic expression.
- How to determine the number of roots of a quadratic equation.

What you will learn
In this chapter you will learn how to:

- Apply circle theorems to problems in coordinate geometry.
- Find the equation of a circle.
- Find the number of intersection points of a line and circle and find their coordinates.

In the real world...

The planets orbit the sun in elliptical (oval-shaped) orbits. Most of the planets, however, have orbits that are almost circular. This allows astronomers to make quick calculations about the approximate positions of the planets.

By solving equations involving circles and straight lines, it is even possible to estimate whether asteroids and meteors are likely to pose any significant danger.

A collision with an asteroid 50 metres in diameter could have the same effect as a nuclear bomb! In 1908, an object roughly 100 metres wide appears to have hit a remote area of Siberia, flattening 2000 square kilometres of forest. An even larger impact probably wiped out the dinosaurs 65 million years ago.

Worked Examples

1. Find the midpoint M of the points (–7, 3) and (9, 15)

   To find the midpoint of two points we find the average of the two x-coordinates and the average of the two y-coordinates:

   Therefore the coordinates of M are $\left(\dfrac{-7+9}{2}, \dfrac{3+15}{2}\right)$.

   So M is the point (1, 9).

2. Find the equation of the line joining the points (1, 3) and (−5, 4).

   $(x_1, y_1) = (1, 3)$ and $(x_2, y_2) = (−5, 4)$.

   The gradient of the line is given by:

   $$m = \frac{y_2 - y_1}{x_2 - x_1}$$

   $$m = \frac{4 - 3}{-5 - 1}$$

   $$m = -\frac{1}{6}$$

   The equation of a straight line passing through point (x_1, y_1) is:

   $$y - y_1 = m(x - x_1)$$

   $$y - 3 = -\frac{1}{6}(x - 1)$$

   $$x + 6y - 19 = 0$$

3. A diameter of a circle has end points A and B. The centre of the circle is at point C. Given that points A and C have coordinates (−3, 5) and (−5, 9) respectively, find the coordinates of B.

Let B be (x, y).

Since C is the midpoint of AB:
$$\frac{-3 + x}{2} = -5 \text{ and } \frac{5 + y}{2} = 9$$
$\Rightarrow x = -7, y = 13$
So B has coordinates (−7, 13).

4. Complete the square to solve for x: $x^2 - 4x + 3 = 0$

$x^2 - 4x + 3 = 0$

Half the coefficient of x is 2:
$(x - 2)^2 - 4 + 3 = 0$

Collect the number terms on the right:
$(x - 2)^2 = 1$

Square root each side:
$x - 2 = \pm 1$
So $x = 3$ or $x = 1$.

5. Determine the number of roots to the equation $2x^2 + 7x + 9 = 0$.

Find the discriminant:
$$b^2 - 4ac = 7^2 - 4(2)(9)$$
$$= 49 - 72$$

This is less than zero; therefore there are no roots to this equation.

Note: The question did not ask for the roots, just the number of them.

Exercise 7A (Revision)

1. For the following pairs of points:
   (i) Find the equation of the straight line joining the points.
   (ii) Find the midpoint of the two points.
   (a) (1, 1) and (−1, −1)
   (b) (10, 3) and (0, 6)
   (c) (−2, −1) and (4, 1)
   (d) (12, 2) and (−12, 4)
   (e) (6, 7) and (−7, −6)

2. A diameter of a circle has end points A and B. Given that the coordinates of A are (−5, −6) and the coordinates of the centre C are (10, −7), find the coordinates of B.

Exercise 7A (Revision)...

3. Complete the square for the following functions.
   (a) $f(x) = x^2 + 4x$
   (b) $f(x) = x^2 + 8x + 6$
   (c) $f(x) = -x^2 - 10x + 6$

4. Solve the following for x by completing the square.
   (a) $x^2 + 6x = -8$
   (b) $-x^2 - 4x = -5$
   (c) $x^2 + 2x - 17 = 0$

5. By calculating the discriminant, find the number of roots of the following quadratic equations.
   (a) $x^2 + x - 1 = 0$
   (b) $x^2 + 5x + 25 = 0$
   (c) $x^2 - 8x + 16 = 0$
   (d) $-x^2 - 2x = 3$
   (e) $(x - 1)^2 = -1$

7.2 Circle Theorems

Note: You may sometimes hear the word **subtended**. In the first diagram below, the angle shown at A is *subtended* by the chord BC at the circumference. The angle shown at O is *subtended* by the chord BC at the centre.

Angles at the centre and the circumference
Point O is the centre of the circle shown below.

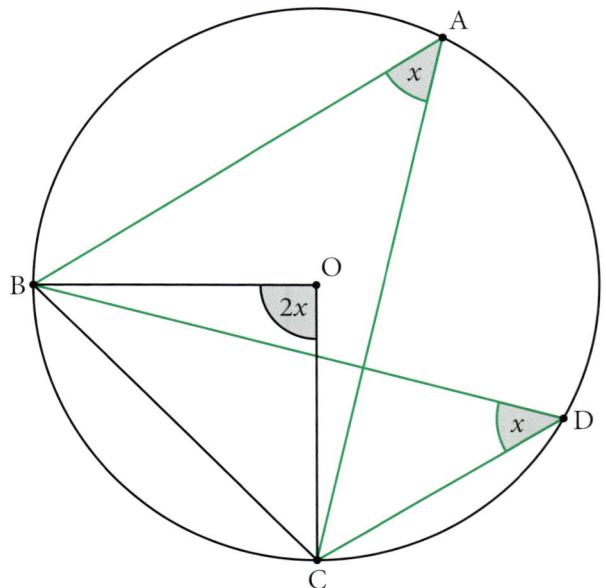

The diagram illustrates two important points.

- Two angles both subtended at the circumference by the same chord are **equal**. In the diagram, the angles at A and D are equal because they are both subtended by the chord BC.

- The angle subtended by a chord at the centre of a circle is **twice** the angle subtended by the same chord at the circumference. In the diagram, the angle at O is twice the angle at A and D.

Worked Example

6. Find the angles marked *a* and *b* in the diagram below.

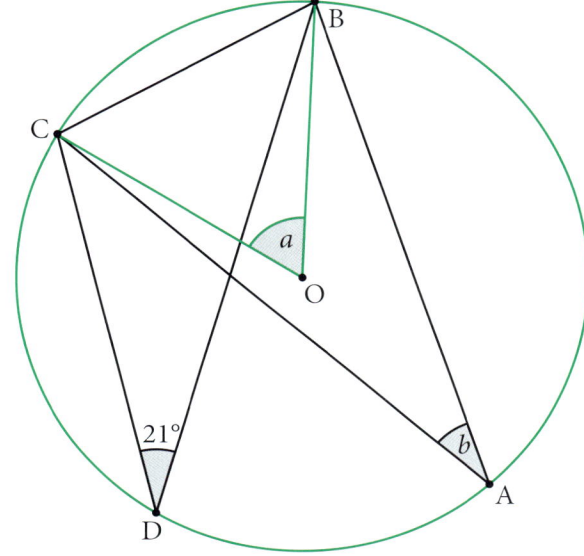

The angle BOC subtended by chord BC at the centre is twice the angle BDC subtended by the same chord at the circumference. So *a* = 42°.

Angle BAC is equal to angle BDC. They are both subtended by chord BC at the circumference. So *b* = 21°.

An angle in a semicircle is a right angle

You may remember from GCSE Mathematics that an angle at the circumference of a semicircle is always a right angle. Consider the circle below.

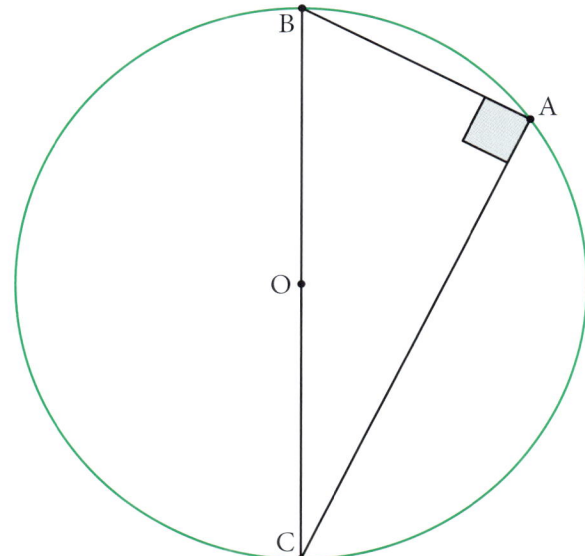

Angle A is 90° because the chord BC is a diameter of the circle. Another way of stating this is that an angle subtended at the circumference by a diameter is a right angle.

Worked Examples

7. The circle C, shown below, has centre (0, 0). Point Y has coordinates (−5, 0) and Z (5, 0). Angle XZY = 70°. What is the size of angle XYZ?

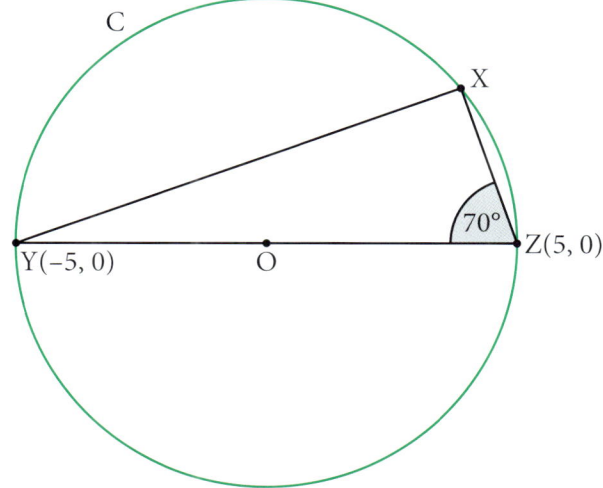

Chord YZ passes through the centre, O, so it is a diameter. Hence XYZ is a triangle in a semicircle.

Therefore angle YXZ is 90°.

Angles in the triangle add up to 180°, so angle XYZ is 20°.

8. Points X(−2, −2), Y(2p, 2p + 10) and Z(4, 2) lie on the circumference of the circle shown, with centre A.

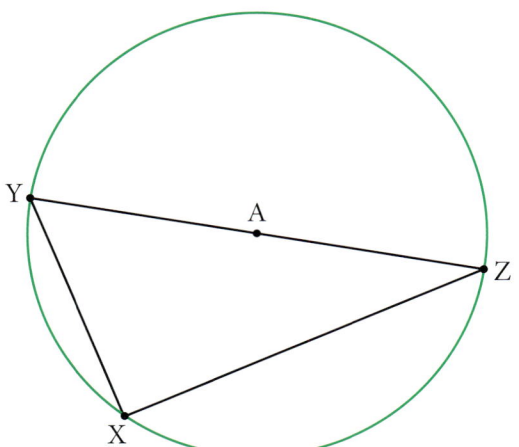

(a) Find the gradient of the chord XZ.
(b) Hence find the gradient of the chord XY.
(c) Find the value of p.

(a) Gradient of XZ:
$$m = \frac{y_2 - y_1}{x_2 - x_1} = \frac{-2 - 2}{-2 - 4}$$
$$= \frac{2}{3}$$

(b) YZ is a diameter, so angle YXZ is 90° (because it is in a semicircle). This means XY and XZ are perpendicular.

So the gradient of XY is $-\frac{3}{2}$.

This is the negative reciprocal of $\frac{2}{3}$ since XY and XZ are perpendicular.

(c) For the gradient of XY:
$$m = \frac{y_2 - y_1}{x_2 - x_1}$$
$$-\frac{3}{2} = \frac{2p + 10 - (-2)}{2p - (-2)}$$
$$-\frac{3}{2} = \frac{2p + 12}{2p + 2}$$

Cross-multiplying gives:
$$4p + 24 = -6p - 6$$
$$10p = -30$$
$$p = -3$$

Perpendicular from centre to a chord

The perpendicular from the centre of a circle to a chord will always bisect the chord, as shown in the following diagram.

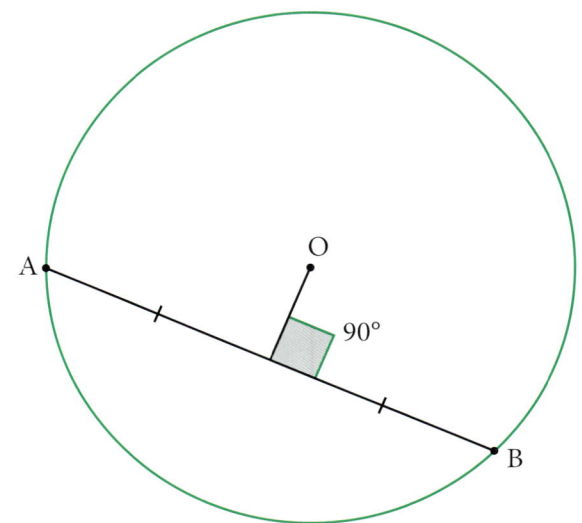

Worked Examples

9. In the circle shown below, the chord AB cuts the radius OD at 90° at point C. The coordinates of points B and C are (4, 2) and (3, 3) respectively. What are the coordinates of A?

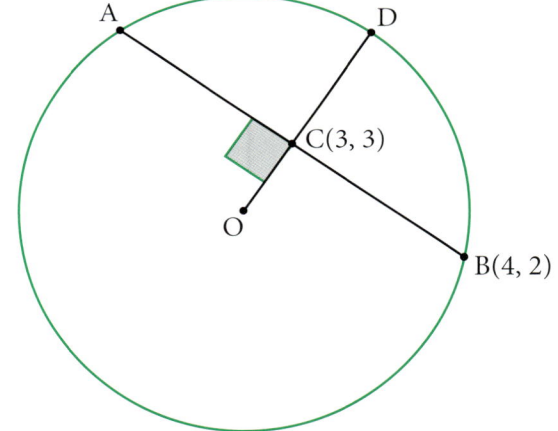

Using the theorem that the perpendicular from the centre to a chord always bisects the chord, C must be the midpoint of AB.

The average of the x-coordinates of A and B gives the x-coordinate of C. Then repeat for the y-coordinates.

Therefore, if the coordinates of A are (x, y):
$$\frac{x + 4}{2} = 3 \text{ and } \frac{y + 2}{2} = 3$$
giving $x = 2, y = 4$

So the coordinates of A are (2, 4).

10. Find the equation of the perpendicular bisector of the chord AB, where A is (10, 5) and B is (4, 8).

Gradient of chord AB $= \dfrac{8-5}{4-10} = -\dfrac{1}{2}$

Therefore the gradient of the perpendicular bisector is 2.

The midpoint, M, of AB is $\left(\dfrac{4+10}{2}, \dfrac{5+8}{2}\right)$.

Therefore the coordinates of M are $\left(7, \dfrac{13}{2}\right)$.

So the equation of the line is given by:
$$y - y_1 = m(x - x_1)$$
$$y - \dfrac{13}{2} = 2(x - 7)$$
$$4x - 2y - 15 = 0$$

Perpendicularity of radius and tangent

A tangent to a circle meets a radius of the circle at 90°, as shown in the following diagram.

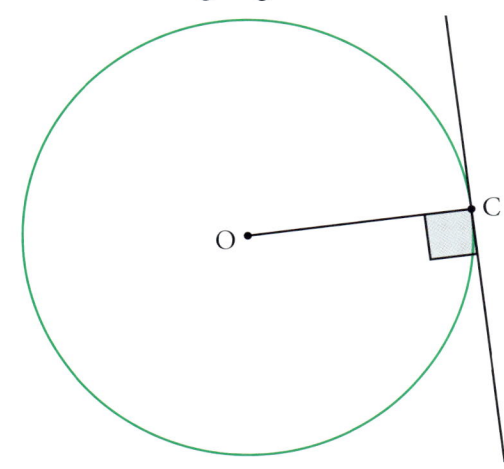

Worked Example

11. A tangent and radius to the circle C meet at the point (4, 3). The gradient of the tangent is $-\dfrac{4}{3}$. What is the gradient of this radius?

Tangent and radius are perpendicular; therefore the gradient of the radius is $\dfrac{3}{4}$.

12. A tangent and radius to the circle C meet at the point (1, 4). The gradient of the radius is $-\dfrac{1}{5}$. What is the equation of the tangent?

Tangent and radius are perpendicular, therefore the gradient of the tangent is 5.

So the equation of tangent is given by:

$$y - y_1 = m(x - x_1)$$
$$y - 4 = 5(x - 1)$$
$$y = 5x - 1$$

Tangents from a point to a circle

The two tangents from a point to a circle are equal in length. In the diagram below, AB = AD.

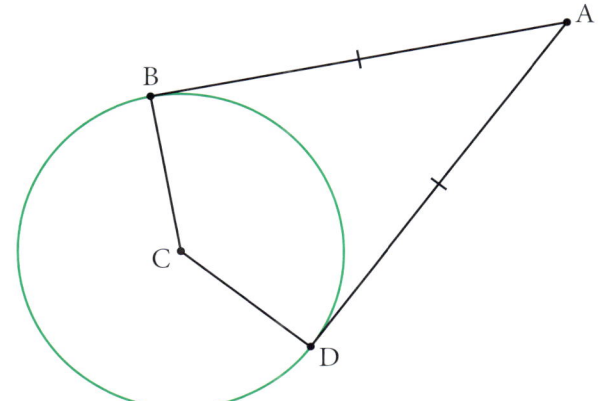

Tangent kites

In the previous diagram, the sides BC and CD are equal in length as they are both the radius of the circle. The quadrilateral ABCD is called a **tangent kite**.

Angles ABC and ADC (where each tangent meets a radius) are both 90°.

The sum of the angles in any quadrilateral is 360°. Since there are two right angles in opposite corners in a tangent kite, the sum of the remaining two angles BCD and BAD must be 180°.

Worked Example

13. In the following diagram, angle PSR is 42°. Tangents from Q meet the circle at P and R. Find the size of angle PQR.

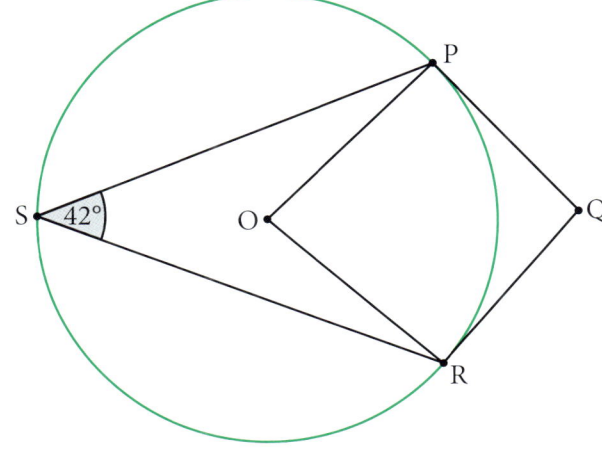

Firstly, note that angle POR is 84°. (The angle subtended by PR at the centre is double the angle subtended at the circumference.)

Quadrilateral OPQR is a tangent kite. The two angles OPQ and ORQ (where the tangents meet the two radii) are both 90°.

Therefore angles POR and PQR must have a sum of 180°. So:

POR + PQR = 180
       PQR = 180 – POR
       PQR = 180 – 84
       PQR = 96°

In the following example, the area of a tangent kite is required. It is calculated as two right-angled triangles.

Worked Example

14. The following diagram shows a circle with centre C(8, 3) and radius 5. From the point A(24, 15), two tangents are drawn to the circle, meeting the circle at the points B and D. Show that the area of the kite ABCD is $25\sqrt{15}$.

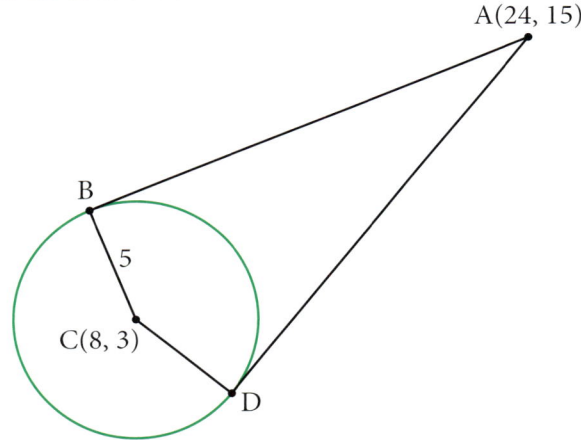

A(24, 15)

We can work out the length AC:
$$AC = \sqrt{(24-8)^2 + (15-3)^2}$$
$$= 20$$

We also know BC = 5.

Triangle ABC has a right angle at B, since the tangent and radius meet at 90°. So we can use Pythagoras' Theorem in triangle ABC to calculate the length AB:
$$AB = \sqrt{20^2 - 5^2}$$
$$= \sqrt{375}$$
$$= 5\sqrt{15}$$

Calculate the area of triangle ABC using:
Area = ½ × base × perpendicular height
$$= \frac{1}{2} \times 5\sqrt{15} \times 5$$
$$= \frac{25\sqrt{15}}{2}$$

The kite ABCD comprises two identical triangles, therefore:
$$\text{Area ABCD} = 2 \times \frac{25\sqrt{15}}{2}$$
$$= 25\sqrt{15}$$

Exercise 7B

1. Find the equation of the perpendicular bisector to each chord, given the coordinates of the two end points of the chord.
   (a) A(–2, 7), B(6, 1)
   (b) A(–5, 2), B(–2, 7)
   (c) A(15, 15), B(10, 20)
   (d) A(3, –4), B(1, –4)
   (e) A(2, 1), B(1, 2)

2. In the circle with the centre given, the angle A is subtended by the chord BC. State whether angle A is a right angle.
   (a) B(–8, 4), C(4, –8), centre (–2, –2)
   (b) B(7, –5), C(–7, 7), centre (0, 1)
   (c) B(–3, 6), C(6, –10), centre (0.5, –2)
   (d) B(–6, –7), C(–6, –2), centre (–6, –4.5)
   (e) B(–2, 9), C(–8, –2), centre (–5, –3.5)

3. The line $y = 2x - 4$ is a tangent to the circle C, touching C at the point P(3, 2). The point Q is the centre of C.
   (a) Find an equation for the straight line through P and Q.
   (b) Given that Q lies on the line $y = 1$, show that the x-coordinate of Q is 5.

4. A circle passes through the points (10, 10), (16, 10) and (10, 20).
   (a) Find the coordinates of the centre of the circle.
   (b) Find the exact radius of the circle.

5. The points A and B lie on a circle with centre P, as shown in the diagram opposite. The point A has coordinates (3, –2) and the mid-point M of AB has coordinates (4, 2). The line L_1 passes through the points M and P.

Exercise 7B...

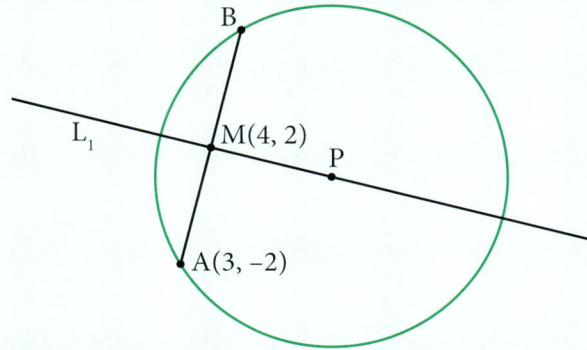

(a) Find an equation for L_1.
(b) Given that the x-coordinate of P is 8, use your answer to part (a) to show that the y-coordinate of P is 1.

6. The circle shown has centre M, with AB as a diameter. A, B and C all lie on the circle and have coordinates $A(1, 2 + 4\sqrt{2})$, $B(q, -2q)$ and $C(3, 2 + 2\sqrt{2})$.

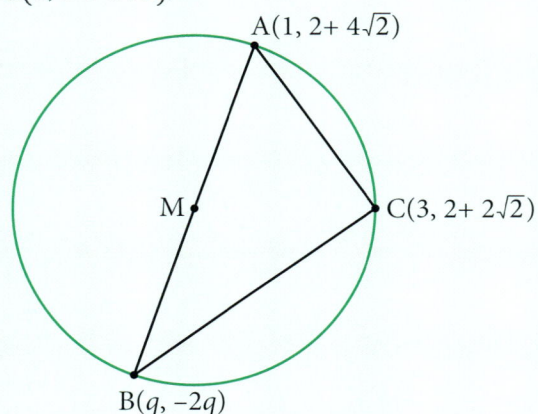

(a) Find the exact gradient of AC.
(b) Hence find the exact gradient of BC.
(c) Find the value of q.

7. A radio transmitter located at C can send signals to three spies X, Y and Z as long as they are within a 13 km radius. Each spy is now located somewhere on the 13 km circle, with spy X being the furthest north. When drawn on a map, spy X is located at (18, 10). The distance between X and Y is $\sqrt{26}$ km and the gradient of the line between them is -5.
(a) What are the coordinates of spy Y?
Given that the spies X and Z are directly opposite each other on the 13 km circle:
(b) Find the gradient of the line between Y and Z. Z has x-coordinate -6.
(c) Find the y-coordinate of Z.

Exercise 7B...

(d) Find the coordinates of the transmitter.
(e) In which direction would somebody have to travel from the transmitter to reach spy Y?

8. In the diagram below, the six points A, B, C, D, E and F are equally spaced around the circle. Tangents are drawn at points B and C. These two tangents meet at the point P.

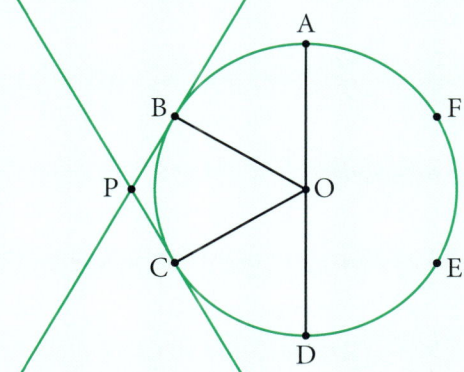

(a) Find the angle BOC.
(b) Hence find the angle BPC.
(c) The radius of the circle is 9 cm. Use trigonometry in triangle OBP to find the length of BP, giving your answer in surd form.
(d) Hence find the exact area of the tangent kite OBPC.

7.3 The Equation of a Circle

The general equation of a circle is:
$$(x - a)^2 + (y - b)^2 = r^2$$

where (a, b) are the coordinates of the circle's centre and r is its radius.

Proof of the equation of a circle

Note: The CCEA specification (at the time of publication) does not require you to know this proof.

Consider a circle with radius r and centre (a, b). Consider a general point $P(x, y)$ on the circle. Construct a right-angled triangle between C and P as shown in the diagram overleaf:

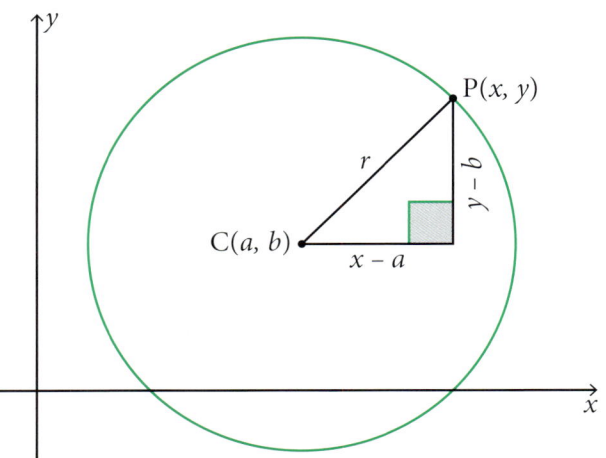

Using Pythagoras' Theorem: $(x - a)^2 + (y - b)^2 = r^2$

Centre and radius

Given the equation of a circle, you can find its centre and radius.

Worked Example

15. Find the centre and radius of the circle C with equation $(x - 7)^2 + (y - 4)^2 = 25$.

    Comparing the equation of C with the general equation of a circle, $(x - a)^2 + (y - b)^2 = r^2$, we can see that the centre is $(7, 4)$ and the radius is 5.

Given the centre and radius of a circle, you can find its equation.

Worked Example

16. The circle C has centre $(10, -5)$ and radius 3. Find its equation.

    We use the general equation of a circle, $(x - a)^2 + (y - b)^2 = r^2$.

    $(a, b) = (10, -5)$ and $r = 3$.

    Therefore the equation of C is:
    $(x - 10)^2 + (y + 5)^2 = 9$

There is a second form of the equation of a circle, which is obtained by expanding the brackets:

$x^2 + y^2 + 2gx + 2fy + c = 0$

Sometimes you will need to solve problems using this equation, by rewriting the equation in the standard form. You will do this by **completing the square**.

Worked Examples

17. The equation of a circle is $x^2 + y^2 + 2x - 4y + 1 = 0$. Find its centre and radius.

    Complete the square for both x and y:
    $(x + 1)^2 - 1 + (y - 2)^2 - 4 + 1 = 0$

    Re-arrange:
    $(x + 1)^2 + (y - 2)^2 = 4$

    Hence, the circle has centre $(-1, 2)$ and radius 2.

18. Determine whether the points A$(1, 9)$ and B$(2, 8)$ lie on the circle C whose equation is:
    $(x + 5)^2 + (y - 9)^2 = 36$

    Point A

    Using $x = 1$ and $y = 9$ in the equation of the circle, the left-hand side becomes:
    $(1 + 5)^2 + (9 - 9)^2 = 36$

    Hence the coordinates of point A satisfy the equation of the circle C; therefore the point A lies on the circle.

    Point B

    Using $x = 2$ and $y = 8$ in the equation of the circle, the left-hand side becomes:
    $(2 + 5)^2 + (8 - 9)^2 = 50$

    Hence the coordinates of point B do not satisfy the equation of the circle C; therefore the point B does not lie on the circle.

19. The point A, with coordinates $(2, -4)$, lies on the circle C, whose equation is: $(x - 4)^2 + (y + 4)^2 = p$. Find the value of p. State the centre and radius of the circle.

    Since A lies on the circle:
    $(2 - 4)^2 + (-4 + 4)^2 = p$
    $(-2)^2 + 0^2 = p$
    $\Rightarrow p = 4$

    So the circle has equation:
    $(x - 4)^2 + (y + 4)^2 = 4$

    Comparing the equation of the circle with the general form, $(x - a)^2 + (y - b)^2 = r^2$, we can see that
    $a = 4, b = -4, r^2 = 4$

    Therefore, the centre of the circle is $(4, -4)$ and its radius is 2.

20. A circle has centre M$(-5, 7)$ and passes through the point A$(-5, -1)$.
    (a) Find the equation of circle.
    (b) Find the coordinates of the points where the circle passes through the x-axis and y-axis, giving exact answers.

(a) The radius of the circle is the distance between points M and A. Recall the formula for the length of a line between two points:

$$l = \sqrt{(x_2 - x_1)^2 + (y_2 - y_1)^2}$$
$$\therefore r = \sqrt{(-5 - -5)^2 + (-1 - 7)^2}$$
$$= \sqrt{0^2 + (-8)^2}$$
$$= 8$$

The general form for the equation of a circle is $(x - a)^2 + (y - b)^2 = r^2$, where (a, b) are the coordinates of the centre and r is its radius

Therefore the equation of the circle is:
$(x + 5)^2 + (y - 7)^2 = 64$

(b) The circle passes through the x-axis when $y = 0$. So:
$$(x + 5)^2 + (0 - 7)^2 = 64$$
$$(x + 5)^2 + 49 = 64$$
$$(x + 5)^2 = 15$$
$$x + 5 = \pm\sqrt{15}$$
So $x = \sqrt{15} - 5$ or $x = -\sqrt{15} - 5$

There are two points where the circle intersects the x-axis: $\left(\sqrt{15} - 5, 0\right)$ and $\left(-\sqrt{15} - 5, 0\right)$. The circle passes through the y-axis when $x = 0$. So:
$$(0 + 5)^2 + (y - 7)^2 = 64$$
$$25 + (y - 7)^2 = 64$$
$$(y - 7)^2 = 39$$
$$y - 7 = \pm\sqrt{39}$$
So $y = 7 + \sqrt{39}$ or $y = 7 - \sqrt{39}$

There are two points where the circle intersects the y-axis: $\left(0, 7 + \sqrt{39}\right)$ and $\left(0, 7 - \sqrt{39}\right)$.

---

21. The chord AB is a diameter of circle C, as shown below.

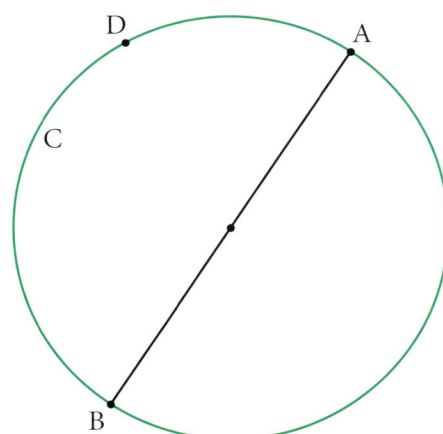

(a) Given that the coordinates of A and B are A(6, 5) and B(2, −1), find the equation of C.

The point D lies on the circle.
(b) Write down the size of angle ADB.
(c) The length of AD is $\sqrt{13}$. Find the exact length of BD.

(a) The midpoint of the diameter is the centre of the circle. Therefore the centre has coordinates:
$$\left(\frac{6 + 2}{2}, \frac{5 - 1}{2}\right) = (4, 2)$$

The diameter's length is:
$$d = \sqrt{(x_2 - x_1)^2 + (y_2 - y_1)^2}$$
$$d = \sqrt{(6 - 2)^2 + (5 - -1)^2}$$
$$= \sqrt{4^2 + 6^2}$$
$$= \sqrt{52}$$
$$= 2\sqrt{13}$$

The radius of the circle is half the length of the diameter. $\therefore r = \sqrt{13}$

The general form for the equation of a circle is $(x - a)^2 + (y - b)^2 = r^2$ where (a, b) are the coordinates of the centre and r is its radius. Therefore the equation of C is:
$(x - 4)^2 + (y - 2)^2 = 13$

(b) Angle ADB is 90°, since it is an angle subtended by the diameter AB at the circumference.

(c) Since triangle ABD has a right angle at D, we can use Pythagoras' Theorem. The radius of the circle is $\sqrt{13}$, so the diameter AB has length $2\sqrt{13}$. If AD $= \sqrt{13}$, then:
$$BD^2 = \left(2\sqrt{13}\right)^2 - \left(\sqrt{13}\right)^2$$
$$= 4(13) - 13$$
$$= 39$$
Hence BD $= \sqrt{39}$

....

Exercise 7C

1. Determine whether the point A, with coordinates given, lies on the circle C whose equation is also given.
   (a) A(−4, −9), C: $(x + 7)^2 + (y - 8)^2 = 64$
   (b) A(−1, −5), C: $(x + 8)^2 + (y + 5)^2 = 49$

2. The point A, with coordinates given, lies on the circle C, whose equation is also given. Find the value of p. Write down the coordinates of the centre and the radius of C.
   (a) A(4, −10), C: $(x + 4)^2 + (y + 10)^2 = p$
   (b) A(−2, −8), C: $(x - 6)^2 + (y + 2)^2 = p$

Exercise 7C...

3. Find the equation of the circle with centre M, which passes through the point A.
   (a) M(8, 7), A(8, 3)
   (b) M(−2, −1), A(−8, −9)

4. The chord AB is a diameter of circle C. Given the coordinates of A and B, find the equation of C.
   (a) A(−2, −2), B(0, −4)
   (b) A(6, −1), B(10, −5)

5. A circle has equation:
   $x^2 + y^2 + 10x − 20y + 100 = 0$.
   (a) Verify that the point A with coordinates (−9, 7) lies on the circle.
   (b) Find the equation of the circle in its standard form.
   (c) Write down the centre of the circle and its radius.

6. Two circles C and D are shown below. The centre of circle D lies vertically above the centre of circle C. The diameter of circle C is twice the diameter of circle D. The equation of circle C is:
   $(x − 9)^2 + y^2 = 16$
   Find the equation of circle D.

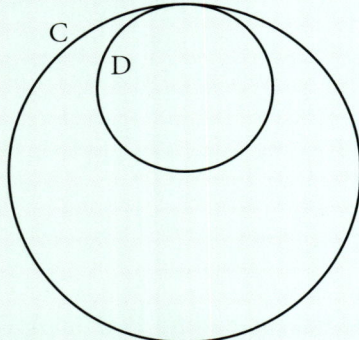

7. The equation of circle C is:
   $x^2 + y^2 − 6x + 2gy − 24 = 0$
   The radius of circle C is 7. Find the value of g.

8. A circle C has the equation:
   $x^2 + y^2 − 12x − 8y − 48 = 0$
   (a) Find the coordinates of the centre of C.
   (b) Find the radius of C.
   (c) The points A and B are both on the circle C. The line AB is a diameter of the circle. The point D also lies on the circle. The length AD = $\sqrt{40}$. Find the length BD, giving your answer as a simplified surd.

Exercise 7C...

9. A circle has centre C with coordinates (−2, 2) and passes through the point A with coordinates (1, 1). Find the coordinates of the points where the circle intersects:
   (a) the x-axis,
   (b) the y-axis.

10. The diagram shows two circles with equations $x^2 + y^2 = 25$ and $(x − 8)^2 + (y − 4)^2 = 4$. Find the shortest distance between the two circles.

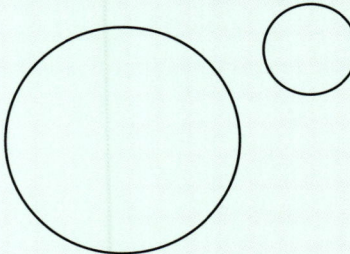

11. The points A(16, −10) and B(14, −12) both lie on a circle. The centre of the circle lies on the line $x = 8$. Find the equation of the circle.

7.4 Intersection of Circles and Straight Lines

You will often have to solve problems involving the intersection points of circles and straight lines. There are three possibilities:

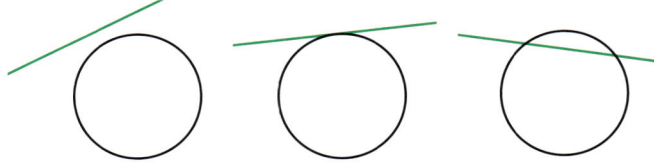

No points of intersection.

One point of intersection (i.e. the line is a tangent to the circle).

Two points of intersection.

You can find the points of intersection by solving the equations of the line and circle simultaneously.

Worked Example

22. Find the points of intersection of the circle C with equation $(x-3)^2 + (y-2)^2 = 25$ and the straight line $y = x$.

$(x-3)^2 + (y-2)^2 = 25$ (1)
$y = x$ (2)

Substitute (2) into (1): $(x-3)^2 + (x-2)^2 = 25$
Expand: $x^2 - 6x + 9 + x^2 - 4x + 4 = 25$
Rearrange: $2x^2 - 10x - 12 = 0$
Divide both sides by 2: $x^2 - 5x - 6 = 0$
Factorise: $(x-6)(x+1) = 0$
So $x = 6$ or $x = -1$

Using (2), when $x = 6$, $y = 6$. When $x = -1$, $y = -1$. Hence the points of intersection are $(6, 6)$ and $(-1, -1)$.

By showing there is only one point of intersection, you can prove that a line is a tangent to a circle.

Worked Example

23. Show that the line $x - 2y - 8 = 0$ is a tangent to the circle C with equation $(x-3)^2 + (y+5)^2 = 5$ and find the coordinates of the point at which the tangent touches the circle.

$x - 2y - 8 = 0$ (1)
$(x-3)^2 + (y+5)^2 = 5$ (2)

Rearrange (1):
$y = \dfrac{x}{2} - 4$

Substitute in (2):
$(x-3)^2 + \left(\dfrac{x}{2} + 1\right)^2 = 5$

Expand brackets:
$x^2 - 6x + 9 + \dfrac{x^2}{4} + x + 1 = 5$

Re-arrange:
$\dfrac{5x^2}{4} - 5x + 5 = 0$
$x^2 - 4x + 4 = 0$
$(x-2)^2 = 0$

There is only one solution: $x = 2$, which indicates that the line and circle intersect at only one point. Therefore, the straight line is a tangent to the circle. When $x = 2$, $y = -3$. So the tangent meets the circle at $(2, -3)$.

You should remember that, when solving a quadratic equation, the number of solutions is determined by the value of the discriminant $b^2 - 4ac$.

Discriminant > 0	two solutions
Discriminant = 0	one solution
Discriminant < 0	no solutions

In the following example, we are asked only to find the number of intersection points, not their coordinates.

Worked Example

24. Find the number of points of intersection between the straight line
$y = 4x - 1$ (1)
and the circle with equation
$(x-3)^2 + (y+6)^2 = 17$ (2)

Substitute (1) into (2):
$(x-3)^2 + (4x+5)^2 = 17$

Expand:
$x^2 - 6x + 9 + 16x^2 + 40x + 25 = 17$

Re-arrange:
$17x^2 + 34x + 17 = 0$
$x^2 + 2x + 1 = 0$

To find the number of solutions, calculate the discriminant:
$b^2 - 4ac = 2^2 - 4(1)(1) = 0$

Hence there is only one solution, i.e. only one point of intersection. The line is a tangent to the circle.

Exercise 7D

1. Find the number of points of intersection between the circle and the straight line, whose equations are given.
   (a) $(x-1)^2 + (y-3)^2 = 4$; $y = -x + 2$
   (b) $x^2 + (y+6)^2 = 12$; $y = -x - 5$
   (c) $(x-9)^2 + y^2 = 2$; $y = x + 3$
   (d) $(x-3)^2 + (y-1)^2 = 20$; $y = 2x + 5$
   (e) $(x-7)^2 + y^2 = 13$; $y = x + 6$

2. Find the coordinates of any points of intersection of the circle and the straight line, whose equations are given. Give exact answers where appropriate.
   (a) $x^2 + y^2 - 8x - 18y + 95 = 0$; $y = x + 7$
   (b) $(x+1)^2 + (y+5)^2 = 2$; $y = -2x - 7$
   (c) $(x-10)^2 + (y+10)^2 = 20$; $y = -2x$

Exercise 7D...

(d) $x^2 + y^2 + 6x - 12y + 25 = 0$; $y = -3x$

(e) $x^2 + y^2 - 8x - 2y + 4 = 0$; $y = 2x + 3$

3. The straight line $y = ax - 6$ touches the circle with equation $(x - 7)^2 + (y - 3)^2 = 2$ at only one point. Find the two possible values of a.

4. The circle $(x - 2)^2 + y^2 = 18$ and the straight line $y = x - 2$ intersect at the points A and B (where the x-coordinate of point B is greater than the x-coordinate of point A).
   (a) Show that the coordinates of point B are $(5, 3)$ and find the coordinates of A.
   (b) Show that the chord AB is a diameter of the circle.

7.5 The Equation of the Tangent to a Circle Through a Point on the Circumference

Worked Examples

25. Find the equation of the tangent to the circle $(x - 6)^2 + (y - 8)^2 = 100$ at the point $P(14, 14)$, giving your answer in the form $ax + by + c = 0$.

The circle has centre $(6, 8)$ and radius 10.
So we can draw:

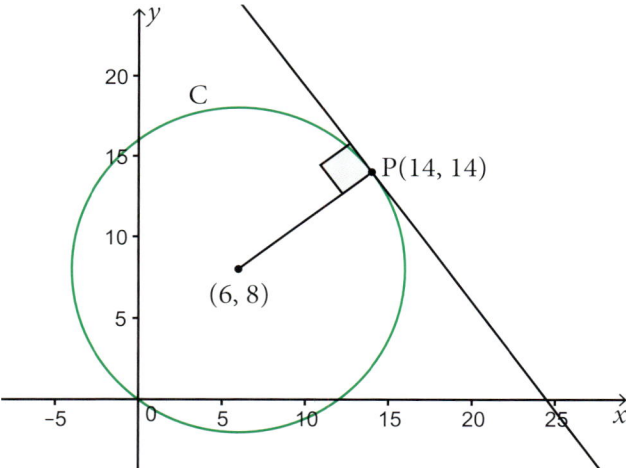

The line joining the centre to the point $P(14, 14)$ has gradient:
$$\frac{rise}{run} = \frac{14 - 8}{14 - 6} = \frac{3}{4}$$

Since the tangent is perpendicular to this radius, the gradient of the tangent is $-\frac{4}{3}$ (the negative reciprocal of $\frac{3}{4}$). The equation of the tangent can be found using:
$$y - y_1 = m(x - x_1)$$
$$y - 14 = -\frac{4}{3}(x - 14)$$
$$3y - 42 = -4(x - 14)$$
$$3y - 42 = -4x + 56$$
$$4x + 3y - 98 = 0$$

26. The equation of the circle C is:
    $x^2 + y^2 - 8x - 6y + 16 = 0$
    (a) Find the coordinates of the centre of C and its radius.
    (b) Circle C passes through the point $P\left(\frac{28}{25}, \frac{96}{25}\right)$. Find an equation for the tangent to C that passes through P. Show that this tangent passes through the origin.
    (c) Find the equation of the other tangent to C that passes through the origin.

(a) Complete the square:
$$x^2 + y^2 - 8x - 6y + 16 = 0$$
$$(x - 4)^2 - 16 + (y - 3)^2 - 9 + 16 = 0$$
$$(x - 4)^2 + (y - 3)^2 = 9$$
Circle C has centre $(4, 3)$ and radius 3.

(b) Gradient of radius passing through the centre and point P is:
$$\frac{\left(\frac{96}{25} - 3\right)}{\frac{28}{25} - 4} = \frac{\frac{21}{25}}{-\frac{72}{25}} = -\frac{7}{24}$$
Since the radius and tangent are perpendicular, the gradient of the tangent is $\frac{24}{7}$.

The equation of the tangent is:
$$y - y_1 = m(x - x_1)$$
$$y - \frac{96}{25} = \frac{24}{7}\left(x - \frac{28}{25}\right)$$
$$y = \frac{24}{7}x$$
The tangent has a y-intercept of zero; therefore, it passes through the origin.

(c) If a tangent is to pass through the origin it has equation $y = mx$ (since $c = 0$). Solving the equation of the tangent and the equation of the circle as simultaneous equations, there should be only one answer for x and y. So:
$$(x - 4)^2 + (y - 3)^2 = 9 \quad (1)$$
$$y = mx \quad (2)$$

Substitute (2) into (1):
$$(x - 4)^2 + (mx - 3)^2 = 9$$
$$x^2 - 8x + 16 + m^2x^2 - 6mx + 9 = 9$$
$$(m^2 + 1)x^2 + (-6m - 8)x + 16 = 0$$

This is a quadratic equation that must have only one solution.

$$\therefore b^2 - 4ac = 0$$
$$(-6m - 8)^2 - 4(m^2 + 1)(16) = 0$$
$$36m^2 + 96m + 64 - 64m^2 - 64 = 0$$
$$28m^2 - 96m = 0$$
$$7m^2 - 24m = 0$$
$$m(7m - 24) = 0$$

So $m = 0$ or $m = \dfrac{24}{7}$

The second tangent that passes through the origin has gradient 0. Its equation is $y = 0$.

Exercise 7E

1. Find the gradient of the tangent to each circle at the point C. In each case O is the centre of the circle.
   (a) O(0, 0), C(2, 1)
   (b) O(10, –1), C(0, –2)
   (c) O(3, 6), C(2, 5)
   (d) O(–2, 7), C(6, 1)
   (e) O(5, 4), C(5, 5)

2. In Exercise 7D question 4, the circle $(x - 2)^2 + y^2 = 18$ and the straight line $y = x - 2$ were shown to intersect at the points A and B, with the coordinates of point B (5, 3). Find the equation of the tangent to the circle at point B.

3. The circle shown has its centre at (–7, 5). The point B(–11, 3) lies on the circle. Line AB is a diameter of the circle.

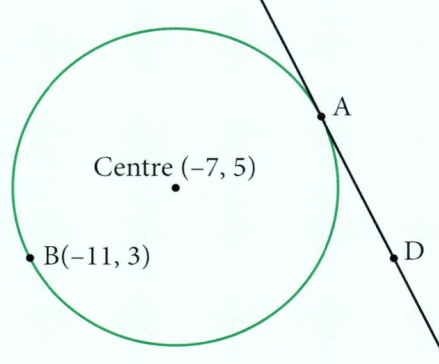

Centre (–7, 5)

B(–11, 3)

A

D

(a) Verify that the coordinates of A are (–3, 7).

Exercise 7E...

   (b) The point D(–1, 3) lies outside the circle. A tangent is drawn from D to the circle, touching the circle at A. Find the gradient of the tangent AD.
   (c) Hence find the equation of the tangent, giving your answer in the form $ax + by + c = 0$, where a, b and c are integers.
   (d) Find the exact length of the line segment AD.

4. The circle C has centre (5, 13) and touches the x-axis.
   (a) Find an equation of C in terms of x and y.
   (b) Find an equation of the tangent to C at the point (10, 1) giving your answer in the form $ax + by + c = 0$, where a, b and c are integers to be found.

5. A circle passes through the point A(–4, 7). A tangent T to the circle touches the circle at point A. The equation of T is $3x + 2y - 2 = 0$. Find the equation of the diameter of the circle that passes through point A. Give your answer in the form $ax + by + c = 0$, where a, b and c are integers.

6. The circle C has equation $x^2 + y^2 - 4x - 8y + 4 = 0$.
   (a) By completing the square for x and y, find the coordinates of the centre and the radius of C.
   (b) The circle C passes through the point P$\left(-\dfrac{6}{5}, \dfrac{8}{5}\right)$. Find an equation for the tangent to C that passes through P. Show that this tangent passes through the origin.
   (c) Find the equation of the other tangent to C that passes through the origin.

7.6 Summary

You need to understand and use the following circle theorems:

- An angle in a semicircle is always a right angle.

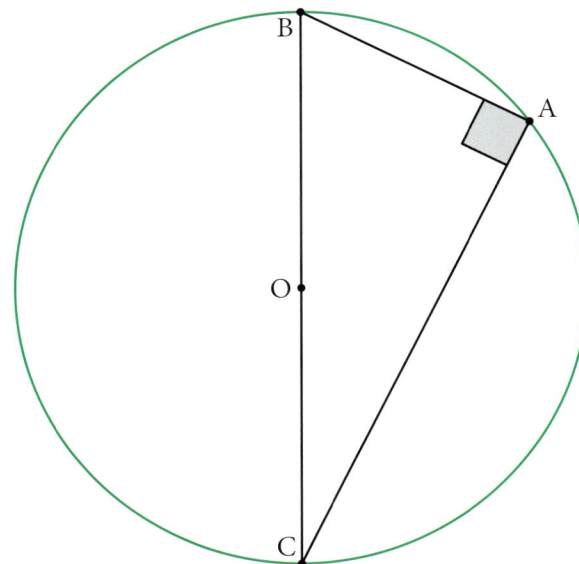

- The perpendicular from the centre of a circle to a chord bisects the chord.

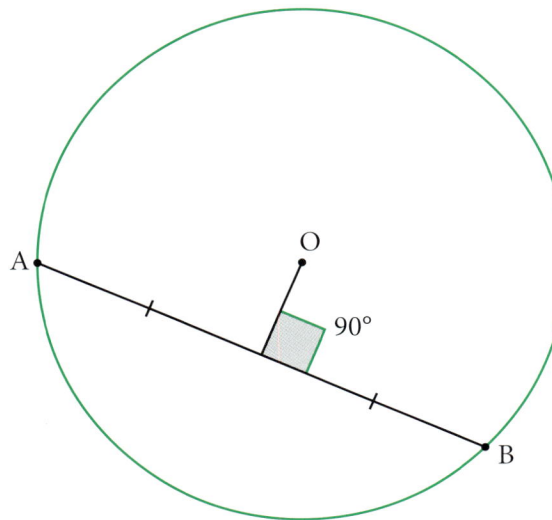

- The tangent to a circle is perpendicular to the radius it touches.

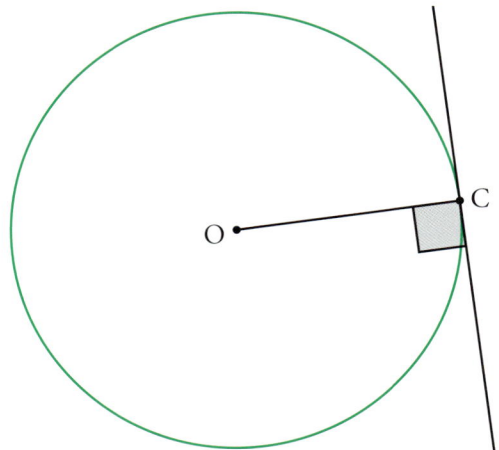

The second and third theorems are often useful when working out the gradient or equation of a line.

The general equation of a circle is:

$$(x - a)^2 + (y - b)^2 = r^2$$

where (a, b) are the coordinates of the centre and r is the circle's radius. This is sometimes written as:

$$x^2 + y^2 + 2gx + 2fy + c = 0$$

You will use the first form most often, especially when finding the centre and radius of a circle.

You can find the points of intersection of a circle with a straight line by solving the equations of the line and circle simultaneously. Eliminate y to form a quadratic equation in x. You can find the number of points of intersection by finding the value of the discriminant $b^2 - 4ac$.

- Discriminant > 0: two solutions, i.e. there are two points of intersection.
- Discriminant = 0: one solution, i.e. the line is a tangent to the circle.
- Discriminant < 0: no solutions, i.e. the line and circle do not intersect.

You can find the equation of a tangent to a circle at a point. First find the gradient of the radius to that point. Then use the fact that the tangent and radius are perpendicular lines to find the gradient of the tangent. Then use $y - y_1 = m(x - x_1)$ to obtain the equation of the tangent.

Chapter 8
Binomial Expansion

8.1 Introduction

Before you start
You should know:

- How to substitute values into formulae.
- How to solve simultaneous equations in 2 and 3 variables.

Worked Examples

1. The formula to convert a temperature measured in degrees Celsius (°C) to a temperature in degrees Fahrenheit (°F) is: $F = \dfrac{9C}{5} + 32$

   Find the temperature in degrees Fahrenheit, given that it is 20 °C.

   $F = \dfrac{9 \times 20}{5} + 32$

   $F = 68$

   So the temperature in degrees Fahrenheit is 68 °F.

2. Solve the following simultaneous equations for a and b:

   $2a - 3b = -17$ (1)
   $3a - 2b = -8$ (2)

Multiply (1) by 3:	$6a - 9b = -51$	(3)
Multiply (2) by 2:	$6a - 4b = -16$	(4)
Subtract (3) from (4):	$5b = 35$	
	$b = 7$	
Substitute into (1):	$2a - 3(7) = -17$	
	$2a = 4$	
	$a = 2$	

   Now check these values by substituting into equation (2): $3(2) - 2(7) = 6 - 14 = -8$

What you will learn
In this chapter you will learn:

- About factorial and combinatorial notation.
- How to use the binomial expansion.

In the real world...

In October 1971, physicist Joseph Hafele and astronomer Richard Keating took four atomic clocks on board aeroplanes and flew twice around the world. They compared the times measured by the atomic clocks with the United States Naval Observatory's clocks.

This was one of the most rigorous tests of Einstein's theories of Special and General Relativity, which state that time is distorted by velocity and also by gravitational fields. For the distortion due to velocity, relativity predicts that the time is given by:

$$T = T_0 \left(1 - \frac{v^2}{c^2}\right)^{-\frac{1}{2}}$$

where T_0 is the 'proper time', v is the velocity and c is the speed of light. A similar equation describes the distortion expected due to gravitational differences.

Using the binomial expansion, it is possible to expand the brackets in the equation above. In this way, the scientists approximated the time they expected to pass according to the atomic clocks. The predictions came very close to the actual times recorded.

Today, GPS (the Global Positioning System) can provide incredibly accurate data on your exact position on Earth. Because the satellites used, however, are travelling at high velocities and are subjected to weaker gravity, their on-board clocks have to be corrected for the strange effects of time dilation.

Time may fly when you're having fun, but it slows down when you're travelling at high speeds!

Exercise 8A (Revision)

1. (a) The speed of a wave is given by the formula $v = f\lambda$, where λ is the wave's wavelength in metres and f is the frequency in s^{-1}. Find v when $f = 0.02 \ s^{-1}$ and $\lambda = 2 \times 10^6$ m.

   (b) The formula for the volume of a sphere is $V = \dfrac{4}{3}\pi r^2$. Calculate V (to 3 significant figures) when $r = 0.5$ m.

Exercise 8A...

(c) Find s given $u = 0, a = -10, t = 3$ and

$$s = ut + \frac{1}{2}at^2$$

2. Solve the following sets of simultaneous equations:
   (a) $-5x + 5y = -25$ $5x - 2y = 40$
   (b) $6x - 4y = 64$ $-4x - 2y = -38$
   (c) $x - 10y = 71$ $x - 8y = 55$
   (d) $-9x + 4y = 14$ $-6x + 9y = 3$
   (e) $-2x + y = 3$ $8x - 10y = 30$
   (f) $-4x - 7y - 3z = 19$
       $-6x - 2y + z = -8$
       $-2x - 2y + 7z = -12$

8.2 Factorials and Combinatorials

Before we discuss the binomial expansion, we need to introduce some new mathematical notation.

> The **factorial** of a number n is the product of all the positive integers up to n.

We denote factorials with an exclamation mark, for example 5!.

It is important to remember that, by definition, $0! = 1$.

Worked Example

3. Find $5!$

$$5! = 5 \times 4 \times 3 \times 2 \times 1$$
$$= 120$$

When dividing factorials, there is often a lot of cancelling.

Worked Example

4. Find $\frac{7!}{3!}$.

$$\frac{7!}{3!} = \frac{7 \times 6 \times 5 \times 4 \times 3 \times 2 \times 1}{3 \times 2 \times 1}$$

Note that the $3 \times 2 \times 1$ cancel out. So:

$$\frac{7!}{3!} = 7 \times 6 \times 5 \times 4$$

$$= 840$$

The second new piece of notation is **combinatorial notation**. You will see a combinatorial written as either ^nC_r or $\binom{n}{r}$.

The definition of this notation is as follows:

$$^nC_r = \frac{n!}{(n-r)!\,r!}$$

This calculation gives the number of ways you could choose r objects from a total of n. (The order in which you choose the objects does not matter.)

For this reason, we often read ^nC_r as "n choose r".

Worked Example

5. Out of a class of 15 pupils, a PE teacher must choose 11 of them to play for the school team. How many different ways could she choose the team?

$$^{15}C_{11} = \frac{15!}{(15-11)!\,11!}$$

$$= \frac{15 \times 14 \times 13 \times 12 \times 11 \times 10 \times 9 \times 8 \times 7 \times 6 \times 5 \times 4 \times 3 \times 2 \times 1}{(4 \times 3 \times 2 \times 1)(11 \times 10 \times 9 \times 8 \times 7 \times 6 \times 5 \times 4 \times 3 \times 2 \times 1)}$$

Note that the last 11 integers cancel out. So:

$$^{15}C_{11} = \frac{15 \times 14 \times 13 \times 12}{4 \times 3 \times 2 \times 1}$$

We can do some more cancelling, since we have 12 in the numerator and 4×3 in the denominator.

$$^{15}C_{11} = \frac{15 \times 14 \times 13}{2 \times 1}$$

Finally, cancel a factor of 2:

$$^{15}C_{11} = 15 \times 7 \times 13$$

$$= 1365$$

There should be an ^nC_r button on your calculator.

> **Note:** n must be greater than or equal to r. If not, $(n - r)$ is negative. The factorial of a negative number is not defined. Try something like $^6C_8$ on your calculator and see what the result is.

Worked Example

6. Evaluate:

(a) $^5C_2$ (b) $\binom{10}{9}$

(a) $^5C_2 = \dfrac{5!}{3!\,2!}$

$= \dfrac{5 \times 4 \times 3 \times 2 \times 1}{(3 \times 2 \times 1)(2 \times 1)}$

$= \dfrac{5 \times 4 \times 3}{3 \times 2 \times 1}$

$= \dfrac{5 \times 4}{2 \times 1}$

$= 10$

(b) $\binom{10}{9} = \dfrac{10!}{1!\,9!}$

The 9! cancels out. So:

$= \dfrac{10}{1}$

$= 10$

This means there are 10 ways to choose 9 items from a collection of 10. This seems to be correct, because the 10 different ways are to leave out each item in turn.

Exercise 8B

1. Calculate:

(a) $2!$ (b) $\dfrac{8!}{4!}$

(c) $\dfrac{3!}{5!}$ (d) $2! \times 3! \times 5!$

(e) $\dfrac{6!}{2!\,4!}$ (f) $1! + 3! + 5!$

(g) $0! + 1!$ (h) $\dfrac{1!}{0!\,1!}$

(i) $\dfrac{100!}{99!}$ (j) $\dfrac{6!\,8!}{5!\,7!}$

2. Evaluate:

(a) $\binom{8}{7}$ (b) $\binom{5}{2}$

(c) $\binom{10}{2}$ (d) $\binom{8}{3}$

(e) $\binom{7}{3}$ (f) $^{100}C_1$

(g) $^8C_4$ (h) $^5C_0$

(i) $^6C_3$ (j) $^{20}C_{20}$

8.3 The Binomial Expansion

Consider the following:

$(1 + x)^0 = 1$

$(1 + x)^1 = 1 + x$

$(1 + x)^2 = 1 + 2x + x^2$

$(1 + x)^3 = 1 + 3x + 3x^2 + x^3$

$(1 + x)^4 = 1 + 4x + 6x^2 + 4x^3 + x^4$

All of these expansions are examples of the **binomial expansion** (so called because there are two terms inside the brackets).

It takes a long time to expand out brackets, particularly with large integer powers. The formula for the binomial expansion provides a shortcut.

Looking at the expansions above, the coefficients of the terms in the expansion of $(1 + x)^n$ are the values of $\binom{n}{0}$, $\binom{n}{1}$, ..., $\binom{n}{n}$. For example, the coefficients of the terms in the expansion of $(1 + x)^3$ are 1, 3, 3, 1, which are the values of $\binom{3}{0}$, $\binom{3}{1}$, $\binom{3}{2}$ and $\binom{3}{3}$.

In this section you will learn how to perform a binomial expansion for positive integer values of n. Later in your studies you may learn how to extend this method to cases where n is a fraction or a negative integer.

Worked Example

7. Work out the binomial expansion of $(1 + x)^4$.

The coefficients of the terms are $\binom{4}{0}$, $\binom{4}{1}$, $\binom{4}{2}$, $\binom{4}{3}$ and $\binom{4}{4}$. So:

$(1 + x)^4 = \binom{4}{0}(1) + \binom{4}{1}x + \binom{4}{2}x^2 + \binom{4}{3}x^3 + \binom{4}{4}x^4$

$= 1 + 4x + 6x^2 + 4x^3 + x^4$

In general:

$(1 + x)^n =$

$\binom{n}{0} + \binom{n}{1}x + \binom{n}{2}x^2 + \cdots + \binom{n}{n-1}x^{n-1} + \binom{n}{n}x^n$

This can be generalised further. In some questions, the first term inside the brackets may not be 1 and the second term may not be x. In these cases, the following formula can be used:

$(a + bx)^n =$

$\binom{n}{0}a^n + \binom{n}{1}bxa^{n-1} + \binom{n}{2}(bx)^2a^{n-2} + \cdots + \binom{n}{n}(bx)^n$

There is another way to write the binomial expansion, using factorials:

$$(1 + x)^n = 1 + nx + \frac{n(n-1)}{2!}x^2 + \frac{n(n-1)(n-2)}{3!}x^3$$
$$+ \cdots + \frac{n(n-1)}{2!}x^{n-2} + nx^{n-1} + x^n$$

These two formulae both appear on the formula sheet, but it is a good idea to memorise at least one of them.

Worked Example

8. Write down the binomial expansion for $(1 + y)^4$.

Using the factorial form of the binomial expansion:

$$(1 + y)^4 = 1 + 4y + \frac{4(3)}{2!}y^2 + \frac{4(3)(2)}{3!}y^3 + y^4$$
$$= 1 + 4y + 6y^2 + 4y^3 + y^4$$

You must take care when the second term is something other than x.

Worked Example

9. Expand $(1 + 3x)^3$.

$$(1 + 3x)^3 = 1 + (3)(3x) + \frac{(3)(2)}{2!}(3x)^2 + (3x)^3$$
$$= 1 + 3(3x) + 3(3x)^2 + (3x)^3$$
$$= 1 + 9x + 27x^2 + 27x^3$$

In the next example, the first term inside the brackets is not 1. There are two methods for handling this.

Worked Example

10. Find the binomial expansion for $(2 + z)^4$.

First method

The formula for the binomial expansion (using combinatorials) is:

$$(a + bx)^n =$$
$$\binom{n}{0}a^n + \binom{n}{1}bxa^{n-1} + \binom{n}{2}(bx)^2a^{n-2} + \cdots + \binom{n}{n}(bx)^n$$

So:

$$(2 + z)^4 = \binom{4}{0}2^4 + \binom{4}{1}z \times 2^3 + \binom{4}{2}z^2 \times 2^2$$
$$+ \binom{4}{3}z^3 \times 2 + \binom{4}{4}z^4$$
$$= 16 + 32z + 24z^2 + 8z^3 + z^4$$

Second method

This involves factorising.

$$(2 + z)^4 = 2^4\left(1 + \frac{z}{2}\right)^4$$

Note: When 2 is taken outside the bracket, it becomes 2^4. Both terms inside the brackets are divided by 2.

Now you can apply the binomial expansion formula. Leave 2^4 (or 16) outside the brackets until the end.

$$= 2^4\left[1 + (4)\left(\frac{z}{2}\right) + \frac{(4)(3)}{2!}\left(\frac{z}{2}\right)^2 + \frac{(4)(3)(2)}{3!}\left(\frac{z}{2}\right)^3 + \left(\frac{z}{2}\right)^4\right]$$
$$= 16\left[1 + 4\left(\frac{z}{2}\right) + 6\left(\frac{z}{2}\right)^2 + 4\left(\frac{z}{2}\right)^3 + \left(\frac{z}{2}\right)^4\right]$$
$$= 16\left[1 + 2z + \frac{3z^2}{2} + \frac{z^3}{2} + \frac{z^4}{16}\right]$$
$$= 16 + 32z + 24z^2 + 8z^3 + z^4$$

It is important to learn one or both of these methods.

You may be asked for only one term of the expansion, for example the term in x^3.

Worked Example

11. Find the term that is independent of x in the expansion of $\left(x + \frac{6}{x}\right)^4$.

The general formula is:
$$(a + bx)^n =$$
$$\binom{n}{0}a^n + \binom{n}{1}bxa^{n-1} + \binom{n}{2}(bx)^2a^{n-2} + \cdots + \binom{n}{n}(bx)^n$$

In this case, $n = 4$, $a = x$ and $bx = \frac{6}{x}$. Therefore:

$$\left(x + \frac{6}{x}\right)^4 =$$
$$\binom{4}{0}x^4 + \binom{4}{1}\left(\frac{6}{x}\right)x^3 + \binom{4}{2}\left(\frac{6}{x}\right)^2x^2 + \binom{4}{1}\left(\frac{6}{x}\right)^3x + \binom{4}{4}\left(\frac{6}{x}\right)$$

We are interested in the third term of the expansion.

$$\text{Third term} = \binom{4}{2}\left(\frac{6}{x}\right)^2(x)^2$$
$$= 6 \times 36 \qquad \text{(The } x^2 \text{ cancels out)}$$
$$= 216$$

Note: If x is small (i.e. less than 1), the terms to higher powers will not be very important to the sum. Some questions will, therefore, ask you to find only the first few terms in the expansion.

Once you have found an expansion, you may be asked to use it to find a value.

······································

Worked Example

12. (a) Find the first 4 terms in the binomial expansion of $(1 - x^2)^8$.

(b) Use your answer to part (a) to estimate the value of 0.99^8.

(a) Be careful with the minus sign here.

$$(1 - x^2)^8 = \left(1 + (-x^2)\right)^8$$

Now we can apply the binomial expansion:

$$(1 - x^2)^8$$

$$= 1 + 8(-x^2) + \frac{8(7)}{2!}(-x^2)^2 + \frac{8(7)(6)}{3!}(-x^2)^3 + \cdots$$

$$= 1 - 8x^2 + 28x^4 - 56x^6 + \cdots \quad (1)$$

(b) We are asked to find an estimate for 0.99^8. The left-hand side of (1) becomes 0.99^8 if $(1 - x^2) = 0.99$. Solving this equation gives the value of x that we should substitute:

$$(1 - x^2) = 0.99$$

$$x^2 = 0.01$$

$$x = 0.1$$

Therefore substitute $x = 0.1$ into (1):

$$0.99^8 \approx 1 - 8(0.1)^2 + 28(0.1)^4 - 56(0.1)^6$$

$$= 0.922744$$

> **Note:** This is an estimate because we have only taken the first four terms.

······································

In the following example you are given some of the terms in the expanded form. You are asked to find the coefficient of x and the power in the unexpanded form. To do this you may require simultaneous equations.

······································

Worked Example

13. (a) Write down the first 4 terms of the binomial expansion, in ascending powers of x, of $(1 + ax)^n$ where $n > 2$.

(b) Given that in this expansion the coefficient of x is 8 and the coefficient of x^2 is 30, calculate the value of n and the value of a.

(c) Find the coefficient of x^3.

(a) $(1 + ax)^n =$

$$1 + nax + \frac{n(n-1)}{2!}(ax)^2 + \frac{n(n-1)(n-2)}{3!}(ax)^3$$

$$= 1 + nax + \frac{n(n-1)}{2}a^2x^2 + \frac{n(n-1)(n-2)}{6}a^3x^3$$

(b) $na = 8 \Rightarrow a = \dfrac{8}{n}$ \hfill (1)

$$\frac{n(n-1)a^2}{2} = 30 \Rightarrow a^2n(n-1) = 60 \quad (2)$$

Substitute (1) into (2):

$$\left(\frac{8}{n}\right)^2 n(n-1) = 60$$

$$\frac{64n(n-1)}{n^2} = 60$$

$$64n(n-1) = 60n^2$$

$$64n^2 - 64n = 60n^2$$

$$4n^2 - 64n = 0$$

$$n^2 - 16n = 0$$

$$n(n - 16) = 0$$

$$n = 16$$

(n cannot be 0 in a binomial expansion)

Substituting n into (1) gives $a = \dfrac{1}{2}$.

(c) The coefficient of x^3 is:

$$\frac{n(n-1)(n-2)a^3}{6}$$

$$= \frac{16(15)(14)\left(\frac{1}{2}\right)^3}{6}$$

$$= 70$$

······································

Exercise 8C

1. Find the first four terms in the binomial expansion of the following:

(a) $(1 + x)^6$ (b) $(1 + 2x)^4$

(c) $(1 - x)^4$ (d) $\left(1 + \dfrac{x}{2}\right)^3$

(e) $(1 - 2x)^5$ (f) $(1 + x)^{10}$

(g) $(1 + 5x)^3$ (h) $\left(1 - \dfrac{x}{10}\right)^3$

(i) $(1 + 10x)^4$ (j) $\left(1 - \dfrac{19x}{27}\right)^6$

2. Find the first 3 terms of the binomial expansion of the following:

(a) $(2 + x)^7$ (b) $(2 + 2x)^3$

(c) $\left(10 - \dfrac{x}{10}\right)^3$ (d) $\left(1 - \dfrac{1}{x}\right)^3$

Exercise 8C...

(e) $(4 + 3x)^4$ (f) $(2 + x^2)^4$

(g) $\left(x + \dfrac{1}{x}\right)^4$ (h) $\left(\sqrt{2} + \dfrac{x}{\sqrt{2}}\right)^4$

(i) $(5 + 2x)^4$ (j) $\left(\dfrac{1}{a} + a^2x\right)^3$

3. (a) Expand $\left(1 + \dfrac{x}{2}\right)^6$ in ascending powers of x as far as the term in x^3, simplifying each term.

   (b) Hence find 1.05^6, correct to 3 decimal places.

4. (a) Write down the first 4 terms of the binomial expansion, in ascending powers of x, of $(1 + ax)^n$ where $n > 2$.

   Given that in this expansion the coefficient of x is 14 and the coefficient of x^2 is 93.1:

   (b) calculate the value of n and the value of a;

   (c) find the coefficient of x^3.

5. (a) Find the first 3 terms, in ascending powers of x, of the binomial expansion of $(1 + px)^9$ where p is a positive constant.

   (b) Given that, in this expansion, the coefficients of x and x^2 are $-q$ and $4q$ respectively, find the value of p and the value of q.

6. The expansion of $(4 + px)^6$ in ascending powers of x, as far as the term in x^2 is $4096 + Ax + 60x^2$. Given that $p > 0$, find the value of p and the value of A.

7. Find the term that is independent of x in the expansion of $\left(x + \dfrac{4}{x}\right)^6$.

8. Neglecting terms in x^4 and higher, find an approximation in ascending powers of x for $(1 - x)(1 + 3x)^5$.

9. (a) Using the binomial expansion, find an approximation for $(1 - x)^n$ up to and including the term in x^3, in the form $1 + ax + bx^2 + cx^3$, where a, b and c are expressions in terms of n.

   (b) Given that n is a positive integer and that $2a + b - 3c = 0$, find n.

10. (a) Find the binomial expansion for $(1 - 2x)^4$ up to and including the term in x^3.

    (b) Use your answer to part (a) to find an approximation for 0.99^4 to 3 decimal places.

8.4 Summary

The factorial of a number n is the product of all the positive integers up to n. For example:

$$5! = 5 \times 4 \times 3 \times 2 \times 1 = 120$$

The number of ways you could choose r objects from a total of n is given by:

$$^nC_r = \frac{n!}{(n - r)!\, r!}$$

For example, to choose 3 pupils from an A-Level class of 10, there are $\dfrac{10!}{7!\, 3!} = 120$ ways to do it.

The binomial expansion provides an efficient way to expand brackets. There are two formulas:

$$(a + bx)^n =$$
$$\binom{n}{0} a^n + \binom{n}{1} bx a^{n-1} + \binom{n}{2} (bx)^2 a^{n-2} + \cdots + \binom{n}{n} (bx)^n$$

and

$$(1 + x)^n = 1 + nx + \frac{n(n - 1)}{2!} x^2 + \frac{n(n - 1)(n - 2)}{3!} x^3$$
$$+ \cdots + \frac{n(n - 1)}{2!} x^{n-2} + nx^{n-1} + x^n$$

Chapter 9
Trigonometry

9.1 Introduction

Key words

- **Period**: The period of a function is the distance between repeating parts of its curve.
- **Asymptote**: is a straight line that a curve approaches, but never touches.
- **Trigonometric ratio**: Any of the trigonometric functions acting on an angle, for example sin 30°.

Before you start

You should know:

- How to solve quadratic equations.
- How to change the subject of an equation.

Worked Examples

1. Find the values of x that satisfy: $x^2 - 3x - 5 = 0$

   Use the quadratic formula:

   $x = \dfrac{-b \pm \sqrt{b^2 - 4ac}}{2a}$

   $x = \dfrac{3 \pm \sqrt{(-3)^2 - 4(1)(-5)}}{2}$

   $x = \dfrac{3 \pm \sqrt{9 + 20}}{2}$

   $x = \dfrac{3 \pm \sqrt{29}}{2}$

2. Make x the subject of the equation: $x - 1 = 3y(2 - x)$

   Expand brackets:
   $x - 1 = 6y - 3xy$

   Take all the terms in x to one side:
   $x + 3xy = 1 + 6y$

   Factorise the left-hand side:
   $x(1 + 3y) = 1 + 6y$

   Divide by $(1 + 3y)$:
   $x = \dfrac{1 + 6y}{1 + 3y}$

What you will learn

In this chapter you will learn:

- How to use the sine and cosine rules.
- About two 'special triangles'.
- How to use the CAST diagram.
- The important characteristics of the trigonometric graphs.
- How to perform some transformations on those graphs.
- How to prove trigonometric identities.
- How to solve trigonometric equations.

In the real world...

In 1977, NASA launched two small space probes, Voyager I and Voyager II.

Their trajectories had been carefully planned to bring them close to the outer planets of our Solar System. For the first time, these worlds would be photographed and studied at close proximity.

The software in the two on-board computers has been updated many times since the launch. But trigonometry played a key role in many aspects of the missions from the initial launch to setting the craft on the correct course and using the gravity of the giant planets to increase the velocity. How to take a clear photograph when travelling at many thousands of metres per second is a considerable problem – mathematically and logistically.

Throughout the 1980s, the two Voyager spacecraft provided breath-taking pictures of Jupiter, Saturn, Uranus, Neptune and many of their moons. Scientists were amazed at the success of these two tiny spacecraft.

Along with three other space probes now leaving the Solar System, the two Voyagers are now the furthest man-made objects from Earth, but they continue to send back important information about their surroundings.

On board are pictures and data about planet Earth and human civilisation, in case the machines ever come into contact with intelligent extra-terrestrial beings.

Exercise 9A (Revision)

1. Solve these quadratic equations.
   (a) $(4x - 5)^2 = 36$
   (b) $3x^2 - 24x + 7 = 10$
   (c) $4x^2 - 2x - 1 = 0$
   (d) $x^2 = 3x + 29$

2. Make x the subject of these equations.
   (a) $1 + 3x = 3(1 - x)$
   (b) $2x + p = 3p(x - 1)$
   (c) $xy = \dfrac{2(1 + y)}{x}$
   (d) $\dfrac{(x + c)}{d} = \dfrac{2(x + e)}{f}$

9.2 The Sine and Cosine Rules and the Area of a Triangle

Revision

You will encounter the Greek letter θ (pronounced 'theta') frequently in this chapter. It is often used as an angle variable, just as x is often used for numbers.

At GCSE, you learnt how to calculate a missing side or a missing angle in a **right-angled** triangle, using these three formulae:

$$\sin \theta = \frac{\text{opposite}}{\text{hypotenuse}}$$

$$\cos \theta = \frac{\text{adjacent}}{\text{hypotenuse}}$$

$$\tan \theta = \frac{\text{opposite}}{\text{adjacent}}$$

The **sine rule** and the **cosine rule** are useful for finding lengths or angles in triangles that **do not have any right angles**.

Remember: if a triangle has right angles, you should use the above formulae for sine, cosine and tangent.

The sine rule

The **sine rule** links two angles and the two sides opposite those angles.

Consider the triangle below. The angles are A, B and C, none of which are right angles. The side lengths are a, b and c.

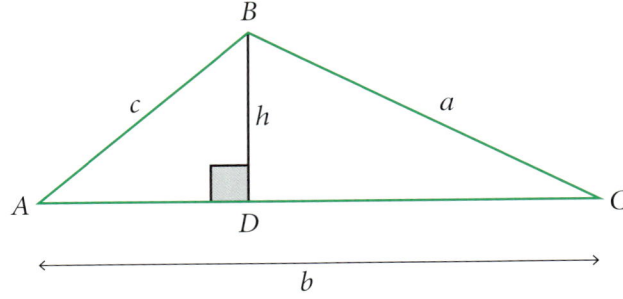

Note: Observe that angle A is opposite the side with length a, etc. This is a very common way to label triangles.

Based on this triangle, we can write the sine rule in two forms:

The sine rule

- Use this form of the sine rule when calculating a side length:

$$\frac{a}{\sin A} = \frac{b}{\sin B} = \frac{c}{\sin C}$$

- Use this form when calculating an angle:

$$\frac{\sin A}{a} = \frac{\sin B}{b} = \frac{\sin C}{c}$$

Proof of the sine rule

Note: The CCEA specification (at the time of publication) does not require you to know this proof.

In the previous diagram, consider triangle ABD.

We have: $\qquad\qquad \sin A = \dfrac{h}{c}$

Re-arrange: $\qquad\quad h = c \sin A \qquad (1)$

Now consider triangle BCD.

We have: $\qquad\qquad \sin C = \dfrac{h}{a}$

Re-arrange: $\qquad\quad h = a \sin C \qquad (2)$

Substitute (2) into (1): $a \sin C = c \sin A$

Re-arrange: $\qquad\quad \dfrac{a}{\sin A} = \dfrac{c}{\sin C}$

A similar process can be used to show that $\dfrac{a}{\sin A} = \dfrac{b}{\sin B}$.

Worked Examples

3. In $\triangle ABC$, the angle A is 35°, the angle B is 40° and the side length a is 5 cm. Calculate the side length b.

   It is a good idea to draw a sketch of the triangle:

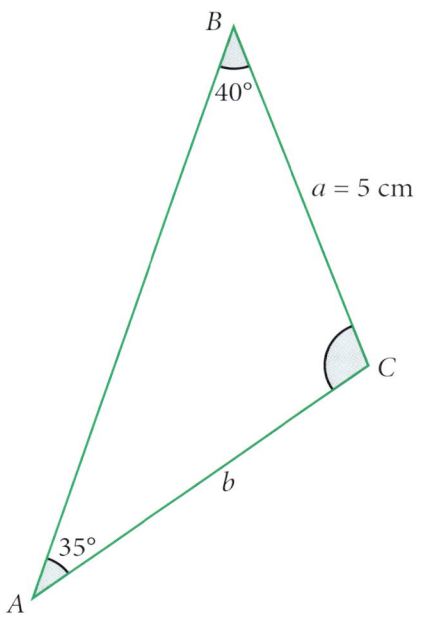

$$\frac{a}{\sin A} = \frac{b}{\sin B}$$

$$b = \frac{a}{\sin A} \times \sin B$$

$$= \frac{5}{\sin 35} \times \sin 40$$

$$= 5.60 \text{ cm (3 s.f.)}$$

Note: Remember to work to at least 4 significant figures in your calculations. This way you will not lose any accuracy when rounding to 3 significant figures in your final answer.

4. In ΔABC, the angle A is 52°, the side length a is 5 cm and the side length c is 6 cm. Calculate the acute angle C.

Sketch the triangle:

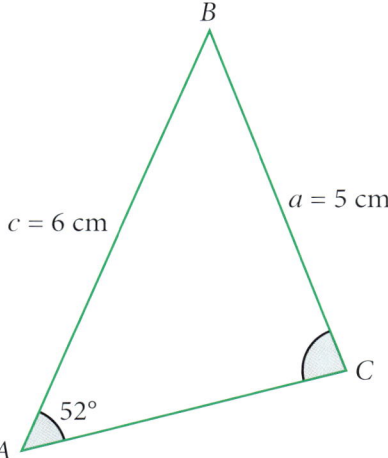

We use the second form of the sine rule, since we are calculating an angle:

$$\frac{\sin C}{c} = \frac{\sin A}{a}$$

Re-arrange:

$$\sin C = c \times \frac{\sin A}{a}$$

$$\sin C = 6 \times \frac{\sin 52°}{5}$$

$$\sin C = 0.9456 \ldots$$

$$C = \sin^{-1}(0.9456 \ldots) = 71.0°$$

Note: Give all answers to 3 significant figures unless you are told otherwise. Sometimes you may be asked to round angles to 1 decimal place.

Beware! When calculating an angle using the sine rule, it is possible that there will be **two** solutions. This is known as the **ambiguous case**.

Worked Example

5. Calculate the angle B in triangle ABC, given that angle $A = 50°$, side $a = 10$ cm and $b = 12$ cm.

Sketch the triangle:

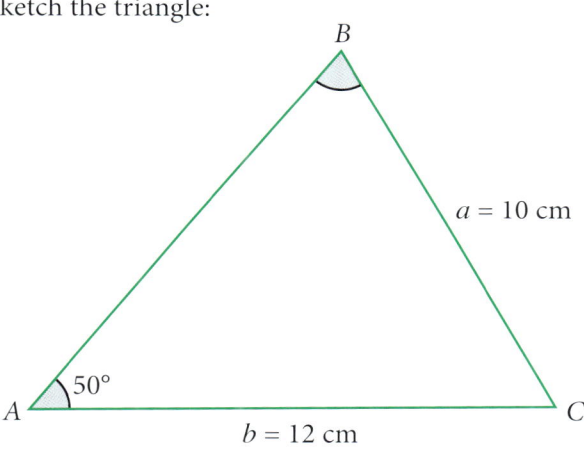

$$\frac{\sin B}{b} = \frac{\sin A}{a}$$

$$\sin B = b \times \frac{\sin A}{a}$$

$$\sin B = 0.919 \ldots$$

$$B = \sin^{-1}(0.919 \ldots) = 66.8°$$

If there is a second solution, it will always be found by subtracting the first solution from 180°. So:

$$B_2 = 180 - 66.8$$

$$= 113.2°$$

We can check that both these solutions are possible by calculating C. Use the fact that angles in a triangle add up to 180°.

First solution:
$$C = 180 - (50 + 66.8)$$
$$= 63.2°$$

Second solution:
$$C = 180 - (50 + 113.2)$$
$$= 16.8°$$

Both these angles are between 0 and 180°, so they create possible triangles. If your second value for B resulted in a negative value of C, for example, it would show that this was not a possibility.

The two possible triangles ABC and AB_2C are shown:

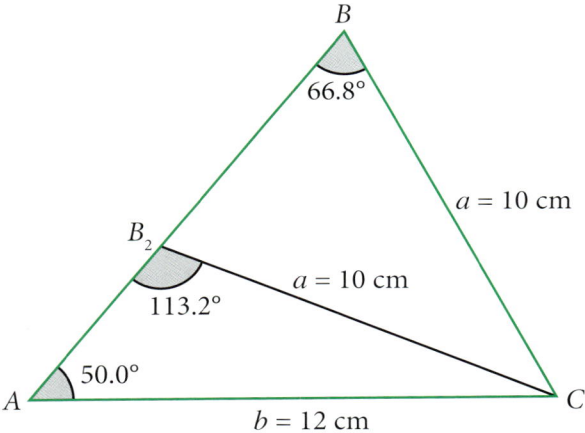

Exercise 9B

For each question in this exercise give all lengths to 3 significant figures and angles to 1 decimal place.

1. Find the missing length b in these triangles:
   (a) Angles $A = 123°$, $B = 10°$, side length $a = 5$ cm.
   (b) Angles $A = 84°$, $B = 76°$, side length $a = 10$ cm.
   (c) Angles $A = 61°$, $B = 47°$, side length $a = 3$ cm.
   (d) Angles $A = 121°$, $B = 45°$, side length $a = 13$ cm.

2. Find the missing angle in each triangle:
   (a) Angle $A = 36°$, side lengths $a = 14$ cm, $b = 2$ cm. Find B.
   (b) Angle $C = 123°$, side lengths $c = 8$ cm, $b = 7$ cm. Find B.
   (c) Angle $A = 44°$, side lengths $a = 12$ cm, $c = 9$ cm. Find C.
   (d) Angle $A = 163°$, side lengths $a = 14$ cm, $b = 5$ cm. Find B.
   (e) Angle $B = 55°$, side lengths $b = 5$ cm, $c = 3$ cm. Find C.

3. Find the two possible values for the specified angle in these triangles (the ambiguous case). Find also the size of the third angle in both cases.
   (a) Angle $B = 32°$, side lengths $b = 9$ cm, $a = 13$ cm. Find A.
   (b) Angle $A = 22°$, side lengths $a = 7$ cm, $b = 14$ cm. Find B.
   (c) Angle $B = 38°$, side lengths $b = 13$ cm, $c = 17$ cm. Find C.
   (d) Angle $C = 57°$, side lengths $c = 6$ cm, $a = 7$ cm. Find A.
   (e) Angle $A = 53°$, side lengths $a = 12$ cm, $c = 13$ cm. Find C.

4. In the triangle ABC, $AB = 6$ cm, $AC = 4$ cm, angle $ABC = 17.2°$ and angle $ACB = x°$.
   (a) Use the sine rule to find the value of $\sin x$, giving your answer to 3 decimal places.
   (b) Given that there are two possible values of x, find these values, giving your answers to 1 decimal place.

5. A ship at point S has a bearing of 120° from lighthouse L and a bearing of 040° from coastguard C. Given that the lighthouse is situated due north of the coastguard, and that the distance from the ship to the lighthouse is 17 km find:
   (a) The angle, when viewed from the ship, between the coastguard and lighthouse;
   (b) The distance between the coastguard and the lighthouse.

6. In the diagram, AB and CD are parallel lines.

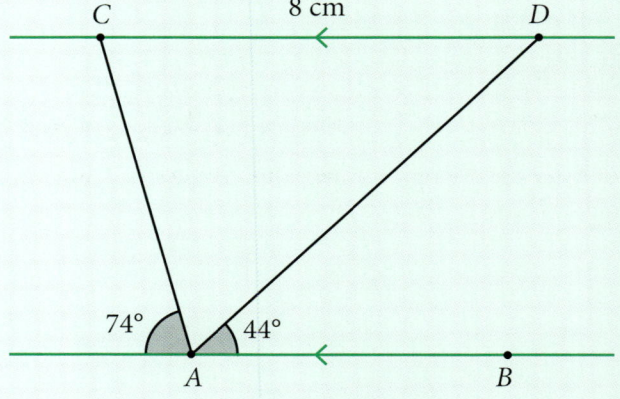

Calculate the lengths of AC and AD.

Exercise 9B...

7. The diagram shows the side elevation of a stadium. It is symmetrical about a vertical line through point F.

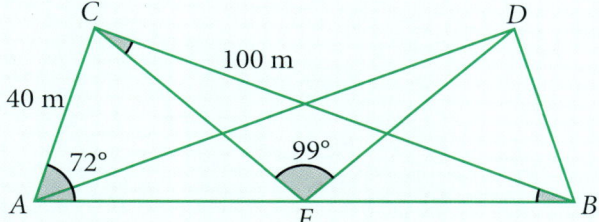

The steel supports AC and BC measure 40 m and 100 m respectively. Angle CAF is 72° and CFD measures 99°. Find the size of the two angles CBF and BCF.

The cosine rule

The **cosine rule** links three sides and one angle.

> **The cosine rule**
>
> - Use this form of the cosine rule to find a side length:
>
> $$a^2 = b^2 + c^2 - 2bc \cos A$$
>
> - Use this form to find an angle:
>
> $$\cos A = \frac{b^2 + c^2 - a^2}{2bc}$$

As usual, the angle A is the angle opposite side a.

The cosine rule looks complicated at first, but it is easy to remember if you think of it as an extension of Pythagoras' Theorem.

Proof of the cosine rule

> **Note:** The CCEA specification (at the time of publication) does not require you to know this proof.

Consider the triangle below, with vertices A, B and C and sides a, b and c.

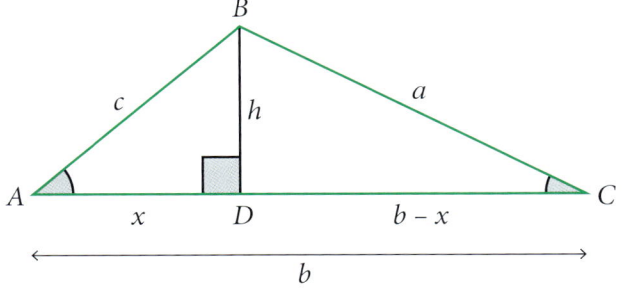

The vertical height h has been added to the diagram, and the base b has been divided into two sections measuring x and $(b - x)$.

Using the formula for cosine in $\triangle ABD$:
$$\cos A = \frac{x}{c}$$
Re-arrange:
$$x = c \cos A \qquad (1)$$

Using Pythagoras' Theorem in $\triangle BCD$ and $\triangle ABD$:
$$a^2 = h^2 + (b - x)^2 \qquad (2)$$
$$c^2 = h^2 + x^2 \qquad (3)$$

Subtract (2) – (3):
$$a^2 - c^2 = (b - x)^2 - x^2$$

Expand brackets and simplify:
$$a^2 - c^2 = b^2 - 2bx$$

Substitute for x from (1):
$$a^2 - c^2 = b^2 - 2bc \cos A$$
$$a^2 = b^2 + c^2 - 2bc \cos A$$

....

If you know three sides of a triangle, you can use the cosine rule to work out any angle.

....

Worked Example

6. The diagram shows triangle ABC, in which sides $a = 5$ cm, $b = 6$ cm and $c = 7$ cm. Find the size of angle A.

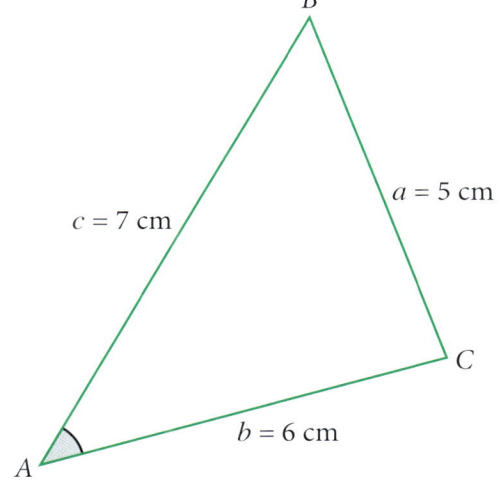

$$a^2 = b^2 + c^2 - 2bc \cos A$$
$$\Rightarrow \cos A = \frac{b^2 + c^2 - a^2}{2bc}$$
$$= \frac{6^2 + 7^2 - 5^2}{2(6)(7)}$$
$$= \frac{5}{7}$$

So: $A = 44.4°$ (3 s.f.)

If you know two of the sides and **the angle between them**, you can calculate the missing side.

Worked Example

7. In $\triangle ABC$, $c = 12$ cm, $b = 16$ cm and $A = 46°$. Calculate side length a.

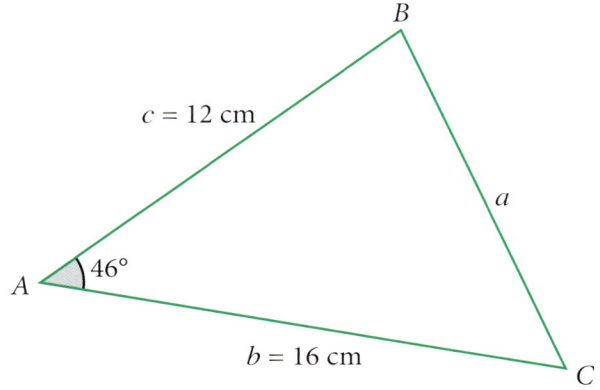

$a^2 = b^2 + c^2 - 2bc \cos A$

$\quad = 16^2 + 12^2 - 2(16)(12) \cos 46$

$\quad = 133.25 \dots$

$a = 11.5$ cm (3 s.f.)

In all questions involving the cosine rule, there is a lot of calculator work. Remember: work to at least 4 significant figures in your working. If you round the numbers further than this in your working, your final answer to 3 significant figures may not be accurate.

If you know two of the sides and an angle that is not the angle between the two known sides, you will need to use a combination of the sine and cosine rules.

Worked Example

8. The straight road between points A and B is 3.8 km long. The straight road between A and C is 6 km long. Given angle ABC is 104°, find the length of the straight road between B and C.

Draw a sketch:

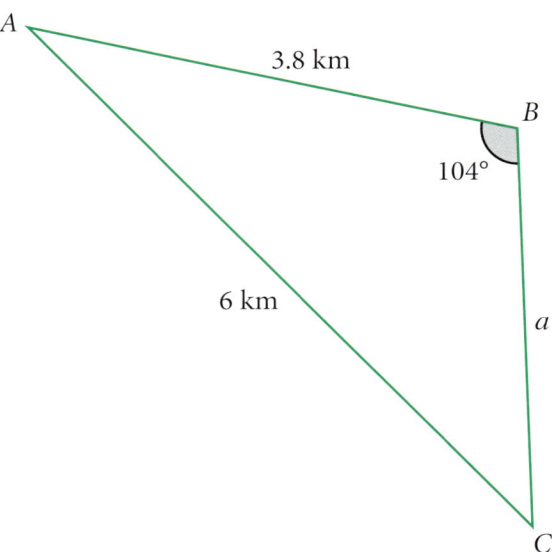

We cannot use the cosine rule directly to find a because we do not know angle A.
So first use the sine rule to find angle C:

$$\frac{\sin C}{c} = \frac{\sin B}{b}$$

$\sin C = 3.8 \times \dfrac{\sin 104}{6}$

$\quad\quad = 0.6145 \dots$

$\quad C = 37.92 \dots$

Keep this number to at least 4 significant figures, since it is not the final answer.
Now we can calculate angle A:

$A = 180 - (B + C)$

$\quad = 180 - (104 + 37.9 \dots)$

$\quad = 38.08 \dots$

Again, keep at least 4 significant figures.
Finally use the cosine rule:

$a^2 = b^2 + c^2 - 2bc \cos A$

$\quad = 6^2 + 3.8^2 - 2(6)(3.8) \cos(38.08 \dots)$

$\quad = 14.55 \dots$

$a = 3.81$ km (3 s.f.)

Sometimes you will be asked to 'solve the triangle'. This means finding all of the missing sides and angles. You may also be required to re-label a diagram to use the cosine rule formula.

Worked Example

9. A ship is anchored at port Z. On a bearing of 335° lies port X and on a bearing of 029° is port Y. The ship's captain knows that ports X and Y are 74 and 90 kilometres away respectively. Solve the triangle to

find all three distances between ports X, Y and Z, and all three angles.

Draw a sketch:

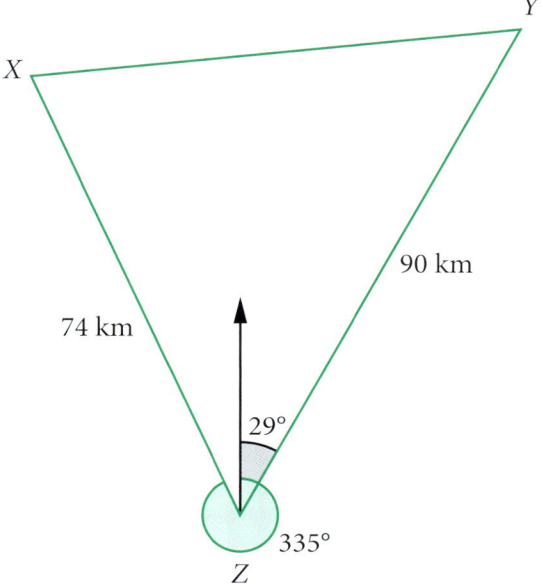

Firstly, angle $XZY = (360 - 335) + 29 = 54°$
So we can re-label the diagram:

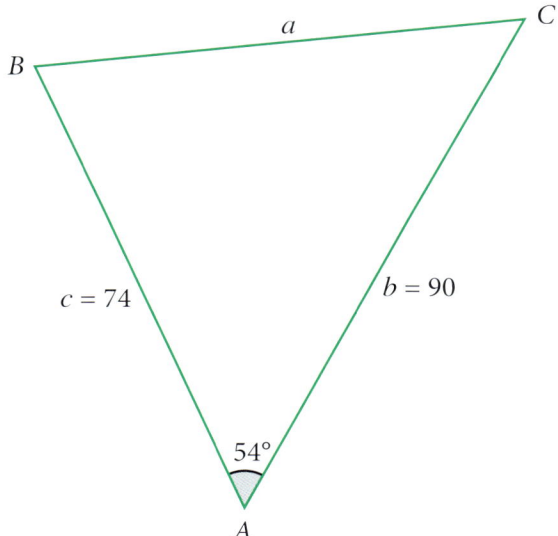

Now use the cosine rule:
$a^2 = b^2 + c^2 - 2bc \cos A$
$= 90^2 + 74^2 - 2(90)(74) \cos 54$
$= 5746.7 \dots$
$a = 75.81 \dots$
$= 75.8$ (3 s.f.)

Therefore, ports X and Y are 75.8 kilometres apart.

Now use the sine rule to find angle B:
$$\frac{\sin B}{b} = \frac{\sin A}{a}$$

$$\sin B = 90 \times \frac{\sin 54}{75.81 \dots}$$

Use at least 4 significant figures for the value of a in this calculation; do not use the answer rounded to 3 significant figures.
$\sin B = 0.9605 \dots$
$\quad B = 73.8°$ (3 s.f.)

Finally find angle C:
$C = 180 - (54 + 73.8 \dots)$
$\quad = 52.2°$ (3 s.f.)

We should give all our answers in terms of the original letters:
$XY = 75.8$ km
$X = 73.8°$, $Y = 52.2°$ (all answers to 3 s.f.)

Exercise 9C

1. Find the lengths of the missing sides in the following triangles to 3 significant figures.
   (a) $b = 11$ cm, $c = 8$ cm, $A = 33°$
   (b) $b = 7$ m, $c = 5$ m, $A = 75°$
   (c) $c = 6$ km, $a = 2$ km, $B = 33°$
   (d) $a = 12$ cm, $b = 9$ cm, $C = 64°$
   (e) $a = 11$ mm, $b = 6$ mm, $C = 36°$

2. Find the size of the angle specified in these triangles, to 1 decimal place.
   (a) $a = 6$, $b = 9$, $c = 8$ cm. Find A.
   (b) $x = 10$, $y = 7$, $z = 10$ cm. Find Y.
   (c) $p = 9$, $q = 11$, $r = 5$ m. Find P.
   (d) $a = 4$, $b = 5$, $c = 6$ mm. Find C.
   (e) $a = 5$, $b = 7$, $c = 7$ cm. Find B.

3. Solve the following triangles. Round your answers to 1 decimal place where necessary.
   (a) $a = 14$ cm, $b = 12$ cm, $c = 7$ cm
   (b) $a = 0.02$ mm, $b = 0.04$ mm, $c = 0.03$ mm
   (c) $b = 13$ cm, $c = 14$ cm, $A = 43°$
   (d) $c = 12$ feet, $a = 13$ feet, $B = 142°$
   (e) $c = 7$ km, $a = 7$ km, $C = 68°$
   (f) $a = 1.1$ cm, $b = 0.8$ cm, $A = 37°$

4. Is it possible to solve the following triangle? Explain your answer.
   $A = 55°$, $B = 45°$, $C = 80°$

5. Is it possible to solve the following triangle? Explain your answer.
   $a = 1.3$, $b = 0.2$, $c = 0.4$ cm

Exercise 9C...

6. A park is laid out in the shape of a trapezium, with gates at each corner, as shown. The distance between gates A and B is $2\sqrt{29}$ m, between B and C is 24 m, between C and D $\sqrt{149}$ m and between D and A is 35 m.

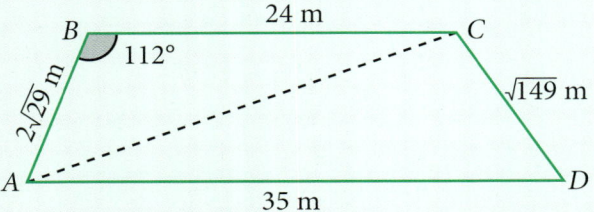

(a) Calculate the length of the path shown between gates A and C.

(b) Calculate the size of the angle ADC.

7. A lifeguard notices a man in trouble in the middle of a swimming pool. The pool is in the shape of a parallelogram, with the longest side 25 m and the shortest 10 m. The smallest corner angle of this quadrilateral is 60°. If the lifeguard is sitting at the corner measuring 120°, how far is he from the man?

8. An unmanned space probe takes a photograph of two moons of a planet, managing to get them both in the same picture. The probe is at point A and has reliable data that the moon Charion is 50 000 km away and the moon Ballisto is 80 000 km away. On-board sensors estimate the angle between the two moons to be 65°. Scientists analysing the photograph and data need to calculate the distance between the two moons. What is this distance?

Area of a triangle

Until now, you have used the formula:

$$A = \frac{1}{2} \text{base} \times \text{height}$$

to calculate the area of a triangle.

Using trigonometry, the area of a triangle can also be found using the formula:

$$A = \frac{1}{2} ab \sin C$$

where a and b are adjacent sides and C is the angle between them.

This formula is useful where the perpendicular height is not known.

Proof of $A = \frac{1}{2} ab \sin C$

Note: The CCEA specification (at the time of publication) does not require you to know this proof.

Consider the triangle below.

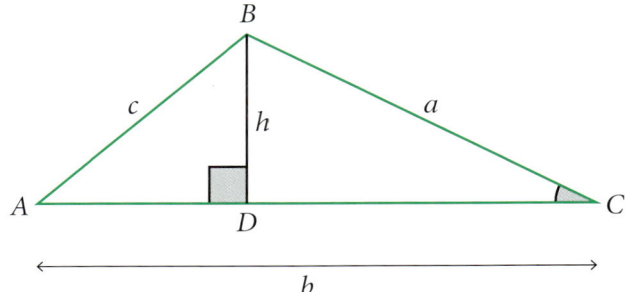

$$\text{Area} = \frac{1}{2} b \times h \qquad (1)$$

Using ΔBCD: $\qquad \sin C = \dfrac{h}{a}$

Re-arrange: $\qquad h = a \sin C \qquad (2)$

Substitute in (1): $\text{Area} = \dfrac{1}{2} b \times a \sin C$

$$\text{Area} = \frac{1}{2} ab \sin C$$

You can show similar results using any two adjacent sides and the angle between them.

> **Area of a triangle**
>
> $$= \frac{1}{2} ab \sin C \quad = \quad \frac{1}{2} bc \sin A \quad = \quad \frac{1}{2} ac \sin B$$

Worked Example

10. Find the area of the triangle in which $a = 7$ cm, $b = 2$ cm and C = 84°.

Firstly, if you have not been given a diagram, it is always helpful to draw a sketch of the triangle:

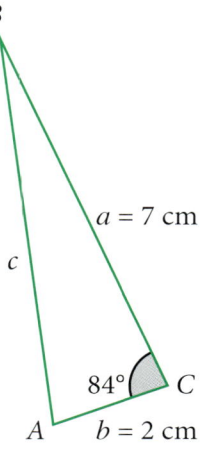

$$\text{Area} = \frac{1}{2}ab\sin C$$

$$= \frac{1}{2}(7)(2)\sin 84$$

$$= 6.96 \text{ cm}^2$$

You may need to calculate the angle before using the area formula.

Worked Example

11. Calculate the area of triangle ABC shown below.

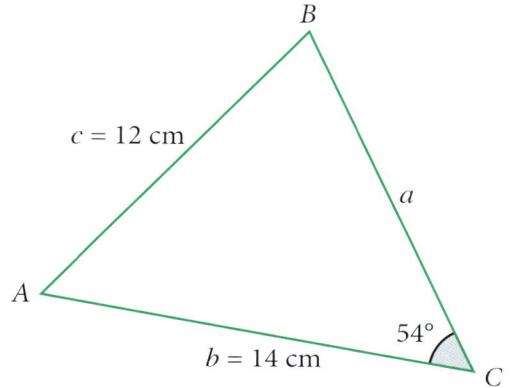

Here, we know two of the sides, but not the angle between them. Use the sine rule to find angle B:

$$\frac{\sin B}{b} = \frac{\sin C}{c}$$

$$\sin B = 14 \times \frac{\sin 54}{12}$$

$$= 0.94\ldots$$

$$B = 70.71\ldots°$$

Now work out angle A:

$$A = 180 - (B + C)$$

$$= 180 - (70.71\ldots + 54)$$

$$= 55.29\ldots°$$

Now use the area formula:

$$\text{Area} = \frac{1}{2}bc\sin A$$

$$= \frac{1}{2}(14)(12)\sin(55.29\ldots)$$

$$= 69.1 \text{ m}^2 \text{ (3 s.f.)}$$

Exercise 9D

1. Calculate the area of the following triangles to 3 significant figures.
   (a) $a = 5$ cm, $b = 6$ cm, $C = 59°$
   (b) $a = 600$ m, $b = 400$ m, $C = 85°$
   (c) $x = 1.2$ km, $y = 4.6$ km, $Z = 25°$
   (d) $a = 1.2$ cm, $b = 4.6$ cm, $B = 25°$
   (e) $c = 10$ m, $a = 4$ m, $B = 16°$
   (f) $p = 9$ cm, $q = 9$ cm, $Q = 68°$

2. Find the length of the side b to 3 significant figures in each of these triangles.
   (a) $a = 11$ cm, Area $= 18$ cm², $C = 120°$
   (b) $a = 6$ cm, Area $= 42$ cm², $C = 75°$
   (c) $a = 30$ mm, Area $= 46$ mm², $C = 30°$
   (d) $a = 10$ km, Area $= 49$ km², $C = 18°$

3. Find the acute angle C in the following triangles ABC. You are given the lengths of two sides and the triangle's area. Give your answers to 1 decimal place.
   (a) $a = 20$ cm, $b = 6$ cm, Area $= 27$ cm²
   (b) $a = 6$ cm, $b = 9$ cm, Area $= 25$ cm²
   (c) $a = 3$ cm, $b = 23$ cm, Area $= 34$ cm²
   (d) $a = 16$ cm, $b = 5$ cm, Area $= 11$ cm²

4. Find the area of the triangle PQR in which $PQ = 4$ cm, $QR = 5$ cm and angle $Q = 30°$.

5. A man runs around the perimeter of a forest, which is triangular in shape. He knows the area of the forest is 25 km², and the product of the two shorter sides is 56 km². Find the size of the largest angle in the triangle, given that it is acute.

6. Two sides of a triangle measure $(x + 5)$cm and $(x + 11)$cm. If the angle between these two sides is 60° and the area of the triangle is $10\sqrt{3}$ cm², find x.

7. A child's drawing of a house is made up of an equilateral triangle on top of a square. If the base of the drawing is 5 cm long, calculate the total area of the drawing, giving an exact answer.

Exercise 9D...

8. In the trapezium shown, $BC = p$, $AC = q$ and $AD = r$. Angle $ACB = \theta$.

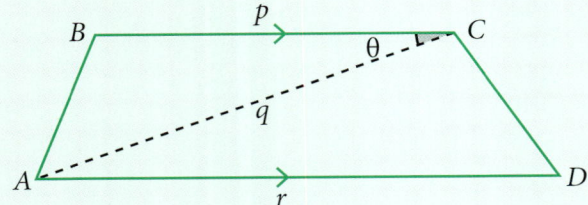

(a) Write down an expression involving $\sin \theta$ for the area of triangle ABC.
(b) Write down an expression involving $\sin \theta$ for the area of triangle ACD.
(c) Given that the area of $\triangle ABC$ is ¾ of the area of $\triangle ACD$, show that $4BC = 3AD$.

9.3 Special Triangles

Two **special triangles** are helpful for finding some trigonometric ratios.

The first special triangle is drawn with two equal sides of 1 unit and an angle of 45°. By Pythagoras' Theorem, this means the hypotenuse is $\sqrt{2}$:

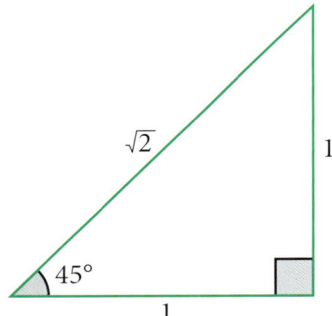

From this triangle, it can be seen that:

$$\sin 45° = \frac{1}{\sqrt{2}} = \frac{\sqrt{2}}{2}$$

$$\cos 45° = \frac{1}{\sqrt{2}} = \frac{\sqrt{2}}{2}$$

$$\tan 45° = \frac{1}{1} = 1$$

The second special triangle is half of an equilateral triangle of side length 2. The two shorter sides are 1 and $\sqrt{3}$ units:

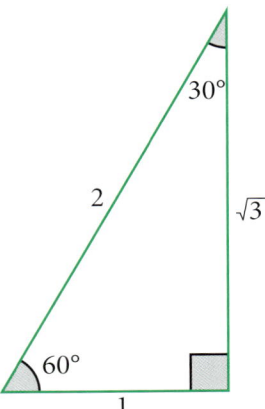

From this triangle, we can work out all three trigonometric ratios for 30° and for 60°, for example

$$\tan 30° = \frac{1}{\sqrt{3}} = \frac{\sqrt{3}}{3}.$$

All of these results are summarised in the following table:

Table 1	30°	45°	60°
$\sin \theta$	$\dfrac{1}{2}$	$\dfrac{\sqrt{2}}{2}$	$\dfrac{\sqrt{3}}{2}$
$\cos \theta$	$\dfrac{\sqrt{3}}{2}$	$\dfrac{\sqrt{2}}{2}$	$\dfrac{1}{2}$
$\tan \theta$	$\dfrac{\sqrt{3}}{3}$	1	$\sqrt{3}$

Remembering these results, or knowing how to find them quickly from the special triangles, can speed up your work and help when giving exact answers.

9.4 The Graphs of the Sine, Cosine and Tangent Functions

Symmetries and periodicities
You should be familiar with the key features of the sine, cosine and tangent graphs.

$y = \sin \theta$

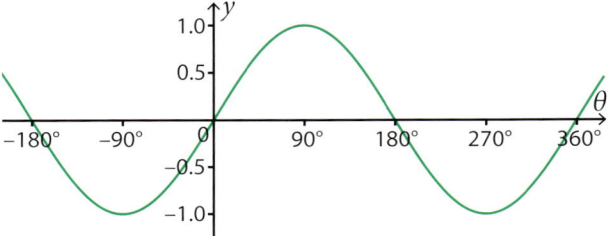

The curve $y = \sin \theta$ passes through the origin. It reaches a maximum value of 1 when $\theta = 90°$ and a minimum value of -1 when $\theta = 270°$. It has a period of 360°, meaning the curve has:

- maxima at $\theta = \ldots -270°, 90°, 450°, \ldots$
- minima at $\theta = \ldots -90°, 270°, 630°, \ldots$
- a value of $y = 0$ when $\theta = \ldots -360°, -180°, 0°, 180°, 360°, \ldots$

Because of the periodicity:

- $\sin(\theta - 360°) = \sin \theta = \sin(\theta + 360°)$.

The sine curve has symmetry about the line $\theta = 90°$, meaning that:

- $\sin(90° + \theta) = \sin(90° - \theta)$

$y = \cos \theta$

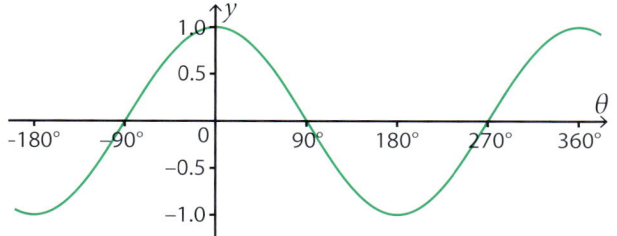

The curve $y = \cos \theta$ has a maximum value of 1 when $\theta = 0°$ and a minimum value of -1 when $\theta = 180°$. It has a period of 360°, meaning the curve has:

- maxima at $\theta = \ldots -360°, 0°, 360°, \ldots$
- minima at $\theta = \ldots -540°, -180°, 180°, 540°, \ldots$
- a value of $y = 0$ when $\theta = \ldots -270°, -90°, 90°, 270°, \ldots$

Because of the periodicity:

- $\cos(\theta - 360°) = \cos \theta = \cos(\theta + 360°)$

The cosine curve has symmetry about the line $\theta = 0°$, meaning that:

- $\cos \theta = \cos(-\theta)$

$y = \tan \theta$

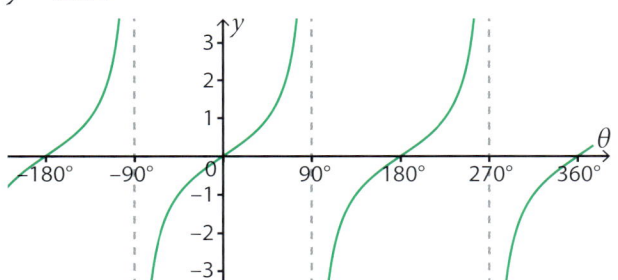

The curve $y = \tan \theta$ has a period of 180°. The curve has:

- a value of $y = 0$ when $\theta = \ldots -180°, 0, 180°, \ldots$

There are no maximum or minimum points. Instead:

- the curve approaches **asymptotes** at $\theta = \ldots, -270°, -90°, 90°, 270°, \ldots$ We write that $y \to \infty$ as $x \to 90°$.

Because of the periodicity:

- $\tan(\theta - 180°) = \tan \theta = \tan(\theta + 180)$

The tangent curve does not have any lines of symmetry.

Some important results
The following table summarises the key values from the three graphs above. You have already seen some of these results in Table 1.

Table 2	0°	30°	45°	60°	90°
$\sin \theta$	0	$\dfrac{1}{2}$	$\dfrac{\sqrt{2}}{2}$	$\dfrac{\sqrt{3}}{2}$	1
$\cos \theta$	1	$\dfrac{\sqrt{3}}{2}$	$\dfrac{\sqrt{2}}{2}$	$\dfrac{1}{2}$	0
$\tan \theta$	0	$\dfrac{\sqrt{3}}{3}$	1	$\sqrt{3}$	$\pm\infty$

Worked Example

12. How many solutions are there within the range $0 < x < 360°$ to the following equations?
    (a) $\sin \theta = -0.4$
    (b) $\cos \theta = 2.5$
    (c) $\tan \theta = 2.5$

(a) Draw the sine curve and the line $y = -0.4$ on the same diagram. Observe how many times they intersect within the given interval:

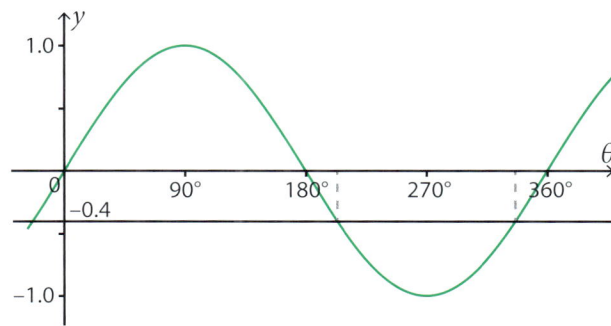

The graph shows that there are two solutions. We are not asked to find these solutions.

(b) There are no solutions. The cosine curve has a maximum value of 1. So $\cos \theta$ is never equal to 2.5.

(c) Draw a sketch of the tan curve and the line $y = 2.5$ on the same diagram:

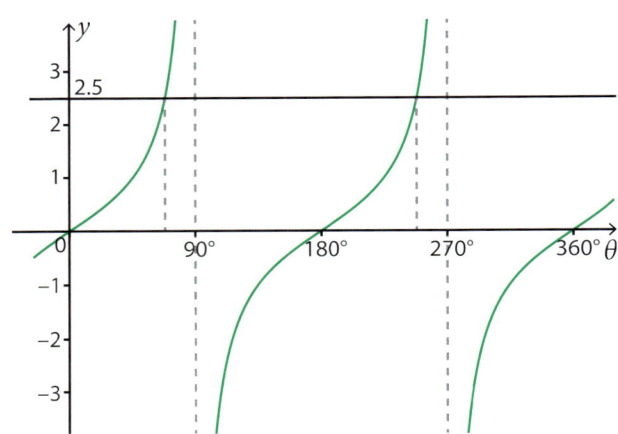

The sketch shows there are two solutions to $\tan \theta = 2.5$ within the interval specified.

Exercise 9E

1. Sketch the graph of $y = \sin x$, where $-180° \leq x \leq 180°$.

2. Sketch the graph of $y = \cos x$, where $-180° \leq x \leq 180°$.

3. Sketch the graph of $y = \tan x$, where $-180° \leq x \leq 180°$.

4. Using the graph of $y = \sin x$, state how many solutions there are for $-180° \leq x \leq 180°$ to the equations:

    (a) $\sin x = \dfrac{1}{2}$ (b) $\sin x = 0$

    (c) $\sin x = 2$ (d) $\sin x = 1$

5. Using the graph of $y = \cos x$, state how many solutions there are for $-180° \leq x \leq 180°$ to the equations:

    (a) $\cos x = -\dfrac{1}{2}$ (b) $\cos x = 0$

    (c) $\cos x = -2$ (d) $\cos x = -1$

6. Using the graph of $y = \tan x$, state how many solutions there are for $-180° \leq x \leq 180°$ to the equations:

    (a) $\tan x = -\dfrac{1}{2}$ (b) $\tan x = 0$

    (c) $\tan x = 2$ (d) $\tan x = -1$

Transformations of trigonometric graphs

In chapter 5 you learnt about **transformations** of curves:

Translations

- To translate an object means to move it without changing its shape.

- Any curve can be translated in these two ways:
  - add a constant to perform a translation parallel to the y-axis;
  - replace x with $(x \pm a)$ to perform a translation parallel to the x-axis.

Reflecting and stretching

- The graph of $y = -f(x)$ is a reflection in the x-axis of $y = f(x)$.
- The graph of $y = f(-x)$ is a reflection in the y-axis of $y = f(x)$.
- The graph of $y = af(x)$ is a stretch parallel to the y-axis of $y = f(x)$.
- The graph of $y = f(ax)$ is a stretch of the graph of $y = f(x)$ parallel to the x-axis, with a stretch factor of $\dfrac{1}{a}$.

All of these transformations can be applied to the trigonometric functions.

Note: If you work towards A2 level Mathematics, you will learn how these transformations can be combined.

Worked Examples

13. Sketch the graph of $y = \cos(x + 30°)$ for $0 \leq x \leq 360°$. State the coordinates of any maximum and minimum points in this interval and write down the period of the curve.

    When compared with $y = \cos x$, we have replaced x with $(x + 30°)$. This is a translation by $30°$ in the **negative x-direction**:

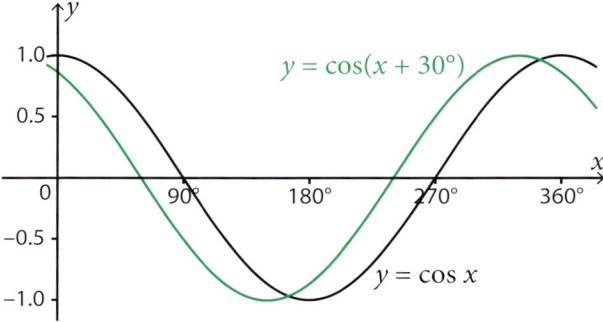

    The graph of $y = \cos(x + 30°)$ has a maximum at $(330°, 1)$. It has a minimum at $(150°, -1)$. The period is $360°$.

14. Sketch the graph of $y = 3 \sin x$ for $0 \leq x \leq 360°$. State the coordinates of any maximum and minimum points in this interval and write down the period of the curve.

When compared with $y = \sin x$, this is a stretch, scale factor 3, in the **y-direction**:

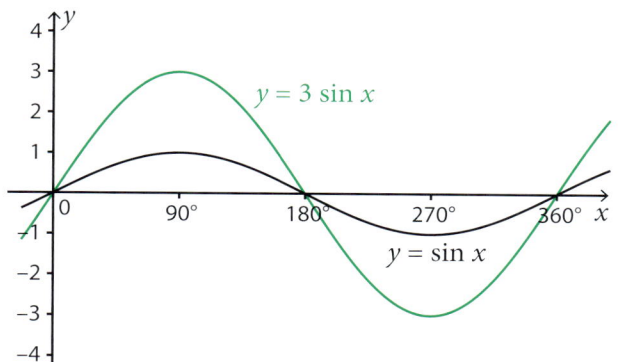

The graph of $y = 3 \sin x$ has a maximum at (90°, 3) and a minimum at (270°, −3). The period of is 360°.

---

15. Write down the maximum value and minimum value of $\sin x + 0.5$. In each case give the smallest positive value of x (in degrees) for which it occurs.

This question is best answered by sketching the graph $y = \sin x + 0.5$. It is a translation of $y = \sin x$ by 0.5 units in the positive y-direction:

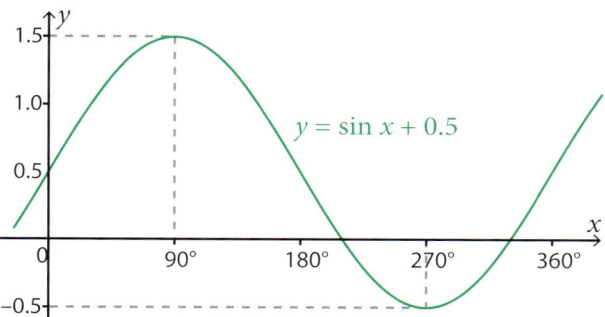

From the graph it can be seen that:

• The maximum value of $\sin x + 0.5$ is 1.5. This occurs when $x = 90°$.

• The minimum value of $\sin x + 0.5$ is −0.5. This occurs when $x = 270°$.

··

Exercise 9F

1. Sketch each pair of curves on the same diagram for $0 \le x \le 360°$.
   - **(a)** $y = \sin x$ $y = 1 + \sin x$
   - **(b)** $y = \cos x$ $y = -1 + \cos x$
   - **(c)** $y = \tan x$ $y = 1 + \tan x$
   - **(d)** $y = \sin x$ $y = \sin(x + 45°)$
   - **(e)** $y = \cos x$ $y = \cos(x - 30°)$
   - **(f)** $y = \tan x$ $y = \tan(x + 90°)$

Exercise 9F...

2. Sketch each pair of curves on the same diagram for $0 \le x \le 360°$.
   - **(a)** $y = \sin x$ $y = -\sin x$
   - **(b)** $y = \cos x$ $y = -\cos x$
   - **(c)** $y = \tan x$ $y = -\tan x$

3. Sketch each pair of curves on the same diagram for $0 \le x \le 360°$ and write down the period of each.
   - **(a)** $y = \cos x$ $y = \cos 2x$
   - **(b)** $y = \sin x$ $y = \sin \dfrac{x}{2}$
   - **(c)** $y = \tan x$ $y = \tan 2x$
   - **(d)** $y = \cos x$ $y = \cos 3x$

4. Write down the equations for the functions sketched here.

   (a)

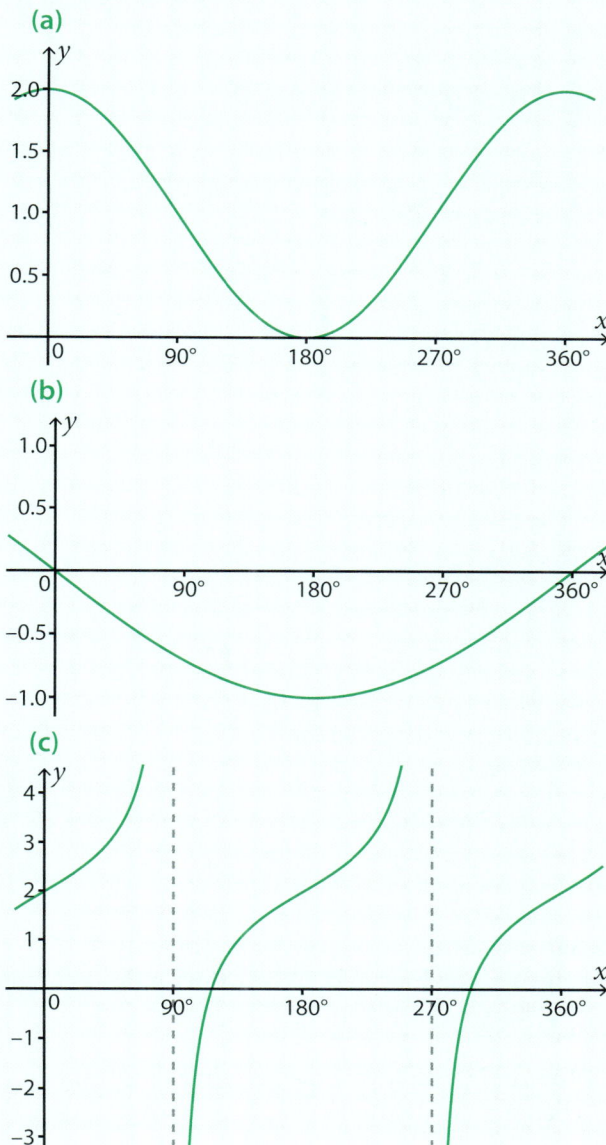

   (b)

   (c)

Exercise 9F...

5. Write down the maximum value and minimum value of each of the following expressions. In each case give the smallest non-negative value of x (in degrees) for which it occurs..
   (a) $\cos(-x)$
   (b) $2 + \sin x$
   (c) $3 \sin x$

6. Sketch the two graphs $y = \cos x$ and $y = \sin(x + 90°)$ on the same diagram. What do you notice?

Later in this chapter we will use the graphs of the trigonometric functions to help us solve equations involving the trigonometric functions. There is, however, another way to solve trigonometric equations: the CAST diagram.

9.5 The CAST Diagram

The graphs in section 5.4 show that the sine, cosine and tangent functions apply to all angles, not just those in the range 0 – 180°. The **CAST diagram** helps you to find the sine, cosine and tangent of angles outside this range. It is often used between 0° and 360° or between –180° and 180°.

The diagram can also help you to find the solutions to trigonometric equations.

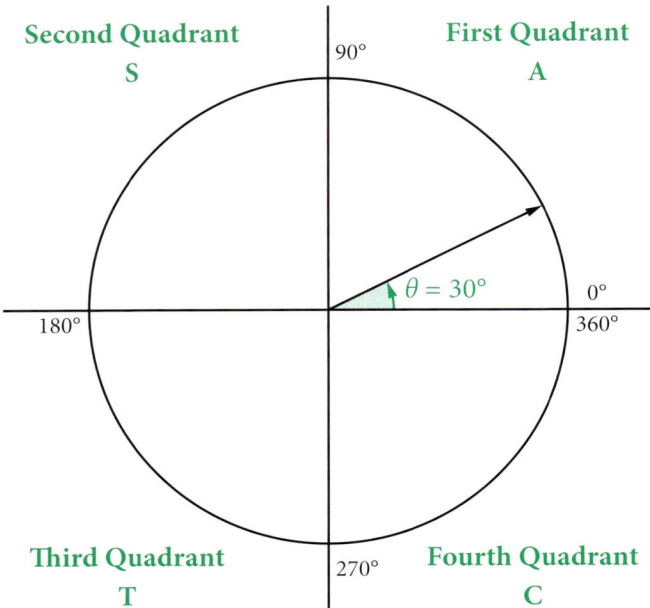

In the CAST diagram – shown above – the angle 0° is aligned with the positive x-axis. From this reference line, all positive angles are measured anticlockwise: for

example the angle θ shown in the diagram is 30°. An angle of 180° is aligned with the negative x-axis and 360° is in the same position as 0°.

The CAST diagram takes its name from the four quadrants. In the C (fourth) quadrant, cosine is positive (e.g. cos 300°). In the A quadrant, all functions (sine, cosine and tangent) are positive. In the S quadrant only sine is positive; in the T quadrant, only tan is positive. This information is summarised in this table:

	θ	Positive	Negative
First Quadrant (A)	0 – 90°	All	
Second Quadrant (S)	90 – 180°	$\sin \theta$	$\cos \theta$, $\tan \theta$
Third Quadrant (T)	180 – 270°	$\tan \theta$	$\sin \theta$, $\cos \theta$
Fourth Quadrant (C)	270 – 360°	$\cos \theta$	$\sin \theta$, $\tan \theta$

Worked Example

16. Using the CAST diagram, state whether the sine of the following angles are positive or negative.
    (a) 40°   (b) 120°   (c) 190°   (d) 335°

    (a) 40° lies within the first quadrant, so sin 40° is positive.
    (b) 120° lies within the second quadrant, so sin 120° is positive.
    (c) 190° lies within the third quadrant, so sin 190° is negative.
    (d) 335° lies within the fourth quadrant, so sin 335° is negative.
    Check these results on your calculator.

You can find the sine, cosine or tangent of an angle in quadrants 2, 3 or 4 by finding its **related acute angle**.

The related acute angle can be found by:

• Plotting the angle on the CAST diagram.
• Working out the acute angle between the line plotted and the horizontal.

Worked Examples

17. (a) Draw the angles 150°, 210° and 330° on the CAST diagram.
    (b) For these three angles, state the related acute angles.
    (c) Given $\sin 30° = \dfrac{1}{2}$, find:

(i) sin 150°
(ii) sin 210°
(iii) sin 330°

(a)

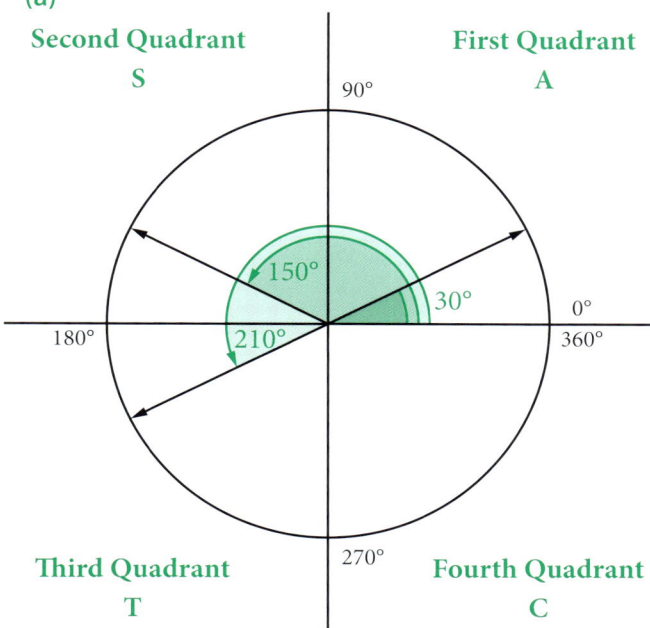

(b) The **related acute angle** is the angle between the line drawn and the horizontal line. For each of these three angles, the related acute angle is 30°. The angle 330° has not been marked on the diagram. This is left as an exercise.

This means that we can work out sine, cosine and tangent of these three angles using sine, cosine and tangent of 30°.

(c) Begin by considering the related acute angle, $\sin 30° = \dfrac{1}{2}$:

(i) 150° lies in the second quadrant, so sin 150° is positive: $\sin 150° = \dfrac{1}{2}$

(ii) 210° lies in the third quadrant, so sin 210° is negative: $\sin 210° = -\dfrac{1}{2}$

(iii) 330° lies in the fourth quadrant, so sin 330° is negative: $\sin 330° = -\dfrac{1}{2}$

Check these results on your calculator.

18. Given $\cos \theta = \dfrac{\sqrt{2}}{2}$, where θ is an acute angle:

(a) Find θ using your calculator.
(b) Use the CAST diagram to find the exact value of cos 315°.
(c) Use the CAST diagram to find the exact value of cos (−45°).

(d) Use the CAST diagram to find the exact value of cos (−135°)

(a)

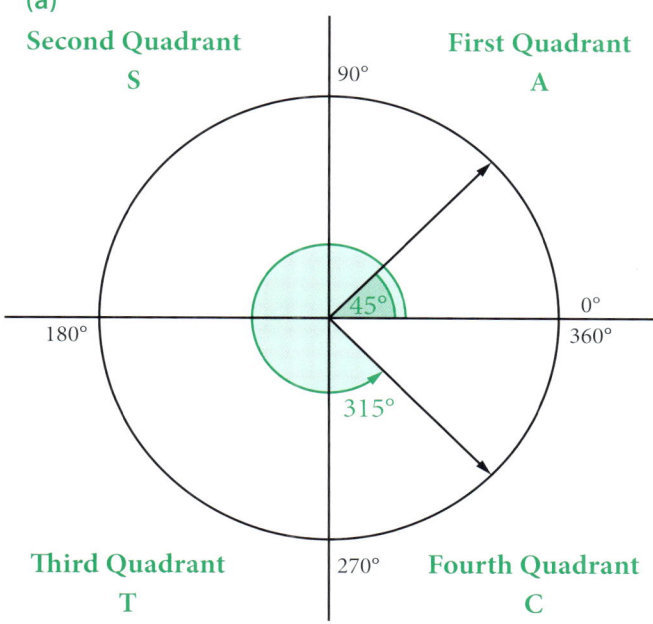

(b) For 315°, the related acute angle is 45°. This means we can work out the cosine of 315° using the cosine of 45°.

Cosine is positive in the fourth quadrant, so:

$$\cos 315° = \frac{\sqrt{2}}{2}$$

Note: In its usual form, the CAST diagram is labelled from 0° to 360°. It can also be re-labelled from −180° to 180°, as shown below.

(c) Re-label the CAST diagram from −180° to 180°:

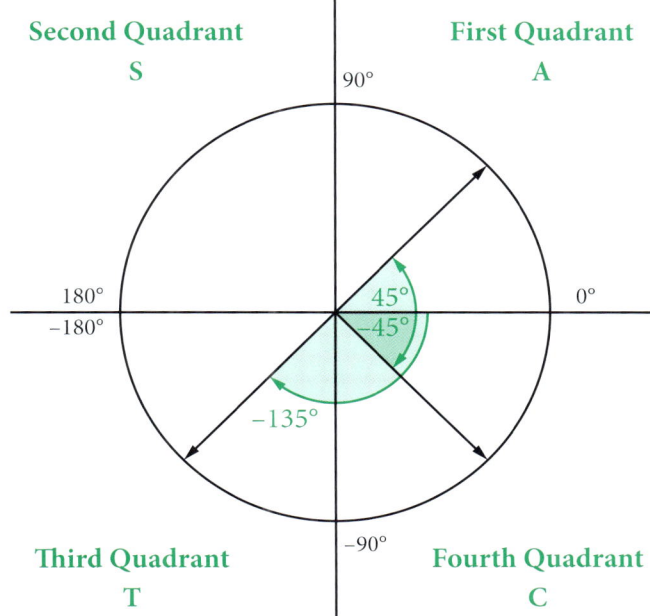

Note the way the CAST diagram has been relabelled and how the angles −45° and −135° have been plotted. For both angles, the related acute angle is 45°. This means we can work out sine, cosine and tangent of these angles using sine, cosine and tangent of 45°.

(b) −45° lies in the fourth quadrant, so cosine is positive:

$$\cos 45° = \frac{\sqrt{2}}{2} \Rightarrow \cos(-45°) = \frac{\sqrt{2}}{2}$$

(c) −135° lies in the third quadrant, so cosine is negative:

$$\cos 45° = \frac{\sqrt{2}}{2} \Rightarrow \cos(-135°) = -\frac{\sqrt{2}}{2}$$

Check these results on your calculator.

Finding one trigonometric ratio from another

If you are given one trigonometric ratio and asked to find another, a sketch of a right-angled triangle is often useful.

Worked Example

19. Given $\sin x = \dfrac{2}{\sqrt{6}}$, where x is an acute angle, find the exact values of $\cos x$ and $\tan x$.

We have been given the opposite and hypotenuse sides in a right-angled triangle. So we can sketch the triangle, as shown on the right.

We can calculate a using Pythagoras' Theorem:

$$a^2 = \left(\sqrt{6}\right)^2 - 2^2$$
$$a = \sqrt{2}$$

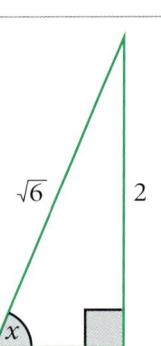

Now we can look at the triangle again to work out $\cos x$ and $\tan x$.

$$\cos x = \frac{\text{adjacent}}{\text{hypotenuse}} = \frac{\sqrt{2}}{\sqrt{6}} = \frac{\sqrt{3}}{3}$$

$$\tan x = \frac{\text{opposite}}{\text{adjacent}} = \frac{2}{\sqrt{2}} = \sqrt{2}$$

> **Note:** The question asked for exact values. This means we should leave the answers in surd form.

> **Note** that this question does not ask you to find the angle, x, itself.

If you are asked for trigonometric ratios of an obtuse angle, first consider the related acute angle.

Worked Example

20. Given that x is obtuse and $\cos x = -\dfrac{3}{5}$, find $\sin x$ and $\tan x$.

The angle x is obtuse, so it lies in the second quadrant. $\cos x$ is always negative in the second quadrant. The related acute angle y lies in the first quadrant and $\cos y$ is positive, i.e. $\cos y = \dfrac{3}{5}$.

So we can sketch the triangle, as shown on the right.

Calculate b using Pythagoras' Theorem:
$$b^2 = 5^2 - 3^2$$
$$b = 4$$

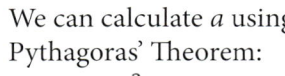

Look at the triangle to work out $\cos y$ and $\tan y$ for the acute angle y:

$$\sin y = \frac{\text{opposite}}{\text{hypotenuse}} = \frac{4}{5}$$

$$\tan y = \frac{\text{opposite}}{\text{adjacent}} = \frac{4}{3}$$

Since the angle x is obtuse, we know it lies in the second quadrant, where sine is always positive.

Therefore $\sin x = \dfrac{4}{5}$.

The tan function is always negative in the second quadrant. Therefore $\tan x = -\dfrac{4}{3}$.

(The angle x is 126.8°, but you are not asked to find this.)

If you have to find trigonometric ratios for reflex angles, use the same technique, i.e. consider first the related acute angle.

Exercise 9G

You should not need a calculator for this exercise.

1. For each of the following angles θ:
   (i) Sketch θ on the CAST diagram, showing which quadrant it lies in.
   (ii) State whether $\sin \theta$, $\cos \theta$ and $\tan \theta$ are positive or negative.
   (iii) Find the related acute angle.

Exercise 9G...

    (a) 30°   (b) 45°   (c) 100°
    (d) 210°   (e) 260°   (f) 320°

2. For each of the following trigonometric ratios:
    (i) Using the CAST diagram, determine the sign (i.e. positive or negative) of each.
    (ii) Find the related acute angle.
    (iii) By using Table 2 in section 9.4, evaluate the ratio.

    (a) sin 135°   (b) cos(−45°)   (c) tan 120°
    (d) cos 150°   (e) sin(−120°)   (f) tan(−30°)
    (g) cos(−135°)   (h) sin(−330°)

3. Using the CAST diagram, find the following:

    (a) Given $\sin 60° = \dfrac{\sqrt{3}}{2}$, find sin 120°.

    (b) Given $\cos 45° = \dfrac{\sqrt{2}}{2}$, find cos 135°.

    (c) Given tan 45° = 1, find tan 225°.

4. Find the following trigonometric ratios using the information given and Pythagoras' Theorem:

    (a) Given $\cos x = \dfrac{3}{7}$ and x is acute, find sin x and tan x.

    (b) Given $\tan x = \dfrac{4}{\sqrt{3}}$ and x is acute, find cos x and sin x.

    (c) Given $\sin x = \dfrac{10}{11}$ and x is acute, find cos x and tan x.

    (d) Given $\cos x = \sqrt{\dfrac{3}{7}}$ and x is acute, find sin x and tan x.

    (e) Given $\tan x = \dfrac{\sqrt{3}+1}{\sqrt{3}-1}$ and x is acute, find cos x and sin x.

    (f) Given $\cos x = \dfrac{\sqrt{5}}{3}$ and x is acute, find sin x and tan x.

    (g) Given tan x = 1 and x is acute, find cos x and sin x.

    (h) Given $\cos x = -\dfrac{1}{3}$ and x is obtuse, find sin x and tan x.

    (i) Given $\sin x = \dfrac{3}{8}$ and x is obtuse, find cos x and tan x.

    (j) Given $\tan x = -\dfrac{1}{6}$ and x is obtuse, find cos x and sin x.

    (k) Given $\tan x = \dfrac{2}{5}$ and x is reflex, find cos x and sin x.

9.6 Trigonometric Identities

An equation is true for certain values of the variable involved. An **identity** is true for all values.

Notation

Identities are often written with the **identity sign** or **equivalence sign** ≡ instead of an equals sign. It indicates that something is always true, not just for certain values of x or θ.

The identity $\tan \theta \equiv \dfrac{\sin \theta}{\cos \theta}$

> **Note:** The CCEA specification (at the time of publication) does not require you to know this proof.

Consider the triangle below:

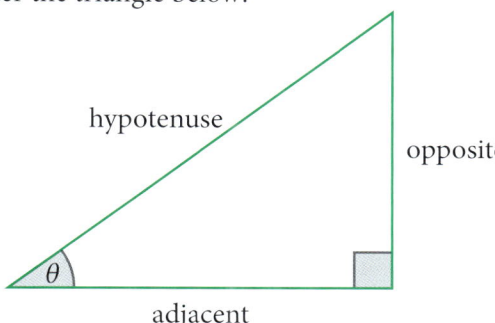

From the triangle: $\sin \theta = \dfrac{\text{opposite}}{\text{hypotenuse}}$

$\cos \theta = \dfrac{\text{adjacent}}{\text{hypotenuse}}$

$\tan \theta = \dfrac{\text{opposite}}{\text{adjacent}}$

Therefore:

$$\frac{\sin \theta}{\cos \theta} = \frac{\text{opposite}}{\text{hypotenuse}} \div \frac{\text{adjacent}}{\text{hypotenuse}}$$

$$= \frac{\text{opposite}}{\text{hypotenuse}} \times \frac{\text{hypotenuse}}{\text{adjacent}}$$

$$= \frac{\text{opposite}}{\text{adjacent}}$$

$$= \tan \theta$$

$$\therefore \tan \theta \equiv \frac{\sin \theta}{\cos \theta}$$

> **Note:** Do not use this result when cos θ = 0 (i.e. 90°, 270°, …). At these values of θ, the tan function is undefined.

The identity $\sin^2 \theta + \cos^2 \theta \equiv 1$

Note: The CCEA specification (at the time of publication) does not require you to know this proof.

Consider the triangle below:

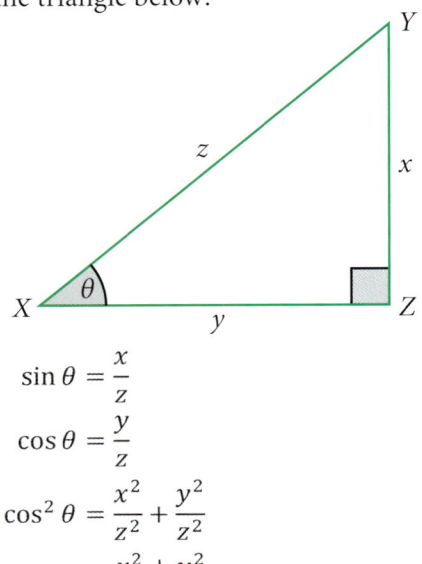

$$\sin \theta = \frac{x}{z}$$

$$\cos \theta = \frac{y}{z}$$

$$\therefore \sin^2 \theta + \cos^2 \theta = \frac{x^2}{z^2} + \frac{y^2}{z^2}$$

$$= \frac{x^2 + y^2}{z^2}$$

Using Pythagoras' Theorem:

$$x^2 + y^2 = z^2$$

$$\therefore \sin^2 \theta + \cos^2 \theta = \frac{z^2}{z^2}$$

$$\therefore \sin^2 \theta + \cos^2 \theta \equiv 1$$

You will use $\sin^2 \theta + \cos^2 \theta \equiv 1$ frequently, both in solving trigonometric equations and when proving other trigonometric identities.

Proving trigonometric identities

The two results proved above can be used to simplify many other trigonometric expressions and to prove many identities.

$$\tan \theta \equiv \frac{\sin \theta}{\cos \theta}$$

$$\sin^2 \theta + \cos^2 \theta \equiv 1$$

Worked Example

21. Simplify: $\cos x + \sqrt{1 - \sin^2 x}$

Use: $\sin^2 x + \cos^2 x = 1$
Re-arranging gives: $1 - \sin^2 x = \cos^2 x$

$$\therefore \cos x + \sqrt{1 - \sin^2 x} = \cos x + \sqrt{\cos^2 x}$$

$$= \cos x + \cos x$$

$$= 2 \cos x$$

When proving an identity, take the expression on one side of the identity, then work on it one step at a time until you reach the expression on the other side. It is a good idea to begin with the expression that looks the most complicated. We use the abbreviations LHS for left-hand side and RHS for right-hand side.

Worked Examples

22. Prove the following identity:

$$\sqrt{1 - \cos^2 \theta \tan^2 \theta} \equiv \cos \theta$$

$$\text{LHS} = \sqrt{1 - \cos^2 \theta \tan^2 \theta}$$

$$= \sqrt{1 - \frac{\cos^2 \theta \sin^2 \theta}{\cos^2 \theta}}$$

$$= \sqrt{1 - \sin^2 \theta}$$

$$= \sqrt{\cos^2 \theta}$$

$$= \cos \theta$$

$$= \text{RHS}$$

$$\therefore \sqrt{1 - \cos^2 \theta \tan^2 \theta} \equiv \cos \theta$$

23. Prove the identity:

$$\tan x \cos x \sin x \equiv \sin^2 x$$

$$\text{LHS} = \tan x \cos x \sin x$$

$$= \frac{\sin x}{\cos x} \cos x \sin x$$

$$= \sin x \sin x \qquad \text{(cancelling } \cos x\text{)}$$

$$= \sin^2 x$$

$$= \text{RHS}$$

$$\therefore \tan x \cos x \sin x \equiv \sin^2 x$$

24. Prove the identity:

$$\tan x + \frac{1}{\tan x} \equiv \frac{1}{\sin x \cos x}$$

$$\text{LHS} = \tan x + \frac{1}{\tan x}$$

$$= \frac{\sin x}{\cos x} + \frac{\cos x}{\sin x} \quad \text{(using } \tan x = \frac{\sin x}{\cos x}\text{)}$$

$$= \frac{\sin^2 x + \cos^2 x}{\sin x \cos x}$$

$$= \frac{1}{\sin x \cos x}$$

$$= \text{RHS}$$

$$\therefore \tan x + \frac{1}{\tan x} \equiv \frac{1}{\sin x \cos x}$$

1. Simplify the following trigonometric expressions.
   (a) $\dfrac{\cos x}{\sin x}$
   (b) $\sin^2 3x + \cos^2 3x$
   (c) $\sqrt{\tan^2 x \cos^2 x}$
   (d) $\dfrac{1-\sin^2 A}{\cos^2 A} - \dfrac{1-\cos^2 A}{\sin^2 A}$
   (e) $\sin^2 A + 2\cos^2 A$
   (f) $(\cos x + \sin x)^2 + (\cos x - \sin x)^2$
   (g) $1 + \dfrac{1}{\tan^2 x}$
   (h) $(\tan A \cos A)^2 + \left(\dfrac{\sin A}{\tan A}\right)^2$
   (i) $(\sin x - 1)(\sin x + 1)(\cos x - 1)(\cos x + 1)$
   (j) $\dfrac{\sin \theta}{\dfrac{1}{\sin \theta} - \sin \theta}$

2. Prove the following identities.
   (a) $\dfrac{1-\cos^2 x}{\tan x} \equiv \sin x \cos x$
   (b) $(\cos A - \sin A)^2 \equiv 1 - 2\sin A \cos A$
   (c) $2\sin^2 \theta + 14\cos^2 \theta - 2 \equiv 12\cos^2 \theta$
   (d) $\sin^2 x (1 - \sin^2 x)\left(1 + \dfrac{1}{\tan^2 x}\right) \equiv \cos^2 x$
   (e) $\dfrac{\sqrt{1-\cos^2 x}}{\cos x} \equiv \tan x$
   (f) $\dfrac{-\sin x + 2\cos x}{\cos x} \equiv 2 - \tan x$
   (g) $\dfrac{\sqrt{1-\sin^2 x}}{\cos x} \equiv 1$
   (h) $\tan B + \dfrac{1}{\tan B} \equiv \dfrac{1}{\sin B \cos B}$
   (i) $\dfrac{\sin \theta}{\cos \theta \tan \theta} + \dfrac{6}{\tan \theta} - \dfrac{6\sin^2 \theta}{\tan \theta} \equiv \dfrac{6\cos^2 \theta}{\tan \theta} + 1$
   (j) $\tan x \equiv \sqrt{\sin^2 x \tan^2 x + \sin^2 x}$

3. $x = t\cos \theta$ and $y = t\sin \theta$. Find a simplified expression for $\sqrt{x^2 + y^2}$.

4. Prove the following trigonometric identities.
   (a) $1 - \dfrac{1}{\cos^2 \theta} \equiv -\tan^2 \theta$
   (b) $\sin^3 \theta (1 - \cos^2 \theta) = \sin^4 \theta \tan \theta \cos \theta$
   (c) $\tan^2 \theta + 1 \equiv \dfrac{\tan^2 \theta}{\sin^2 \theta}$
   (d) $\cos x + 2\sin x + \tan x \sin x \equiv \dfrac{(\cos x + \sin x)^2}{\cos x}$

9.7 Solution of Trigonometric Equations

You will often be asked to solve a trigonometric equation, for example to find all solutions to:

$3 - 3\cos \theta - \sin^2 \theta = 0$ for $-180° < \theta < 180°$

Because of the periodic nature of the trigonometric functions, there will usually be more than one solution.

To find all the solutions within the range specified, follow these steps:

1. You may need to use a substitution and adjust the range, for example if you are solving an equation involving 2θ, instead of θ.

2. Find the first solution on your calculator, often an acute angle. This is called the **principal value**.

3. Use the CAST diagram, or a sketch of the trigonometric graph to find the second solution.

4. To find subsequent solutions within the range:
   - for questions involving cosine and sine, add and subtract 360° from your first two solutions;
   - for questions involving the tan function, add and subtract 180° from your first two solutions.

5. If you used a substitution in step 1, you will need to reverse it.

> **Note:** In total, there will usually be an even number of solutions. If you have an odd number of solutions, check your work.

Questions are usually of one of the following five types:

1. Simple equations with multiple solutions, for example:
   $\sin \theta = \dfrac{1}{2}$

2. Equations involving multiple angles, for example:
   $\cos(3\theta - 45°) = \dfrac{\sqrt{3}}{2}$

3. Quadratics involving just one trigonometric function, for example:
   $\tan^2 \theta - 2\tan \theta + 1 = 0$

4. Equations requiring the identity:
   $\tan \theta \equiv \dfrac{\sin \theta}{\cos \theta}$

5. Quadratics requiring the identity:
   $\sin^2 \theta + \cos^2 \theta \equiv 1$

Both identities 4 and 5 above are used extensively when solving trigonometric equations. You can substitute 1 in place of $\sin^2 \theta + \cos^2 \theta$, for example, or $\sin^2 \theta$ for

$1 - \cos^2 \theta$, etc. A 'Cheat Sheet' for solving trigonometric equations can be found at the end of this chapter.

Worked Example

25. Solve the equation $\cos x = \dfrac{\sqrt{3}}{2}$ for $-360° \leq x \leq 360°$.

Find the first solution (the principal value) from the calculator:

$$x = \cos^{-1}\left(\frac{\sqrt{3}}{2}\right)$$

$x = 30°$ This solution is an acute angle.

> **Note:** Some calculators have buttons marked arcsin, arccos and arctan, instead of $\sin^{-1}$, $\cos^{-1}$ and $\tan^{-1}$. You will usually press SHIFT-sin, SHIFT-cos, etc to access these functions.

There are two methods to find the second solution:

Method 1

Use the CAST diagram to find the other answers in the range specified. Cosine is positive in quadrants 1 and 4. Therefore, a second solution can be found by reflecting $x = 30°$ in the horizontal line:

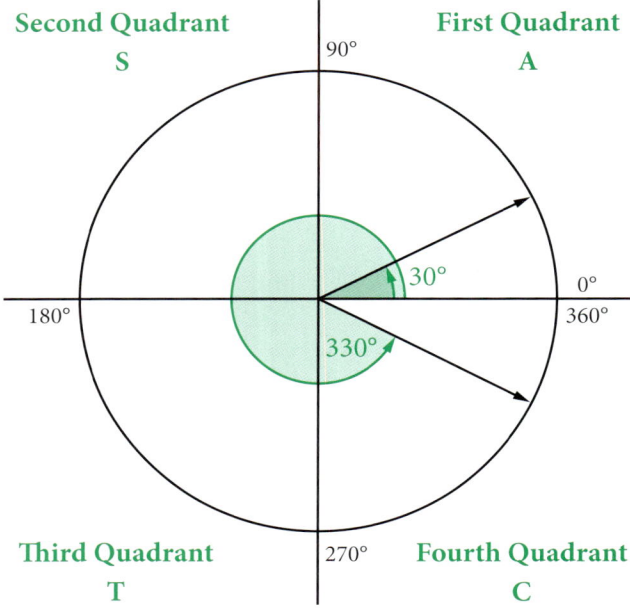

So $x = 330°$ is the second solution within the range.

Method 2

Use the symmetry of the graph of the cosine function:

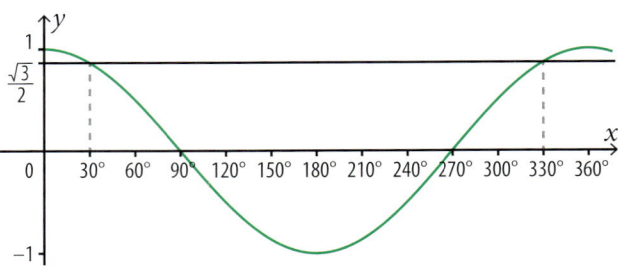

We know the first solution is $x = 30°$.
The graph shows us that the second solution is $x = 360 - 30 = 330°$.

To find further solutions

The cosine curve has a period of 360°. Therefore, any subsequent solutions can be found by adding or subtracting 360° from the two solutions found. Bear in mind the range specified in the question is $-360° \leq x \leq 360°$. So:

- $30° + 360° = 390°$ – not in the specified range.
- $330° + 360° = 690°$ – not in the specified range.
- $30° - 360° = -330°$ – within the specified range.
- $330° - 360° = -30°$ – within the specified range.

Subtracting 360° again would take us outside the range. Therefore, our four solutions are $-330°$, $-30°$, $30°$ and $330°$.

It is a good idea to check your answers on your calculator. Enter $\cos(-330)$ for example.

You will often have to find the solutions to trigonometric equations involving multiple angles. For these problems, use a substitution.

Worked Example

26. Find all solutions to: $\tan 2\theta = \sqrt{3}$ within the range $-180° \leq \theta \leq 180°$.

Use the substitution $x = 2\theta$. Then $\tan x = \sqrt{3}$.

Adjust the range: $-180° \leq \theta \leq 180°$
Since $x = 2\theta$, then $-360° \leq x \leq 360°$

Use the calculator to find the first solution or principal value: $x = 60°$.

There are two methods to find the second solution:

Method 1

The tangent function is positive in the first and third quadrants. So we find the second solution by adding 180°:

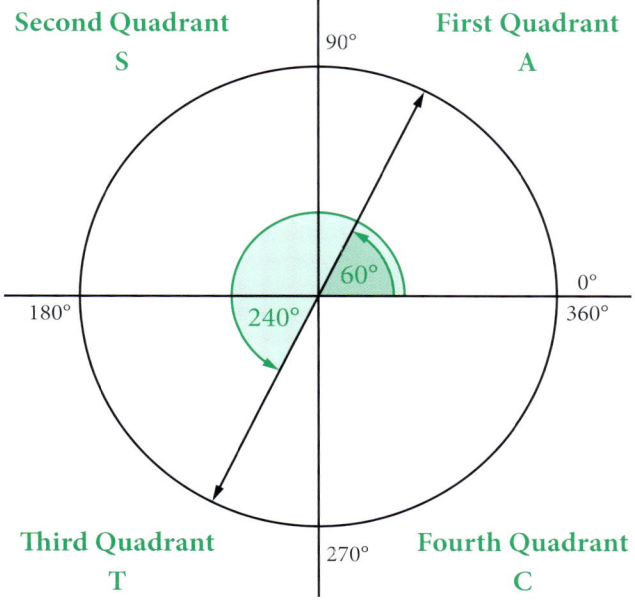

So $x = 240°$ is the second solution.

Method 2

Draw a sketch of the tangent function:

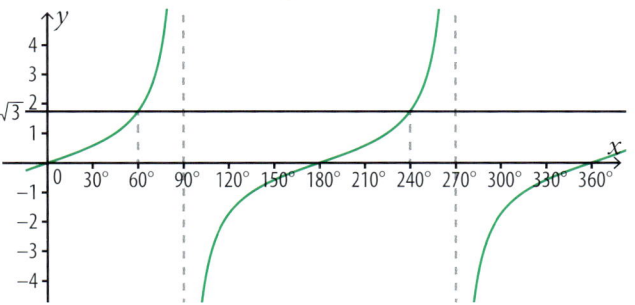

This shows that the second solution is at 240° because the period of the tan curve is 180°.

To find further solutions

The tangent function has period 180°, so further solutions can be found by repeatedly adding or subtracting 180°:
$x = ..., -480°, -300°, -120°, 60°, 240°, 420°, ...$

Finally, reverse the substitution

Now $x = 2\theta \Rightarrow \theta = \dfrac{x}{2}$.

So solutions for θ are found by dividing our answers for x by 2:
$x = ..., -240°, -150°, -60°, 30°, 120°, 210°, ...$

Within the range $-180° \le \theta \le 180°$:
$\theta = -150°, -60°, 30°, 120°$

Check your answers on your calculator.

You can solve equations where the angle is a sum or a difference in a similar way.

Worked Example

27. Find all solutions to: $\cos(x + 60°) = \dfrac{1}{2}$
for $-180° \le x \le 180°$.

Use a substitution $\theta = x + 60°$.

Now we must solve $\cos \theta = \dfrac{1}{2}$

From the calculator, the first solution is $\theta = 60°$. Since cosine is positive in the first and fourth quadrants, a second solution for θ can be found by reflecting the first solution in the horizontal 0° line. This gives a second solution of 300°:

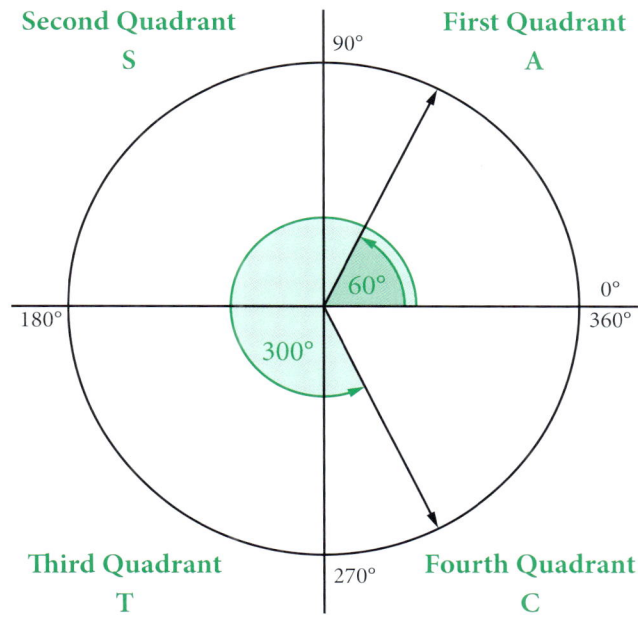

So $\theta = 60°, 300°$.

Since the cosine function has a period of 360°, subsequent solutions can be found by adding or subtracting 360° from the two solutions already found:
$\theta = ..., -300°, -60°, 60°, 300°, 420°, 660°, ...$

Now $\theta = x + 60° \Rightarrow x = \theta - 60°$. So:
$x = ..., -360°, -120°, 0°, 240°, 360°, 600°, ...$

Since the specified range is $-180° \le x \le 180°$, there are only two solutions:
$x = -120°, 0°$.

Note: Do not fall into the trap of replacing $\cos(x + 60°)$ with $\cos x + \cos 60°$. These two expressions are **not** equal. To use mathematical language, the cosine function is **not linear**. Neither are the other trigonometric functions.

Equations of the form $a \sin x + b \cos x = 0$ can be re-arranged to form an equation involving $\tan x$.

Worked Example

28. Solve: $2 \sin x + \cos x = 0$ for $0 \le x \le 360°$.

Dividing by $\cos x$ gives:
$2 \tan x + 1 = 0$

Rearranging gives:
$\tan x = -\dfrac{1}{2}$

From the calculator, the principal value is $-26.6°$.

Using the CAST diagram, the solutions within the specified range are $153.4°$ and $333.4°$.

You will often have to re-arrange a trigonometric equation before solving it. Use the usual rules of algebra, treating $\sin x$ (for example) as the unknown.

Worked Example

29. Find solutions to the equation:
$\dfrac{3 - 5 \sin x}{2} + \cos^2 x = 1$
for $0 \le x \le 360°$.

This equation involves $\sin x$ and $\cos^2 x$. Use the identity $\sin^2 \theta + \cos^2 \theta \equiv 1$ to replace $\cos^2 x$:
$\dfrac{3 - 5 \sin x}{2} + (1 - \sin^2 x) = 1$

$$\sin^2 x = \frac{3 - 5 \sin x}{2}$$

$$2 \sin^2 x = 3 - 5 \sin x$$

$$2 \sin^2 x + 5 \sin x - 3 = 0$$

We now have a quadratic equation in $\sin x$. You may find it simpler to use the substitution $y = \sin x$. Then:
$2y^2 + 5y - 3 = 0$

Factorising gives:
$(2y - 1)(y + 3) = 0$

$y = \dfrac{1}{2}$ or $y = -3$

so $\sin x = \dfrac{1}{2}$ or $\sin x = -3$

There are no solutions to $\sin x = -3$, since the sine function only gives answers between -1 and 1. (Consider the sine graph to convince yourself of this!)

We solve $\sin x = \dfrac{1}{2}$ in the usual way. The first answer is obtained from the calculator: $x = 30°$. The second answer can be obtained from the CAST diagram:

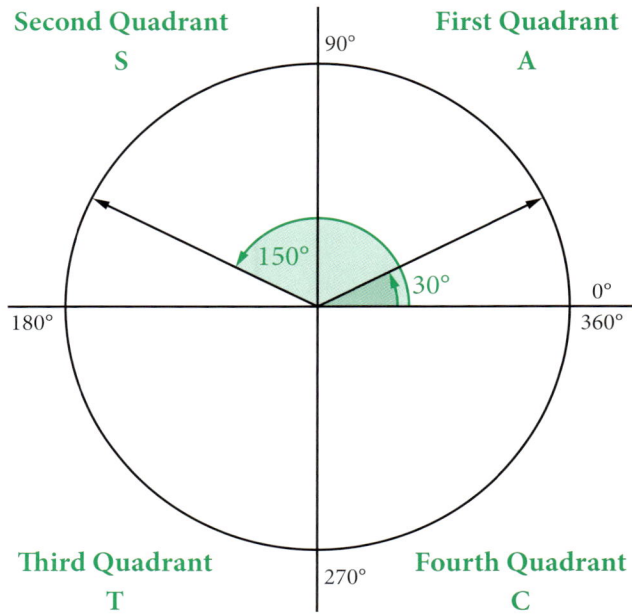

The sine function is positive in the second quadrant, so the second solution is $150°$.

The sine function has period $360°$, but adding and subtracting $360°$ to our two solutions does not give any additional results within the specified range.

Therefore $x = 30°, 150°$.

When re-arranging your equation, you will often make use of trigonometric identities, as in the following example.

Worked Example

30. Find all the values of θ in the range $0 \le \theta \le 360°$ satisfying: $4 \sin \theta \tan \theta = 15$.

$$4 \sin \theta \tan \theta = 15$$

Using $\tan \theta \equiv \dfrac{\sin \theta}{\cos \theta}$:

$$4 \sin \theta \left(\frac{\sin \theta}{\cos \theta} \right) = 15$$

$$\Rightarrow \frac{4 \sin^2 \theta}{\cos \theta} = 15$$

Use $\sin^2 \theta = 1 - \cos^2 \theta$ to obtain a quadratic equation in $\cos \theta$:

$$\Rightarrow 4(1 - \cos^2 \theta) = 15 \cos \theta$$
$$\Rightarrow 4 \cos^2 \theta + 15 \cos \theta - 4 = 0$$

Let $y = \cos \theta$:

$$\Rightarrow 4y^2 + 15y - 4 = 0$$
$$\Rightarrow (4y - 1)(y + 4) = 0$$
$$y = \frac{1}{4} \text{ or } y = -4$$
$$\Rightarrow \cos \theta = \frac{1}{4}$$

There are no solutions to $\cos \theta = -4$. Therefore:
$\theta = 75.5°, 284° (3 \text{ s.f.})$

You may need to use the quadratic formula if you cannot factorise a quadratic.

Worked Example

31. Find solutions to: $4(\tan^2 \theta - \tan \theta) = 1$ in the range $-180° \leq \theta \leq 180°$. Give your answers correct to 1 decimal place.

$4(\tan^2 \theta - \tan \theta) = 1$
Re-arranging gives: $4 \tan^2 \theta - 4 \tan \theta - 1 = 0$

Again, you may use a substitution, $y = \tan \theta$. Here we solve directly for $\tan \theta$, using the quadratic formula:

$$\tan \theta = \frac{4 \pm \sqrt{16 - 4(4)(-1)}}{8}$$

$$\tan \theta = \frac{4 \pm \sqrt{32}}{8}$$

$$\tan \theta = \frac{1 \pm \sqrt{2}}{2}$$

First, consider $\tan \theta = \frac{1 + \sqrt{2}}{2}$.

From the calculator, $\theta = 50.36 \ldots°$. Use the CAST diagram or the graph of the tan function to obtain $\theta = -129.6°, 50.4°$. Adding and subtracting $180°$ gives no more solutions within the specified range.

Next, consider $\tan \theta = \frac{1 - \sqrt{2}}{2}$.

From the calculator, $\theta = -11.70 \ldots°$. Use the CAST diagram again to obtain $\theta = -11.7°, 168.3°$. Adding and subtracting $180°$ gives no more solutions within the specified range.

Therefore: $\theta = -129.6°, -11.7°, 50.4°, 168.3° (1 \text{ d.p.})$

Warning

When solving a trigonometric equation, be careful when dividing by a trigonometric function. Consider this example:
$\sin x \cos x = \sin x$

Dividing both sides of the equation by $\sin x$ may seem sensible. But this approach will result in losing solutions to the equation.

Instead, you should bring all terms to the left-hand side:
$\sin x \cos x - \sin x = 0$

and factorise:
$\sin x(\cos x - 1) = 0$

To obtain all solutions, we must solve both $\sin x = 0$ and $\cos x - 1 = 0$. If you cancel $\sin x$ as your first step, you lose all the solutions resulting from $\sin x = 0$.

Exercise 9I

1. Find all the values of x satisfying the following within the range specified.
   (a) $\tan x = \sqrt{3}, 0° \leq x < 360°$
   (b) $\cos x = -\frac{\sqrt{3}}{2}, 0° \leq x < 360°$
   (c) $\sin x = \frac{1}{2}, -180° \leq x < 180°$
   (d) $\tan x = 1, -180° \leq x < 180°$
   (e) $\cos x = -\frac{1}{\sqrt{2}}, -180° \leq x < 180°$

2. Solve these equations, giving all solutions between $0°$ and $360°$, correct to 3 significant figures where appropriate.
   (a) $\sin x = \frac{\sqrt{3}}{2}$ (b) $\cos x = -\frac{1}{2}$
   (c) $\cos \theta = -0.43$ (d) $\tan \theta = 2$
   (e) $\cos A = 0.25$ (f) $\sin y = \frac{\sqrt{5}}{5}$
   (g) $\tan x = 0.2$ (h) $\cos A = 0.77$
   (i) $\cos x = 0.99$ (j) $\tan t = \frac{11}{7}$
   (k) $\cos \theta = \frac{1}{3}$ (l) $\sin z = \frac{1 - \sqrt{3}}{2}$
   (m) $\cos y = \sqrt{2} - 1$ (n) $\cos \theta = -0.6$
   (o) $\sin x = 0.15$

3. Solve these equations, giving all solutions between $0°$ and $180°$, correct to 3 significant figures where appropriate.
   (a) $\tan 2\theta = 2$ (b) $\sin 2x = 0.8$
   (c) $\cos 2x = -0.5$ (d) $\sin 3x = \frac{\sqrt{2}}{2}$

Exercise 9I...

(e) $\tan 3\theta = 30$ (f) $\sin\left(\frac{x}{2}\right) = \frac{3}{4}$

(g) $\cos\left(\frac{x}{3}\right) = -\frac{\sqrt{3}}{2}$ (h) $\cos(4y) = \frac{1}{2}$

(i) $\tan\left(\frac{x}{3}\right) = -1$ (j) $\sin\left(\frac{4}{2}\right) = 0.6$

4. Solve these equations, giving all solutions between 0° and 360°. Give your answers to 3 significant figures where appropriate.
(a) $\tan(x - 45°) = \sqrt{3}$
(b) $\cos(x - 90°) = \frac{1}{\sqrt{2}}$
(c) $1 + \sin(x - 30°) = \frac{1}{2}$
(d) $\tan(x + 20°) = \frac{1}{\sqrt{2}}$
(e) $\tan(2x) = 1$
(f) $\sin(3x - 30°) = \frac{1}{2}$
(g) $\cos(2x - 120°) + 1 = 1$
(h) $\tan(10° - 2x) = \frac{\sqrt{3}}{3}$

5. Solve the following equations, giving answers in the interval $-180° \leq x \leq 180°$.
(a) $\sin x = \cos x$
(b) $4\cos x = \sin x$
(c) $\sin 3x = \frac{1}{\sqrt{3}}\cos 3x$
(d) $\sin(2x - 15°) - \sqrt{3}\cos(2x - 15°) = 0$
(e) $\left(\sqrt{\cos x} - \sqrt{\frac{1}{2}\sin x}\right)\left(\sqrt{\cos x} + \sqrt{\frac{1}{2}\sin x}\right) = 0$

6. Solve these equations, giving all solutions between 0° and 360°. Give your answers to 3 significant figures where appropriate.
(a) $\cos^2 \theta = \frac{3}{4}$
(b) $\sin^2 x = \frac{1}{9}$
(c) $\tan^2 y = 3$

7. Solve the following quadratics by re-arranging, if necessary, then factorising. Give your answers in degrees, to 3 significant figures where appropriate, between 0° and 360°.
(a) $\sin^2 x + \sin x - 2 = 0$
(b) $2\cos^2 \theta + \cos \theta - 1 = 0$
(c) $\tan^2 t - \tan t - 6 = 0$

Exercise 9I...

(d) $\tan^2 x - 3\tan x = 4$
(e) $6\sin^2 y - 16\cos y = 0$
(f) $\sin^2 x = 1 + \cos x$
(g) $3\cos^2 \theta - 2\cos \theta - 1 = \sin^2 \theta$
(h) $\cos^2 x - 3(1 + \sin x) = 0$

8. Use the quadratic formula to solve the following. Give your answers in degrees, to 3 significant figures where appropriate, between 0° and 360°.
(a) $2\tan^2 x - \tan x - 3 = 0$
(b) $\sin^2 x - 5\sin x - 2 = 0$
(c) $2\cos^2 x + 3\cos x - 4 = 0$
(d) $7\cos^2 x - 2\cos x - 4 = 0$

9. Use the quadratic formula to solve the following. Give answers to 3 significant figures where appropriate, between −180° and 180°.
(a) $\sin^2 \theta + 2\sin \theta - 2 = 0$
(b) $\cos^2 x - 4\cos x = -1$
(c) $2\tan^2 y - 2\tan y - 3 = 0$
(d) $2\sin^2 x + \sin x = 2$
(e) $2\tan \theta = \sqrt{3}(\tan \theta - 1)(\tan \theta + 1)$

10. Given that: $5\sin 2\theta = \cos 2\theta$, find the values of θ, to two decimal places, in the interval $0° \leq \theta \leq 360°$.

11. Show that the equation: $14\cos^2 \theta = 12 + 12\sin \theta$ may be written as a quadratic equation in $\sin \theta$. Hence solve the equation, giving all values of θ such that $0° \leq \theta \leq 360°$.

12. Find all the values of θ in the range $0° \leq \theta \leq 360°$ satisfying: $5\sin \theta \tan \theta = 24$

9.8 Summary

When labelling the sides and angles in a triangle, angle A is opposite side a, etc.

The **sine rule** and **cosine rule** are used to find missing sides or angles in non-right-angled triangles:

Sine rule: $\dfrac{a}{\sin A} = \dfrac{b}{\sin B} = \dfrac{c}{\sin C}$

Cosine rule: $a^2 = b^2 + c^2 - 2bc \cos A$

The sine rule links two angles and two sides. Therefore, if you know two angles and a side, you can work out the missing side. Or if you know two sides and an angle, you can calculate the missing angle.

The cosine rule links three sides and one angle. Therefore, if you know three sides of a triangle, you can work out any angle. If you know two of the sides and one angle, you can calculate the missing side.

To find the **area of a triangle**, this formula can be used:

$\text{Area} = \dfrac{1}{2} ab \sin C$

You should be familiar with the graphs of $y = \sin x$, $y = \cos x$ and $y = \tan x$. You should remember the key points of these graphs, such as their periods, where the maximum and minimum points lie, etc.

You should be familiar with the identities:

$\sin^2 \theta + \cos^2 \theta \equiv 1$

and

$\tan \theta \equiv \dfrac{\sin \theta}{\cos \theta}$

and how to use these identities when proving further trigonometric identities and in solving trigonometry equations.

The 'Cheat Sheet' at the end of this chapter summarises the processes involved in solving trigonometric equations. After you have found the **principal value** on a calculator, use the CAST diagram or the trigonometric graphs to find subsequent solutions.

Solving Trigonometric Equations – 'Cheat Sheet'

Type	How to spot it	Method	Example
1. Equations involving a more complicated function of x.	Instead of $\sin x$, $\cos x$ or $\tan x$ these equations have something more complicated in place of x, for example $\cos 2x$ or $\sin(3x - 15°)$.	1. Use a substitution, e.g. $y = 3x - 15°$ and find the correct range for y. 2. Use $\sin^{-1}$, $\cos^{-1}$ or $\tan^{-1}$ on your calculator to get principal value. 3. Use the CAST diagram or graph to find the second value for y. 4. For questions involving sin and cos, repeatedly add and subtract $360°$ to both of the first two solutions. For tan, add and subtract $180°$. 5. Substitute back to get values of x.	Q. Solve: $\sin(2x - 15°) = \dfrac{1}{2}$ for $0 \leq x \leq 360°$. A. $y = 2x - 15$ and $-15° \leq y \leq 705°$ Principal value is $y = 30°$. Second solution is $y = 150°$. Add and subtract $360°$ to find any other solutions in range: $y = 30°, 150°, 390°, 510°$ $y = 2x - 15° \Rightarrow x = \dfrac{y + 15°}{2}$ $x = 22.5°, 82.5°, 202.5°, 262.5°$
2. Equations requiring $\tan x = \dfrac{\sin x}{\cos x}$	These equations involve $\sin x$ **and** $\cos x$, but not $\sin^2 x$ or $\cos^2 x$.	1. Divide the whole equation by $\cos x$. 2. Rearrange into the form $\tan x = constant$. 3. Use $\tan^{-1}$ on your calculator to get the principal value. 4. Use the CAST diagram to obtain all values in the required range.	Q. Solve $3 \sin x + \cos x = 0$ for $0 \leq x \leq 360°$. A. Dividing by $\cos x$ and rearranging gives us: $\tan x = -\dfrac{1}{3}$. Principal value is $-18.4°$. From CAST diagram, solutions within the range are $161.6°, 341.6°$.
3. Quadratics involving just one trigonometric function.	These have a squared trigonometric function, e.g. $\sin^2 x$, but only involve one of the three trigonometry functions, not a mixture.	1. Rearrange equation so that all the terms are on one side, equal to zero. 2. Factorise the equation. It may be helpful to use a substitution, e.g. $y = \sin x$. 3. Find up to 2 solutions to the quadratic in the normal way. 4. If a substitution has been used, don't forget to substitute back.	Q. Solve $\sin^2 x = 2 - \sin x$ for $0 \leq x \leq 360°$. A. Re-arrange to give: $\sin^2 x + \sin x - 2 = 0$ Let $y = \sin x$, then: $y^2 + y - 2 = 0$ Factorise: $(y - 1)(y + 2) = 0$ So $y = 1$ or $y = -2$. There are no solutions for $\sin x = -2$. Solving $\sin x = 1$ gives only one solution, $x = 90°$.
4. Quadratics requiring the identity $\sin^2 x + \cos^2 x \equiv 1$	These equations involve **either** $\sin^2 x$ and $\cos x$ **or** $\cos^2 x$ and $\sin x$.	1. If the equation has $\sin^2 x$, replace with $1 - \cos^2 x$. If equation has $\cos^2 x$, replace with $1 - \sin^2 x$. 2. Re-arrange and solve the quadratic as in case 3 (above).	Q. Solve $- \cos^2 x = 1 - \sin x$ for $0 \leq x \leq 360°$. A. Replace $\cos^2 x = 1 - \sin^2 x$. Re-arranging gives: $\sin^2 x + \sin x - 2 = 0$ Then proceed as in 3 (above).

Chapter 10
Exponentials and Logarithms

10.1 Introduction

Key words

- **Exponential growth**: A relationship in which the growth rate is proportional to the current value.
- **Logarithm**: The logarithm of a number is the power to which a base must be raised in order to make the number. For example, using base 10, the logarithm of 1000 is 3.

Before you start

You should know:

- How to solve quadratic equations.
- How to manipulate indices.
- How to sketch curves and recognise asymptotes.

Worked Examples

1. Solve: $x^2 - 7x + 10 = 0$

   $x^2 - 7x + 10 = 0$
   $(x - 5)(x - 2) = 0$
   So: $x = 5$ or $x = 2$.

2. Simplify: $(3x^2)^3 \times (2x^3)^2$

   $(3x^2)^3 \times (2x^3)^2$
   $= 27x^6 \times 4x^6$
   $= 108x^{12}$

3. Find x, where: $2^6 = 4^x$

   $2^6 = 4^x$
   $\Rightarrow 2^6 = (2^2)^x$
   $\Rightarrow 2^6 = 2^{2x}$
   $\Rightarrow 6 = 2x$
   $x = 3$

What you will learn

In this chapter you will learn how to:

- Understand and sketch exponential curves.
- Use the laws of logarithms.
- Solve equations involving logarithms.

In the real world...

Thomas Malthus was an English scholar and clergyman of the nineteenth century. He became well-known through his writings on population growth and the ability of society and the world to cope.

Malthus believed that populations tend to grow in an **exponential** way (which you will learn about in this chapter). Because of this growth, he argued, sooner or later the population will be overcome by famine and disease.

Malthus' ideas were controversial at the time. Other scholars believed that society could continue improving indefinitely: that slowly, through new technology and innovation, society will become ever more perfect.

Since then, the world's population has increased beyond what Malthus would have considered possible. Many people think this is evidence Malthus has been proved wrong.

Was he? The world may now be at a critical point in its history, when the ingenuity of man to cope with an ever-growing population will be tested as never before. If we can succeed, we could prove Malthus wrong again.

Exercise 10A (Revision)

1. Simplify the following.
   (a) $x^2 \times x^3$
   (b) $y^7 \div y^4$
   (c) $(z^2)^5 \times z^3$
   (d) $p^{-1} \times p^{-2}$
   (e) $\left(q^{\frac{3}{2}}\right)^2 \div q^{-2}$

2. Find x, where:
   (a) $100^5 = 10000^x$
   (b) $2^8 = 4^x$
   (c) $4^x = \dfrac{1}{64}$

Exercise 10A...

3. Solve the following equations for x.
   (a) $x(x + 3) = 0$
   (b) $x^2 + 3x - 4 = 0$
   (c) $2x^2 + 5x - 3 = 0$
   (d) $x^3 + x^2 - 6x = 0$
   (e) $3x^2 + 5x - 2 = 0$

4. Sketch the following curves and state the equations of any asymptotes.
   (a) $y = \dfrac{1}{x}$ (b) $y = \dfrac{2}{x}$
   (c) $y = \dfrac{1}{x^2}$ (d) $y = \dfrac{1}{x} + 1$

10.2 The Exponential Function and its Graph

The general equation of an exponential graph is $y = a^x$ (with $a > 0$).

The graph of $y = a^x$

Worked Example

4. Using a table of values, plot the graphs of $y = 2^x$ and $y = 1.5^x$, using $-5 \leq x \leq 5$.

x	-5	-4	-3	-2	-1
2^x	0.0313	0.0625	0.125	0.25	0.5
1.5^x	0.132	0.198	0.296	0.444	0.667

x	0	1	2	3	4	5
2^x	1	2	4	8	16	32
1.5^x	1	1.5	2.25	3.375	5.06	7.59

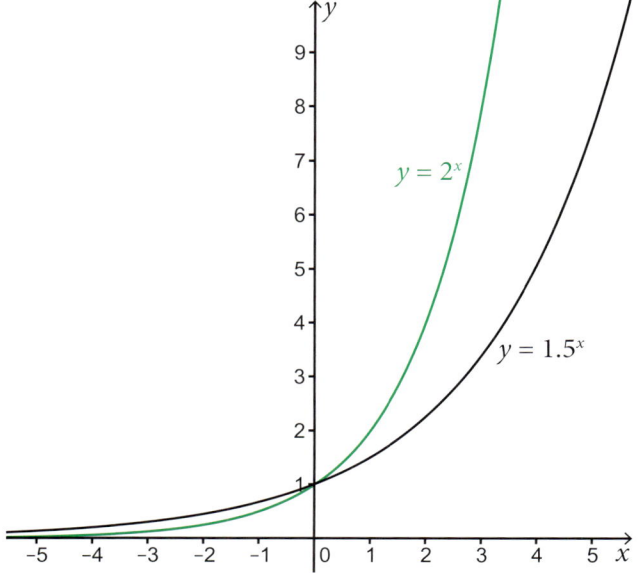

These are both examples of an exponential curve.

Key points of the graph of an exponential function

Many of the key points of the exponential curve $y = a^x$ can be seen in example 4.

- The x-axis is an asymptote; $y = a^x$ approaches this asymptote for small values of x.
- The greater the value of a, the steeper the curve.
- The curve $y = a^x$ (where $a > 0$) rises more and more steeply.
- All curves of this type cross the y-axis at $(0, 1)$.

The function e^x and its graph

The family of curves $y = a^x$ are known as **exponential curves**. Some of them are shown below.

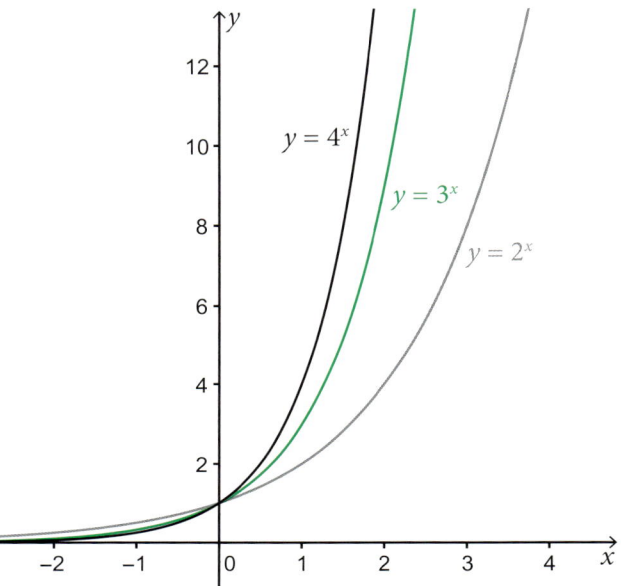

The gradient of an exponential curve is greater as the value of a increases.

All of these curves cross the y-axis at the point $(0, 1)$. What is the value of the gradient of these curves at this point? In the next chapter you will learn how to differentiate $y = a^x$ to obtain the gradient at any point on the curve. For now, these values are summarised in the table below.

Curve	Gradient at $(0, 1)$
$y = 2^x$	0.6931
$y = 3^x$	1.0986
$y = 4^x$	1.3863

This table suggests there is a curve in the family $y = a^x$ whose gradient is exactly 1 at the point $(0, 1)$. This curve is $y = e^x$ where $e = 2.718$.

In fact, the gradient of the curve $y = e^x$ is equal to the value of y at every point on the curve.

> $y = e^x$ is the curve whose gradient equals its y value at every point.

The value of e is just over 2.718. Like π, it is an irrational number, which means it cannot be written exactly as a fraction.

> **Note:** You may also see the notation $y = \exp(x)$.

Transformations of the graph of the exponential function

You can perform transformations of the graph of $y = a^x$ (including $y = e^x$) using the rules you learnt in Chapter 5.

- $y = f(x) + b$: Translation by b units in the positive y-direction.

  The curve $y = a^x + b$ is a translation of the curve $y = a^x$ by b units in the **positive** y-direction (upwards).

- $y = f(x + b)$: Translation by b units in the negative x-direction

  The curve $y = a^{x+b}$ is a translation of the curve $y = a^x$ by b units in the **negative** x-direction (to the left).

- $y = bf(x)$: Stretch in the y-direction, scale factor b.

  The curve $y = ba^x$ is a stretch of the curve $y = a^x$ by a factor of b, parallel to the y-axis.

- $y = f(bx)$: Stretch in the x-direction, scale factor $\frac{1}{b}$.

  The curve $y = a^{bx}$ is a stretch of the curve $y = a^x$ by a factor of $\frac{1}{b}$, parallel to the x-axis.

- $y = -f(x)$: Reflection in the x-axis.

  The curve $y = -a^x$ is a reflection of the curve $y = a^x$ in the x-axis.

- $y = f(-x)$: Reflection in the y-axis.

  The curve $y = a^{-x}$ is a reflection of the curve $y = a^x$ in the y-axis.

Worked Examples

5. Sketch the curve $y = \left(\frac{5}{2}\right)^x + 3$.

   Mark clearly where the curve intersects the y-axis and the equation of the asymptote.

This is a translation of the curve $y = \left(\frac{5}{2}\right)^x$, by 3 units in the positive y-direction. So we sketch:

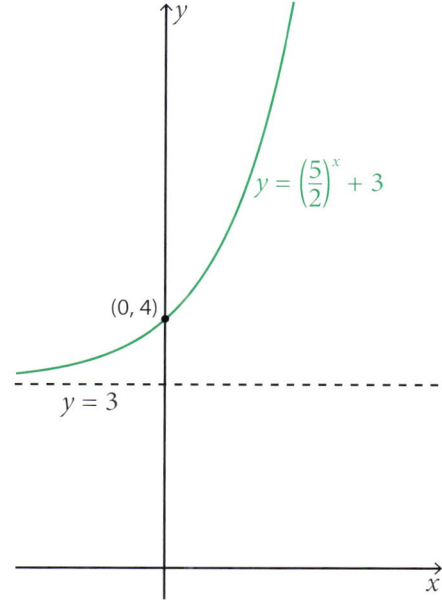

The point of intersection with the y-axis is $(0, 4)$. The equation of the horizontal asymptote is $y = 3$.

6. Sketch the curve $y = 2(4^x)$.

When compared with $y = 4^x$ this represents a stretch, scale factor 2, parallel to the y-axis. So we sketch:

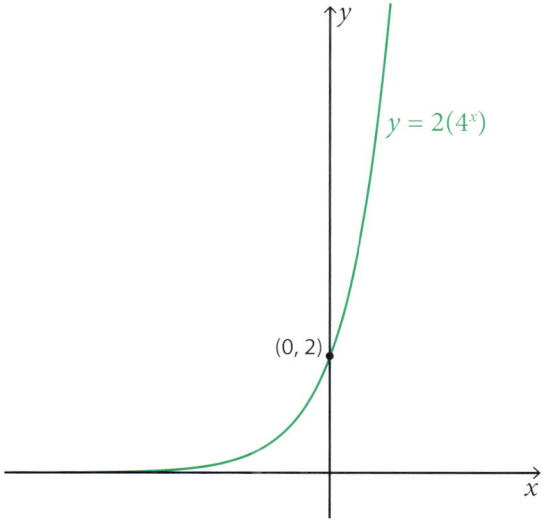

7. Sketch the curves $y = e^x$ and $y = 2e^x$ on the same diagram.

The curve $y = 2e^x$ is a stretch of the curve $y = e^x$ parallel to the y-axis. It passes through the point $(0, 2)$. So we sketch:

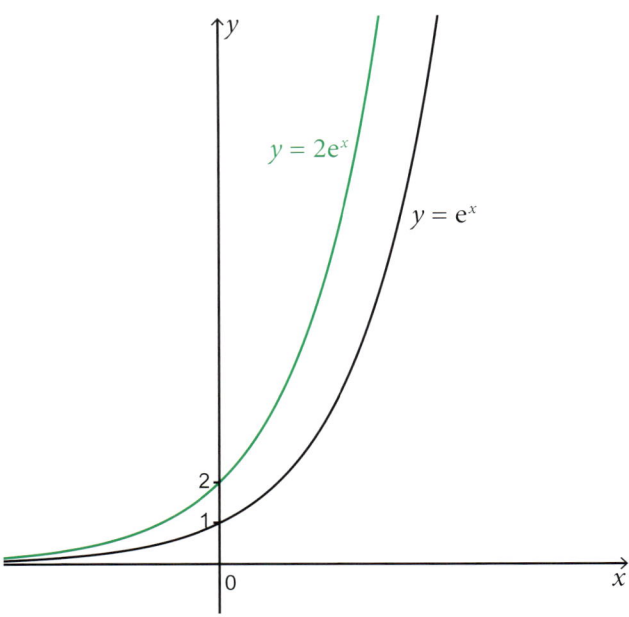

8. Sketch the three curves $y = e^x$, $y = e^{-x}$ and $y = -e^x$ on the same diagram.

$y = e^{-x}$ is a transformation of the form $y = f(-x)$. It represents a reflection of $y = e^x$ in the y-axis.

$y = -e^x$ is a transformation of the form $y = -f(x)$. It represents a reflection of $y = e^x$ in the x-axis.

So we sketch:

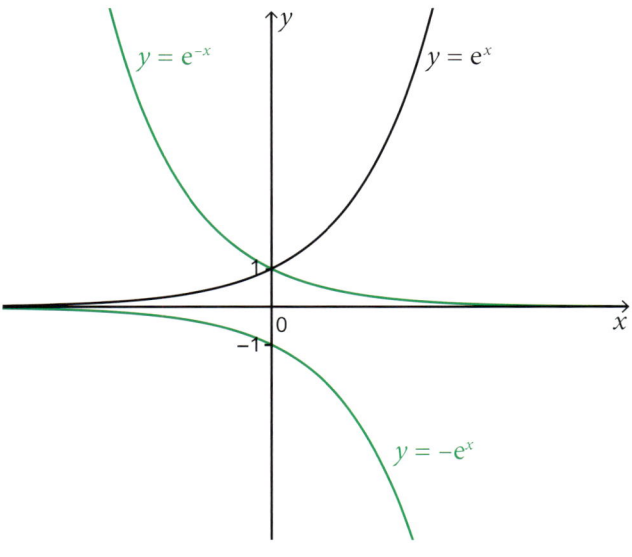

Exercise 10B

Questions 1 to 3 of this exercise require an accurate plot of the graph in question. Begin by drawing up a table of values. Subsequently in this exercise you will be asked for sketches only.

Exercise 10B...

1. Plot these curves on the same diagram. Use $-5 \leq x \leq 5$.
    (a) $y = 2^x$
    (b) $y = 3^x$

2. (a) Plot the graphs of $y = 3^x$ and $y = x + 3$ on the same diagram. Use $0 \leq x \leq 3$.
    (b) Show that there is one solution in this range to the equation $3^x = x + 3$. Estimate this value of x.
    (c) By extending your graph to the range $-3 \leq x \leq 3$, show that there is a second solution. Estimate this value of x.

3. (a) Show, using the rules of indices, that $2^{2x} = 4^x$.
    (b) Hence plot the curve $y = 2^{2x}$. Show the curve $y = 2^x$ on the same diagram.

4. On separate diagrams, sketch the graphs of the following curves. Sketch also the curve $y = 3^x$ on each diagram. Mark clearly where each curve crosses the y-axis.
    (a) $y = 3^{2x}$ (b) $y = 3^{\frac{x}{2}}$ (c) $y = 2(3^x)$

5. On separate diagrams, sketch the graphs of the following curves. Sketch also the curve $y = 2^x$ on each diagram. Mark clearly where each curve crosses the y-axis.
    (a) $y = 2^{-x}$ (b) $y = -2^x$

6. On separate diagrams, sketch the graphs of the following curves. Sketch also the curve $y = 2^x$ on each diagram. Mark clearly where each curve crosses the y-axis and the equations of any asymptotes.
    (a) $y = 2^x - 1$ (b) $y = 2^{x+1}$

7. Consider the following table of values. For lines (a) and (b), write down an equation that could have given these results.

x	-2	-1	0	1	2
(a) $y =$?	$\frac{1}{9}$	$\frac{1}{3}$	1	3	9
(b) $y =$?	$-\frac{1}{9}$	$-\frac{1}{3}$	-1	-3	-9

8. Sketch each curve and the curve $y = e^x$ on the same diagram. In each case, state which transformation could transform the graph of $y = e^x$ into the graph of the equation given.

Exercise 10B...

(a) $y = e^{2x}$ (b) $y = e^{x+1}$
(c) $y = e^{x-1}$ (d) $y = -e^x$
(e) $y = 3e^x$ (f) $y = e^{\frac{x}{2}}$
(g) $y = \dfrac{e^x}{2}$ (h) $y = e^x - 1$

9. The curve $y = e^x$ has a gradient of 1 at the point $(0, 1)$. By referring to your sketches in question 1, or otherwise, state the gradient of the following curves at the point where the curve crosses the y-axis.

(a) $y = e^{2x}$ (b) $y = -e^x$
(c) $y = 3e^x$ (d) $y = e^{\frac{x}{2}}$
(e) $y = \dfrac{e^x}{2}$ (f) $y = e^x - 1$

10. (a) Draw up a table of values for the function $f(x) = e^x + e^{-x}$. Use integer values of x from -3 to 3. Use an accuracy of 2 decimal places for $f(x)$.
   (b) Sketch the curve $y = f(x)$.

10.3 Logarithms

The definition of $\log_a x$ as the inverse of a^x (where $a > 0$ and $x \geq 0$)

Consider the exponential equation $y = a^x$. How could we re-arrange this to make x the subject? For this, we need some new notation. We say that x is the **logarithm** of y, base a.

As an equation, we write: $x = \log_a y$

> **Note:** It is important to remember the relationship between exponentials and logarithms:
>
> If $y = a^x$ then $x = \log_a y$
> (You can think of this as taking logs (base a) on both sides of the equation.)
>
> Going the other way, if $x = \log_a y$ then $y = a^x$ (setting a to the power of each side.)

Worked Examples

9. Without a calculator, evaluate the following.
   (a) $\log_9 81$ (b) $\log 100000$

   (a) $\log_9 81 = 2$ (because $9^2 = 81$)

(b)
> **Note:** If you are not given the base of a logarithm, you can assume it is base 10.

The base is 10, so:
$\log_{10} 100000 = 5$ (because $10^5 = 100000$)

10. Write equivalent statements using logarithms.
   (a) $2^6 = 64$ (b) $3^5 = 243$ (c) $1000 = 10^3$

   (a) $2^6 = 64 \Leftrightarrow \log_2 64 = 6$
   (b) $3^5 = 243 \Leftrightarrow \log_3 243 = 5$
   (c) $1000 = 10^3 \Leftrightarrow \log_{10} 1000 = 3$

11. Write equivalent statements using indices.
   (a) $\log_3 9 = 2$
   (b) $\log_5 125 = 3$
   (c) $\log_{10} 1000000 = 6$

   (a) $3^2 = 9$
   (b) $5^3 = 125$
   (c) $10^6 = 1000000$

It is also important to remember that for any value of a:

$$\log_a a = 1$$
$$\log_a 1 = 0$$

On your calculator, you may have three buttons to calculate logarithms. They will probably look similar to the following:

| log | | ln |

The first of these buttons performs logarithms to base 10. With the second button, you can enter the base. The purpose of the third button will be explained when we look at **natural logarithms** later in this chapter.

Worked Example

12. Use your calculator to work out:
   (a) $\log_{10} 100$ (b) $\log_4 64$ (c) $\log_6 6$
   (d) $\log 10$ (e) $\log_6 216$

   (a) On your calculator, enter: | log | 100
   Answer: 2
   The answer is the power you would need to raise the base to in order to get the answer 100.

   (b) On your calculator, enter: 4 64
   Answer: 3
   (c) $\log_6 6 = 1$
   (d) $\log 10 = 1$
   (e) $\log_6 216 = 3$

Exercise 10C

1. Without a calculator, find the value of:
   (a) $\log_{10} 1$ (b) $\log_6 216$
   (c) $\log 10000$ (d) $\log_3 27$
   (e) $\log_8 64$ (f) $\log_2 \dfrac{1}{16}$
   (g) $\log_{10} 0.01$ (h) $\log_3 3\sqrt{3}$
   (i) $\log_8 2$ (j) $\log_9 3$

2. Use your calculator to work out the following. Give your answers to 3 significant figures.
   (a) $\log 450$ (b) $\log_8 65$
   (c) $\log_5 2$ (d) $\log_{10} 8$
   (e) $\log_3 10$ (f) $\log_9 4$

3. Write equivalent statements using logarithms.
   (a) $100 = 10^2$ (b) $5^{-3} = 0.008$
   (c) $\dfrac{1}{4} = 4^{-1}$ (d) $9^0 = 1$
   (e) $2^2 = 4$ (f) $8^1 = 8$
   (g) $6^5 = 7776$ (h) $7^{10} = 282475249$
   (i) $10^7 = 10000000$ (j) $5^3 = 125$

4. Write equivalent statements using equations involving indices.
   (a) $\log_7 7 = 1$ (b) $\log_4 1 = 0$
   (c) $\log_2 128 = 7$ (d) $\log_2 \dfrac{1}{16} = -4$
   (e) $\log_6 \left(\dfrac{1}{6}\right) = -1$ (f) $\log_8 64 = 2$
   (g) $\log_4 64 = 3$ (h) $\log_7 2401 = 4$
   (i) $\log_5 625 = 4$ (j) $\log_3 \left(\dfrac{1}{59049}\right) = -10$
   (k) $\log_2 8\sqrt{2} = \dfrac{7}{2}$

5. Do you think it makes any sense to talk about logarithms with base 1? Explain your answer.

6. By drawing up a suitable table of values, plot the graph of $y = \log_{10} x$. (Hints: you do not need a negative x-axis, since the logarithm of a negative number is not defined. Choose several values of x between 0 and 1 and a few greater than 1.) Show clearly where your graph crosses either of the coordinate axes and also give the equation of the asymptote. Do you have any observations about your graph?

10.4 The Function $\ln x$ and its Graph

$\ln x$ as the inverse function of e^x

We have seen that the inverse of the function $y = a^x$ is the function $y = \log_a x$. This also applies when $a = e$.

> The inverse of the function $y = e^x$ is the function $y = \ln x$ (where $\ln x$ is another way of writing $\log_e x$). $\ln x$ is sometimes referred to as the **natural log** of x.

You can see this by inspecting the graphs of the two functions. One is the reflection of the other in the line $y = x$:

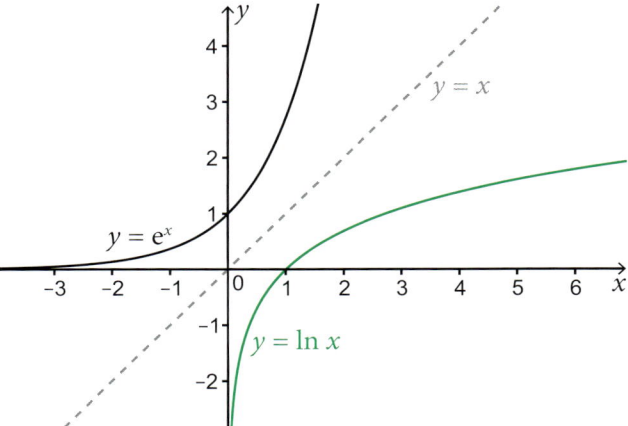

The key points of the graph of $y = \ln x$:

- It crosses the x-axis at $(1, 0)$.
- The y-axis is an asymptote.
- The value of the function is always increasing, but the gradient is always decreasing.
- The function is only defined for positive values of x.
- Any y-value is possible.

Transformations

You can use the usual rules when making transformations of the $\ln x$ function.

....

Worked Example

13. The graph of $y = \ln x$ is shown opposite. Sketch the graphs of the three functions:
    (a) $y = \ln(x + 1)$
    (b) $y = -\ln x$
    (c) $y = 1 + \ln x$
    marking clearly where each of the curves cross the coordinate axes.

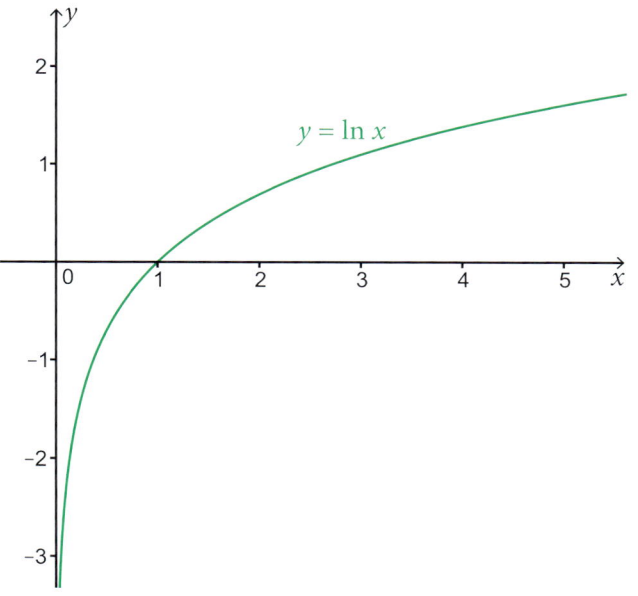

(b) We are being asked to draw the graph of $y = -f(x)$. This is a reflection in the x-axis:

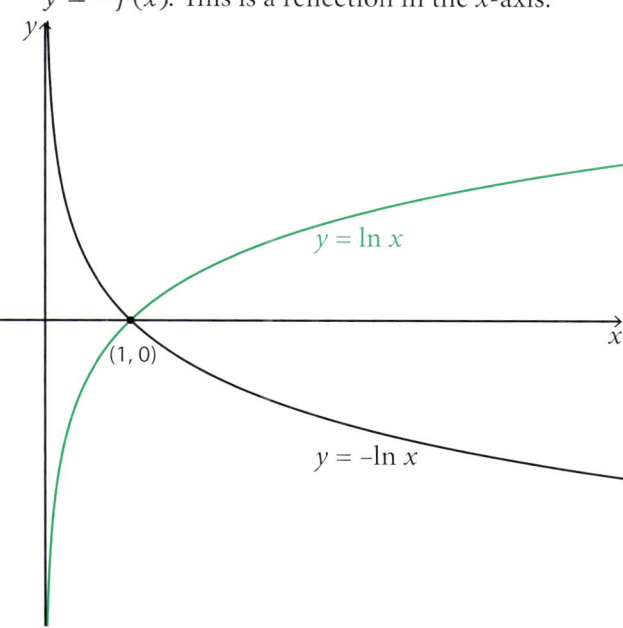

(a) If the given graph is $y = f(x)$, then we must draw the graph of $y = f(x + 1)$. This transformation causes a translation by 1 unit in the negative x-direction:

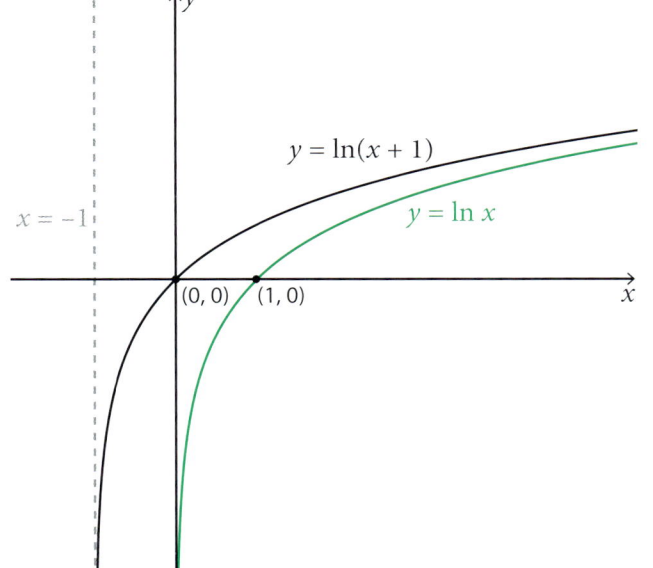

(c) We are being asked to draw the graph of $y = 1 + f(x)$. This is a translation by 1 unit in the positive y-direction.

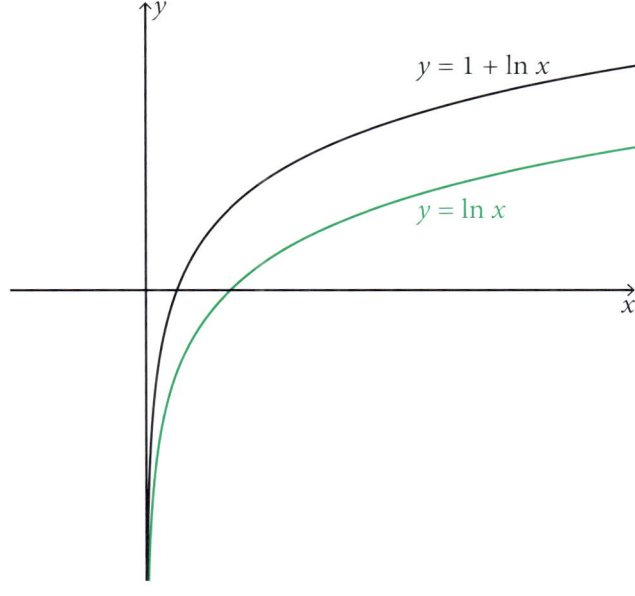

The exponential function and the ln function are inverses of each other. Because of this:

$$\ln e^a = a \text{ and } e^{\ln a} = a$$

Worked Example

14. Simplify: $\ln e^{3x} + e^{\ln 2x}$.

$\ln e^{3x} + e^{\ln 2x}$
$= 3x + 2x$
$= 5x$

Exercise 10D

1. Using your calculator, evaluate the following to 3 significant figures.
   (a) $\ln 10$　　(b) $\ln 2.7$　　(c) $\ln 0.1$

2. Use your calculator to find the value of e correct to 5 decimal places. (Hint: On many calculators e can also be found using ALPHA–×10^x. Alternatively type e^1 using SHIFT–ln then 1).

3. Using your calculator, evaluate the following. Obtain e on the calculator using one of the methods mentioned in question 2.
   (a) $\ln e$　　(b) $\ln e^2$　　(c) $\ln \dfrac{1}{e}$
   (d) $e^{\ln 2}$　　(e) $e^{3\ln 2}$　　(f) $e^{-\ln 2}$

4. Simplify the following.
   (a) $e^{\ln x}$　　(b) $ae^{\ln b}$　　(c) $\ln e^{2x}$
   (d) $\ln e^{\frac{x}{2}} + e^{\ln\frac{x}{2}}$

5. Sketch the following curves.
   (a) $y = \ln(x - 1)$　　(b) $y = 2\ln x$
   (c) $y = \ln \dfrac{x}{3}$　　(d) $y = \ln(-x)$

10.5 Laws of Logarithms

There are three important laws of logarithms that you should learn:

Addition law:	$\log_a x + \log_a y = \log_a(xy)$
Subtraction law:	$\log_a x - \log_a y = \log_a\left(\dfrac{x}{y}\right)$
Power law:	$n\log_a x = \log_a x^n$

Note: When using the addition and subtraction laws, the two bases must be equal.

Note: You need to learn the following three proofs.

Proof of Law 1 – the addition law

Let $p = \log_a x \Rightarrow x = a^p$　　(1)
and let $q = \log_a y \Rightarrow y = a^q$　　(2)

$(1) \times (2)$ gives:
$\quad xy = a^{p+q}$ (using the rules of indices)
$\Rightarrow p + q = \log_a(xy)$　　(3)

$(1) + (2)$ gives:
$\quad \log_a x + \log_a y = p + q$
$\quad\quad\quad\quad\quad\quad\quad = \log_a(xy)$ from (3)
$\therefore \log_a x + \log_a y = \log_a(xy)$

Proof of Law 2 – the subtraction law

Again let $p = \log_a x \Rightarrow x = a^p$　　(1)
and let $q = \log_a y \Rightarrow y = a^q$　　(2)

$(1) \div (2)$ gives:
$\quad \dfrac{x}{y} = a^{p-q}$ (using the rules of indices)
$\Rightarrow p - q = \log_a\left(\dfrac{x}{y}\right)$　　(3)

$(1) - (2)$ gives:
$\quad \log_a x - \log_a y = p - q$
$\quad\quad\quad\quad\quad\quad\quad = \log_a\left(\dfrac{x}{y}\right)$ from (3)
$\therefore \log_a x - \log_a y = \log_a\left(\dfrac{x}{y}\right)$

Proof of Law 3 – the power law

Let $p = \log_a x \Rightarrow x = a^p$　　(1)

Raise both sides to the power n:
$\quad x^n = (a^p)^n = a^{pn}$ (using the rules of indices)
$\Rightarrow \log_a(x^n) = pn$
$\Rightarrow \log_a(x^n) = n\log_a x$

Worked Examples

15. Write $\log_3 4 + \log_3 5$ as a single logarithm.

$\log_3 4 + \log_3 5 = \log_3(4 \times 5)$ (using the addition law)
$\quad\quad\quad\quad\quad\quad = \log_3 20$

16. Write $\log 12 + \log 5 - \log 30$ as a single logarithm.

$\log 12 + \log 5 - \log 30 = \log(12 \times 5) - \log 30$
(using the addition law)
$= \log 60 - \log 30$
$= \log 2$ (using the subtraction law)

17. Prove that:
   (a) $\log_a\left(\dfrac{1}{x}\right) = -\log_a x$　(b) $\log_a(\sqrt{x}) = \dfrac{1}{2}\log_a x$

(a) Use the power law: $k \log_a x = \log_a x^k$
When $k = -1, -\log_a x = \log_a x^{-1}$
i.e. $\log_a \left(\dfrac{1}{x}\right) = -\log_a x$

(b) Again, use the power law: $k \log_a x = \log_a x^k$
When $k = \dfrac{1}{2}, \dfrac{1}{2} \log_a x = \log_a x^{1/2}$
i.e. $\dfrac{1}{2} \log_a x = \log_a (\sqrt{x})$

18. Write the following as a single logarithm:
(a) $2 \log_5 3 + \log_5 10$
(b) $7 \log a + 6 \log b - 4 \log c$

(a) $2 \log_5 3 + \log_5 10 = \log_5 3^2 + \log_5 10$
$= \log_5 9 + \log_5 10$
$= \log_5 90$

(b) $7 \log a + 6 \log b - 4 \log c = \log a^7 + \log b^6 - \log c^4$
$= \log a^7 b^6 - \log c^4$
$= \log \left(\dfrac{a^7 b^6}{c^4}\right)$

19. Simplify the following expression by writing it in terms of $\log_5 2$ only: $2 \log_5 8$

$2 \log_5 8 = 2 \log_5 (2^3)$
$= 2 \times 3 \log_5 2$
$= 6 \log_5 2$

20. Write the following in terms of $\log a$, $\log b$ and $\log c$:
$\log \left(\dfrac{b^3 c^2}{a^{1/4}}\right)$

$\log \left(\dfrac{b^3 c^2}{a^{1/4}}\right) = \log b^3 + \log c^2 - \log a^{1/4}$
$= 3 \log b + 2 \log c - \dfrac{1}{4} \log a$

Exercise 10E

1. Simplify the following using the power law. There may be more than one correct answer.
(a) $\log_2 1000$ (b) $\log_3 243$ (hint: $3^5 = 243$)
(c) $\log_3 16$ (d) $\log_7 27$
(e) $\log_4 \left(\dfrac{1}{1024}\right)$ (f) $\log 125$
(g) $2 \log_4 100$ (h) $4 \log_2 81$
(i) $\log_4 \left(\dfrac{1}{10}\right)$ (j) $\log_{10} \left(\dfrac{1}{8}\right)$

2. If possible, express the following as a single logarithm using the addition law.
(a) $\log_a 30 + \log_a 2$ (b) $\log_9 23 + \log_5 3$
(c) $\log_2 15 + \log_2 6$ (d) $\log_3 10 + \log_3 17$

Exercise 10E...

(e) $\log_5 13 + \log_{13} 5$ (f) $\log_p 12 + \log_p 3$
(g) $\log 20 + \log 5$ (h) $\log_6 9 + \log_6 4$

3. If possible, express the following as a single logarithm using the subtraction law.
(a) $\log_a 30 - \log_a 2$ (b) $\log_8 2 - \log_7 3$
(c) $\log_2 18 - \log_2 6$ (d) $\log_3 70 - \log_3 7$
(e) $\log_4 13 - \log_5 13$ (f) $\log_q 36 - \log_q 3$
(g) $\log 20 - \log 5$ (h) $\log_6 11 - \log_6 4$

4. Simplify:
(a) $\log_2 7 + 2 \log_2 3$
(b) $2 \log_5 2 + \log_5 20$
(c) $2 \log \sqrt{3} - 2 \log \sqrt{2}$
(d) $\log \sqrt{50} + \log \sqrt{2}$
(e) $2 \log_3 6 + \log_3 2$
(f) $3 \log_2 2 + 2 \log_2 3 - \log_2 18$
(g) $\dfrac{1}{2} \log_5 64 + \log_5 \left(\dfrac{125}{8}\right)$
(h) $5 \log a + 2 \log b - 4 \log c$
(i) $6 \ln a + 4 \ln b + 2 \ln c$
(j) $\exp(2 \ln x + 3 \ln y)$

5. Write the following in terms of $\log a$, $\log b$ and $\log c$.
(a) $\log abc$ (b) $\log \left(\dfrac{ab}{c}\right)$
(c) $\log(a^2 bc)$ (d) $\log(a^2 \sqrt{bc})$
(e) $\log \left(\dfrac{a^{1/3}}{b^{1/2}}\right)$ (f) $\log_5 (5ab)$
(g) $\log_2 \left(\dfrac{a^2}{32 c^2}\right)$ (h) $\log_3 (27 b^3)$

6. Simplify:
(a) $6 \log x + 2 \log y$
(b) $3 \log p - 3 \log q$
(c) $7 \log a + 6 \log b - 4 \log c$

7. (a) Write down the value of $\log_2 8$.
(b) Given that $\log_2 x = a$, find, in terms of a, the simplest form of:
(i) $\log_2 (8x)$ (ii) $\log_2 \left(\dfrac{x^2}{2}\right)$

8. Given that $p = \log_q 256$, express in terms of p:
(a) $\log_q 4$ (b) $\log_q (64q)$

9. Express: $4 \log_a 3 + \log_a 11$ as a single logarithm with base a.

10. Prove that the value of x that satisfies:
$2 \log_2 x + \log_2 (x - 1) = 1 + \log_2 (12x + 18)$
is a solution of the equation:
$x^3 - x^2 - 24x - 36 = 0$

10.6 Solving Equations Using Logarithms

You may have to solve an equation in which the unknown is an index, for example $2^x = 20$. To do this, take logs of both sides of the equation. The power law of logs can then be used to obtain a standard equation in the unknown. When taking logs on both sides, you can use any base.

Worked Example

21. Solve:
    (a) $2^x = 20$ (b) $e^{2x} - 2 = 0$

    (a) Take logs (base 10) of both sides: $\log 2^x = \log 20$
       Use the power law on the left hand side:
       $$x \log 2 = \log 20$$
       $$x = \frac{\log 20}{\log 2}$$
       $$= 4.32 \, (3 \text{ s.f.})$$

    (b) $e^{2x} - 2 = 0$
       $\Rightarrow e^{2x} = 2$
       Take logs (base e) on both sides:
       $$2x = \ln 2$$
       $$x = \frac{1}{2} \ln 2$$
       $$= 0.347 \, (3 \text{ s.f.})$$

> **Note:** When solving any equation, it is a good idea to check your answer by substituting it back into the original equation.

Both sides of the equation may involve the unknown as an index.

Worked Example

22. Solve for x: $5^x = 6^{x-1}$

    Take logs:
    $$\log 5^x = \log 6^{x-1}$$

    Use the power law on both sides:
    $$x \log 5 = (x - 1) \log 6$$

    Expand the RHS:
    $$x \log 5 = x \log 6 - \log 6$$

    Note that $\log 5$ and $\log 6$ are constants. You can treat these as you would treat any other constants in an equation.

    Collect terms involving x on the left-hand side:

$$x \log 6 - x \log 5 = \log 6$$
$$x(\log 6 - \log 5) = \log 6$$
$$x = \frac{\log 6}{(\log 6 - \log 5)}$$
$$= \frac{0.77815 \ldots}{0.07918 \ldots}$$
$$= 9.83 \, (3 \text{ s.f.})$$

> **Note:** Here we worked to 5 decimal places in the working. Only round the final answer to 3 significant figures.

You may be asked to solve an equation involving logarithms. Firstly, use the laws of logarithms to combine all the terms involving logarithms into a single term. Then raise both sides to a power to eliminate logarithms from the equation. This is the inverse of taking logs of both sides.

Worked Example

23. Solve for x: $\log_5 x - \log_5(2x - 3) = 2$

    Using the subtraction law:
    $$\log_5 \left(\frac{x}{2x - 3} \right) = 2$$

    Raise both sides to power 5:
    $$\frac{x}{2x - 3} = 25$$
    $$x = 25(2x - 3)$$
    $$x = 50x - 75$$
    $$49x = 75$$
    $$x = \frac{75}{49}$$

If you are asked to solve an equation involving both a^{2x} and a^x, you will have to solve a quadratic equation, remembering that $a^{2x} = (a^x)^2$.

It is often best to use a substitution to solve this type of problem.

Worked Example

24. (a) Solve: $3^{2x} - 5(3^x) + 4 = 0$. Give your answers to 3 significant figures where appropriate.
    (b) Solve: $e^{2x} - 6e^x + 5 = 0$, giving exact answers.

    (a) Let $y = 3^x$.
       Then: $y^2 = (3^x)^2 = 3^{2x}$
       Then we must solve:
       $$y^2 - 5y + 4 = 0$$
       $$(y - 1)(y - 4) = 0$$

$y = 1$ or $y = 4$

Substitute back for x:

$3^x = 1$ or $3^x = 4$

Take logs:

$\log 3^x = \log 1$ or $\log 3^x = \log 4$

Use the power law:

$x \log 3 = 0$ or $x \log 3 = \log 4$

$x = 0$ or $x = \dfrac{\log 4}{\log 3}$

$x = 0$ or $x = 1.26 \,(3 \text{ s.f.})$

(b) Let $y = e^x$.

Then: $y^2 - 6y + 5 = 0$

$(y - 1)(y - 5) = 0$

$y = 1$ or $y = 5$

Substitute back for x:

$e^x = 5$ or $\ln e^x = \ln 1$

Take logs:

$\ln e^x = \ln 1$ or $\ln e^x = \ln 5$

Use the power law:

$x \ln e = 0$ or $x \ln e = \ln 5$

$\Rightarrow x = 0$ or $x = \ln 5$

> **Note:** Exact answers are required, so we don't give a rounded decimal for the second solution.

Sometimes in an equation involving logarithms the unknown may be in the base. Again, combine all logarithm terms into a single term.

Worked Example

25. Solve: $2 \log_x 2 + 3 \log_x 4 = 4$

$\log_x 2^2 + \log_x 4^3 = 4$ (power law)

$\log_x 4 + \log_x 64 = 4$

$\log_x(4 \times 64) = 4$ (addition law)

$\log_x(256) = 4$

$x^4 = 256$

$x = \sqrt[4]{256} = 4$

You may have to solve simultaneous equations. Eliminate logarithms from both equations as a first step.

Worked Example

26. Solve the following simultaneous equations, giving your answers as simplified surds.

$\log_4 x + \log_4 y = 2$ (1)

$\log_9 x - \log_9 y = \dfrac{1}{2}$ (2)

First consider equation (1):

$\Rightarrow \log_4 xy = 2$

$\Rightarrow 4^2 = xy$

$\Rightarrow y = \dfrac{16}{x}$

Now consider equation (2):

$\Rightarrow \log_9\left(\dfrac{x}{y}\right) = \dfrac{1}{2}$

$\Rightarrow 9^{1/2} = \dfrac{x}{y}$

$\Rightarrow y = \dfrac{x}{3}$

Therefore:

$\dfrac{16}{x} = \dfrac{x}{3}$

$\Rightarrow x^2 = 48$

$\Rightarrow x = 4\sqrt{3}, \quad y = \dfrac{4\sqrt{3}}{3}$

We can ignore the other solution, $x = -4\sqrt{3}$. This would not work in the original equations because the logarithm of a negative number is not defined.

If the equation involves the natural log of an unknown, take e to the power of each side.

Worked Example

27. Solve the following for x: $\dfrac{1}{3}\ln(2x - 1) = 1$

$\dfrac{1}{3}\ln(2x - 1) = 1$

$\ln(2x - 1) = 3$

Take e to the power of each side:

$2x - 1 = e^3$

$x = \dfrac{e^3 + 1}{2}$

$= 10.5 \,(3 \text{ s.f.})$

Exercise 10F

1. By forming a log equation, solve the following equations to find x. Give your answers to 3 significant figures where appropriate.

   (a) $3^x = 27$ (b) $6^x = \dfrac{1}{6}$

   (c) $10^x = 1000000000$ (d) $4^x = \dfrac{1}{2}$

   (e) $5^x = 1$ (f) $9^x = 12$ (g) $2^x = 97$

   (h) $10^x = 72$ (i) $7^x = 78$ (j) $8^x = 32$

2. Take logs of each side of the equation and use the power law to solve these equations. Give your answers to 3 significant figures where appropriate.

   (a) $4^x = 15$ (b) $2^x = 15$

   (c) $4^x = 8$ (d) $3^x = 11$

   (e) $2^x = \dfrac{1}{2}$ (f) $9^x = 0.6$

   (g) $8^x = 21$ (h) $5^x = 19$

   (i) $2 = 2^x$ (j) $\dfrac{1}{100} = 0.5^x$

3. Take logs of each side of the equation and use the power law to solve these equations. Give your answers to 3 decimal places where appropriate.

   (a) $4^{x+4} = 7^x$ (b) $3^{x+2} = 7^x$

   (c) $6^{x-4} = 2^{7x}$ (d) $4^{x-4} = 6^{3x}$

   (e) $3^{x-4} = 5^{6x}$ (f) $5^{x-2} = 4^{4x}$

   (g) $7^{x-3} = 3^{6x}$ (h) $2^{x+3} = 5^x$

   (i) $7^{x-4} = 6^{7x}$ (j) $3^{x-2} = 6^{7x}$

4. Solve the following equations. Give your answers to 3 significant figures where appropriate.

   (a) $e^x = 3$ (b) $e^x = 10.75$

   (c) $3e^x = \dfrac{3}{4}$ (d) $-e^t = -\dfrac{5}{2}$

   (e) $\ln x = 2$ (f) $\ln x + \ln 3x = \ln 12$

   (g) $\ln y + \ln(2y - 1) = 0$

5. Solve the following equations. Give exact answers where appropriate.

   (a) $e^{2x} - 3e^x + 2 = 0$

   (b) $e^{2x} - 9 = 0$

   (c) $\ln(x + 5) - \ln x = \ln 6$

6. Solve the following equation for x, giving your answer in terms of e:
   $\ln(x^2 + 5x + 6) - \ln(x^2 + 3x) = 3$

Exercise 10F...

7. By solving simultaneous equations, find the coordinates of the intersection point of the two curves $y = 5e^{3x} - 4$ and $y = 4e^{3x} - 3$.

8. Given that $\ln x = a$, find, in terms of a, the simplest form of:

   (a) $\ln(xe^4)$ (b) $\ln\left(\dfrac{x^4}{e}\right)$

   (c) Hence, or otherwise, solve:

   $$\ln(xe^4) - \ln\left(\dfrac{x^4}{e}\right) = \dfrac{1}{2}$$

   giving your answer in terms of e.

9. Find the base a in the following equations.

   (a) $\log_a 9 = 2$ (b) $\log_a 9 = 1$

   (c) $\log_a 64 = 6$ (d) $\log_a 16 = 2$

   (e) $\log_a 256 = 4$ (f) $\log_a\left(\dfrac{1}{8}\right) = -3$

   (g) $\log_a 0.01 = -2$ (h) $\log_a\left(\dfrac{1}{4}\right) = -2$

   (i) $\log_a 256 = 8$ (j) $\log_a\left(\dfrac{1}{1000000}\right) = -6$

10. Solve: $\log_4(14x + 3) - \log_4 x = 2$

11. Given that $\log_2 x = a$, find, in terms of a, the simplest form of:

    (a) $\log_2(32x)$ (b) $\log_2\left(\dfrac{x^2}{2}\right)$

    (c) Hence, or otherwise, solve:

    $$\log_2(32x) - \log_2\left(\dfrac{x^2}{2}\right) = \dfrac{1}{2}$$

    giving your answer in the simplest surd form.

12. Solve the equation $8^{x+2} = 2^{x+10}$.
    (a) By taking logs of both sides.
    (b) Using the laws of indices.
    Which method do you prefer? Is it always possible to solve equations like this using both methods?

13. (a) Using the substitution $u = 3^x$, show that the equation $9^x - 3^{x+1} - 180 = 0$ can be written in the form $u^2 - 3u - 180 = 0$.
    (b) Hence solve $9^x - 3^{x+1} - 180 = 0$ giving your answers to 2 decimal places.

14. Solve the equation:
    $2\log_4 x - \log_4 3x = 1$

15. Solve for x:
    $\log_2(x^2 + 13x + 42) - \log_2(x^2 + 6x) = 3$

Exercise 10F...

16. A savings scheme pays interest at a rate of 2% per year. Hence, after x years, the total value of an initial £1 investment is £y, where $y = 1.02^x$. Using logarithms, find the number of years it takes to double the total value of any initial investment.

17. Solve: $6\log_x 4 + 4\log_x 2 = 8$

10.7 Inequalities Involving Exponential Functions

You may have to solve an inequality in which the unknown is in the index, for example $a^x < b$.

There are many similarities between solving an inequality and solving an equation. However, multiplying or dividing both sides by a negative number will result in the inequality sign being reversed.

....

Worked Examples

28. Find the range of values of x that satisfy:
(a) $3^x < 20$ (b) $0.5^x < 20$

(a) Take logs of both sides:
$$\log 3^x < \log 20$$
$$x\log 3 < \log 20$$
$$x < \frac{\log 20}{\log 3}$$
$$x < 2.73 \ (3 \text{ s.f.})$$

(b) $\log 0.5^x < \log 20$
$$x\log 0.5 < \log 20$$
$$x > \frac{\log 20}{\log 0.5}$$
(Note: the inequality sign has been reversed because we have divided by $\log 0.5$, which is negative.)
$$x > -4.32 \ (3 \text{ s.f.})$$

29. Solve: $5^x \times 5^{2x+1} > 2000$

$$5^x \times 5^{2x+1} > 2000$$

Add the indices on the left-hand side:
$$5^{3x+1} > 2000$$
$$\log 5^{3x+1} > \log 2000$$

Use the power law, remembering to write $(3x + 1)$ in brackets:
$$(3x + 1)\log 5 > \log 2000$$

Expand brackets:
$$3x\log 5 + \log 5 > \log 2000$$
$$3x\log 5 > \log 2000 - \log 5$$
$$x > \frac{\log 2000 - \log 5}{3\log 5}$$
$$x > 1.24 \ (3 \text{ s.f.})$$

30. Solve: $\log x < 5$

$$\log x < 5$$

Take 10 to the power of each side:
$$x < 10^5$$
$$x < 100000$$

31. Find the range of values of x satisfying the following: $2^x < 3 \leq 5^x$

We split this into two inequalities: $2^x < 3$ and $3 \leq 5^x$.

First, consider $2^x < 3$:
$$x\log 2 < \log 3$$
$$x < \frac{\log 3}{\log 2}$$
$$x < 1.58 \quad (1)$$

Now, consider $3 \leq 5^x$:
$$\log 3 \leq x\log 5$$
$$x \geq \frac{\log 3}{\log 5}$$
$$x \geq 0.683 \quad (2)$$

Combining (1) and (2) gives:
$$0.683 \leq x < 1.58 \ (3 \text{ s.f.})$$

32. Solve: $\log_4 x - \log_4 x^2 < 3$

$$\log_4 x - \log_4 x^2 < 3$$
$$\log_4\left(\frac{x}{x^2}\right) < 3$$
$$\log_4\left(\frac{1}{x}\right) < 3$$

Take 4 to the power of each side:
$$\frac{1}{x} < 4^3$$
$$64x > 1$$
$$x > \frac{1}{64}$$

33. A man invests £1000 in a savings account. At the end of each year he is paid 4% interest on his balance and he does not make any withdrawals. Calculate how many full years it will take before his balance is £2000.

Use the compound interest formula, $T = P \times r^n$ where T is the total after n years; P is the principle (or starting) amount; and r is the multiplying factor, which is 1 plus the interest rate (expressed as a decimal). Since we are interested in the total exceeding £2000:

$$1000 \times 1.04^n > 2000$$

Divide by 1000:

$$1.04^n > 2$$

Take logs on both sides:

$$\log 1.04^n > \log 2$$

Using the power law:

$$n \log 1.04 > \log 2$$

$$n > \frac{\log 2}{\log 1.04}$$

$$n > \frac{\log 2}{\log 1.04}$$

$$n > 17.67 \text{ years}$$

After 18 years the balance will exceed £2000.

Exercise 10G

1. Find the range of values of x that satisfies each inequality.
   (a) $2^x < 30$
   (b) $0.4^x < 10$
   (c) $0.92^x < 0.1$
   (d) $\left(\frac{1}{4}\right)^x > 10$
   (e) $1.25^x \geq 2$
   (f) $1.5^x < 100$
   (g) $3^x \leq 27$
   (h) $10^x < 1$
   (i) $2^{-x} \geq 3$
   (j) $\left(\frac{3}{2}\right)^{-x} > 4$

2. Solve the following inequalities.
   (a) $\left(1\frac{1}{4}\right)^{-x+1} \leq 16$
   (b) $3^x \times 3^{2x} > 9$
   (c) $(4^x)^2 < 5$
   (d) $\left(\frac{1}{2}\right)^3 \times \left(\frac{1}{2}\right)^x \geq 9$

3. Find the range of values of x that satisfy the following.
   (a) $2^x < 3 < 7^x$
   (b) $3^{x+1} < \frac{7}{2} < 3^{x+2}$
   (c) $4 < 3^x < 9$
   (d) $1 < 2^{-x} < 2$

4. A pendulum is held 64 cm from its equilibrium position and then released. On its first swing it reaches three quarters of this distance from the equilibrium position, and on the next swing three quarters of this distance, and so on. Find how many full swings it takes for the pendulum's swing to be less than 10 cm.

10.8 Exponential Growth and Decay

You will often see questions involving **exponential growth or decay**.

Exponential growth is a relationship of the form $y = y_0 a^{kt}$.

Exponential decay is a relationship of the form $y = y_0 a^{-kt}$.

In both cases, the value of y depends on its initial value y_0 and time t. k is a positive constant. a is also a positive constant and is often, but not always, e.

You will usually find the values of the constants k and y_0 in the question. These will then be used to find the value of y at a particular time.

Worked Example

34. After being released onto an island, the population P of a group of beetles grows exponentially according to the formula $P = P_0 e^{kt}$ where P_0 is the initial population, k is a constant and t is the time from release in days.
    (a) Given that the population of beetles doubles within three days, show that the value of k is 0.23105 to 5 decimal places.
    (b) Calculate how long it will take for the population to reach 3 times its initial size.
    (c) Given the initial population of beetles is 10, calculate the number of beetles on the island after 5 days.
    (d) Sketch a graph of the number of beetles on the island against time in days.
    (e) Do you think this model could be used to predict the number of beetles on the island in 2 months' time? Explain your answer.

(a) $\dfrac{P}{P_0} = e^{kt}$

   When $t = 3$, $P = 2P_0$

   $\therefore 2 = e^{3k}$

   $3k = \ln 2$

   $k = \dfrac{1}{3} \ln 2 = 0.23105 \,(5 \text{ d.p.})$

(b) $\dfrac{P}{P_0} = e^{kt}$

   When population has trebled, $P = 3P_0$

   $\therefore 3 = e^{kt}$

   $3 = e^{0.23105t}$

   $0.23105t = \ln 3$

   $t = \dfrac{\ln 3}{0.23105} = 4.75 \text{ days } (3 \text{ s.f.})$

(c) $P = P_0 e^{kt}$

$P = 10e^{(0.23105)(5)}$

$P = 31.75$

32 beetles

> **Note:** In an exam question, 31 or 32 may be accepted, provided there were no mistakes in the working.

(d)

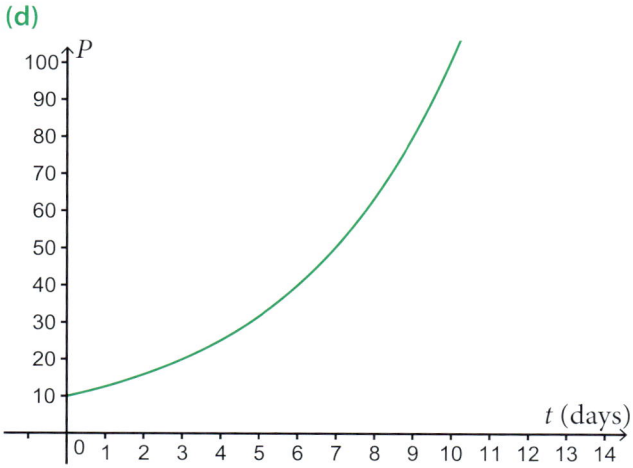

(e) No, the model is only suitable for the first few days. Other factors, such as finite food resources, will prevent the beetle population rising exponentially indefinitely.

Example 34 contains an example of a **discrete** variable rising exponentially. A discrete variable is one that can only take particular values. In this case, the number of beetles can take an integer value (a whole number), but cannot take an intermediate value, such as 2.4. Another example of a discrete variable is a scoring system that takes values of 0.1, 0.2, 0.3, … up to 1.0.

A **continuous** variable is one that can take any value within a range, for example a height or weight.

You will be asked questions about exponential growth and decay involving both discrete and continuous variables.

Exponential growth rarely continues indefinitely. There are usually limiting factors that mean it applies only for a certain amount of time.

Exponential decay, however, may continue indefinitely. When a material undergoes radioactive decay, for example, the number of radioactive particles halves in a certain time, then halves again, and so on. (The time taken for the number of particles to halve is called the half-life of the substance.) In theory, the number of radioactive particles never reaches zero.

Worked Example

35. After an explosion at a nuclear power plant, an area of land is contaminated with radioactive material. Scientists estimate that the concentration C of radioactive particles will fall according to an exponential decay formula: $C = C_0 e^{-kt}$ where C_0 is the initial concentration (immediately after the explosion), t is the time in years and k is a positive constant.

(a) After 4 years, the concentration of particles is ⅓ of the initial concentration. Show that $k = 0.275$ to 3 significant figures.

(b) Hence find the half-life of this particular radioactive material, giving your answer in years to 3 significant figures.

(c) Find what percentage of the initial concentration remains after 4 years.

(d) The initial concentration of particles was measured as 100 000 particles per square metre. Find the number of particles per square metre expected to remain after 10 years.

(e) The area will be declared safe when the concentration reaches 1% of its initial concentration. How long will this take? Give your answer in years to 3 significant figures.

(a) $\qquad C = C_0 e^{-kt}$

When $t = 4$, $\ C = \dfrac{1}{3}C_0$

$\dfrac{1}{3}C_0 = C_0 e^{-4k}$

$\dfrac{1}{3} = e^{-4k}$

Take logs of both sides:

$\ln\left(\dfrac{1}{3}\right) = -4k$

$k = -\dfrac{1}{4}\ln\left(\dfrac{1}{3}\right)$

$k = 0.27465\ …$

$k = 0.275$ (3 s.f.)

(b) The half-life is the time taken for C to become half of its initial value, i.e. the time at which $C = \dfrac{1}{2}C_0$:

$\qquad C = C_0 e^{-kt}$

$\dfrac{1}{2}C_0 = C_0 e^{-0.275t}$

$\dfrac{1}{2} = e^{-0.275t}$

Take logs of both sides:

$$\ln\left(\frac{1}{2}\right) = -0.275t$$

$$t = -\frac{1}{0.275}\ln\left(\frac{1}{2}\right)$$

$$t = 2.52 \text{ years}$$

(c) $C = C_0 e^{-kt}$

When $t = 4$:

$C = C_0 e^{-0.275 \times 4}$

$C = 0.332 C_0$

So 33.2% of the radiation remains after 4 years. (3 s.f.)

(d) We must find C when $t = 10$.

$C = C_0 e^{-kt}$

$C = 100000 e^{-10 \times 0.275}$

$C = 6390$ (3 s.f.)

(e) We must find t when $C = \frac{1}{100}C_0$.

$$C = C_0 e^{-kt}$$

$$\frac{1}{100}C_0 = C_0 e^{-0.275t}$$

$$\frac{1}{100} = e^{-0.275t}$$

$$\ln\left(\frac{1}{100}\right) = -0.275t$$

$$t = -\frac{1}{0.275}\ln\left(\frac{1}{100}\right)$$

$$t = 16.7 \text{ years (3 s.f.)}$$

Exercise 10H

1. Every pound invested in a savings scheme gains interest at a rate of 7% per year. Hence, after t years, the total value of an initial investment of £S_0 is £S, where $S = S_0 \times 1.07^t$.
   (a) Calculate, to the nearest pound, the total value of an initial £800 investment after 14 years.
   (b) Use logarithms to find the number of full years it takes to double the total value of any initial investment.

2. A patient takes a dose of the drug Trippozine. The amount D of the drug remaining in her blood after time t hours is given by the exponential decay equation: $D = D_0 e^{-kt}$ where D_0 is the initial amount and k is a positive constant.
   (a) After 3 hours the amount of the drug remaining in the patient's blood is 75% of the initial amount. Show that $k = 0.0959$ to 3 significant figures.

Exercise 10H

   (b) Hence find how long it takes for the amount of the drug remaining in her blood to come down to 50% of the initial amount.
   (c) Find what percentage of the drug remains in the patient's blood after one day.

3. A star explodes in a supernova. After t hours, the radius of the star r can be modelled using the formula: $r = r_0 e^{at}$ where r_0 is the initial radius and a is a constant.
   (a) Given that the star's radius is doubling every four hours, calculate the value of a to 3 significant figures.
   (b) Find, to the nearest minute, how long it will take for the star to become 5 times its original size.
   (c) Given the initial radius of the star is 10^9 m, calculate its radius after 1 day.
   (d) Sketch a graph of the radius of the star against time in hours.
   (e) Do you think this model could be used to predict the radius of the star 1 month after the supernova event?

4. After running a bath, a man forgets to get into it for 20 minutes. Its temperature cools according to the equation: $T = A + (T_0 - A)e^{-at}$ where T_0 is the initial temperature in degrees Celsius, A is the constant air temperature in the bathroom, a is a constant and t is the time in minutes after the bath was run.
   (a) Using the variable D to denote the difference in temperature between the bath water and the air temperature, and the variable D_0 to denote the initial value of this difference, express D in terms of D_0, a and t.
   (b) The difference between the bath water temperature and the air temperature has halved by the time the man gets into the bath. Find the value of a.
   (c) Given that the air temperature is 20 °C and the initial temperature of the bath water was 38 °C, calculate the temperature of the bath water 5 minutes after the man gets into the bath, correct to 1 decimal place.
   (d) The man gets out of the bath when the temperature of the water reaches 26°C. Calculate, to the nearest minute, how long after running the bath he gets out.
   (e) Sketch the graph of T against t.

Exercise 10H...

5. A man buys some meat and puts it into his refrigerator. It contains low levels of bacteria, but these bacteria could potentially cause food poisoning if allowed to multiply to a certain level. The number of bacteria can be approximated using the equation:
    $$N = N_0 e^{pt} \qquad (1)$$
    where N_0 is the initial number of bacteria, p is a constant and t is the time in hours.
    (a) When it is purchased, the meat contains 10 000 bacteria. Given that this number doubles after 2 days, show that $p = \dfrac{\ln 2}{48}$.
    (b) After 2 days, the man cooks the piece of meat. Cooking the meat reduces the number of bacteria by 90%. He then freezes it. While the meat is frozen, the bacteria multiply according to the equation:
    $$N = N_0 e^{qt} \qquad (2)$$
    where $q = \dfrac{p}{100}$.
    How many bacteria are present in the meat when it is removed from the freezer after 4 weeks? Give your answer to 3 significant figures.
    (c) After defrosting, the bacteria population can again be modelled using equation (1). The number of bacteria that could cause food poisoning is thought to be 25 000. For how long after defrosting the meat will it be safe to eat? Give your answer as a whole number of days.

6. The populations of two different species of deer on an island are given by: $P_1 = 2000(1 - e^{-kt})$ and: $P_2 = 5000e^{-kt}$.
    (a) Sketch the graphs of the two populations on the same axes, giving the equations of any asymptotes.
    (b) What does the model predict about the long-term behaviour of these two populations?
    (c) The two populations compete for food and space, but one species of deer is more successful. Make a comment about the model.

Exercise 10H...

7. A population of hedgehogs is introduced into a park. The population P at time t years after the hedgehogs have been introduced is modelled by the equation: $P = \dfrac{2681d^t}{6 + d^t}$ where d is a constant.
    Given that there are 720 hedgehogs in the park after 6 years:
    (a) Calculate, to 4 decimal places, the value of d.
    (b) Predict the number of years needed for the population to increase from 720 to 1390.

10.9 Summary

You should learn the shape of the exponential curve $y = a^x$ and be familiar with its key points:

*   The x-axis is an asymptote; the curve approaches this asymptote as the value of x decreases.
*   The greater the value of a, the steeper the curve.
*   For positive values of x, the curve $y = a^x$ rises more and more steeply.
*   The curves cross the y-axis at $(0, 1)$.
*   The curve $y = a^{-x}$ is a reflection in the y-axis of $y = a^x$.

You can apply the usual transformations to the curve $y = a^x$: translation in both x and y directions, stretching in both x and y directions, reflections in both x and y axes.

Logarithms are the inverse of the exponential function:

* $y = a^x \Leftrightarrow x = \log_a y$
* $y = e^x \Leftrightarrow x = \ln y$

You should know how to use your calculator to calculate logs to any base.

There are three important laws for combining logarithms:

*   Addition law: $\log_a x + \log_a y = \log_a(xy)$
*   Subtraction law: $\log_a x - \log_a y = \log_a\left(\dfrac{x}{y}\right)$
*   Power law: $n \log_a x = \log_a x^n$

You can use logarithms to solve equations and inequalities with the unknown as the power, for example $3^x = 2^{\frac{1}{x}}$.

The curve $y = e^x$ is one member of the family of curves $y = a^x$. The gradient of the curve $y = e^x$ is always equal to the y-value.

e is an irrational number. Its value is just over 2.71.

Transformations of the graphs of $y = e^x$ and $y = \ln x$ are performed using the usual rules for transformations.

Equations involving e^x can be solved by taking natural logs of each side.

Equations involving $\ln x$ can be solved by taking e to the power of each side.

You may need to re-arrange either type of equation before performing these operations, e.g. solve a quadratic equation involving e^x.

Exponential growth is a relationship of the form $y = y_0 a^{kt}$.

Exponential decay is a relationship of the form $y = y_0 a^{-kt}$.

In both cases, the value of y depends on its initial value y_0 and time t. a and k are both positive constants, with the value of a often being e.

Chapter 11
Differentiation

11.1 Introduction

What is differentiation?

Differentiation is a technique used to find the **gradient** of a curve at any point.

The gradient of a curve can also be interpreted as a **rate of change**. For example, if you have a graph of velocity against time, differentiation will give you the rate of change of velocity, or acceleration.

In Chapter 2 we discussed **quadratic** curves. You learnt to solve a quadratic equation using the method called **completing the square**. You were also shown that this technique could help you to find the **turning point** of a quadratic curve.

In this chapter you will learn a more advanced way to find the turning points of any curve using **differentiation**. This will, of course, help you when sketching curves. But there is much more to differentiation than that. You will use the techniques learnt here in a wide variety of mathematics and possibly beyond.

Differentiation is a part of the area of mathematics called **calculus**. At first, these new techniques may seem strange. In fact, calculus may be the most important part of mathematics you will ever learn!

Key words

- **Calculus**: The area of mathematics that includes differentiation.
- **Gradient**: The steepness of a curve at any point.
- **Derivative / gradient function**: A function that allows you to calculate the gradient at any point on a curve.
- **Differentiate**: To find the gradient function.
- **Turning point / stationary point**: A point on a curve where the gradient is zero.
- **Tangent**: A straight line that touches a curve at a point, but does not cross it.
- **Normal**: A straight line at right angles to a tangent, intersecting the tangent at the point where it touches the curve.
- **Increasing**: A function is increasing if its gradient is positive in a certain interval.

- **Decreasing**: A function is decreasing if its gradient is negative in a certain interval.

Before you start

You should know:

- How to manipulate indices.
- How to use the rules of algebraic manipulation.
- How to sketch curves.
- How to solve inequalities.

Worked Examples

1. Write $(x^3)\sqrt{x}$ as x^n where n a fraction.

   The square root is equivalent to the power of a half:
   $(x^3)\sqrt{x} = x^3 x^{1/2}$

   Using the rules of indices, add the powers:
   $$= x^{3+1/2}$$
   $$= x^{7/2}$$

2. Write the following as the sum of two powers of x:
   $$\frac{x^4 + x^2}{\sqrt{x}}$$

   $$\frac{x^4 + x^2}{\sqrt{x}} = \frac{x^4}{\sqrt{x}} + \frac{x^2}{\sqrt{x}}$$
   $$= \frac{x^4}{x^{1/2}} + \frac{x^2}{x^{1/2}}$$

   Using the rules of indices, subtract the powers:
   $$= x^{7/2} + x^{3/2}$$

3. Simplify the following: $(x^2 + 2x - 3) - (3x - 1)$

   $$(x^2 + 2x - 3) - (3x - 1) = x^2 + 2x - 3 - 3x + 1$$
   $$= x^2 - x - 2$$

4. Sketch the curve $y = (x - 1)^3$, marking the coordinates of the point at which the curve is flat and the point where the curve intersects the y-axis.

   The curve is based on the cubic $y = x^3$. It is translated by 1 unit in the positive x-direction.

   Recall the curve $y = x^3$ is flat at the origin. Hence the point at which the curve $y = (x - 1)^3$ is flat is $(1, 0)$.

To find the coordinates of the point where the curve crosses the y-axis, set $x = 0$:

$$y = (0 - 1)^3$$
$$= -1$$

We now have enough information to draw a sketch of the curve:

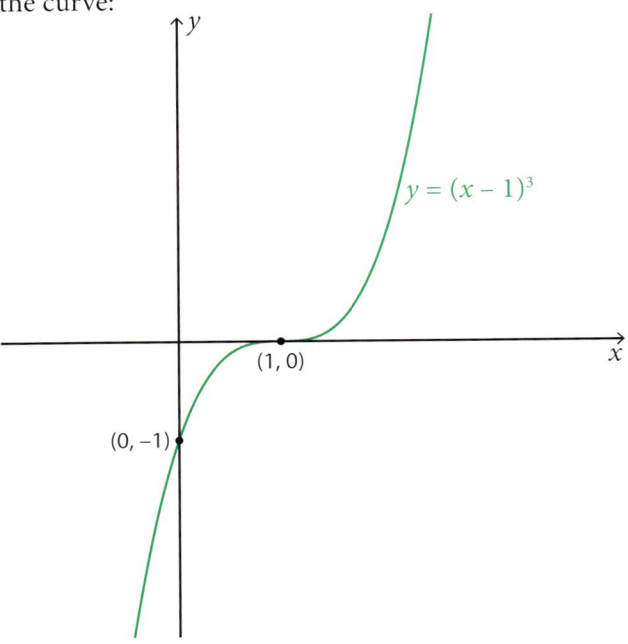

5. Find the range of values of x that make $x(x + 9) < 0$.

First sketch the curve $y = x(x + 9)$:

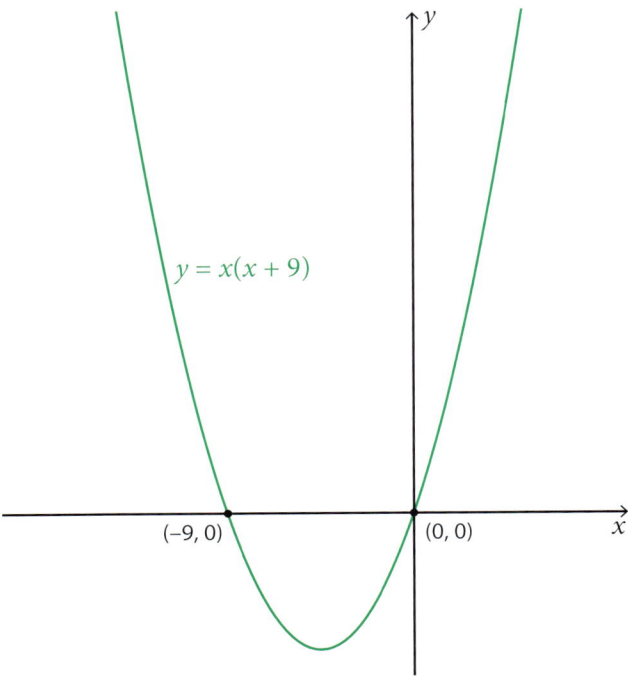

From this we can see that $x(x + 9) < 0$ when x is between -9 and 0. So we write $-9 < x < 0$.

What you will learn

In this chapter you will learn how to:

- Find the derivative function.
- Differentiate expressions involving x^n.
- Solve problems involving rates of change.
- Find second order derivatives.
- Find the gradient of the tangent to a curve at any point.
- Find the equations of tangents and normals.
- Find the maximum and minimum points (turning or stationary points) of curves.
- Investigate whether functions are increasing or decreasing.

In the real world...

Differentiation is calculating a **rate of change**. This includes calculating acceleration, since it is the rate of change of velocity. Calculating acceleration is easy when it is constant, but when it is variable, differentiation becomes essential.

Aircraft pilots are one group of people who need to have precise measurements of acceleration. They need to know their exact acceleration on the runway, because without enough acceleration, they would not be able to take off.

Differentiation is used in many, diverse areas. Geographers use differentiation to work out how quickly populations are changing. Engineers use it to model flows within pipes. Biologists use it to study changes in the populations of species. Investment banks are using derivative products in increasingly sophisticated ways.

Calculus, discovered by Isaac Newton and Gottfried Leibniz, is arguably the greatest mathematical innovation in all of human history.

Exercise 11A (Revision)

1. Find the simplest way to write the following algebraic expressions.
    (a) $(2x - 1) - (3x - 1)$
    (b) $(x^2 + 4x - 3) - (2x + 1)$
    (c) $(x - 1)^2 + (x + 1)^2$
    (d) $(1 - x) - (1 - x^2) + (1 - x^3)$
    (e) $2x(1 - x) + 6x(x - 1)$

Exercise 11A...

2. Write the following in the form x^n.

    (a) $x^2 x$ (b) $\dfrac{x^2}{x^{1/2}}$ (c) $\dfrac{\sqrt{x}}{x^3}$

    (d) $\dfrac{x^{-1/2}}{\sqrt{x}}$ (e) $\dfrac{x^{1/2}}{\sqrt{x}}$

3. Write the following as sums of powers of x.

    (a) $(1 - x)(1 + x^2)$

    (b) $\dfrac{x^{-1} + x^2}{x^3}$

    (c) $x(x - 1)(4x + 1)$

    (d) $\dfrac{2x^2 + 5x^{-2}}{\sqrt{x}}$

    (e) $\dfrac{(1 + x)(1 - x)}{x^2}$

4. Sketch the following curves.

    (a) $y = \dfrac{3}{x}$ (b) $y = \dfrac{1}{x^2}$

    (c) $y = 2x^3$ (d) $y = (x + 2)^3$

5. Find the values of x for which:

    (a) $(x + 1)(x - 3) < 0$

    (b) $x(x + 9) > 0$

    (c) $2x^2 + x - 1 > 0$

    (d) $2x^2 - 18 < 0$

11.2 The Gradient of the Tangent to a Curve

The derivative of $f(x)$ as the gradient of the tangent

Consider how would you work out the gradient of a curve at a point. You already know how to work out the gradient of a straight line, using the formula:

$$m = \frac{rise}{run} = \frac{y_1 - y_0}{x_1 - x_0}$$

You could draw a tangent to the curve at the point and calculate the gradient using this formula. The curve would have the same gradient as the tangent:

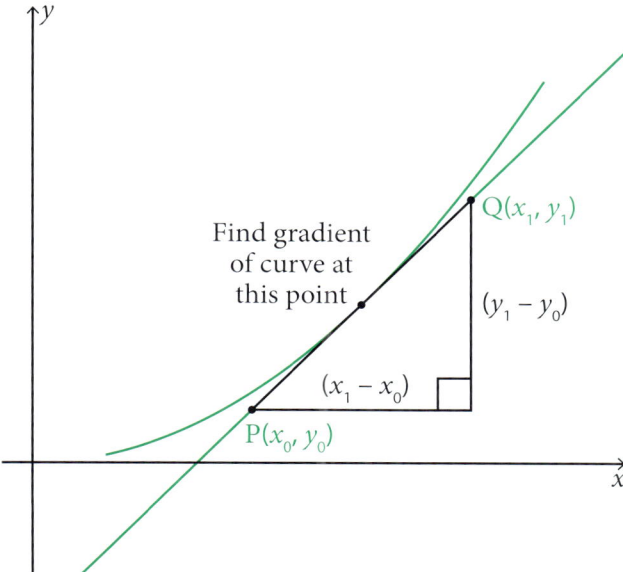

However, there are problems with this method:

- You need to plot the curve to find the gradient.
- There may be inaccuracies in your measurements.

The gradient of the tangent as a limit

Another technique to find the gradient of a curve uses two points close together on the curve.

Suppose we require the gradient of the curve at the point $P(x_0, y_0)$. Consider the point $P(x_0, y_0)$ and another point nearby on the curve, $Q(x_1, y_1)$. A chord between these two points would have approximately the same gradient as the curve at point P:

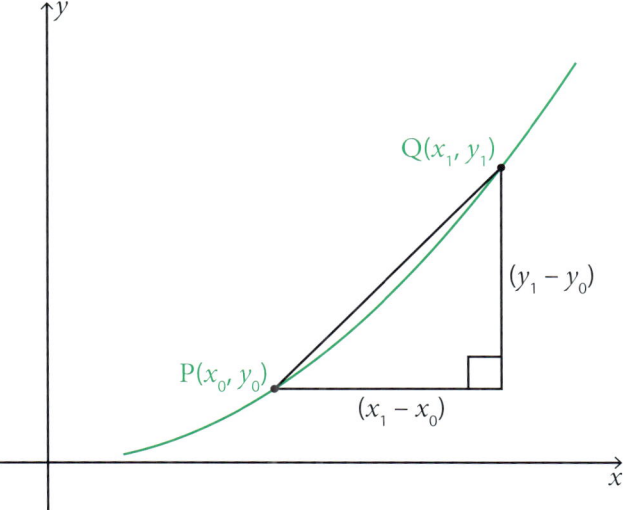

You can see that the gradient of the line PQ is:

$$m = \frac{rise}{run} = \frac{y_1 - y_0}{x_1 - x_0}$$

We can use this as an approximation of the gradient of the curve at P.

The approximation becomes better when the distance PQ becomes smaller:

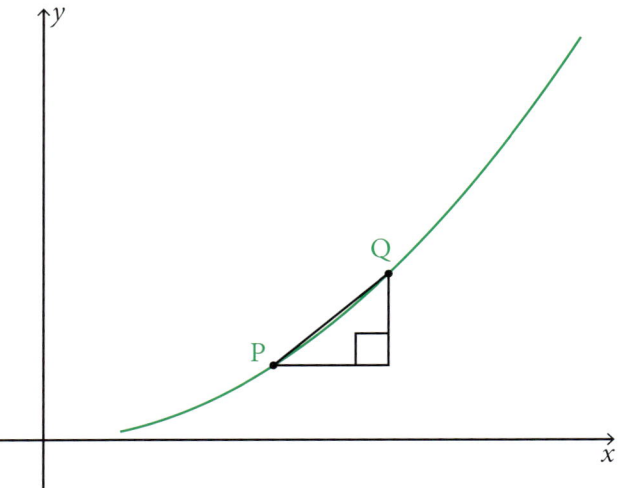

When Q moves closer to P you can see that the gradient of the chord PQ is a better approximation of the gradient of the curve. The closer points P and Q become, the better the approximation becomes.

> As Q approaches P, the gradient of the chord PQ approaches the gradient of the curve.

This technique is known as the **method of small increments**. We can use it to estimate the gradient of a curve at a point.

Worked Example

6. Consider the curve $y = x^2$. By considering smaller and smaller chords, estimate the gradient at point P(1, 1).

    For the point Q, use the following values for x_1 and calculate the y-coordinate y_1.

    $x_1 = 2, 1.1, 1.01, 1.001$

    We draw up the following table, using the equation $y = x^2$ to calculate our y_1 values from the x_1 values given:

x_0	y_0	x_1	y_1	$m = \dfrac{y_1 - y_0}{x_1 - x_0}$
1	1	2	4	3
1	1	1.1	1.21	2.1
1	1	1.01	1.0201	2.01
1	1	1.001	1.002001	2.001

We can see that as our chord gets smaller, our estimate of the gradient m gets closer to 2. This

indicates that the gradient of the curve at (1, 1) is 2.

11.3 Differentiation of Powers of x

In this section, you will learn how to find the **derivative** or **gradient function** for functions of the form $y = x^n$.

The derivative will usually be a function of x. It can be used to calculate the gradient *at any point* on the curve.

Notation

We use the notation $\dfrac{dy}{dx}$ or $f'(x)$ for the derivative.

We usually use $\dfrac{dy}{dx}$ if the original equation involves y.

We would use $f'(x)$ if the original equation is given using function notation: $f(x) = \cdots$. Throughout the rest of this chapter both notations will be used.

Differentiation of x^n

The general rule is:

$$y = x^n \Rightarrow \frac{dy}{dx} = nx^{n-1}$$

Also, a multiplying constant will not affect the differentiation:

$$y = ax^n \Rightarrow \frac{dy}{dx} = anx^{n-1}$$

A proof of these results is beyond the scope of this book, but for the interested reader there are many textbooks that do include a derivation from first principles.

In A-level mathematics, you will not be asked to find a derivative from first principles. Instead, you will use the formula above.

Worked Example

7. Find the gradient function $\dfrac{dy}{dx}$ for the following.

   (a) $y = x^2$ (b) $y = x^3$ (c) $y = x^4$

(a) $y = x^2 \Rightarrow \dfrac{dy}{dx} = 2x$

(b) $y = x^3 \Rightarrow \dfrac{dy}{dx} = 3x^2$

(c) $y = x^4 \Rightarrow \dfrac{dy}{dx} = 4x^3$

---

8. Find the derivative $f'(x)$ when $f(x) = 3x^2$.

$f'(x) = 6x$

---

9. Find $\dfrac{dy}{dx}$ when:

   (a) $y = 4x$ (b) $y = 4$ (c) $y = \dfrac{4}{x}$

(a) $y = 4x^1$

   $\dfrac{dy}{dx} = 4x^0$

   $\dfrac{dy}{dx} = 4$

   This result was expected. We know that the straight line $y = 4x$ has a gradient of 4.

(b) $y = 4x^0$

   $\dfrac{dy}{dx} = 0 \times 4x^{-1}$

   $\dfrac{dy}{dx} = 0$

   This result was also expected. We know that any horizontal line, such as $y = 4$ has a gradient of 0.

> **Note:** Differentiating a constant will always give 0.

(c) $y = 4x^{-1}$

   $\dfrac{dy}{dx} = -4x^{-2}$

   $\dfrac{dy}{dx} = -\dfrac{4}{x^2}$

---

10. A curve has equation $y = 3x^{2/3}$.

   (a) Find $\dfrac{dy}{dx}$.

   (b) Find the gradient of the curve at the point (8, 12).

---

a) $y = 3x^{2/3}$

   Multiply by the power and reduce the power by 1:

   $\dfrac{dy}{dx} = \dfrac{2}{3} \times 3x^{-1/3}$

   $\dfrac{dy}{dx} = 2x^{-1/3}$ or $\dfrac{dy}{dx} = \dfrac{2}{\sqrt[3]{x}}$

(b) When $x = 8$:

$\dfrac{dy}{dx} = \dfrac{2}{\sqrt[3]{8}}$

$\dfrac{dy}{dx} = \dfrac{2}{2}$

$\dfrac{dy}{dx} = 1$

At the point (8, 12) the curve has a gradient of 1.

....

Exercise 11C

1. Find the derivative $\dfrac{dy}{dx}$ for each of the following.

   (a) $y = 3x^2$ (b) $y = 2x$ (c) $y = -7x$

   (d) $y = 2x^5$ (e) $y = \dfrac{3}{7}x^7$ (f) $y = -2x^3$

   (g) $y = -\dfrac{5x}{4}$ (h) $y = \dfrac{1}{3}x^{-3}$

2. By rewriting these equations in the form $y = ax^n$, differentiate to find $\dfrac{dy}{dx}$.

   (a) $y = \dfrac{1}{x}$ (b) $y = \sqrt{x}$ (c) $y = \dfrac{1}{\sqrt{x}}$

   (d) $y = x\sqrt{x}$ (e) $y = \dfrac{1}{x\sqrt{x}}$ (f) $y = -\dfrac{2}{x^2}$

   (g) $y = \dfrac{2}{3x\sqrt{x}}$ (h) $y = -\dfrac{3}{\sqrt[3]{x}}$

3. Find the gradient of each curve at the point given.

   (a) $y = 3x$; $(-1, -3)$ (b) $y = x^2$; $(2, 4)$

   (c) $y = \dfrac{1}{x}$; $(2, 0.5)$ (d) $y = \sqrt{x}$; $(4, 2)$

   (e) $y = \dfrac{4}{\sqrt{x}}$; $(4, 2)$ (f) $y = -\dfrac{4}{x^2}$; $(2, -1)$

   (g) $y = \dfrac{5}{3x\sqrt{x}}$; $\left(4, \dfrac{5}{24}\right)$

   (h) $y = \dfrac{24}{\sqrt[3]{x}}$; $(8, 12)$

4. Consider $y = x^2$.

   (a) What is the derivative $\dfrac{dy}{dx}$?

   (b) What happens to $\dfrac{dy}{dx}$ when x approaches infinity? (Hint: try putting some very large values of x into your expression for $\dfrac{dy}{dx}$.)

Exercise 11C...

(c) What happens to $\frac{dy}{dx}$ when x approaches negative infinity?

5. Consider $y = x^3$.

(a) What is the derivative $\frac{dy}{dx}$?

(b) What happens to $\frac{dy}{dx}$ when x approaches infinity?

(c) What happens to $\frac{dy}{dx}$ when x approaches negative infinity?

(d) How does your answer to part (c) differ from your answer to question 4 part (c)? How do these results relate to the graphs of the two curves?

6. Given $y = 8\sqrt{x}$, show that $2x\left(\frac{dy}{dx}\right)^2 - y\frac{dy}{dx} = 0$.

Differentiation of sums and differences

When differentiating a sum of powers of x, we simply differentiate each term in turn.

If $y = f(x) + g(x)$, then $\frac{dy}{dx} = f'(x) + g'(x)$.

Worked Example

11. Find $\frac{dy}{dx}$ when $y = x^2 + 3x + 1$.

Differentiating x^2 gives $2x$.

Differentiating $3x$ gives 3.

Differentiating 1 gives 0.

So: $\frac{dy}{dx} = 2x + 3$

Note: Remember that differentiating a constant gives zero.

Multiply out brackets before differentiating.

Worked Example

12. $f(x) = (x + 3)(x - 2)$. Find $f'(x)$.

Expanding brackets: $f(x) = x^2 + x - 6$

So: $f'(x) = 2x + 1$.

Sometimes you will need to differentiate with respect to a variable other than x.

Worked Example

13. (a) $y = 4t^3 + 3t^4$. Find $\frac{dy}{dt}$.

(b) Find $f'(\theta)$ when $f(\theta) = \theta^2 - \theta^3$.

(a) Differentiate with respect to t:
$$\frac{dy}{dt} = 12t^2 + 12t^3$$

(b) Differentiate with respect to θ:
$$f'(\theta) = 2\theta - 3\theta^2$$

Exercise 11D

1. Differentiate the following with respect to x.

(a) $y = 3x^2 + 4x$ (b) $y = 3x^4 - x$

(c) $y = \dfrac{1}{x} + \dfrac{4}{x^2}$ (d) $y = \dfrac{x}{3} + \dfrac{x^2}{4}$

(e) $y = (x - 3)(x - 1)$

(f) $y = x^2(x + 3)$

(g) $y = x^2(x^2 - x + 1)$

(h) $y = (1 + x^2)(x^2 - 1)$

(i) $y = \sqrt{x} + 3x$ (j) $y = \dfrac{1 - \sqrt{x}}{x}$

(k) $y = \sqrt{x}(2x - 1)$ (l) $y = \dfrac{1}{\sqrt{x}}(1 - x^2)$

2. Differentiate the following equations with respect to the variable on the right-hand side of the equation.

(a) $y = 4t^2 + 3t$ (b) $P = v^2 - \dfrac{1}{v}$

(c) $v = 3 + 10t$ (d) $s = t + 5t^2$

(e) $p = \dfrac{1}{q}(q - 1)$ (f) $W = \sqrt{x}(x^2 - 1)$

(g) $A = (1 - s)(2s - 1)$

(h) $z = \dfrac{\theta^4 - \theta^2}{\theta^3}$

(i) $m = (n^2 + 1)(3n - 2)$

(j) $A = \pi r^2$ (Note: π is a constant.)

3. Find $f'(x)$ given $f(x)$ in each case:

(a) $f(x) = 1 - 2x^2$ (b) $f(x) = \dfrac{1 - x}{x}$

(c) $f(x) = \dfrac{4x^4 - x^3}{x^2}$ (d) $f(x) = \dfrac{x^2 + 2}{x}$

(e) $f(x) = \dfrac{(x - 2)^2}{x}$ (f) $f(x) = \dfrac{1 - \sqrt{x}}{\sqrt{x}}$

(g) $f(x) = (x - 2)(2x - 1)$

Exercise 11D...

(h) $f(x) = x(2x^2 - x)$

(i) $f(x) = \sqrt{x} + x\sqrt{x} + x$

(j) $f(x) = \dfrac{px^2 + qx}{r}$

(Note: p, q and r are constants.)

4. Given $f(x) = 3x + 2$ and $g(x) = x^2$:
   (a) Find $f'(x)$
   (b) Find $g'(x)$
   (c) Find $f'(x)g'(x)$
   (d) Find $\dfrac{f'(x)}{g'(x)}$
   (e) Work out $h(x)$ where $h(x) = f(x)g(x)$
   (f) Find $h'(x)$
   (g) Does $h'(x) = f'(x)g'(x)$?
   (h) Work out $j(x)$ where $j(x) = \dfrac{f(x)}{g(x)}$.
   (i) Find $j'(x)$
   (j) Does $j'(x) = \dfrac{f'(x)}{g'(x)}$?

5. Match each of the functions with the correct derivative from the table below.

Derivatives	$9x^2$	x^2	$-\dfrac{10}{x^3}$	$10x$	$2x - 1$

   (a) $\dfrac{1}{3}x^3$
   (b) $(x + 1)(x - 2)$
   (c) $3x^3$
   (d) $\dfrac{5}{x^2}$
   (e) $5x^2$

11.4 Differentiation as a Rate of Change

In the previous section, you learnt how to work out the derivative for various functions. You learnt that the derivative measures the gradient of the curve, when one variable is plotted against another.

However, there is another interpretation of the derivative: the rate at which one variable is changing with respect to the other. For example, if A is the surface area of a sphere and r its radius, then $\dfrac{dA}{dr}$ is the rate at which the surface area changes with respect to the radius. In other words it represents how much the surface area is changing for each change of one unit in the radius.

Rate of change questions often involve displacement, velocity, acceleration and time.

Velocity is the rate of change of displacement with respect to time, i.e. $v = \dfrac{ds}{dt}$.

Acceleration is the rate of change of velocity with respect to time, i.e. $a = \dfrac{dv}{dt}$.

....

Worked Examples

14. The velocity of a ball is governed by the equation:
$$v = \dfrac{12}{t} + 6t$$
    where t is the time between 1 and 3 seconds.
    (a) Acceleration is the rate of change of velocity with respect to time. Differentiate v to find an equation for the acceleration of the ball.
    (b) When $t = 1$, is the ball accelerating or decelerating?
    (c) When $t = 2$, is the ball accelerating or decelerating?

    (a) $\dfrac{dv}{dt} = -\dfrac{12}{t^2} + 6$

    (b) When $t = 1$, $\dfrac{dv}{dt} = -\dfrac{12}{1^2} + 6 = -6$
    The acceleration is negative, so the ball is decelerating.

    (c) When $t = 2$, $\dfrac{dv}{dt} = -\dfrac{12}{2^2} + 6 = 3$
    The acceleration is positive, so the ball is accelerating.

15. Consider a circle, which is increasing in size. What is the rate of change of the area with respect to the radius when the radius is:
    (a) 1 cm
    (b) 2 cm
    (c) 3 cm?

    The formula for the area of a circle is $A = \pi r^2$. Differentiate with respect to r:
    $$\dfrac{dA}{dr} = 2\pi r \text{ (remember } \pi \text{ is a constant)}.$$
    (a) When $r = 1$, $\dfrac{dA}{dr} = 2\pi \approx 6.28$.
    (b) When $r = 2$, $\dfrac{dA}{dr} = 4\pi \approx 12.57$.
    (c) When $r = 3$, $\dfrac{dA}{dr} = 6\pi \approx 18.85$.

    In other words, the area changes at a smaller rate when the radius is small, and a higher rate as the radius increases.

    When the radius is 3 cm, the area increases by about 18.85 cm² every time the radius increases by 1 cm.

16. A box in the shape of a cube increases in size.
  (a) If each side of the cube has length x cm, and the volume of the box is V cm³, write down an equation linking the volume and side length.
  (b) Differentiate to find an equation for the rate of change of the volume with respect to the side length.
  (c) What is the rate of change of the volume when the side length is 1 cm?
  (d) What is the rate of change of the volume when the side length is 2 cm?

(a) $V = x^3$
(b) $\dfrac{dV}{dx} = 3x^2$
(c) When $x = 1$, $\dfrac{dV}{dx} = 3$
(d) When $x = 2$, $\dfrac{dV}{dx} = 12$

In other words:
  • when the cube has side length 1 cm, the volume is increasing at a rate of 3 cm³ per 1 cm increase in side length;
  • when the cube has side length 2 cm, the volume is increasing at a rate of 12 cm³ per 1 cm increase in side length.

Exercise 11E

1. Find the rate of change of the variable on the left with respect to the variable on the right-hand side of the equation.
  (a) $y = 2x^2$
  (b) $F = p^4 + \dfrac{1}{p}$
  (c) $A = \dfrac{5}{2}r^2 + \dfrac{7}{2}r$
  (d) $b = \dfrac{\sqrt{c} + c}{c^2}$
  (e) $x = \dfrac{5}{y^2}$

2. Find the rate of change of y with respect to x when x takes the value given.
  (a) $y = 2x$; $x = 1$
  (b) $y = 3x^2$; $x = 2$
  (c) $y = \dfrac{1}{3}x^3$; $x = 3$
  (d) $y = 2\sqrt{x}$; $x = 4$
  (e) $y = \dfrac{3}{4}x^4 + \dfrac{2}{3}x^3 + \dfrac{3}{2}x^2 - 2x$; $x = -1$

Exercise 11E...

3. The volume of water flowing in a pipe is related to the pressure by the formula $V = 3p^2 + \dfrac{4}{p}$ (where V is measured in m³ s⁻¹ and p in bars). Find the rate of change of the volume when the pressure is 2 bars.

4. The surface area of a cylinder is given by the formula $A = 2\pi r^2 + 2\pi rh$, where r is the radius and h is the height.
  (a) Eliminate h from this equation by considering the case when the height is equal to the radius (i.e. $h = r$).
  (b) The cylinder increases in size, but the height remains equal to the radius. Differentiate your answer to part (a) to find the rate of change of A with respect to the radius r.
  (c) How fast is the area changing per centimetre increase in the radius when the radius is 2 cm? Leave π in your answer.

5. A tourist drops a coin from a tall building. The distance (in metres) it has fallen is given by the equation $x = 24t + 5t^2$, where t is the time (in seconds). Find the velocity of the coin after 10 seconds. (Hint: velocity is the rate of change of distance with respect to time.)

6. The formula $c = 2s + \sqrt[3]{s}$ links two of the variables in an experiment, where $s \geq 0$.
  (a) Find the rate of change of c with respect to s.
  (b) What is the value of s when the rate of change of c with respect to s is $\dfrac{10}{3}$?

7. The velocity of a stone falling off a cliff reaches 30 m s⁻¹ as it hits the sea. Given that its vertical distance from the cliff-top is given by the formula $s = 5t^2$, find the height of the cliff. (Hint: velocity is the rate of change of distance with respect to time.)

8. The formula $b = 3q - \dfrac{2}{\sqrt{q}}$ links the number of bacteria to the quantity of nutrients supplied in a laboratory experiment.
  (a) Find the rate of change of b with respect to q.
  (b) What is the value of q when the rate of change of b with respect to q is 11?

11.5 Tangents and Normals

In section 11.2 we saw that the gradient of a curve at a point is equal to the gradient of the tangent at the same point:

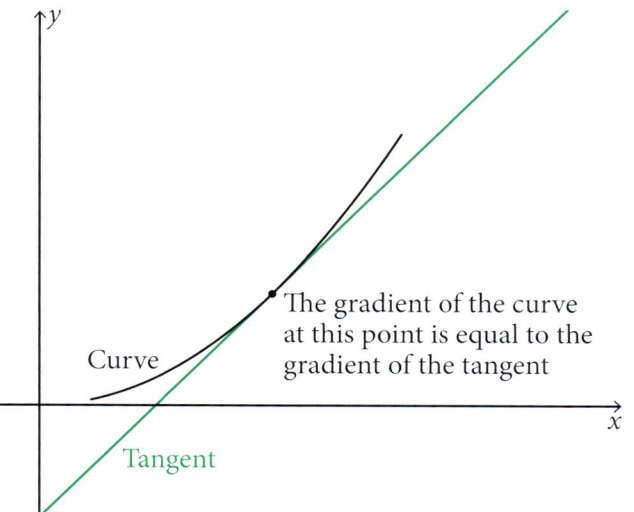

Curve

The gradient of the curve at this point is equal to the gradient of the tangent

Tangent

Therefore, if we can work out the gradient of the curve at a point using differentiation, we also know the gradient of the tangent. This helps us to find the equation of the tangent.

Worked Examples

17. Find the gradient of the tangent at the point (2, 4) on the curve $y = x^2$.

A sketch of the curve and the tangent is shown below.

> **Note:** You do not have to draw a sketch; it has been included here to explain the question graphically.

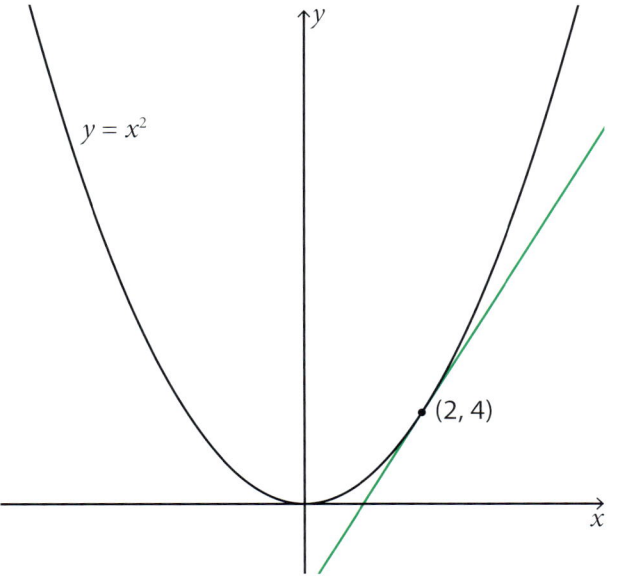

$y = x^2$

(2, 4)

The equation of the curve is $y = x^2$. Differentiate to find the gradient function: $\dfrac{\mathrm{d}y}{\mathrm{d}x} = 2x$

At point (2, 4) $x = 2$, therefore $\dfrac{\mathrm{d}y}{\mathrm{d}x} = 4$.

Since the gradient of the tangent equals the gradient of the curve at this point, the gradient of the tangent is also 4.

---

18. Find the equation of the tangent to the curve $y = x^3 - 4x$ at the point (1, −3).

A sketch of the curve is below.

> **Note:** As in the previous example, you do not have to draw a sketch; it has been included here to explain the question graphically.

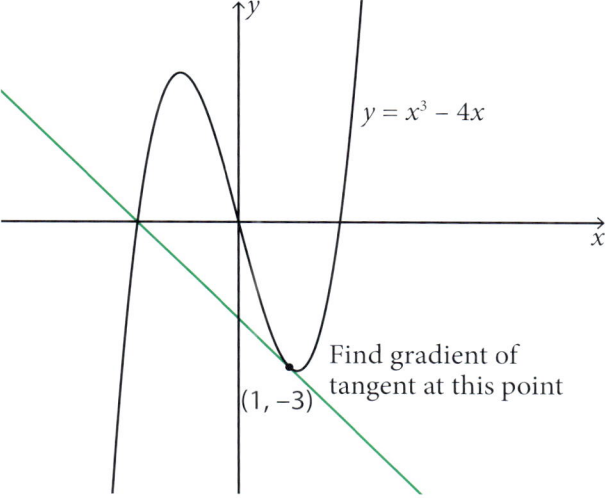

$y = x^3 - 4x$

(1, −3)

Find gradient of tangent at this point

Equation of curve: $y = x^3 - 4x$. Differentiate to find gradient function: $\dfrac{\mathrm{d}y}{\mathrm{d}x} = 3x^2 - 4$

At point (1, −3) $x = 1$, therefore $\dfrac{\mathrm{d}y}{\mathrm{d}x} = 3(1)^2 - 4 = -1$

Since the gradient of the tangent equals the gradient of the curve at this point, the gradient of the tangent is also −1.

However, this question asks for the equation of the tangent. We use the equation of a straight line: $y - y_1 = m(x - x_1)$

We know both the gradient, $m = -1$ and a point on the line, (1, −3). Therefore:

$$y - (-3) = -1(x - 1)$$
$$y + 3 = -x + 1$$
$$y = -x - 2$$

Hence the equation of the tangent is: $y = -x - 2$.

The equation of the tangent indicates that the gradient is –1 and the y-intercept is –2. This agrees with our sketch.

The **normal** to a curve is the straight line at right angles to the tangent at a point on the curve. The normal also cuts the curve at right angles:

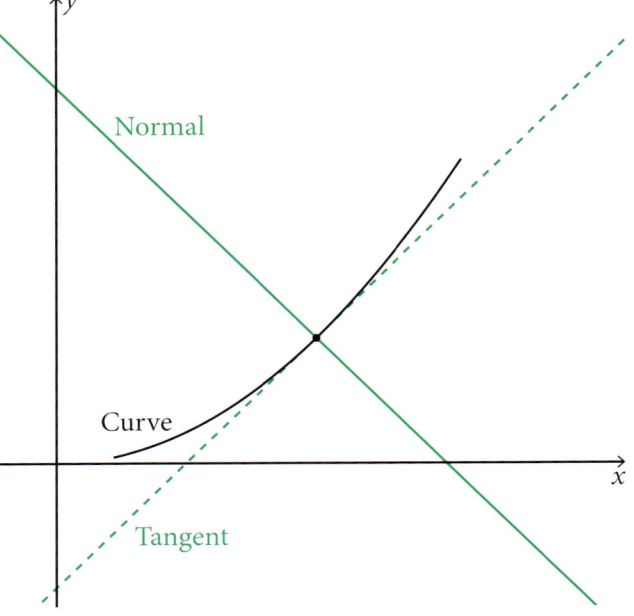

Recall from chapter 6 that:

> Two straight lines are perpendicular if the product of their gradients is –1.

Hence, using the gradient of the tangent, it is also possible to find the gradient of the normal to the curve.

If we call the gradient of the tangent m_1 and the gradient of the normal m_2, then:

$$m_1 m_2 = -1 \quad \text{or} \quad m_2 = -\frac{1}{m_1}$$

We could also find the **equation** of the normal.

Worked Examples

19. Find the equation of the normal to the curve $y = x^2 - 4x + 1$ at the point (3, –2).

The curve is shown in the following sketch.

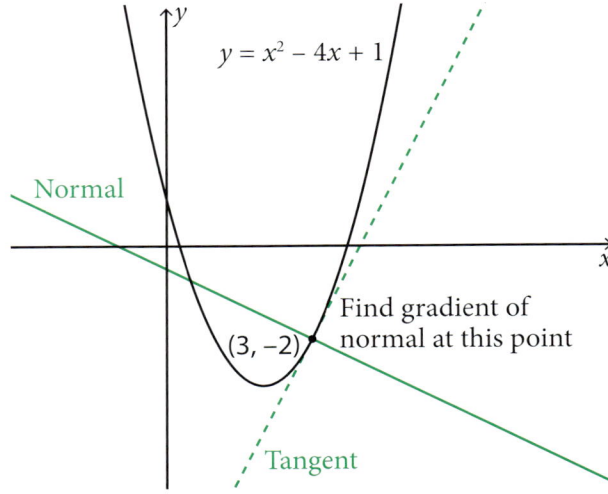

Equation of curve: $y = x^2 - 4x + 1$. Differentiate to find the gradient function: $\dfrac{dy}{dx} = 2x - 4$

At point (3, –2) $x = 3$, so $\dfrac{dy}{dx} = 2(3) - 4 = 2$

So the gradient of the tangent is $m_1 = 2$.

Using $m_2 = -\dfrac{1}{m_1}$ to find the gradient of the normal,

we find $m_2 = -\tfrac{1}{2}$.

However, this question asks for the **equation** of the normal. From the equation of a straight line:
$y - y_1 = m(x - x_1)$

We know the gradient is –½ and that a point on the line is (3, –2). Therefore:

$$y - (-2) = -\tfrac{1}{2}(x - 3)$$
$$y + 2 = -\tfrac{1}{2}x + \tfrac{3}{2}$$
$$y = -\tfrac{1}{2}x - \tfrac{1}{2}$$

Hence the equation of the normal in its general form is: $x + 2y + 1 = 0$.

> **Note:** Once again, drawing a sketch is not essential to answer this type of question. Doing so may, however, help you to visualise the problem.

Exercise 11F

1. Consider the curve $y = x^2$.
   (a) Find the gradient function $\dfrac{dy}{dx}$.
   (b) Find the gradient of the curve at the point (1, 1).
   (c) Find the equation of the tangent to the curve at this point.

Exercise 11F...

2. Find the equation of the tangent to the curve $y = x^4 - 4x^2 + 3$ where $x = 2$.

3. Find the equation of the tangent at the point $x = 4$ on the curve $y = x^3 - 7x^2 + 5$.

4. Find, in general form, the equation of the normal at the point $x = 2$ on the curve $y = x^4 - 4x^2 + 4$.

5. The curve C has equation $y = x^3 - 3x + \dfrac{3}{x}$.

   The points A and B both lie on C and have coordinates $(1, -3)$ and $(-1, 3)$ respectively.
   (a) Show that the gradient of C at A is equal to the gradient of C at B.
   (b) Find the equation for the normal to C at A in its general form.

6. The curve C has equation $y = 4x^2 + \dfrac{5 - x}{x}$. The point P on C has x-coordinate 1.

   (a) Show that the value of $\dfrac{dy}{dx}$ at P is 3.

   (Hint: Rewrite the equation for C. Split the fraction part into two separate fractions.)
   (b) Find an equation of the tangent to C at P.

7. The curve C is given by the equation $y = x^4(4x^6 + 4x^3)$. Calculate the gradient of the tangent at the point $x = 1$ on C.

8. The curve C has equation $y = (x - 2)(x^2 - 16)$. The curve cuts the x-axis at the points P(2, 0), Q and R.
   (a) Write down the x-coordinates of Q and R.
   (b) Show that $\dfrac{dy}{dx} = 3x^2 - 4x - 16$.
   (c) Show that $y = -9x + 36$ is an equation of the tangent to C at the point $(-1, 45)$.

9. The curve C is given by the equation $y = x^3(3x^2 + 2x)$. Calculate the gradient of the tangent at the point where $x = 1$ on C.

10. The curve C has equation $y = x^3 - 3x + \dfrac{4}{x}$.

    The points A and B both lie on C and have coordinates $(2, 4)$ and $(-2, -4)$ respectively.
    (a) Show that the gradient of C at A is equal to the gradient of C at B.
    (b) Find the equation for the normal to C at A in its general form.

11.6 Finding Coordinates of a Point on a Curve, Given the Gradient

You can also use the gradient at a point on a curve to find out the coordinates of the point.

....

Worked Example

20. Find the coordinates of the point on the curve $y = x^2 + 4x - 2$ where the gradient of the curve is 2.

    _____

    Equation of curve: $y = x^2 + 4x - 2$. Differentiate to find the gradient function: $\dfrac{dy}{dx} = 2x + 4$

    We need to know where the gradient is 2, so we must solve:
    $2x + 4 = 2$
    $x = -1$

    To find the y-coordinate, substitute $x = -1$ into the equation of the curve:
    $y = x^2 + 4x - 2$
    $y = (-1)^2 + 4(-1) - 2$
    $y = -5$

    So the coordinates of the point are $(-1, -5)$.

....

Exercise 11G

1. Find the coordinates of the point on the curve $y = x^2$ where the gradient of the curve is -2.

2. Consider the curve $y = -\dfrac{1}{x^2}$.

   (a) Differentiate to find $\dfrac{dy}{dx}$.

   (b) Find the coordinates of the point where the gradient of the curve is ¼.

3. The curve C has equation $y = 2\sqrt{x}$. What are the coordinates of the points where:
   (a) $\dfrac{dy}{dx} = \dfrac{1}{2}$ (b) $\dfrac{dy}{dx} = \dfrac{1}{3}$

4. The curve C has equation $y = \dfrac{4}{\sqrt{x}}$. What are the coordinates of the points where:
   (a) $\dfrac{dy}{dx} = -2$ (b) $\dfrac{dy}{dx} = -16$

5. There are two points on the curve $y = \dfrac{1}{3}x^3 - 2x^2 - 8$ at which the gradient is 5.

   What are the x-coordinates of those points?

Exercise 11G...

6. If $y = 6x + 2x^3$:

   (a) Find $\dfrac{dy}{dx}$.

   (b) Hence find the coordinates of the points where the gradient of the curve is 12.

7. There are two points P and Q on the curve $y = x(x^2 - 51)$ where the gradient of the curve is −3. What are the x-coordinates of P and Q?

8. What are the coordinates of the two points at which the gradient of the curve $y = \dfrac{1}{x}$ is −4?

9. There are two points on the curve $y = \dfrac{1}{3}x^3 - 4x^2 + 2$ at which the gradient is −12. What are the coordinates of those points?

10. A curve C has equation $y = 4x^3 - 42x^2 + 125x + 12$.

    (a) Find $\dfrac{dy}{dx}$ in terms of x.

    (b) The points P and Q lie on C. The gradient of C at both P and Q is 5. The x-coordinate of P is 2. Find the x-coordinate of Q.

    (c) Find an equation for the tangent to C at P, giving your answer in the form $y = mx + c$.

11. The Cheshire Cat's face slowly disappears, leaving only its smile, which then also disappears. The amount of face remaining is governed by the equation $F = 5(9 - \sqrt{t})$ where F is the area of face in cm² and t is the time in seconds.

    (a) How big is the Cheshire Cat's face in cm² initially?

    (b) Find the time at which the rate of change of facial area is −½ cm² s⁻¹.

    (c) How long does it take for the entire face to disappear?

11.7 Stationary Points: Maxima and Minima

A **stationary point** (or **turning point**) of a curve is where the curve has a gradient 0, i.e. the curve is flat at this point. Here are some examples of stationary points:

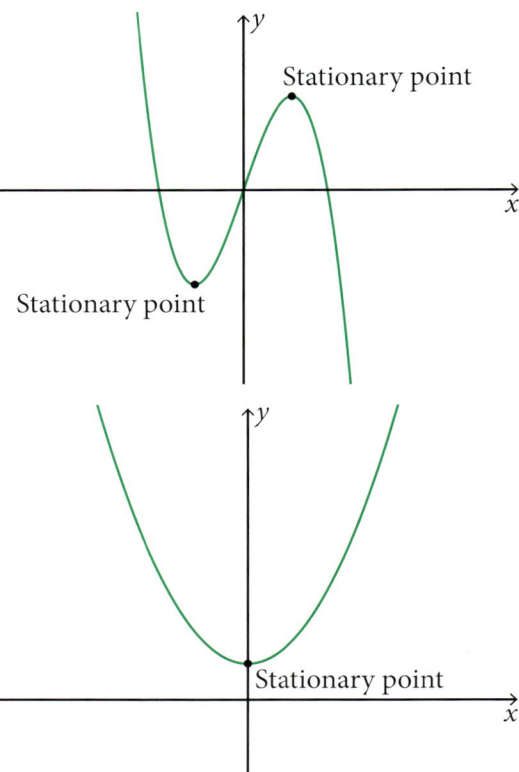

We can work out the position of a stationary point by finding the gradient function $\dfrac{dy}{dx}$ and setting it equal to zero.

....

Worked Examples

21. Find the coordinates of the stationary point of the curve $y = x^2 - 4x + 5$.

    $$y = x^2 - 4x + 5$$
    $$\frac{dy}{dx} = 2x - 4$$

    At stationary points, the gradient is zero, so:
    $$2x - 4 = 0$$
    $$x = 2$$

    Use the equation of the curve to find the y-coordinate:
    $$y = 2^2 - 4(2) + 5$$
    $$= 1$$

    So the coordinates of the stationary point are (2, 1).

Note: You can also use completing the square to find the turning point of a quadratic function.

22. The curve $f(x) = (x + a)(x + 1)$ has a turning point where $x = 4$. Find the value of a.

$$f(x) = (x + a)(x + 1)$$
$$f(x) = x^2 + (a + 1)x + a$$
$$f'(x) = 2x + (a + 1)$$

At the turning point $f'(x) = 0$ and $x = 4$. So:
$$2(4) + (a + 1) = 0$$
$$a = -9$$

You should be familiar with three types of stationary point: a **maximum point**, a **minimum point** and a **point of inflection**. The meanings of these terms are best explained with the aid of diagrams.

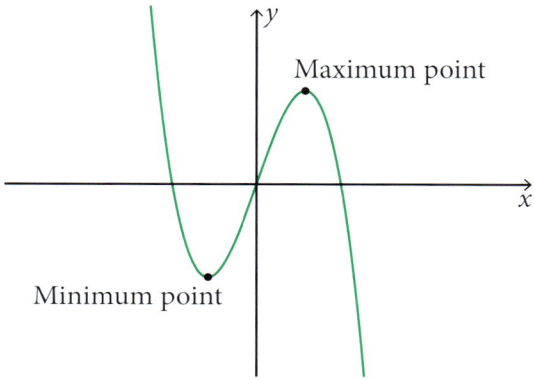

At a **maximum point**, the y-value reaches a local maximum.

At a **minimum point**, the y-value reaches a local minimum.

A **point of inflection** is the type of stationary point you often see in cubic curves:

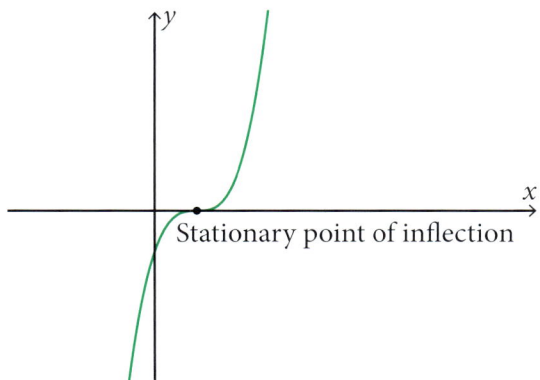

At a stationary point of inflection, the gradient of the curve is zero, but it is neither a local maximum, nor a local minimum.

At all stationary points $\dfrac{dy}{dx} = 0$.

You can also see that:

- At a maximum point, the gradient changes from positive to negative.
- At a minimum point, the gradient changes from negative to positive.
- The gradient is either positive on both sides of a stationary point of inflection, or negative on both sides.

Exercise 11H

1. Find the coordinates of the stationary points of the following curves:
   (a) $y = x^2 + 2$
   (b) $y = x^2 + 4x$
   (c) $y = -x^2 + 8x$
   (d) $y = x^3 - 3x + 3$
   (e) $y = x(x + 5)$
   (f) $y = 2x^2 - 20x$
   (g) $y = 2x^2 - 8x + 6$
   (h) $y = -2x^2 + 20x + 1$
   (i) $y = 2x^3 - 15x^2 + 36x - 91$
   (j) $y = x(x + 1)(x - 1)$
   (k) $y = (x - 1)^3 - 1$

2. Find the coordinates of the turning points of the curve $y = 2x^3 - 24x^2 + 72x - 61$.

3. At a point P on the curve $y = 4x^2 - 16x$ the tangent to the curve is parallel to the x-axis. What are the coordinates of the point P? (Hint: if the tangent is parallel to the x-axis, the gradient of the tangent is zero.)

4. The curve C has equation $y = 2 + 9x^2 - 4x^3$.
   (a) Find $\dfrac{dy}{dx}$.
   (b) Find the coordinates of the two stationary points of the curve.

5. The curve C has equation:
   $$f(x) = \frac{(x^2 - 4)^2}{x^3}, x \neq 0$$
   (a) Show that $f(x) = x - 8x^{-1} + 16x^{-3}, x \neq 0$.
   (b) Hence differentiate $f(x)$.
   (c) Verify that the graph of $y = f(x)$ has turning points at $x = \pm 2$.

Exercise 11H...

6. The function $f(x)$ is defined as
   $f(x) = x^{2/3}(20 - x)$.
   (a) Find the derivative function $f'(x)$.
   (b) Find the coordinates of the stationary point of $y = f(x)$.

7. The curve $y = 3x^2 + kx$ has a turning point at $x = 3$. Find the value of k.

8. The curve with equation $y = px^2 - qx$ (where p and q are constants) has a stationary point at $(4, -48)$.
   (a) Differentiate to find $\dfrac{dy}{dx}$.
   (b) Find the values of p and q. (Hint: you will need to solve two simultaneous equations: one from the original equation, one from your answer to part (a).)

9. The curve $y = x^3 + bx^2 + cx + 2$ has a stationary point of inflection at the point $(-1, 1)$. What are the values of the constants b and c?

11.8 Second Order Derivatives

Differentiation of $\dfrac{dy}{dx}$ gives the **second derivative**.

We write the second derivative as $\dfrac{d^2y}{dx^2}$.

Using function notation, we write $f'(x)$ for the first derivative and $f''(x)$ for the second.

Worked Example

23. (a) Find the first and second derivatives of
       $y = 2x^3 - 5x^2 + 4x - 3$.
    (b) Given $f(x) = \dfrac{1}{x} - \dfrac{1}{x^2}$, find the second derivative.

(a) $\dfrac{dy}{dx} = 6x^2 - 10x + 4$

   $\dfrac{d^2y}{dx^2} = 12x - 10$

(b) $f(x) = x^{-1} - x^{-2}$
    $f'(x) = -x^{-2} + 2x^{-3}$
    $f''(x) = 2x^{-3} - 6x^{-4}$

The second derivative can be used to determine the **nature** of stationary points, i.e. whether a stationary point is a maximum point, a minimum point or a point of inflection.

For example, the nature of the stationary point on the curve $f(x) = x^2$ is **minimum**. The nature of the stationary point on the curve $f(x) = -x^2$ is **maximum**. The nature of the stationary point in the cubic $f(x) = x^3$ is a **point of inflection**.

> - If the second derivative is positive at a stationary point, the stationary point is a minimum.
> - If the second derivative is negative at a stationary point, the stationary point is a maximum.
> - If the second derivative is zero at a stationary point, the stationary point may be a maximum, a minimum or a point of inflection.

Worked Example

24. (a) Find the coordinates of the stationary points of the curve $y = \dfrac{1}{3}x^3 - 2x^2 + 3x + 1$.
    (b) By finding the second derivative, determine the nature of the stationary points.
    (c) Sketch the curve, marking clearly the stationary points and the coordinates of the point at which the curve intercepts the y-axis.

(a) Differentiate:
   $\dfrac{dy}{dx} = x^2 - 4x + 3$

   At stationary points $\dfrac{dy}{dx} = 0$. So:
   $x^2 - 4x + 3 = 0$
   $(x - 1)(x - 3) = 0$

   Therefore, there are stationary points at $x = 1$ and $x = 3$. When $x = 1$, $y = \frac{7}{3}$; when $x = 3$, $y = 1$.

   So the stationary points are: $(1, \frac{7}{3})$, $(3, 1)$.

(b) Differentiate again: $\dfrac{d^2y}{dx^2} = 2x - 4$
   When $x = 1$:

   $\dfrac{d^2y}{dx^2} = 2(1) - 4 = -2$

   $\dfrac{d^2y}{dx^2} < 0$, hence the stationary point at $x = 1$ is a maximum.

   When $x = 3$:

   $\dfrac{d^2y}{dx^2} = 2(3) - 4 = 2$

   $\dfrac{d^2y}{dx^2} > 0$, hence the stationary point at $x = 3$ is a minimum.

(c) When $x = 0$, $y = 1$. Hence the curve intercepts the y-axis at $(0, 1)$.

Recall (from chapter 5) that because the term in x^3 is positive, the general direction of the curve is bottom left to top right.

With the locations and nature of the two stationary points, we now have enough information to sketch the curve:

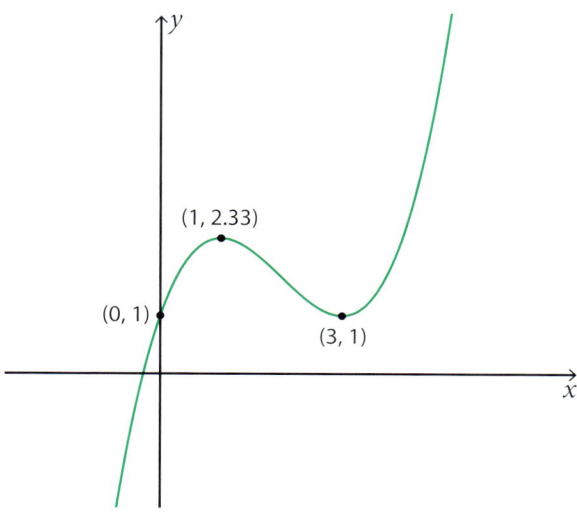

When investigating the nature of a stationary point, it is possible that $\dfrac{d^2y}{dx^2} = 0$ at this point. This does not give us a clear indication about the nature of the turning point; so we must use other techniques. The most common method is to calculate the gradient (the value of $\dfrac{dy}{dx}$) on either side of the stationary point:

- Gradient changes from negative to positive: minimum turning point.

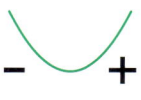

- Gradient changes from positive to negative: maximum turning point.

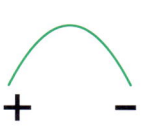

- Gradient is negative to the left and to the right: stationary point of inflection.

- Gradient is positive to the left and to the right: stationary point of inflection.

Worked Example

25. Find the stationary points on the curve $y = x^4 - x^3$ and determine their nature.

$$y = x^4 - x^3$$
$$\frac{dy}{dx} = 4x^3 - 3x^2$$

To find stationary points, set $\dfrac{dy}{dx}$ equal to zero:
$$4x^3 - 3x^2 = 0$$
$$x^2(4x - 3) = 0$$
$$x = 0 \text{ or } x = ¾$$

Therefore there are two stationary points, with x-coordinates 0 and ¾ (or 0.75). Find their y-values:
$$y = x^4 - x^3$$
$$\text{So } y = 0 \text{ or } y = -0.105 \text{ (3 s.f.)}$$

So the two stationary points are $(0, 0)$ and $(0.75, -0.105)$.

To investigate their nature, consider $\dfrac{d^2y}{dx^2}$:
$$\frac{d^2y}{dx^2} = 12x^2 - 6x$$

When $x = 0.75$, $\dfrac{d^2y}{dx^2} = 2.25$, which is positive, so $(0.75, -0.105)$ is a minimum turning point.

When $x = 0$, $\dfrac{d^2y}{dx^2} = 0$. In this case we need to use a different technique to determine the nature of this stationary point. Investigate the gradient either side of the stationary point.

When $x = -0.1$:
$$\frac{dy}{dx} = 4(-0.1)^3 - 3(-0.1)^2$$
$$= -0.034$$

When $x = 0.1$:
$$\frac{dy}{dx} = 4(0.1)^3 - 3(0.1)^2$$
$$= -0.026$$

Since the gradient is negative on either side of the stationary point $(0, 0)$, it is a point of inflection.

The second derivative as the rate of change of gradient

The second derivative $\dfrac{d^2y}{dx^2}$ is obtained by differentiating the gradient function $\dfrac{dy}{dx}$. Hence, it can be thought of as the **rate of change of the gradient**.

Worked Example

26. The curve C has equation $y = x^3 + 3x$. Find the rate of change of the gradient of this curve at the point where $x = 1$.

We are being asked to find the rate of change of the gradient, which is the second derivative $\dfrac{d^2y}{dx^2}$.

$\dfrac{dy}{dx} = 3x^2 + 3$

$\dfrac{d^2y}{dx^2} = 6x$

When $x = 1$, $\dfrac{d^2y}{dx^2} = 6(1) = 6$.

Therefore at this point on the curve, the gradient is increasing by 6 units for every increase of 1 unit in the value of x.

Exercise 11I

1. Find the first and second derivatives of each of these functions.

(a) $f(x) = 2x^2 + 1$ (b) $f(x) = \dfrac{1}{4}x^4 + \dfrac{1}{3}x^3$

(c) $f(x) = x + \dfrac{1}{x}$ (d) $f(x) = \dfrac{x}{2}$

(e) $f(x) = 3\sqrt{x}$ (f) $f(x) = \dfrac{3}{\sqrt{x}}$

(g) $f(x) = 2x^6 - 2x^{-6}$

(h) $f(x) = (2x + 1)(1 - x)$

(i) $f(x) = x(1 - x^2)$

(j) $f(x) = \dfrac{1}{x}(x + x^2)$

2. Find the first and second derivatives of these curves when $x = -1$.

(a) $y = \dfrac{1}{2}x^2$ (b) $y = 2x^3 - 2x$

(c) $y = 5x$ (d) $y = \dfrac{1}{2x}$

(e) $y = (3x + 1)(2x + 1)$

3. Find the first and second derivatives of these curves when $x = 1$.

(a) $y = x(1 - x + x^2)$

(b) $y = 3\sqrt{x}$

(c) $y = 3\sqrt{x} + \dfrac{3}{\sqrt{x}}$

(d) $y = \dfrac{4 - 2\sqrt{x}}{\sqrt{x}}$

(e) $y = \dfrac{5}{2}cx - \dfrac{3}{4}$, where c is a constant.

Exercise 11I...

4. Find the coordinates and nature of the stationary points of the curve $y = 2x^3 - 24x^2 + 72x - 63$

5. Find the coordinates and nature of the stationary point on the curve with equation $y = 4x^2 - 24x$

6. Show that the curve with equation $y = 7x^2 - 14x + 3$ has a minimum stationary point at $(1, -4)$.

7. Find $\dfrac{dy}{dx}$ where $y = -4x^2 - \dfrac{1}{x}$

Hence find the coordinates of the stationary point of the curve $y = -4x^2 - \dfrac{1}{x}$ and determine its nature.

8. The curve C has equation $y = 2x^3 - 5x^2 - 4x + 3$

(a) Find $\dfrac{dy}{dx}$.

(b) Using the result from part (a), find the x-coordinates of the stationary points of C.

(c) Find $\dfrac{d^2y}{dx^2}$.

(d) Hence or otherwise, determine the nature of the stationary points of C.

9. Given $f(x) = 3 + 9x^2 - 3x^3$, find the coordinates of the two stationary points on the curve $y = f(x)$ and determine the nature of these stationary points.

10. The curve with equation $y = (4x + 2)(x^2 - k)$, where k is a constant, has a stationary point where $x = 1$.

(a) Determine the value of k.

(b) Find the x-coordinates of the stationary points and determine the nature of each.

(c) Find the rate of change of the gradient of the curve at the point where $x = 0$.

11. Given $f(x) = \dfrac{(x^2 - 6)^2}{x^3}, x \neq 0$,

(a) Show that $f(x) = x - 12x^{-1} + 36x^{-3}$.

(b) Hence or otherwise differentiate $f(x)$ with respect to x.

(c) Verify that the graph of $y = f(x)$ has stationary points at $x = \pm\sqrt{6}$.

(d) Determine the nature of the stationary point at $x = \sqrt{6}$.

Exercise 11I...

12. Find the coordinates of any stationary points on the curve $y = x^5 - x^3$ and determine their nature. Give your answers to 3 significant figures where appropriate.

13. A curve has the equation $y = 3x^4 - 8x^3$.

    (a) Find $\dfrac{dy}{dx}$.

    (b) Find the coordinates of the stationary points of the curve and determine their nature.

14. The curve with equation $y = (6x + 3)(x^2 - k)$, where k is a constant, has a stationary point where $x = 1$.

    (a) Determine the value of k.

    (b) Find the coordinates of the stationary points and determine the nature of each.

11.9 Practical Applications

There are many practical applications of calculus, in many diverse areas. In this section you will learn how to use your knowledge of stationary points to solve real-life problems.

The fact that the gradient of a curve is zero at maximum and minimum points is used widely in this section.

··

Worked Example

27. A car's velocity is given by the equation:

$$v = \frac{3}{1000}t^2 - \frac{3}{100000}t^3$$

where t is measured in seconds and $0 < t < 100$.
A graph of the car's velocity against time is shown:

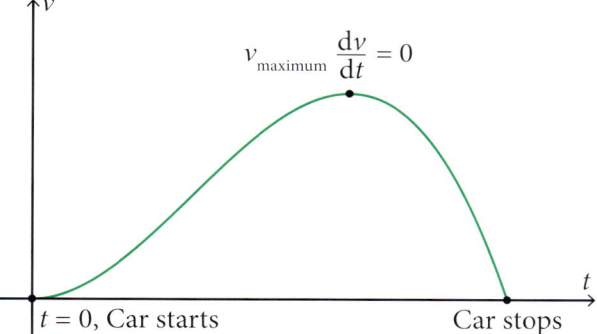

(a) Determine the time at which the car reaches its maximum velocity.

(b) Show that the car stops after 100 seconds.

(a) v reaches its maximum at the turning point on the graph above. We need to find the point on the curve where the gradient is zero, i.e. $\dfrac{dv}{dt} = 0$.

Differentiate to obtain $\dfrac{dv}{dt}$:

$$\frac{dv}{dt} = \frac{3}{500}t - \frac{9}{100000}t^2$$

Maximum and minimum v occur when $\dfrac{dv}{dt} = 0$, i.e.:

$$\frac{3}{500}t - \frac{9}{100000}t^2 = 0$$

$$\frac{3}{500}t\left(1 - \frac{3}{200}t\right) = 0$$

So $t = 0$ or $t = \dfrac{200}{3} = 66.7$ s (3 s.f.)

From the graph, it is clear that the car has its minimum velocity when $t = 0$ and its maximum velocity when $t = 66.7$. However, we will not always be given a graph, so we must check using the second derivative:

$$\frac{d^2v}{dt^2} = \frac{3}{500} - \frac{18}{100000}t$$

When $t = 0$, $\dfrac{d^2v}{dt^2} = \dfrac{3}{500}$, which is positive, so this is the time at which v is at its minimum.

When $t = \dfrac{200}{3}$, $\dfrac{d^2v}{dt^2} = -\dfrac{3}{500}$, which is negative, so this is the time at which v is at its maximum.

(b) To find the time at which the car stops, set $v = 0$ in the equation of the curve. (No differentiation is needed here.)

$$\frac{3}{1000}t^2 - \frac{3}{100000}t^3 = 0$$

$$\frac{3}{1000}t^2\left(1 - \frac{1}{100}t\right) = 0$$

So $t = 0$ or $t = 100$ s. The car is stationary when $t = 0$ (at the start of its journey) and again after 100 seconds.

··

In the following example we are interested in the maximum value of variable A. It is dependent on two variables, x and y. To differentiate we must find A as a function of just one variable.

Worked Examples

28. A farmer has 800 metres of fencing and plans to make a rectangular enclosure for his animals. Show that, to give his animals the greatest amount of space, the enclosure should be square.

Let the length of the enclosure be x and the width y:

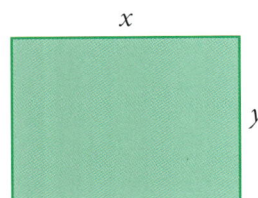

The area A is given by:
$$A = xy \qquad (1)$$

If the amount of fencing available is 800 m, then
$$2x + 2y = 800$$
$$x + y = 400$$
$$y = 400 - x \qquad (2)$$

Substituting (2) into (1) gives A as a function of x only:
$$A = x(400 - x)$$
$$A = 400x - x^2$$

Differentiate:
$$\frac{dA}{dx} = 400 - 2x$$

The area is at a maximum when $\frac{dA}{dx} = 0$. So:
$$400 - 2x = 0$$
$$x = 200$$

Substituting into (2): $y = 200$

The length and width of the enclosure should both be 200 m; therefore the enclosure will be square.

However, we do not have a graph of A against x. How do we know that A is a maximum, not a minimum? To complete this question, differentiate again:
$$\frac{d^2 A}{dx^2} = -2$$

The value of $\frac{d^2 A}{dx^2}$ is negative, which shows that the stationary point is a maximum.

> **Note:** In this example $\frac{d^2 A}{dx^2}$ is not a function of x.
>
> If it were, we would evaluate $\frac{d^2 A}{dx^2}$ when $x = 200$.

29. I think of a number, subtract 2, square and add 1. What is the smallest possible answer?

Let my number be x. Let the answer be y. We are looking for the smallest possible value for y.
$$y = (x - 2)^2 + 1$$
$$y = x^2 - 4x + 5$$
$$\frac{dy}{dx} = 2x - 4 \qquad (1)$$

The value of y reaches a minimum when $\frac{dy}{dx} = 0$.
$$2x - 4 = 0$$
$$x = 2$$

This is the number I originally thought of. So
$$y = (x - 2)^2 + 1$$
$$y = (2 - 2)^2 + 1$$
$$y = 1$$

The smallest possible answer is 1. How do we know this is a minimum, not a maximum?

Differentiate (1): $\frac{d^2 y}{dx^2} = 2$

The positive value means we have found a minimum value of y.

Again, note that the second derivative is a constant value. If it were a function of x, we would need to evaluate $\frac{d^2 y}{dx^2}$ when $x = 2$.

Exercise 11J

1. A stone is thrown into the air and after t seconds its distance s metres above the ground is given by the equation $s = 30t - 5t^2$.
   (a) Using calculus, find the time taken for the stone to reach its maximum height.
   (b) What is the maximum height?

2. In a laboratory, a particle is accelerated such that its acceleration a m s^{-2} after t seconds is governed by the equation $a = 3t(2 - t)$.
   (a) After how many seconds does the particle reach its maximum acceleration?
   (b) What is the maximum acceleration?

3. If I add a positive real number to its reciprocal, what is the smallest possible answer I could get?

4. A lorry is driven from Belfast to Dublin at a steady speed of v kilometres per hour. The total cost of the journey £C is given by:
$$C = \frac{1000}{v} + \frac{2v}{5}$$

Exercise 11J...

(a) Find the value of v for which C is a minimum.

(b) Find $\dfrac{d^2 C}{dv^2}$ and hence verify that C is a minimum for this value.

(c) Calculate the minimum total cost of the journey.

5. In a wind tunnel, the wind speed is set to v m s⁻¹. For $v > 0.5$, the force exerted on a model building, F Newtons, is modelled by:

$$F = \frac{2}{v} + \frac{v^2}{125}$$

(a) Show by calculus that there is a value of v for which F has a stationary value, and find this value of v.

(b) Find the second derivative of F to show that this value of v gives a minimum value of F.

(c) Find the minimum value of F.

6. A beaker containing water is made in the shape of a cylinder with a hemispherical lid. The cylinder has radius r cm and height h cm.

(a) Given that the volume of the cylinder is 300 cm³, find h in terms of r.

(b) Show that the surface area A of the beaker is given by: $A = 3\pi r^2 + \dfrac{600}{r}$

(c) The beaker's manufacturer wants to minimise the amount of plastic used. Find the value of r that achieves this, giving an exact answer involving π.

7. A running track is built in the shape of a rectangle with a semicircle on either end, as shown in the diagram.

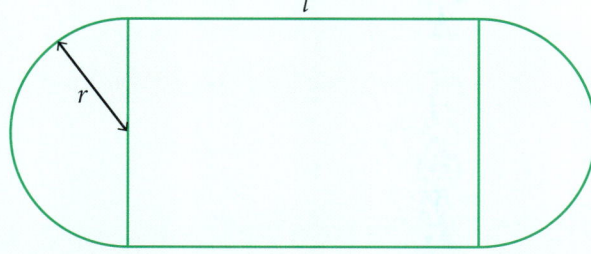

The length of the rectangle is l and the radius of each semicircle is r. The perimeter of the track must be 400 m.

(a) Find an expression for l in terms of r.

(b) Find an expression for the area of the rectangle, A, in terms of r (eliminating l).

Exercise 11J...

(c) The planning committee wish to ensure the rectangular area is maximised. Find the radius r that ensures A is a maximum. Leave π in your answer.

(d) By finding $\dfrac{d^2 A}{dr^2}$, verify that you have found a maximum.

(e) Investigation: Somebody on the planning committee suggests the *entire* enclosed area should be maximised. What value would r take then? Again leave π in your answer. What value would l take? What shape would the track be?

8. A glass box is to be made with a square base and an open top. The box must have a volume of 500 m³. The length and width of the base are x metres and the height is h metres.

(a) Find h in terms of x.

(b) Show that the total surface area A of the box is given by $A = x^2 + \dfrac{2000}{x}$.

(c) Glass for the box costs £10 per square metre. Find the dimensions of the box that minimise the amount of glass used and calculate the cost of the glass using these dimensions.

9. A factory makes matchboxes. The pieces of card used measure 3 cm by 2 cm. Squares of side x cm are cut from each corner of the sheet and the remainder is folded along the dotted lines to make an open tray for the matchbox, as shown.

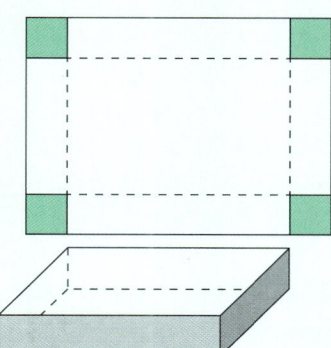

(a) Show that the volume V of the tray is given by $V = 6x - 10x^2 + 4x^3$.

(b) By considering the lengths of the sides of the piece of card, state the range of possible values for x.

Exercise 11J...

(c) Find the value of x for which V is a maximum, leaving your answer in surd form.

(d) By considering the second derivative of V, show that the value of x you have found does give the maximum value of V.

10. The diagram shows the plan of a garden in the shape of a rectangle joined to a semicircle.

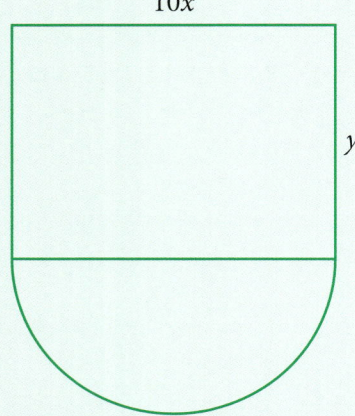

The length of the rectangular part is $10x$ m and the width is y m. The diameter of the semicircular part is $10x$ m. The perimeter of the garden is 20 m.

(a) Show that the area, A, of the garden is given by $A = 100x - \left(50 + \dfrac{25\pi}{2}\right)x^2$.

(b) Use calculus to show that the value of x at which A has a stationary value is given by $x = \dfrac{4}{4 + \pi}$.

(c) Use the second derivative of A to prove that the value of x you found in part (b) gives the maximum value of A.

(d) Calculate the maximum area of the garden, giving your answer in terms of π.

11.10 Increasing and Decreasing Functions

An **increasing function** is a function whose gradient is positive for all values of x. A **decreasing function** is one whose gradient is always negative.

For example, the function $f(x) = 2x$ is an increasing function. It represents a straight line with a positive gradient for all values of x.

A function can also be increasing or decreasing for a certain range of x values, as shown in the following diagram.

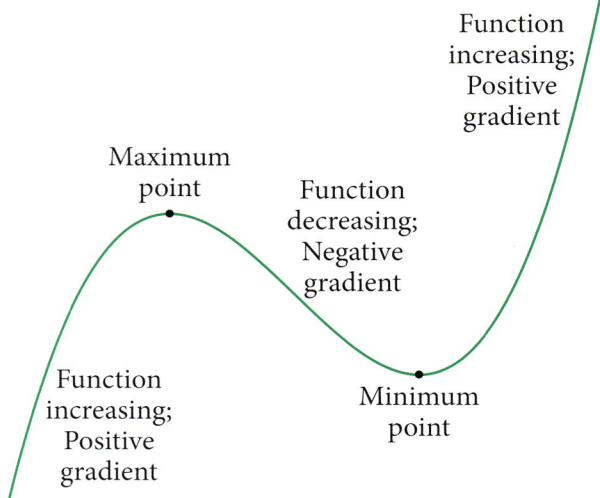

The diagram also shows the two stationary points of this curve, one a maximum point, the other a minimum point.

Worked Example

30. $f(x) = x^2$

For what range of values of x is $f(x)$
(a) decreasing?
(b) increasing?

A sketch of the graph demonstrates the answers:

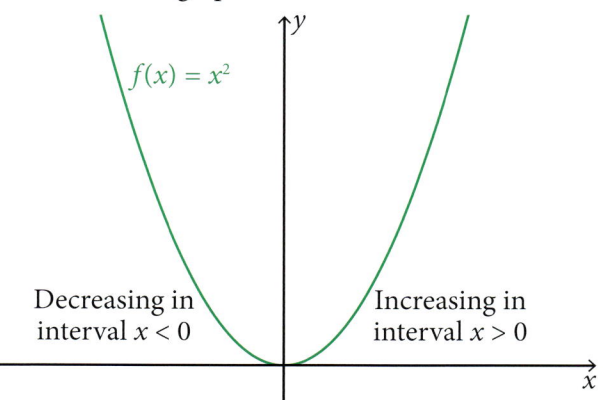

(a) The graph of $y = f(x)$ is decreasing when $x < 0$;
(b) The graph of $y = f(x)$ is increasing when $x > 0$.

The formal definitions are as follows:

> The function $f(x)$ is **increasing** if $f(x_2) > f(x_1)$ when $x_2 > x_1$ for all values of x in the given interval.
>
> The function $f(x)$ is **decreasing** if $f(x_2) < f(x_1)$ when $x_2 > x_1$ for all values of x in the given interval.

> **Note:** At the time of writing, the CCEA specification does not require you to remember these definitions.

You may also hear the expressions **monotonic increasing function** and **monotonic decreasing function**. These expressions have the same meanings as increasing and decreasing functions.

Worked Examples

31. Consider the function $f(x) = x^3 - 3x^2 + 4$. Is the function increasing, decreasing or stationary when:

(a) $x = 1$ (b) $x = 2$ (c) $x = 4$?

$f(x) = x^3 - 3x^2 + 4$

Differentiate:

$f'(x) = 3x^2 - 6x$

(a) When $x = 1$, $f'(x) = 3(1)^2 - 6(1) = -3$
This is a negative gradient, so the function is decreasing when $x = 1$.

(b) When $x = 2$, $f'(x) = 3(2)^2 - 6(2) = 0$
This is a zero gradient, so there is a stationary point when $x = 2$.

(c) When $x = 4$, $f'(x) = 3(4)^2 - 6(4) = 24$
This is a positive gradient, so the function is increasing when $x = 4$.

32. Consider the function $f(x) = \dfrac{3x}{2} - \dfrac{x^3}{8}$.

Find the range of values of x for which $f(x)$ is an increasing function.

$f(x) = \dfrac{3x}{2} - \dfrac{x^3}{8}$

$f'(x) = \dfrac{3}{2} - \dfrac{3x^2}{8}$

When the function is increasing, its gradient is positive. So:

$\dfrac{3}{2} - \dfrac{3x^2}{8} > 0$

$\dfrac{3}{2} > \dfrac{3x^2}{8}$

$24 > 6x^2$

$x^2 < 4$

Re-arrange to give:
$x^2 - 4 < 0$

Factorise the left-hand side using the difference of two squares formula:
$(x - 2)(x + 2) < 0$

Sketch the curve $y = (x - 2)(x + 2)$ and determine where it lies below the x-axis. We find that $-2 < x < 2$.

Hence $f(x)$ is increasing when $-2 < x < 2$.

Exercise 11K

1. Find the gradient of each curve at the point specified. State whether the curve is increasing or decreasing at that point.

   (a) $y = 3x^2$; $x = 2$

   (b) $y = 3x^2$; $x = -2$

   (c) $y = (x - 3)(x + 2)$; $x = 2$

   (d) $y = (x - 3)(x + 2)$; $x = -1$

   (e) $y = 3 - 2x - x^2$; $x = 0$

   (f) $y = 3 - 2x - x^2$; $x = -5$

   (g) $y = 3x$; $x = 2$

   (h) $y = x^3 + 2x$; $x = -1$

   (i) $y = -\dfrac{x}{2}$; $x = 2$

   (j) $y = -\dfrac{1}{x}$; $x = -1$

   (k) $y = \sqrt{x} + 1$; $x = 1$

   (l) $y = \dfrac{\sqrt{x} + 1}{x^{3/2}}$; $x = 1$

2. Find the range of values of x for which each function is increasing or decreasing.

   (a) $f(x) = x^2 + 2x$

   (b) $f(x) = x^3 - 3x + 1$

   (c) $f(x) = 7x$

   (d) $f(x) = -2x + 1$

   (e) $f(x) = (x - 2)(x + 3)$

   (f) $f(x) = x(x - 1)$

   (g) $f(x) = x^{3/2} - 3x, x > 0$

3. Show that the function $f(x) = 5x^3 + 2x + 5$ is always increasing.

4. Show that the function $f(x) = 1 - 3x - 3x^3$ is always decreasing.

5. Is the function $f(x) = 1 - 6x - 4x^3$ always increasing, always decreasing or neither?

Exercise 11K...

6. The equation of a curve is $y = 8 + 8x^2 - 2x^3$. Find the range of values of x for which the curve is increasing.

7. A curve has the equation $y = 2x^3 - 15x^2 + 24x - 43$.
   (a) Find the coordinates of the two turning points of the curve.
   (b) Determine the range of values of x for which the curve is decreasing.

8. Find the range of values of x for which the curve $y = 3x^2 - 6x + 10$ is increasing.

9. A curve has the equation $y = 3 + 9x^2 - 9x^3$.
   (a) Find the coordinates of the two turning points of the curve and determine their nature.
   (b) Find the range of values of x for which the curve is increasing.

10. A curve has the equation $y = 2x^4 - 4x^3$.
   (a) Find $\dfrac{dy}{dx}$.
   (b) Determine the range of values of x for which the curve is increasing.

11.11 Summary

Differentiation is a method used to find the **gradient** of a curve at any point. You can also think of it as finding a **rate of change**.

$f'(x)$ and $\dfrac{dy}{dx}$ are both notations for the **gradient function** or **derivative**.

To differentiate a power of x, the general rule is:

$$y = ax^n \Rightarrow \frac{dy}{dx} = anx^{n-1}$$

For sums and differences, differentiate each term in turn:

$$\text{If } y = f(x) + g(x), \text{ then } \frac{dy}{dx} = f'(x) + g'(x).$$

Having used $\dfrac{dy}{dx}$ to find the gradient of a curve at a point, you can then find the equation of tangents and normal to curves:

- The **gradient of the tangent** is equal to the gradient of the curve at any point on the curve.

- The **gradient of the normal** can be found using $m_2 = \dfrac{-1}{m_1}$ where where m_1 and m_2 are the gradients of the tangent and normal respectively.

- The equation of the tangent and the equation of the normal can be found using $y - y_1 = m(x - x_1)$.

You can find the position of **stationary points** or turning points on the curve by setting $\dfrac{dy}{dx} = 0$.

To determine whether a stationary point is a maximum or a minimum, you must find the **second derivative** $\dfrac{d^2y}{dx^2}$:

- If $\dfrac{d^2y}{dx^2} > 0$ at a stationary point, the stationary point is a minimum.

- If $\dfrac{d^2y}{dx^2} < 0$ at a stationary point, the stationary point is a maximum.

- If $\dfrac{d^2y}{dx^2} = 0$ at a stationary point, the stationary point may be a maximum, a minimum or a point of inflection.

The gradient function can also be used to determine where a function is **increasing** or **decreasing**.

Chapter 12
Integration

12.1 Introduction

What is integration?

In Chapter 11 you learnt about differentiation. You learnt that differentiation gives a way to measure the gradient of a curve at any point. This gradient can also be considered a rate of change. For example, you can differentiate velocity to obtain acceleration, which is the rate of change of velocity.

Integration can also be used in a variety of ways. Firstly, it is the reverse of differentiation – so if you know the gradient function of a curve, integration will tell you the equation of the curve itself.

Secondly, you can use integration to measure the area under a curve. If you progress to A2 mathematics, you will also use integration to calculate volumes.

Together, differentiation and integration form the branch of mathematics known as **calculus**, possibly the greatest innovation in the history of mathematics.

Key words

- **Calculus**: The area of mathematics of which integration is a part.
- **Gradient**: The steepness of a curve at any point.
- **Derivative / gradient function**: A function that allows you to calculate the gradient at any point on a curve.
- **Differentiation**: A technique used to find the gradient function.
- **Integration / indefinite integration**: The reverse of differentiation; finding a function given its gradient function.
- **Definite integration**: A technique used to find the area under a curve.

Before you start

You should know how to:

- Expand brackets.
- Manipulate indices.
- Differentiate polynomials, e.g. $x^2 + 2x + 1$.

Worked Examples

1. Expand the brackets: $(x + 1)(x - 3)$

$$(x + 1)(x - 3)$$
$$= x^2 - 3x + x - 3$$
$$= x^2 - 2x - 3$$

2. Simplify the following: $a\left(a^{\frac{3}{2}}\right)^2$.

$$a\left(a^{\frac{3}{2}}\right)^2 = a(a^3) \quad \text{(because } (a^b)^c = a^{bc}\text{)}$$
$$= a^4 \quad\quad\quad \text{(add powers when multiplying)}$$

3. Differentiate the following to find $\frac{dy}{dx}$:

$$y = 2x^2 - \frac{x}{2} + 3$$

$$y = 2x^2 - \frac{1}{2}x + 3$$
$$\frac{dy}{dx} = 4x - \frac{1}{2}$$

What you will learn

In this chapter you will learn how to:

- Perform integration, the reverse of differentiation.
- Find the equation of a curve from its gradient function.
- Find the area enclosed between a curve and the x or y-axis.

In the real world...

Animated films are constructed almost entirely on computers these days. Special effects are generated using algebra; trigonometry rotates and moves the objects; integration helps to light each scene in a realistic way. There is a lot of mathematics behind the scenes.

Every strand of the *Trolls'* hair, the stunts in *Cars* and the haunting illumination in *Finding Dory* all owe their power to mathematics.

A technique called **Global Illumination** involves simulating how light bounces around in any scene. For every point on screen, software must work out how much light is travelling towards every other point, for every pair of points, for every frame. There are 24 frames for every second of the film. This vast calculation turns into an integral, which animators call the rendering equation.

The rendering equation is approximated as a set of linear equations, one equation for every item on screen, with typically 1 million to 10 million items. Vast computing power is needed to solve all the equations to provide realistic lighting alone. Now you can see why it takes about 6 days of computer time to create every second of each film!

Exercise 12A (Revision)

1. Expand out the brackets in the following expressions.
   (a) $x(x + 1)$ (b) $x^2(x^2 + 2x - 1)$
   (c) $(x - 1)(x - 3)$ (d) $(2x + 1)(3x - 2)$
   (e) $(x^2 - 1)(x^2 + 1)$ (f) $(x + 2)^3$

2. Simplify the following expressions.
   (a) $a^2 \times a^3$ (b) $b^2 \div b^3$
   (c) $\dfrac{c^4}{c \div c^3}$ (d) $\dfrac{(d^2)^4}{d^{-1}}$

3. Write the following in index form.
   (a) $\left(\sqrt{e}\right)^3$ (b) $\dfrac{1}{\sqrt{f}}$
   (c) $g\left(\sqrt[3]{g}\right)$ (d) $\dfrac{h^3}{\left(\sqrt{h}\right)^4}$

4. Differentiate the following with respect to x.
   (a) $y = x^2 + 1$ (b) $y = -x^3 + 4x^2 - 2x$
   (c) $y = \dfrac{1}{x^2} - \dfrac{1}{x}$ (d) $y = \sqrt{x}(2x^2 - 1)$
   (e) $y = (x - 2)^2$

12.2 Indefinite Integration of x^n

Consider the following function:
$y = x^2 + 1$

We can obtain the gradient function by differentiating:
$\dfrac{dy}{dx} = 2x$

We get same gradient function from many different functions:

$$y = x^2 + 2 \Rightarrow \dfrac{dy}{dx} = 2x$$

$$y = x^2 - 1 \Rightarrow \dfrac{dy}{dx} = 2x$$

and so on. Many different functions give the same gradient function when differentiated. Therefore, when we integrate – which is the reverse of differentiating – there are many possible answers.

If: $\dfrac{dy}{dx} = 2x$

then $y = x^2 + c$

where c can be any constant.

We call c the **constant of integration**. It is important to remember c whenever you perform indefinite integration.

Worked Example

4. If $\dfrac{dy}{dx} = 4x$, find y.

$\dfrac{dy}{dx} = 4x$

Increase the power of x by 1 and divide by the new power. Remember to include the constant of integration:

$y = \dfrac{4x^2}{2} + c$

$y = 2x^2 + c$

Check your answer by differentiating y.

When integrating a power of x:

- Increase the power by 1;
- Then divide by the new power.

> If $\dfrac{dy}{dx} = ax^n$
>
> then $y = \dfrac{a}{n + 1}x^{n+1} + c$

These rules apply when the power of x is positive, negative and fractional.

Worked Example

5. Find y where:
   (a) $\dfrac{dy}{dx} = 3x$ (b) $\dfrac{dy}{dx} = -6x^5$ (c) $\dfrac{dy}{dx} = 3x^{-2}$
   (d) $\dfrac{dy}{dx} = 5x^{3/2}$ (e) $\dfrac{dy}{dx} = 3x\sqrt{x}$

In all cases, increase the power by 1, then divide by the new power. Finally, add the constant of integration.

(a) $\dfrac{dy}{dx} = 3x$

$\Rightarrow y = \dfrac{3x^2}{2} + c$

$\Rightarrow y = \dfrac{3}{2}x^2 + c$

b) $\dfrac{dy}{dx} = -6x^5$

$\Rightarrow y = -\dfrac{6x^6}{6} + c$

$\Rightarrow y = -x^6 + c$

(c) $\dfrac{dy}{dx} = 3x^{-2}$

$\Rightarrow y = \dfrac{3x^{-1}}{-1} + c$

$\Rightarrow y = -3x^{-1} + c$

(d) $\dfrac{dy}{dx} = 5x^{3/2}$

$y = \dfrac{5x^{5/2}}{5/2} + c$

$y = 2x^{5/2} + c$

(e) You often have to re-arrange an expression before you can integrate it.

$\dfrac{dy}{dx} = 3x\sqrt{x}$

$= 3x^{3/2}$

$y = \dfrac{3x^{5/2}}{5/2} + c$

$y = \dfrac{6}{5}x^{5/2} + c$

Exercise 12B

1. Integrate the following to find y.

(a) $\dfrac{dy}{dx} = 6x$ (b) $\dfrac{dy}{dx} = x^6$

(c) $\dfrac{dy}{dx} = 2x$ (d) $\dfrac{dy}{dx} = -x^2$

(e) $\dfrac{dy}{dx} = -4x^3$ (f) $\dfrac{dy}{dx} = 6x^5$

(g) $\dfrac{dy}{dx} = 3x^2$ (h) $\dfrac{dy}{dx} = 50x^{99}$

(i) $\dfrac{dy}{dx} = 10x^7$ (j) $\dfrac{dy}{dx} = 12x^3$

(k) $\dfrac{dy}{dx} = -9x^2$

Exercise 12B

2. Integrate the following to find y.

(a) $\dfrac{dy}{dx} = 3x^{-4}$ (b) $\dfrac{dy}{dx} = -2x^{-2}$

(c) $\dfrac{dy}{dx} = \dfrac{1}{3}x^{-4}$ (d) $\dfrac{dy}{dx} = \dfrac{4}{3}x^{\frac{1}{3}}$

(e) $\dfrac{dy}{dx} = ax^{-2}$ (where a is a constant)

(f) $\dfrac{dy}{dx} = 7x^{-15}$ (g) $\dfrac{dy}{dx} = 7x^{\frac{5}{2}}$

(h) $\dfrac{dy}{dx} = -\dfrac{11}{5}x^{-16/5}$ (i) $\dfrac{dy}{dx} = -9x^{-9/8}$

3. Simplify and integrate the following.

(a) $\dfrac{dy}{dx} = \sqrt{x}$ (b) $\dfrac{dy}{dx} = \left(\sqrt{x}\right)^3$

(c) $\dfrac{dy}{dx} = \left(\dfrac{1}{x}\right)^3$ (d) $\dfrac{dy}{dx} = (-x)^2$

(e) $\dfrac{dy}{dx} = (-1)^4 x$ (f) $\dfrac{dy}{dx} = \dfrac{1}{\sqrt{x}}$

(g) $\dfrac{dy}{dx} = (2x)^4$ (h) $\dfrac{dy}{dx} = \left(\dfrac{1}{\sqrt{x}}\right)^4$

(i) $\dfrac{dy}{dx} = \left(\dfrac{1}{x}\right)^4 \left(\dfrac{x}{2}\right)^4$ (j) $\dfrac{dy}{dx} = \dfrac{\left(\sqrt{x}\right)^4 (x^3)^{-2}}{\left(x\sqrt{x}\right)^2}$

4. Sketch three different curves that, when differentiated, have the gradient function $\dfrac{dy}{dx} = 2x$.

12.3 Notation

The integral of a function $f(x)$ is usually represented using this notation:

$$\int f(x)\, dx$$

This should be read as 'the integral of $f(x)$ with respect to x'.

The general result from the previous section can be rewritten using this notation:

$$\int ax^n\, dx = \dfrac{a}{n+1}x^{n+1} + c$$

for $n \neq -1$. (You will learn how to integrate x^{-1} if you later study A2 mathematics.)

In Chapter 11, you learnt that $f'(x)$ and $\dfrac{dy}{dx}$ mean the same thing and are both notations for the derivative.

Therefore, we can write:

$$\int f'(x)\, dx = f(x) + c$$

Worked Example

6. Find $\displaystyle\int \dfrac{x^3}{4}\, dx$.

Firstly re-arrange: $\displaystyle\int \dfrac{x^3}{4}\, dx = \int \dfrac{1}{4}x^3\, dx$

This is another way of saying:

Find $f(x)$ if $f'(x) = \dfrac{1}{4}x^3$.

We proceed in the usual way: increase the power of x by 1, then divide the whole term by the new power. Finally, remember the constant of integration.

$$\int \dfrac{1}{4}x^3\, dx = \left(\dfrac{1}{4}x^4\right) \div 4 + c$$

$$= \dfrac{1}{16}x^4 + c$$

It is important to remember dx when writing an integral. This tells us we are integrating **with respect to** the variable x, i.e. it is the power of x that will increase by one. This becomes important in integrals such as

$\displaystyle\int \pi r^2\, dr$, where dr reminds us that we are integrating with respect to the variable r, and π is a constant.

Worked Example

7. Integrate to find an equation for s: $s = \displaystyle\int 4t\, dt$

We are integrating with respect to t.

Increase the power of t by 1, then divide by the new power. Finally add a constant of integration. So:

$s = 2t^2 + c$

Remember to simplify surds and rewrite using index notation before integrating.

Worked Example

8. Find: $\displaystyle\int 5x\sqrt{x}\, dx$

Rewrite using the rules of indices:

$$\int 5x\sqrt{x}\, dx = \int 5x^{3/2}\, dx$$

Increase the power by one and divide by the new power:

$$= \dfrac{5x^{5/2}}{5/2}$$

And don't forget the constant of integration!

$$= 2x^{5/2} + c$$

When integrating a constant, think of it as multiplying the variable to the power 0. The solution then contains the variable to the power 1.

Worked Example

9. Find $\displaystyle\int 3\, dx$.

$$\int 3\, dx = \int 3x^0\, dx$$

We are integrating with respect to x. The power of x goes up from 0 to 1. Dividing by the new power, 1, leaves the 3 unchanged:

$$= 3x + c$$

Exercise 12C

1. Find the following integrals.

   (a) $\displaystyle\int 4x\, dx$
   (b) $\displaystyle\int x^5\, dx$

   (c) $\displaystyle\int -x^3\, dx$
   (d) $\displaystyle\int -3x^2\, dx$

   (e) $\displaystyle\int 5\, dx$
   (f) $\displaystyle\int 3x^3\, dx$

   (g) $\displaystyle\int 100x^{49}\, dx$
   (h) $\displaystyle\int 10x^5\, dx$

   (i) $\displaystyle\int -12x^5\, dx$
   (j) $\displaystyle\int 9x^5\, dx$

2. Integrate the following.

   (a) $\displaystyle\int 4x^{-5}\, dx$
   (b) $\displaystyle\int -4t^{-2}\, dt$

   (c) $\displaystyle\int -\dfrac{1}{4}x^{-5}\, dx$
   (d) $\displaystyle\int \dfrac{5}{8}y^{\frac{1}{4}}\, dy$

   (e) $\displaystyle\int bx^{-3}\, dx$ (where b is a constant)

Exercise 12C...

3. Integrate the right-hand side of the following equations.

   (a) $y = \int -\dfrac{9}{4}z^{-\frac{13}{4}}\,dz$

   (b) $y = \int -8x^{-17}\,dx$

   (c) $r = \int 6\theta^{\frac{7}{2}}\,d\theta$

   (d) $s = \int -x^{-11/10}\,dx$

4. Simplify and integrate the following.

   (a) $\int \sqrt{y}\,dy$

   (b) $\int -\left(\dfrac{1}{\sqrt{x}}\right)^6 dx$

   (c) $\int \left(\dfrac{1}{s}\right)^3 \left(\dfrac{s}{2}\right)^3 ds$

   (d) $\int (-x)^4\,dx$

5. Integrate the right-hand side of the following equations.

   (a) $y = \int (-1)^2\,dp$

   (b) $z = \int (\sqrt{x})^5\,dx$

   (c) $p = \int \left(\dfrac{2}{z}\right)^4 dz$

   (d) $y = \int \dfrac{4}{\sqrt{x}}\,dx$

   (e) $s = \int (2t)^2\,dt$

   (f) $I = \int \dfrac{(\sqrt{x})^6(x^2)^{-2}}{(x\sqrt{x})^4}\,dx$

12.4 Sums and Differences

You can integrate sums and differences by integrating each term in turn. The general result is:

$$\int \big(f(x) + g(x)\big)\,dx = \int f(x)\,dx + \int g(x)\,dx$$

Worked Example

10. Find y where: $y = \int (x^2 + x^3)\,dx$

    The brackets make it clear that $(x^2 + x^3)$ is being integrated, not just one of these terms.

    Integrate each term:
    $y = \dfrac{1}{3}x^3 + \dfrac{1}{4}x^4 + c$

    Strictly speaking, both terms give constants when integrated. We combine them into a single constant, c.

You may need to expand brackets or rearrange in other ways before integrating.

Worked Examples

11. Expand the brackets and integrate the following:

$$\int \left(x^2 + \dfrac{1}{x}\right)^2 dx$$

$$\int \left(x^2 + \dfrac{1}{x}\right)^2 dx = \int \left(x^4 + 2(x^2)\left(\dfrac{1}{x}\right) + \left(\dfrac{1}{x}\right)^2\right) dx$$

$$= \int (x^4 + 2x + x^{-2})\,dx$$

$$= \dfrac{1}{5}x^5 + x^2 - x^{-1} + c$$

12. Find: $\int \left((\sqrt{x})^3 + \dfrac{1}{\sqrt{x}}\right) dx$

    Rewrite using index notation:

$$\int \left((\sqrt{x})^3 + \dfrac{1}{\sqrt{x}}\right) dx = \int (x^{3/2} + x^{-1/2})\,dx$$

$$= \dfrac{2}{5}x^{5/2} + 2x^{1/2} + c$$

13. Find: $\int (ax^2 + bx + c)\,dx$

$$\int (ax^2 + bx + c)\,dx = \dfrac{a}{3}x^3 + \dfrac{b}{2}x^2 + cx + d$$

    We call the constant d here because c is already being used.

Exercise 12D

1. Integrate the following.

   (a) $\int \left(3 + 4x^{3/4}\right) dx$

   (b) $\int \left(4 + 3\sqrt{x}\right) dx$

   (c) $\int (8x^2 + 7x)\,dx$

   (d) $\int (2x^4 + 3x)\,dx$

   (e) $\int (6x^3 + 4x)\,dx$

   (f) $\int \left(4 + \dfrac{3}{x^2}\right) dx$

   (g) $\int x(4 - x)\,dx$

   (h) $\int x(9 - x)\,dx$

   (i) $\int \left(x^{-7} + 4\sqrt{x}\right) dx$

   (j) $\int \left(x^{-4} + 6\sqrt{x}\right) dx$

   (k) $\int (3x^3 + 5x)\,dx$

   (l) $\int (8x - x^2 - 8)\,dx$

2. Given $f'(x)$, find $f(x)$.

   (a) $f'(x) = 4x^3 + 3x^2 + 6$

   (b) $f'(x) = 16x^3 + 6x^2 + 5$

   (c) $f'(x) = 12x^3 + 6x^2 + 7$

Exercise 12D...

(d) $f'(x) = \dfrac{x}{2} + \dfrac{3}{x^2}$

(e) $f'(x) = \dfrac{x}{3} + \dfrac{4}{x^2}$

(f) $f'(x) = x^2 - 8x + 3$

(g) $f'(x) = x^3 - 24x^2 + 144x$

(h) $f'(x) = x^3 - 7x^2 + 15x + 3$

(i) $f'(x) = x^2 - 4x + 3$

(j) $f'(x) = x^2 + 7x + 19$

3. Expand the brackets to find:

(a) $\displaystyle\int 4(2x^4 + x)\, dx$ (b) $\displaystyle\int (x + 2)^2\, dx$

(c) $\displaystyle\int (x^2 - 2)^2\, dx$ (d) $\displaystyle\int \left(4\sqrt{x} + 9\right)^2 dx$

(e) $\displaystyle\int (2 - x)^2\, dx$ (f) $\displaystyle\int \left(1 - \dfrac{1}{x^2}\right)^2 dx$

(g) $\displaystyle\int (1 - x)(1 + 2x)\, dx$

(h) $\displaystyle\int x(2x^2 + 3x)\, dx$

(i) $\displaystyle\int \dfrac{1}{x^4}(2x + 1)^2\, dx$

(j) $\displaystyle\int x(x^2 + 2x + 1)^2\, dx$

4. If k is a constant, find:

(a) $\displaystyle\int (k + 2)^2\, dx$

(b) $\displaystyle\int (k + 2x)^2\, dx$

(c) $\displaystyle\int (kx + 2)^2\, dx$

(d) $\displaystyle\int (kx + 2x)^2\, dx$

5. Re-arrange or simplify to find the following integrals.

(a) $\displaystyle\int \dfrac{(x^2 + 1)}{x^2}\, dx$ (b) $\displaystyle\int \dfrac{(\sqrt{t} - 2t)}{t}\, dt$

(c) $\displaystyle\int \dfrac{(\sqrt{z} + 3z)}{\sqrt{z}}\, dz$ (d) $\displaystyle\int x\left(\dfrac{\sqrt{x} + 1}{2x^3}\right) dx$

(e) $\displaystyle\int \dfrac{x^2 - 4}{x^3(x + 2)}\, dx$ (f) $\displaystyle\int \dfrac{\theta - 1}{\theta\sqrt{\theta}}\, d\theta$

(g) $\displaystyle\int \dfrac{1 + s}{\sqrt[3]{s}\sqrt{s}}\, ds$

6. Given: $\dfrac{dy}{dx} = 7 + \dfrac{2}{x^2}$

use integration to find y in terms of x.

Exercise 12D...

7. Given:
$$\int 2(p + 3x)^2\, dx = 6x^3 - 24x^2 + 32x + c$$

what is the value of p?

12.5 Finding the Constant of Integration

As mentioned in section 12.2, a constant of integration will always appear in the solution to an indefinite integral. This is because there are an infinite number of curves that have the same gradient function. Consider:

$y = x^2 + 1 \;\Rightarrow\; \dfrac{dy}{dx} = 2x$

$y = x^2 \qquad \Rightarrow\; \dfrac{dy}{dx} = 2x$

$y = x^2 - 4 \;\Rightarrow\; \dfrac{dy}{dx} = 2x$

Therefore the gradient function $2x$ gives many possible solutions when integrated.

$$\int 2x\, dx = x^2 + c$$

The family of curves $y = x^2 + c$ are all translations of each other in the y-direction, as shown by the following graph.

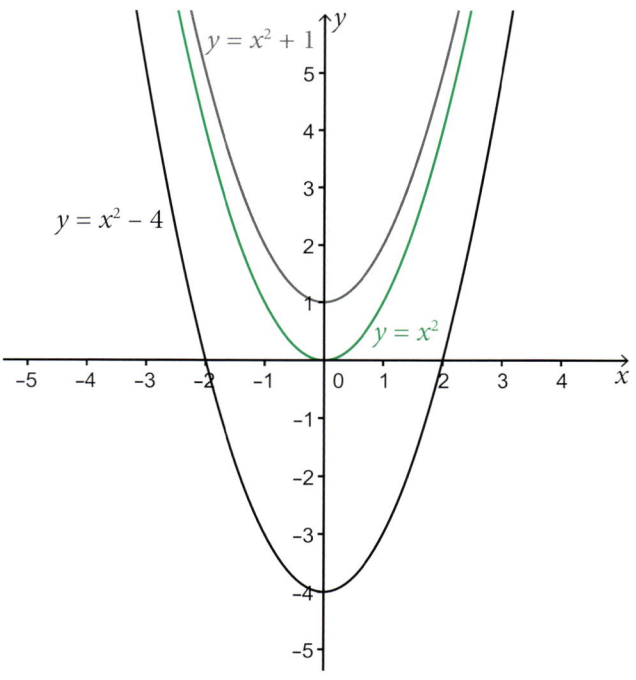

If we have been given the coordinates of a point on the curve, we can work out the constant of integration and the correct equation of the curve.

Worked Examples

14. The gradient function of a curve is given by:

$$\frac{dy}{dx} = 6 + \frac{2}{x^2}$$

(a) Use integration to find y in terms of x and a constant of integration c.

(b) Given also that the point $(2, 7)$ lies on the curve, find the full equation of the curve.

(c) Find the value of y where $x = 3$.

(a) $y = \int \left(6 + \frac{2}{x^2}\right) dx$

$y = \int (6 + 2x^{-2}) \, dx$

$y = 6x - 2x^{-1} + c$, or

$y = 6x - \frac{2}{x} + c$

(b) $y = 7$ when $x = 2$, therefore:

$7 = 12 - 1 + c$

$c = -4$

So:

$y = 6x - \frac{2}{x} - 4$

(c) When $x = 2$:

$y = 6(3) - \frac{2}{3} - 4$

$y = \frac{40}{3}$

---

15. $y = \int 2x \, dx$

Find y in terms of x given that $x = 1$ when $y = 3$.

$y = \int 2x \, dx$

$y = x^2 + c$

When $x = 1$, $y = 3$, therefore:

$3 = 1^2 + c$

$c = 2$

$y = x^2 + 2$

Exercise 12E

1. Given the gradient function $\frac{dy}{dx}$ of a curve and a point on the curve, find y in terms of x.

(a) $\frac{dy}{dx} = 3x, \left(1, -\frac{3}{2}\right)$

(b) $\frac{dy}{dx} = x^2 + 4, \left(1, \frac{16}{3}\right)$

(c) $\frac{dy}{dx} = \frac{1}{x^2}, (1, 0)$

(d) $\frac{dy}{dx} = x^3 + 1, (0, 1)$

(e) $\frac{dy}{dx} = 2x^3 - \frac{3}{2}x^2 + x, (1, 2)$

(f) $\frac{dy}{dx} = \frac{x - 1}{x^3}, \left(1, -\frac{1}{2}\right)$

(g) $\frac{dy}{dx} = \sqrt{x}, (1, 1)$

(h) $\frac{dy}{dx} = 2x^2 + \sqrt{x}, (1, 2)$

(i) $\frac{dy}{dx} = x^2 + 6x + 1, (-2, 8)$

(j) $\frac{dy}{dx} = \frac{1}{x^2} + x^{-5/2}, \left(2, -\frac{2}{5}\right)$

2. Given that $\frac{dy}{dx} = 5 + \frac{3}{x^2}$:

(a) Use integration to find y in terms of x.

(b) Given also that $y = 5$ when $x = 2$, find the value of y at $x = 3$.

3. The gradient function of a curve is given by:

$$\frac{dy}{dx} = 4x^4 + 6x$$

Given that $y = 8$ when $x = 0$, integrate to find y as a function of x.

4. Integrate to find y, given that: $\frac{dy}{dx} = 4x^2 + 7x$ and that $y = 6$ when $x = 1$.

5. The gradient function of a curve is given by

$$\frac{dy}{dx} = ax + b$$

Given that the curve passes through the points $(0, 2)$, $(1, 3)$ and $(2, 2)$, find a, b and the constant of integration. Hence state the equation of the curve.

6. The second derivative of a function can be written as $\frac{d^2y}{dx^2}$ or $f''(x)$. It is obtained by differentiating a function twice. In reverse, you can integrate the second derivative twice

Exercise 12E...

to obtain the original function. Remember to include a constant of integration each time you integrate.

(a) Given $\dfrac{d^2y}{dx^2} = 4x$ and given that $\dfrac{dy}{dx} = 1$ when $x = 1$, find $\dfrac{dy}{dx}$ in terms of x.

(b) Given that $y = 10$ when $x = 3$, find y in terms of x.

12.6 Definite Integration

Indefinite integration, introduced in the previous sections, gives you an integral as a function of x.

You can find the **numerical** value of an integral using a technique called **definite integration.** In the following sections, we will use this technique to find areas enclosed by curves.

Definite integrals are written with an upper and a lower limit, for example:

$$\int_1^3 x^3\, dx$$

These limits are values of x used to find exact values of the integral. The integral between the limits is evaluated by subtracting the value of the integral at the lower limit from the value at the upper limit.

> **Note:** Sometimes you may see the words 'upper bound' and 'lower bound'. These mean the same as 'upper limit' and 'lower limit'.

You do not need a constant of integration when performing definite integration. Write the result of the integration inside square brackets, keeping the limits. In the next step, substitute the limits and subtract.

As an equation, we write:

$$\int_a^b f'(x)\, dx = [f(x)]_a^b$$
$$= f(b) - f(a)$$

Worked Examples

16. Find: $\displaystyle\int_1^3 x^3\, dx$

Put the result of the integration in square brackets with the limits:

$$\int_1^3 x^3\, dx = \left[\frac{1}{4}x^4\right]_1^3$$

In place of x, substitute in the limits. Subtract the result at the lower limit from the result at the upper limit.

$$= \left(\frac{1}{4}(3)^4\right) - \left(\frac{1}{4}(1)^4\right)$$
$$= \frac{81}{4} - \frac{1}{4}$$
$$= 20$$

17. Find: $\displaystyle\int_3^5 (x - 1)\, dx$

$$\int_3^5 (x - 1)\, dx = \left[\frac{1}{2}x^2 - x\right]_3^5$$
$$= \left(\frac{1}{2}(5)^2 - 5\right) - \left(\frac{1}{2}(3)^2 - 3\right)$$
$$= \left(\frac{25}{2} - 5\right) - \left(\frac{9}{2} - 3\right)$$

Be careful with the signs, especially in the second set of brackets.

$$= \frac{15}{2} - \frac{3}{2}$$
$$= 6$$

12.7 Area Enclosed Between a Curve and the x-axis

You can use definite integration to find the area between a curve and either of the coordinate axes.

Most often, you will be asked to find the area between a curve and the x-axis.

Worked Example

18. Find the area A enclosed between the curve $y = x^2$, the x-axis and the lines $x = 2$ and $x = 4$.

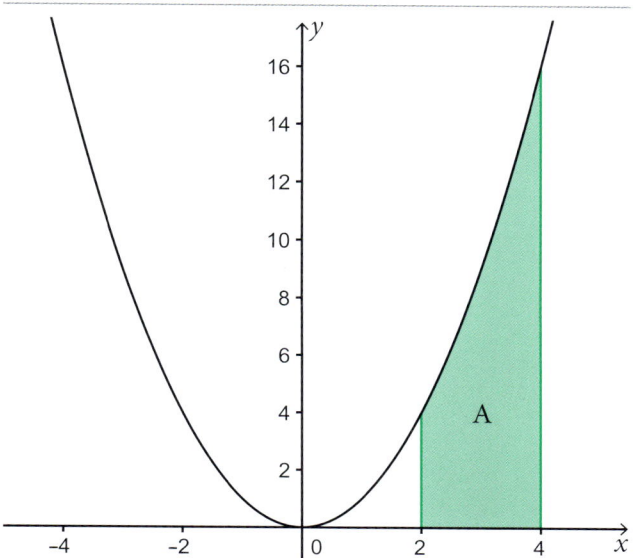

$$A = \int_2^4 x^2 \, dx$$

$$= \left[\frac{1}{3} x^3 \right]_2^4$$

$$= \left(\frac{1}{3}(4)^3 \right) - \left(\frac{1}{3}(2)^3 \right)$$

$$= \frac{64}{3} - \frac{8}{3}$$

$$= \frac{56}{3}$$

> **Note:** There are no units. You may write "square units", but it is not necessary.

Sometimes you will be required to work out the upper and lower limits. In these cases, you must find where the curve intersects the x-axis.

Worked Example

19. Find the area enclosed by the curve $y = x(4 - x)$ and the x-axis.

Firstly, sketch the curve to find out where it intersects the x-axis:

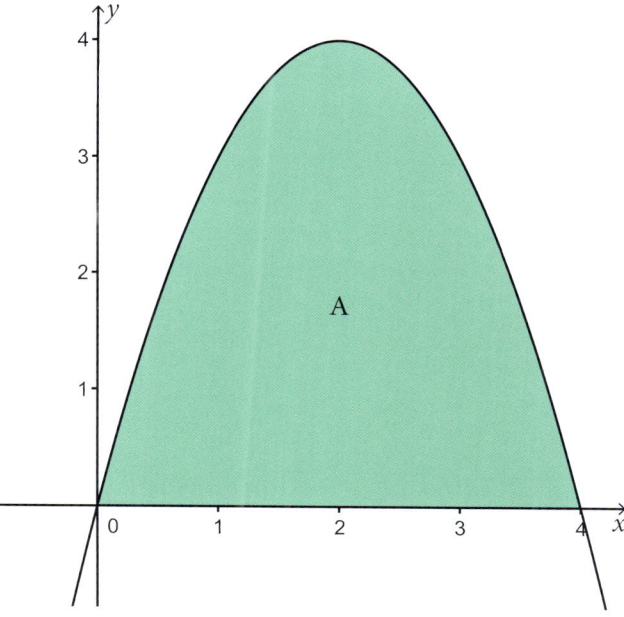

The sketch shows that the curve crosses the x-axis at $(0, 0)$ and $(4, 0)$. Our upper and lower limits are therefore $x = 4$ and $x = 0$.

$$A = \int_0^4 x(4 - x) \, dx$$

$$= \int_0^4 (4x - x^2) \, dx$$

$$= \left[2x^2 - \frac{1}{3} x^3 \right]_0^4$$

$$= \left(2(4)^2 - \frac{1}{3}(4)^3 \right) - \left(2(0)^2 - \frac{1}{3}(0)^3 \right)$$

$$= \left(32 - \frac{64}{3} \right) - (0 - 0)$$

$$= \frac{32}{3}$$

> **Note:** As in most of the A-Level topics, answers are usually left as improper fractions rather than mixed numbers or decimals.

If the curve lies below the x-axis, the result from the definite integration will be negative. When finding an area, you should report the positive value.

Worked Example

20. Find the area enclosed by the curve $y = (x - 1)^3$, the x-axis and the y-axis.

Firstly, sketch the curve to find our limits. Remember that $y = (x - 1)^3$ is a translation by 1 unit in the positive x-direction of the curve $y = x^3$.

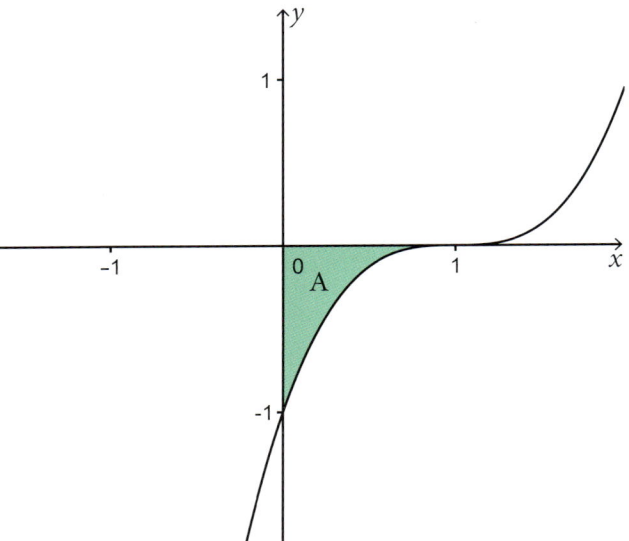

The curve intersects the x-axis at $(1, 0)$, so the upper limit for the integration is $x = 1$.

To the left, the area is enclosed by the y-axis, so the lower limit is $x = 0$.

$$\int_0^1 (x - 1)^3 \, dx = \int_0^1 (x^3 - 3x^2 + 3x - 1) \, dx$$

$$= \left[\frac{x^4}{4} - x^3 + \frac{3x^2}{2} - x \right]_0^1$$

$$= \left(\frac{1^4}{4} - 1^3 + \frac{3(1)^2}{2} - 1 \right) - \left(\frac{0^4}{4} - 0^3 + \frac{3(0)^2}{2} - 0 \right)$$

$$= \left(\frac{1}{4} - 1 + \frac{3}{2} - 1 \right) - 0$$

$$= -\frac{1}{4}$$

The integration gives a negative result because the area lies below the x-axis. When reporting the area, we must give the positive value.

$$A = \frac{1}{4}$$

Note: The lower limit often gives the value zero when substituted into the integrated expression. Be careful though – this is not always the case!

Sometimes, a part of the curve lies above and a part below the x-axis. In these cases, you must consider each part separately. The result from one part will be negative. When finding the total area, make both answers positive and add them.

Worked Example

21. Find the total area enclosed by the curve $y = x(x - 2)$, the line $x = 3$ and the x-axis.

A sketch of the curve is shown below:

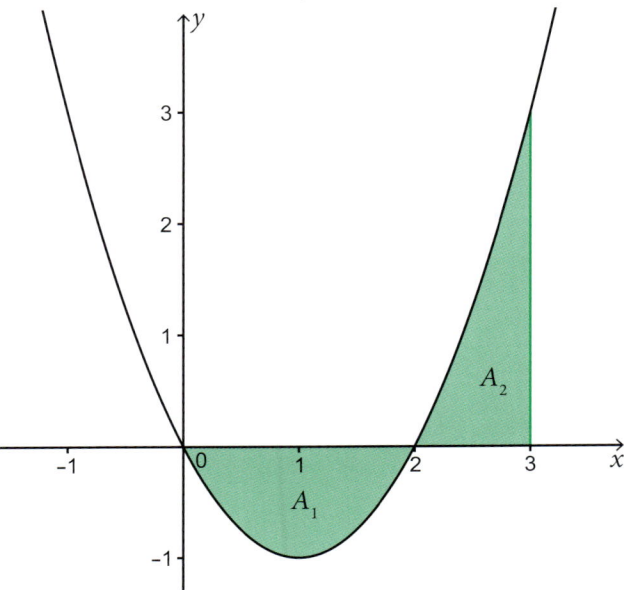

The curve intersects the x-axis at $(0, 0)$ and $(2, 0)$.

- Between $x = 0$ and $x = 2$, the curve lies below the x-axis.
- Between $x = 2$ and $x = 3$, the curve lies above the x-axis.

We must consider these two areas separately.

To find A_1:

$$\int_0^2 x(x - 2) \, dx = \int_0^2 (x^2 - 2x)$$

$$= \left[\frac{1}{3} x^3 - x^2 \right]_0^2$$

$$= \left(\frac{1}{3} 2^3 - 2^2 \right) - \left(\frac{1}{3} 0^3 - 0^2 \right)$$

$$= -\frac{4}{3}$$

So area $\quad A_1 = \frac{4}{3}$.

To find A_2:

$$\int_2^3 x(x-2)\,dx = \int_2^3 (x^2 - 2x)\,dx$$

$$= \left[\frac{1}{3}x^3 - x^2\right]_2^3$$

$$= \left(\frac{1}{3}3^3 - 3^2\right) - \left(\frac{1}{3}2^3 - 2^2\right)$$

$$= 0 - \left(-\frac{4}{3}\right)$$

So area $A_2 = \dfrac{4}{3}$

The total area is $A_1 + A_2 = \dfrac{8}{3}$.

> **Note:** A sketch of the curve is essential here. Without it, it would be difficult to see that a part of the curve lies below the x-axis and a part of it above. The two areas must be found separately.

Exercise 12F

1. Evaluate the following. Give your answers to 3 significant figures where appropriate.

   (a) $\displaystyle\int_0^3 x(4-x)\,dx$

   (b) $\displaystyle\int_0^7 x(8-x)\,dx$

   (c) $\displaystyle\int_4^6 \left(x^{-3} + 10\sqrt{x}\right)dx$

   (d) $\displaystyle\int_1^4 \left(8x^3 + 6x^2 + 4\right)dx$

   (e) $\displaystyle\int_1^2 \left(12x^3 + 9x^2 + 2\right)dx$

   (f) $\displaystyle\int_2^9 \left(5x^3 + 4x\right)dx$

   (g) $\displaystyle\int_1^5 \left(8x^3 + 7x\right)dx$

   (h) $\displaystyle\int_1^4 6\sqrt{x}\,dx$

   (i) $\displaystyle\int_0^4 \left(3\sqrt{x} + x\right)dx$

   (j) $\displaystyle\int_1^2 x^2\left(1 - \frac{1}{x^4}\right)dx$

Exercise 12F...

2. Evaluate the following definite integrals. Give your answer in the form $a + b\sqrt{c}$ where a, b and c are integers.

   (a) $\displaystyle\int_1^8 \frac{2}{\sqrt{x}}\,dx$

   (b) $\displaystyle\int_1^{27} \frac{3}{\sqrt{x}}\,dx$

   (c) $\displaystyle\int_1^{125} \frac{6}{\sqrt{x}}\,dx$

3. The curve C is defined by the equation $y = x^3 - 24x^2 + 144x$, as shown.

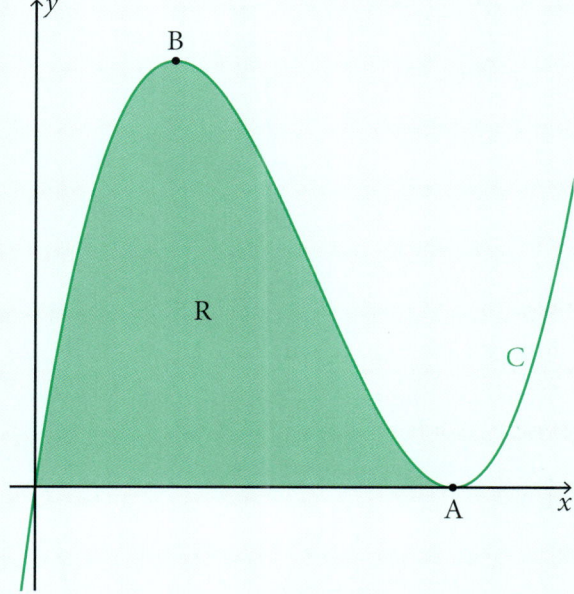

   C touches the x-axis at A and has a maximum turning point at B.
   (a) Show that the equation of the curve may be written as $y = x(x-12)^2$.
   (b) Hence write down the coordinates of A.
   (c) Find the coordinates of B.
   (d) The shaded region R is bounded by the curve and the x-axis. Find the area of R.

Exercise 12F...

4. The diagram shows a sketch of $y = x^2 - 5x + 4$ with areas A and B marked. Find the areas A and B and the total shaded area.

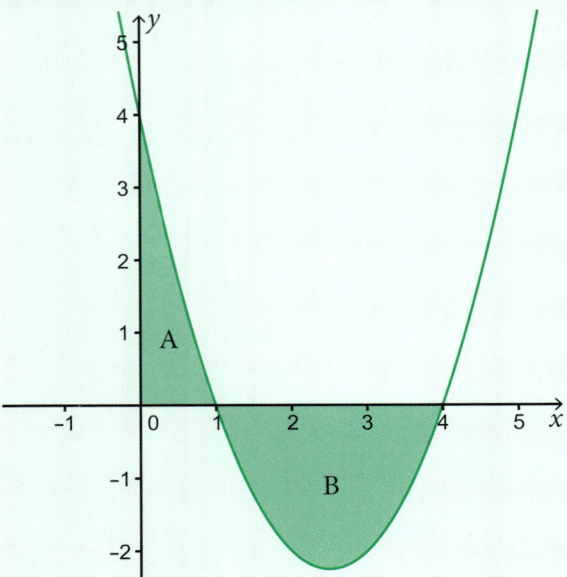

5. The diagram shows a sketch of part of the curve C with equation $y = x(x - 3)(x - 6)$.

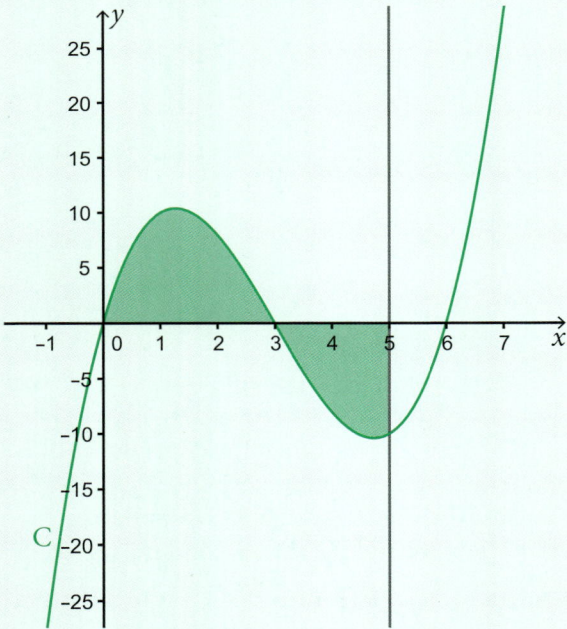

Use calculus to find the total area of the finite region shown, bounded by the lines $x = 0$ and $x = 5$, curve C and the x-axis.

Exercise 12F...

6. The diagram shows the logo of an Olympic ski jump venue.

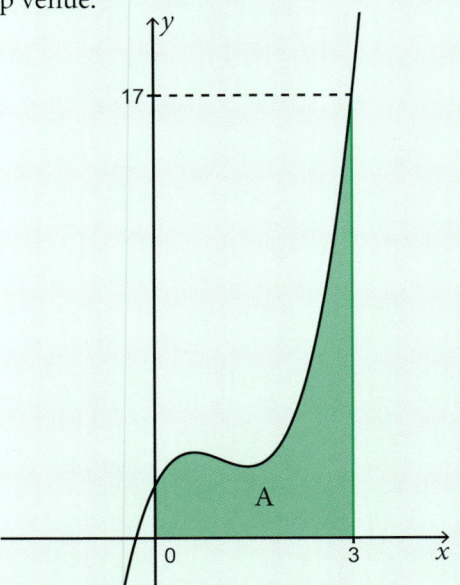

The design is modelled on a curve with equation $y = 2x^3 - 6x^2 + 5x + 2$.

The units on both axes are centimetres. Calculate how much material is required to make the area A of the logo.

7. The diagram shows a part of the curve $y = 2x^3 - 4x^2$.

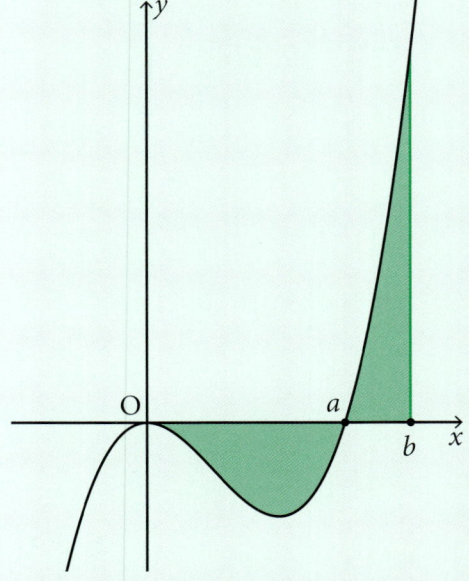

(a) Find the value of a, the x-coordinate of the point where the curve crosses the x-axis.

(b) Given that the two shaded regions are equal in area, find the value of b.

12.8 Area Enclosed Between a Curve and the y-axis

You can also use integration to find the area between a curve and the y-axis.

In this case, you must find x as a function of y, then integrate x with respect to y. The limits will refer to y-values, i.e.:

$$A = \int_a^b x \, dy$$

Worked Example

22. Calculate the area A shown in the diagram, bounded by the curve $y = x^2$, the y-axis and the straight lines $y = 2$ and $y = 4$.

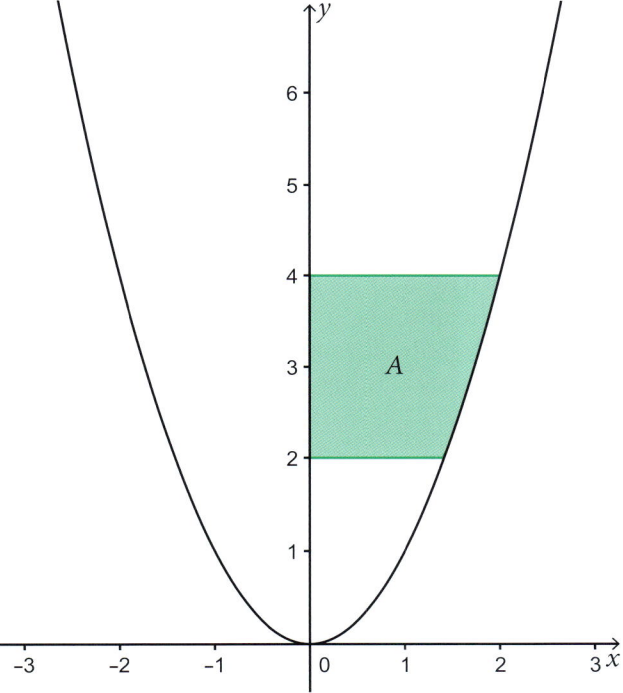

Re-arrange the equation of the curve to obtain x as a function of y:

$$y = x^2 \Rightarrow x = y^{1/2}$$

Now integrate with respect to y between the limits on the y-axis:

$$A = \int_2^4 y^{1/2} \, dy$$

$$= \left[\frac{2}{3} y^{3/2} \right]_2^4$$

$$= \left(\frac{2}{3} (4)^{3/2} \right) - \left(\frac{2}{3} (2)^{3/2} \right)$$

$$= 3.45 \text{ (3 s.f.)}$$

Note: The answer to the integration will be negative if the area lies to the left of the y-axis. As before, if you are finding an area, you must report the positive value.

Exercise 12G

1. The curve C shown represents the graph of $y = \dfrac{x^2}{4}$. The points A and B on the curve C have x-coordinates 2 and 4 respectively.

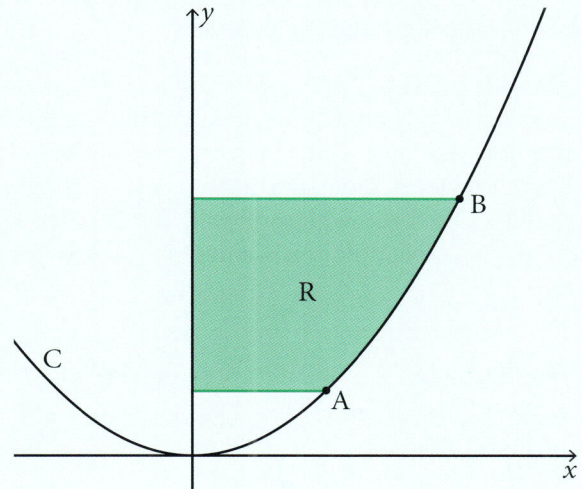

   (a) Write down the y-coordinates of A and B.

   The finite region R is enclosed by C, the y-axis and the lines through A and B parallel to the x-axis.

   (b) Express x in terms of y.

   (c) Use integration to find the area of R.

2. The diagram shows the curve $f(x) = x^3$.

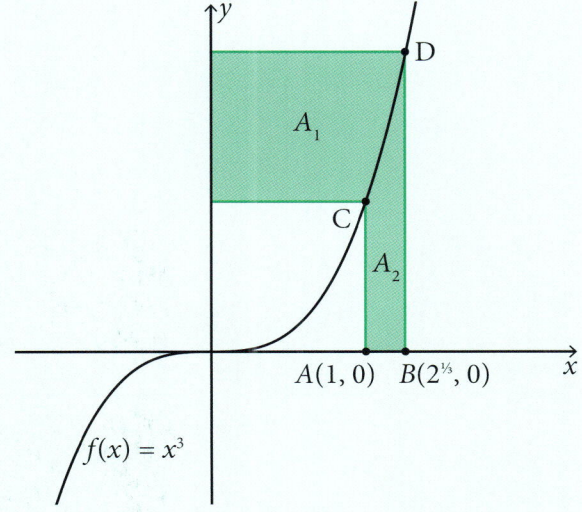

Exercise 12G...

The point A has coordinates $(1, 0)$ and $B(2^{1/3}, 0)$.

The points C and D lie on the curve and have the same x-coordinates as A and B respectively.

(a) Find the y-coordinates of points C and D.

(b) Show that the area A_1 is $\dfrac{3}{4}(2^{4/3} - 1)$.

(c) Find the exact value of the area A_2.

(d) Find the ratio $A_1 : A_2$.

12.9 More Complex Areas

You may be asked to find more complex areas, such as the area between a curve and a straight line. In this type of question you may need to calculate a definite integral, then add or subtract the area of a triangle, rectangle or trapezium. Often you will be given a sketch of the graph, but in the next example you are required to provide the sketch.

Worked Example

23. Find the area enclosed between the curve $y = x^2$ and the straight line $y = x$.

In this question no diagram is given, so we must draw a sketch of the two functions and the area enclosed.

To find out the intersection points, we solve:
$$x^2 = x$$
$$x(x - 1) = 0$$
$$x = 0 \text{ or } x = 1$$

When $x = 0$, $y = 0$. When $x = 1$, $y = 1$. The intersection points are $(0, 0)$ and $(1, 1)$. So we draw:

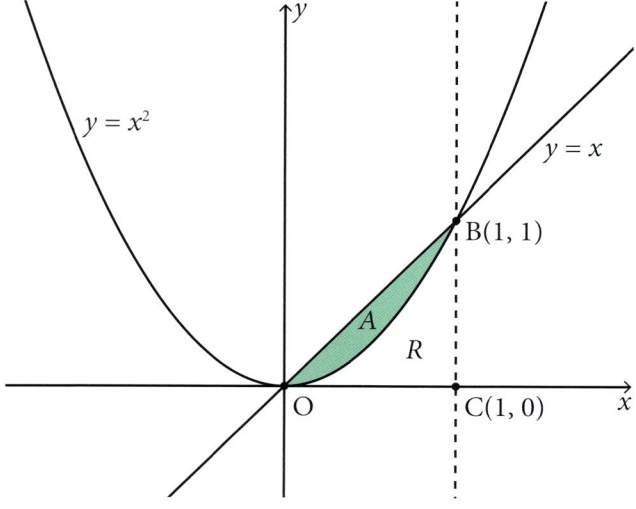

From the diagram, the area A is the difference between the triangle OBC and the area labelled R.

$$\Delta OBC = \frac{1}{2}(1)(1) = \frac{1}{2}$$

Area R can be found by integrating the equation of the curve between limits:

$$R = \int_0^1 x^2 \, dx$$
$$= \left[\frac{x^3}{3}\right]_0^1$$
$$= \left(\frac{1^3}{3}\right) - \left(\frac{0^3}{3}\right)$$
$$= \frac{1}{3}$$

So $A = \dfrac{1}{2} - \dfrac{1}{3} = \dfrac{1}{6}$

Exercise 12H

1. Ollie is standing at point O, at the bottom of a hill with equation $y = \dfrac{x}{3}$.

   His friend Becky is standing on the hill at point B. Ollie throws a snowball at Becky and the snowball flies through the air with equation $y = 4x - x^2$. The snowball makes a direct hit.

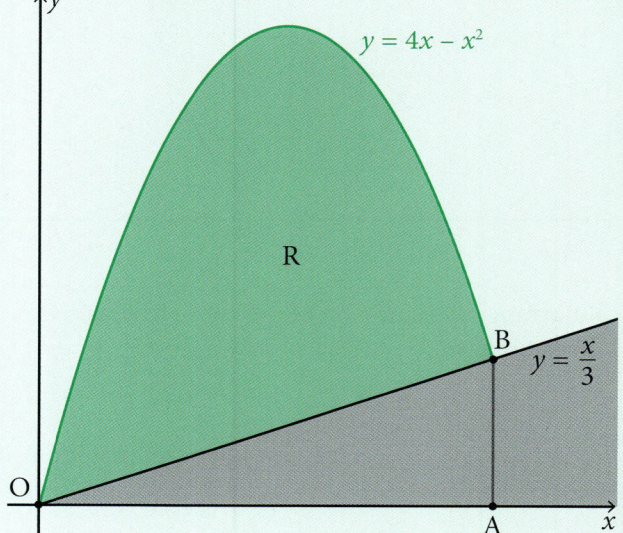

   All distances are measured in metres.

   (a) Calculate Becky's exact position, i.e. the coordinates of point B.

   (b) Find the area of the triangle OAB.

   (c) Find the area of R, the region bounded by the slope and the trajectory of the snowball.

Exercise 12H

2. The diagram shows a sketch of part of the curve C with equation $y = x^3 - 7x^2 + 15x + 4$.

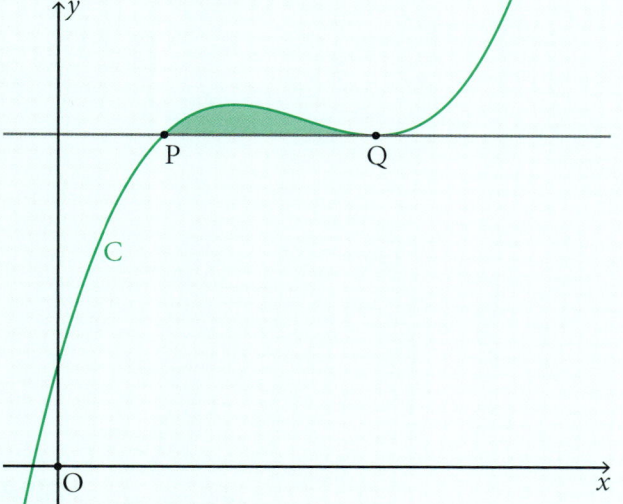

The point P, on C, has x-coordinate 1 and the point Q is the minimum turning point of C.

(a) Find $\dfrac{dy}{dx}$.

(b) Find the y-coordinate of P.

(c) Find the coordinates of Q.

(d) Calculate the area, shown shaded, bounded by C and the line PQ.

3. The curve given by $y = x^3 - 7x^2 + 16x$ has a maximum point at A and a minimum at B, as shown.

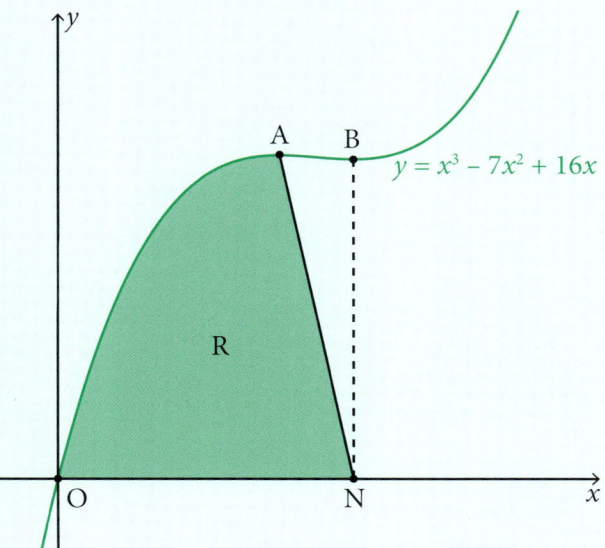

(a) Use calculus to find the x-coordinates of A and B.

The line through B parallel to the y-axis meets the x-axis at the point N. The region R is bounded by the curve, the x-axis and the line from A to N.

(b) Find $\displaystyle\int (x^3 - 7x^2 + 16x)\, dx$

(c) Hence calculate the area of R, giving your answer to 3 significant figures.

4. The diagram shows the line with equation $y = 7 - x$ and the curve $y = x^2 - 2x + 1$.

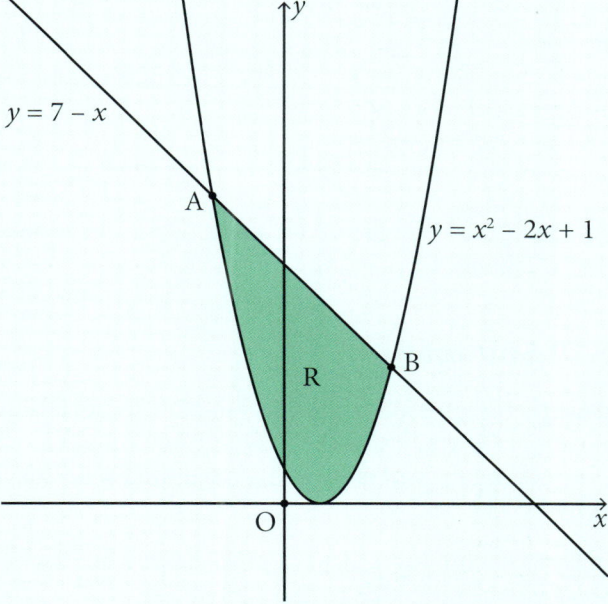

The line and the curve intersect at the points A and B, and O is the origin.

(a) Calculate the coordinates of A and B.

The shaded region R is bounded by the line and the curve.

(b) Calculate the exact area of R.

Exercise 12H...

5. The diagram shows a part of the curve $y = 16x - 8x^2$ and the straight line $y = 7.5$.

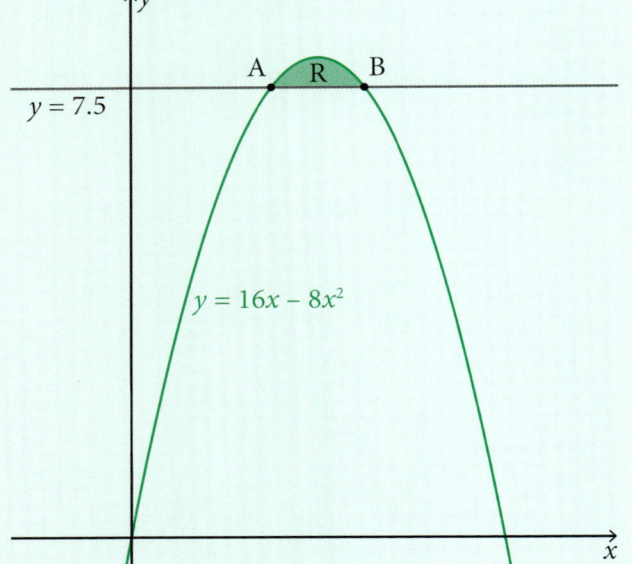

Find the exact area R enclosed by the curve and the line $y = 7.5$.

12.10 Summary

Indefinite integration is the **reverse of differentiation**. For example, if you know the gradient function of a curve, integration will tell you the equation of the curve itself.

To integrate a function that is a power of x, raise the power by one and divide by the new power.

Sums and differences of terms can be integrated by integrating each term in turn.

The result of indefinite integration will always include a **constant of integration**.

Sometimes you will be given enough information to calculate the constant of integration. For example, if the question relates to a curve we may be given the coordinates of a point on it.

Definite integration is a way to find a numerical value of an integral. It can be used to find the area between a curve and either of the coordinate axes.

You may be asked to find more complex areas, such as the area between a curve and a line. To do this you will integrate to find the area between the curve and the x-axis, then combine this with some other area, such as a triangle, rectangle or trapezium.

Chapter 13
Vectors

13.1 Introduction

Key words

- **Vector**: A quantity with both size and direction, such as force or velocity. A vector can be expressed using two or three components, which are scalars (numbers).

- **Magnitude**: The length or size of a vector.

- **Resultant**: The sum of more than one vector.

- **Position vector**: The vector from the origin to a point.

- **Unit vector**: A vector with a magnitude of 1.

- **Scalar**: A numerical quantity without a direction. Mass, length and time are all scalar quantities.

Before you start

You should know:

- How to use vectors to represent translations.

- How to use Pythagoras' Theorem.

- How to solve simultaneous equations in two unknowns.

Worked Examples

1. Find the vector that translates the curve $y = (x - 3)^2$ to the curve $y = x^2 + 4x$.

    Both quadratic curves are parabolas with minimum points (since x^2 is positive).

    The first curve has its minimum point at $(3, 0)$.

    For the second curve, complete the square:
    $y = x^2 + 4x$
    $\quad = (x + 2)^2 - 4$

    This tells us the minimum point is at $(-2, -4)$.

    Hence, the translation vector is $\begin{pmatrix} -5 \\ -4 \end{pmatrix}$, as shown in the following diagram:

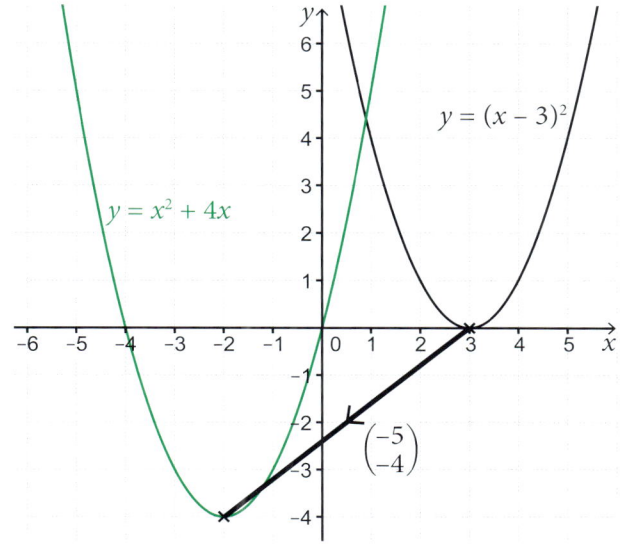

2. Find the distance between the points $(6, 7)$ and $(-1, 2)$, giving your answer as a surd.

    $d = \sqrt{(x_2 - x_1)^2 + (y_2 - y_1)^2}$
    $\quad = \sqrt{(-1 - 6)^2 + (2 - 7)^2}$
    $\quad = \sqrt{49 + 25}$
    $\quad = \sqrt{74}$

What you will learn

In this chapter you will learn how to:

- Express vectors in more than one way.

- Find the magnitude and direction of a vector in 2 dimensions.

- Add and subtract vectors in 2 dimensions.

- Multiply vectors by scalars.

- Use position vectors.

- Find the distance between two points.

In the real world...

Ants use vectors when out of the nest, in order to find their way home.

They keep track of distances by counting their steps, and the position of the sun to calculate the direction for each step of their outward journey. By the process of evolution, the ant's brain has developed the ability to process information about distance and direction and to perform the appropriate vector sums.

Each time they move in a straight line, the vector is added to the **resultant vector** (the total). The resultant gives a vector that points from the nest to their current location. Reversing this vector takes them straight back to the nest. So to find their way back home, ants do not need to remember the precise route they have taken; they simply add each bit of their journey to the last total and take the negative.

The result is a continuously updated home vector. If they find food or come under attack from a predator and need to get back home quickly, the home vector gets them there quickly.

Exercise 13A (Revision)

1. (a) The point $(2, 3)$ is mapped to the point $(-2, -3)$ by a translation. Find the vector that describes this translation.
   (b) The curve $y = x^2$ is translated by the vector $\begin{pmatrix} 1 \\ -2 \end{pmatrix}$. Find the coordinates of the stationary point of the new curve.

2. The line $y = 3x + 2$ is translated to the line l_2 by the vector $\begin{pmatrix} 0 \\ 4 \end{pmatrix}$.
   (a) What is the y-intercept of the new line?
   (b) What is the gradient of the new line?
   (c) Write down the equation of l_2.

3. (a) Use Pythagoras' Theorem to find the length of the line segment between the points $(0, 0)$ and $(2, 2)$. Give your answer as a surd.
   (b) The distance between the points $(1, 1)$ and $(k, 9)$ is 10. Find the two possible values of k.

13.2 Vectors in Two Dimensions

How to draw vectors

The following diagram shows an example of a two-dimensional vector between the points $A(0, 0)$ and $B\left(\dfrac{\sqrt{2}}{2}, \dfrac{\sqrt{2}}{2}\right)$. The vector is marked with an arrowhead.

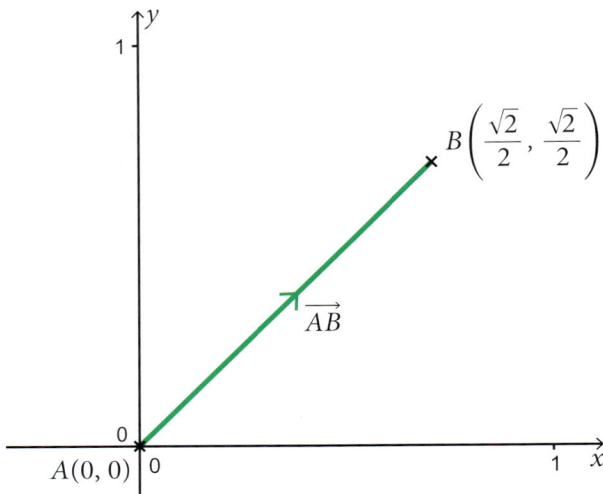

Naming vectors

There are two ways to name vectors:

- Sometimes they are named after two points they connect. In the previous diagram, note that the vector is labelled $\overrightarrow{AB}$ because it represents movement from point A to point B. We could write $\overrightarrow{AB} = \begin{pmatrix} \sqrt{2}/2 \\ \sqrt{2}/2 \end{pmatrix}$.

- Alternatively, a vector can be named with a single lower case letter, e.g. **b**. Lower case letters used to name vectors are either written in bold or underlined (e.g. b̲). In your work, you should underline all your vector names.

Unit vectors

A **unit vector** is any vector of length (or **magnitude**) 1.

A unit vector is often denoted with a 'hat', e.g. $\hat{\mathbf{b}}$.

The special unit vectors **i** and **j** run parallel to the positive x and y axes respectively, as shown in the following diagram:

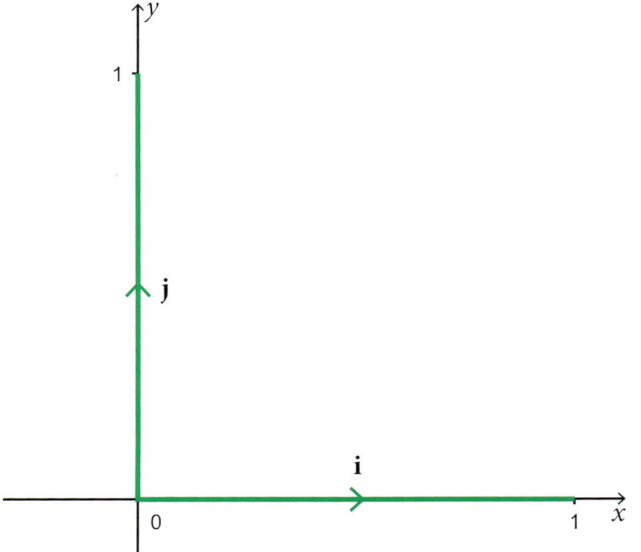

We could write $\mathbf{i} = \begin{pmatrix} 1 \\ 0 \end{pmatrix}$ and $\mathbf{j} = \begin{pmatrix} 0 \\ 1 \end{pmatrix}$.

Vector equality

Note that two vectors are equal if they are the parallel and have the same length (magnitude). The following diagram shows two vectors that are equal. Therefore they are both labelled **a**.

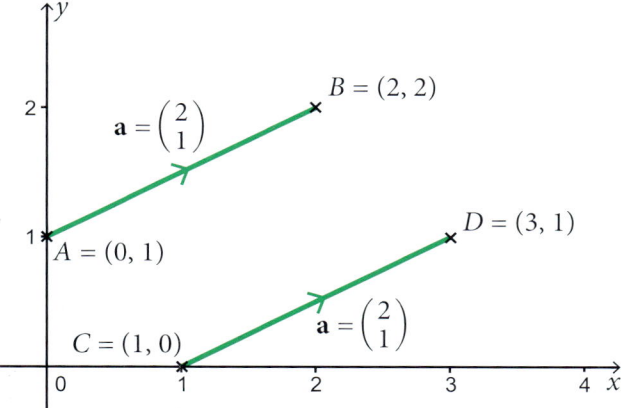

Notation: the components of vectors

There are two ways to denote the components of a vector.

As you have already seen, vectors can be written as a column of numbers, for example $\begin{pmatrix} 2 \\ 1 \end{pmatrix}$. These are known as **column vectors**.

Vectors can also be written using combinations of the unit vectors **i** and **j**:

$\mathbf{p} = \begin{pmatrix} 2 \\ 1 \end{pmatrix} = 2\mathbf{i} + \mathbf{j}$

We will use both notations in this chapter, but you may decide to use only one or the other in your work.

> **Note:** It is important not to confuse vector notation with coordinate notation. For example, do not confuse the vector $\begin{pmatrix} 2 \\ 1 \end{pmatrix}$ with the point (2, 1).

13.3 Algebraic Operations

Vector addition and subtraction

To add two vectors, add the components in turn. The sum of two vectors is called the **resultant**.

To subtract one vector from another, subtract the components in turn.

Worked Example

3. Find the sum and the difference of the two vectors:

$\mathbf{p} = \begin{pmatrix} 9 \\ -1 \end{pmatrix}, \mathbf{q} = \begin{pmatrix} -2 \\ 4 \end{pmatrix}.$

$\mathbf{p} + \mathbf{q} = \begin{pmatrix} 9 \\ -1 \end{pmatrix} + \begin{pmatrix} -2 \\ 4 \end{pmatrix}$

$\quad = \begin{pmatrix} 7 \\ 3 \end{pmatrix}$

$\mathbf{p} - \mathbf{q} = \begin{pmatrix} 9 \\ -1 \end{pmatrix} - \begin{pmatrix} -2 \\ 4 \end{pmatrix}$

$\quad = \begin{pmatrix} 11 \\ -5 \end{pmatrix}$

Geometrical interpretation of vector addition

When drawing a diagram to represent the addition of two vectors, begin the second vector where the first vector finishes ('top to tail'). A resultant vector is usually marked with a double arrowhead.

The following diagram shows that the resultant of the two vectors $\overrightarrow{AB}$ and $\overrightarrow{BC}$ is $\overrightarrow{AC}$.

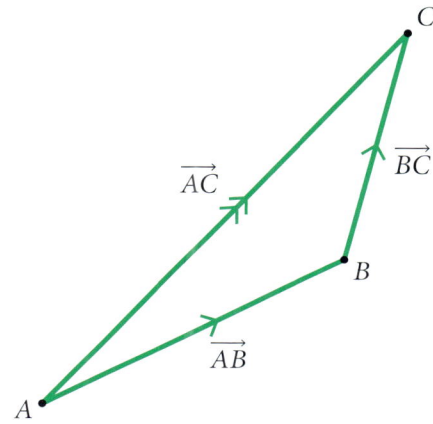

From this diagram, you can see:

$\overrightarrow{AC} = \overrightarrow{AB} + \overrightarrow{BC}$

This is known as the **triangle law** of addition.

You can also find vector $\overrightarrow{AB}$ if you know $\overrightarrow{AC}$ and $\overrightarrow{BC}$:

$\overrightarrow{AB} = \overrightarrow{AC} - \overrightarrow{BC}$

The next diagram shows that it does not matter in which order vectors are added.

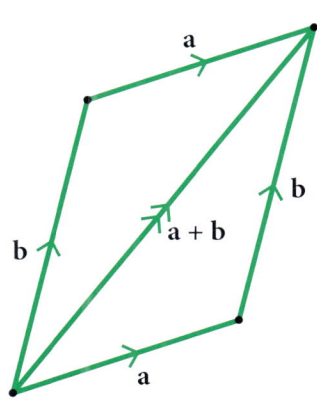

From this diagram, you can see:

$$a + b = b + a$$

This is known as the **parallelogram law** of addition.

Multiplication by scalars

Multiplying a vector $\overrightarrow{AB}$ by a scalar gives a vector parallel to $\overrightarrow{AB}$, as shown in the following diagram.

In this case $\overrightarrow{AC} = 4\overrightarrow{AB}$.

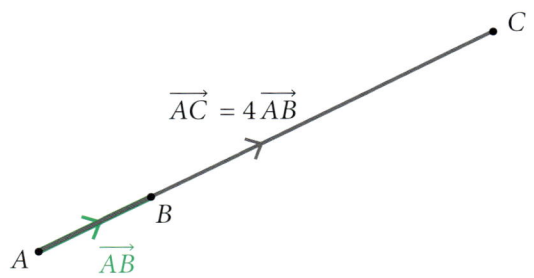

If three points A, B and C are **collinear** (i.e. they all lie on the same straight line), then

$$\overrightarrow{AC} = \lambda\overrightarrow{AB}$$

for some scalar λ.

Conversely, if $\overrightarrow{AC} = \lambda\overrightarrow{AB}$, then we know the three points A, B and C are collinear.

Multiplying by –1

Making a vector negative, or multiplying by –1, results in a vector of the same length, but in the opposite direction, as shown in the following diagram:

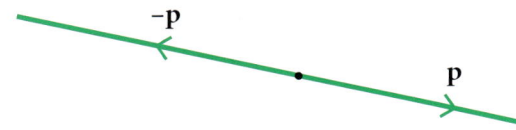

For example, if $p = \begin{pmatrix} 2 \\ -1 \end{pmatrix}$, then $-p = \begin{pmatrix} -2 \\ 1 \end{pmatrix}$.

Worked Examples

4. Find $\overrightarrow{AC}$ if $\overrightarrow{AB} = \begin{pmatrix} 4 \\ 3 \end{pmatrix}$ and $\overrightarrow{BC} = \begin{pmatrix} 2 \\ 7 \end{pmatrix}$.

   $\overrightarrow{AC} = \overrightarrow{AB} + \overrightarrow{BC}$

   $\phantom{\overrightarrow{AC}} = \begin{pmatrix} 4 \\ 3 \end{pmatrix} + \begin{pmatrix} 2 \\ 7 \end{pmatrix}$

   $\phantom{\overrightarrow{AC}} = \begin{pmatrix} 6 \\ 10 \end{pmatrix}$

5. Vector $t = \begin{pmatrix} 5 \\ 3 \\ -2 \end{pmatrix}$. Find a vector that is parallel to t, but 5 times as long.

$$5t = 5\begin{pmatrix} 5 \\ 3 \\ -2 \end{pmatrix} = \begin{pmatrix} 25 \\ 15 \\ -10 \end{pmatrix}$$

Exercise 13B

1. Find the sum of the following vectors.
   (a) $\begin{pmatrix} 1 \\ 0 \end{pmatrix} + \begin{pmatrix} 0 \\ 1 \end{pmatrix}$
   (b) $\begin{pmatrix} 1 \\ 2 \end{pmatrix} + \begin{pmatrix} 1 \\ -6 \end{pmatrix}$
   (c) $(-6i + 6j) + (-i + 2j)$
   (d) $p + q$ where $p = \begin{pmatrix} 6 \\ 0 \end{pmatrix}$, $q = \begin{pmatrix} -15 \\ -7 \end{pmatrix}$

2. Find the resultant of these vectors.
   (a) $\begin{pmatrix} 1 \\ -4 \end{pmatrix}, \begin{pmatrix} -1 \\ 1 \end{pmatrix}, \begin{pmatrix} -6 \\ 1 \end{pmatrix}$
   (b) p, q, r where $p = \begin{pmatrix} 3 \\ 1 \end{pmatrix}$, $q = \begin{pmatrix} -1 \\ -7 \end{pmatrix}$, $r = \begin{pmatrix} 5 \\ 0 \end{pmatrix}$
   (c) $(-i - j), (4i - 2j), (-4i + 2j)$

3. Find the following.
   (a) $\begin{pmatrix} 1 \\ 0 \end{pmatrix} - \begin{pmatrix} 0 \\ 1 \end{pmatrix}$
   (b) $\begin{pmatrix} 2 \\ 1 \end{pmatrix} - \begin{pmatrix} -2 \\ 1 \end{pmatrix}$
   (c) $(-2i + 3j) - (-4i - 2j)$
   (d) $p - q$ where $p = \begin{pmatrix} 6 \\ -1 \end{pmatrix}$, $q = \begin{pmatrix} -10 \\ -1 \end{pmatrix}$

4. If $a = \begin{pmatrix} -3 \\ 2 \end{pmatrix}$ and $b = \begin{pmatrix} 1 \\ 4 \end{pmatrix}$, find:
   (a) $a + b$ (b) $a - b$ (c) $a + 2b$
   (d) $2a - b$ (e) $-a$ (f) $-b$
   (g) $b - a$

5. Find $\overrightarrow{BC}$ if $\overrightarrow{AB} = \begin{pmatrix} -4 \\ 5 \end{pmatrix}$ and $\overrightarrow{AC} = \begin{pmatrix} 2 \\ 1 \end{pmatrix}$.

6. In the following diagram, $ABCD$ is a parallelogram.
   $\overrightarrow{AB} = r = \begin{pmatrix} 5 \\ 3 \end{pmatrix}$ and $\overrightarrow{AD} = s = \begin{pmatrix} 1 \\ 2 \end{pmatrix}$.

   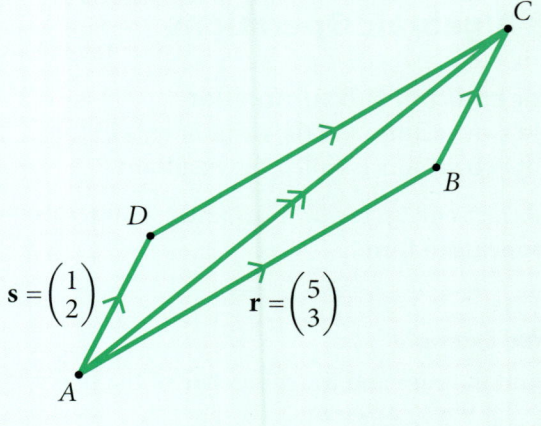

   Find $\overrightarrow{AC}$.

Exercise 13B...

7. In the following diagram, points *A, B* and *C* are collinear. The distance between *B* and *C* is 3 times the distance from *A* to *B*. Find $\overrightarrow{AC}$.

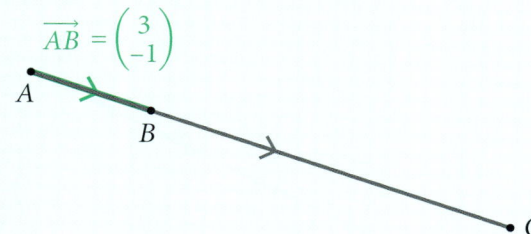

$$\overrightarrow{AB} = \begin{pmatrix} 3 \\ -1 \end{pmatrix}$$

8. Vector $\mathbf{u} = \begin{pmatrix} 10 \\ 3 \end{pmatrix}$.

Find a vector $\mathbf{v}$, such that $\mathbf{v}$ is parallel to $\mathbf{u}$, but has one third of the magnitude (length).

13.4 Magnitude and Direction of a Vector

The magnitude of a vector is its length.

The magnitude of vector $\overrightarrow{AB}$ is written $\left|\overrightarrow{AB}\right|$.

The magnitude of vector $\mathbf{b}$ is written $|\mathbf{b}|$.

We can use Pythagoras' Theorem to find the magnitude of a vector.

> In two dimensions, the magnitude of vector $\begin{pmatrix} x \\ y \end{pmatrix}$ is $\sqrt{x^2 + y^2}$.

Worked Example

6. Show that the vector $\overrightarrow{AB} = \begin{pmatrix} \frac{1}{\sqrt{2}} \\ \frac{1}{\sqrt{2}} \end{pmatrix}$ is a unit vector.

We must show that the length of $\overrightarrow{AB}$ is 1.

Using Pythagoras Theorem:

$$\left|\overrightarrow{AB}\right| = \sqrt{\left(\frac{1}{\sqrt{2}}\right)^2 + \left(\frac{1}{\sqrt{2}}\right)^2}$$

$$= \sqrt{\frac{1}{2} + \frac{1}{2}}$$

$$= 1$$

Hence $\overrightarrow{AB}$ is a unit vector.

To find a unit vector parallel to a given vector, divide the given vector by its own magnitude.

Worked Example

7. The vector $\mathbf{p} = \mathbf{i} - 2\mathbf{j}$.
   (a) Find a unit vector parallel to $\mathbf{p}$.
   (b) Find a vector of magnitude 10 in the same direction as $\mathbf{p}$.

(a) Find the magnitude of $\mathbf{p}$:
$$|\mathbf{p}| = \sqrt{1^2 + (-2)^2}$$
$$= \sqrt{5}$$

The unit vector parallel to $\mathbf{p}$ is:
$$\hat{\mathbf{p}} = \frac{1}{\sqrt{5}}(\mathbf{i} - 2\mathbf{j})$$
$$= \frac{\sqrt{5}}{5}(\mathbf{i} - 2\mathbf{j})$$

(You can check this really is a unit vector by finding its magnitude.)

(b) To find a vector of magnitude 10 in the same direction as $\mathbf{p}$, multiply the unit vector by 10:
$$10\hat{\mathbf{p}} = \frac{10\sqrt{5}}{5}(\mathbf{i} - 2\mathbf{j})$$
$$= 2\sqrt{5}(\mathbf{i} - 2\mathbf{j})$$

Calculating the direction of a vector

You may be asked to find the direction of a vector.

> **Note:** When you are asked for the direction of a vector you should give the angle it makes with the *x*-axis.

Worked Examples

8. The vector $\mathbf{a} = 2\mathbf{i} - 3\mathbf{j}$. Find its magnitude and direction.

First, draw a sketch:

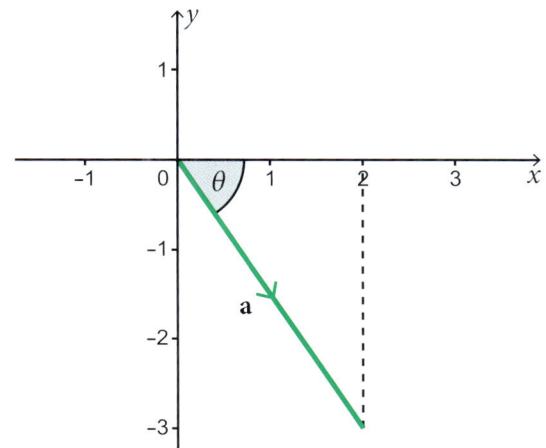

For the magnitude, use Pythagoras' Theorem with the triangle marked in the diagram. The two shorter sides have lengths 2 and 3.

$$|\mathbf{a}| = \sqrt{2^2 + 3^2}$$
$$= \sqrt{13}$$

To find angle θ:
$$\tan \theta = \frac{3}{2}$$
$$\theta = 56.3° \text{ (3 s.f.)}$$

The vector has magnitude $\sqrt{13}$ in the direction 56.3° below the positive x-axis.

9. The vector $\mathbf{a} = \begin{pmatrix} -1 \\ 4 \end{pmatrix}$.
   (a) Find the magnitude of $\mathbf{a}$, giving an exact answer.
   (b) Find its direction.

First, draw a sketch:

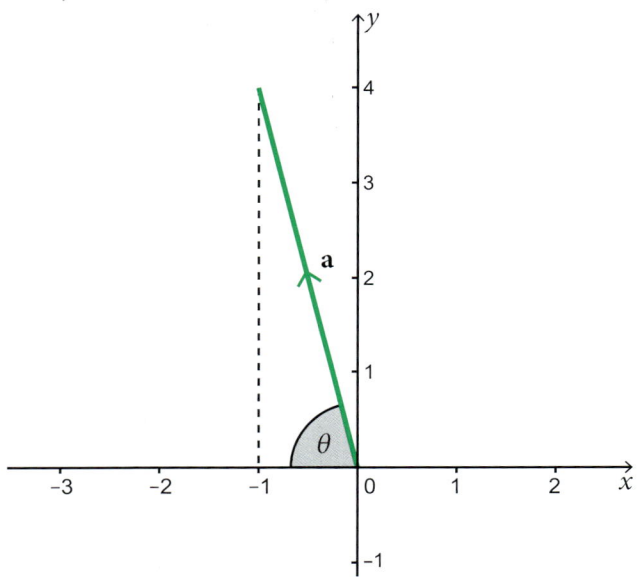

(a) Use Pythagoras' Theorem with the triangle shown:
$$|\mathbf{a}| = \sqrt{1^2 + 4^2}$$
$$= \sqrt{1 + 16}$$
$$= \sqrt{17}$$

(b) To find angle θ, use the triangle shown in the diagram:
$$\tan \theta = \frac{4}{1} = 4$$
$$\theta = 76.0° \text{ (3 s.f.)}$$

The vector has magnitude $\sqrt{17}$ in the direction 76.0° above the negative x-axis.

If you are given the magnitude and direction of a vector, you may have to calculate the vector's two components.

Worked Examples

10. The vector $\mathbf{v}$ has magnitude $2\sqrt{5}$ in the direction 26.57° above the positive x-axis. Find the two components of $\mathbf{v}$.

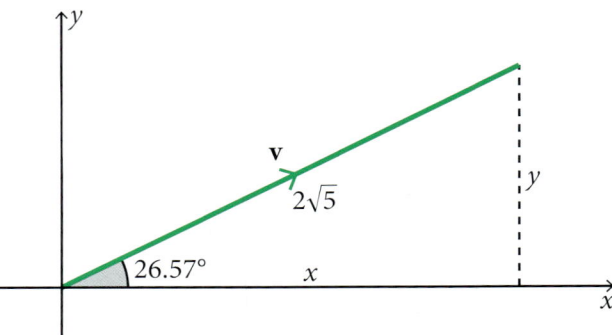

Using the right-angled triangle shown:
$$\cos(26.57) = \frac{x}{2\sqrt{5}}$$
$$x = 2\sqrt{5}\cos(26.57)$$
$$x = 4.00 \text{ (3 s.f.)}$$

$$\sin(26.57) = \frac{y}{2\sqrt{5}}$$
$$y = 2\sqrt{5}\sin(26.57)$$
$$y = 2.00 \text{ (3 s.f.)}$$

So $\mathbf{v} = \begin{pmatrix} 4.00 \\ 2.00 \end{pmatrix}$

11. The vector $\mathbf{w}$ has magnitude 10 in the direction 30° above the negative x-axis. Find the two components of $\mathbf{w}$, giving your answers as simplified surds where appropriate.

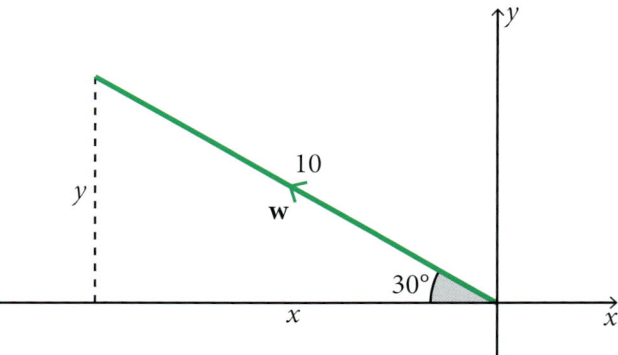

$$\cos 30 = \frac{x}{10}$$
$$x = 10\cos 30$$
$$x = 5\sqrt{3}$$

This value is the length of the base of the triangle. So the x-component of the vector is $-5\sqrt{3}$.

$$\sin 30 = \frac{y}{10}$$
$$y = 10 \sin 30$$
$$y = 5$$

So $\mathbf{w} = \begin{pmatrix} -5\sqrt{3} \\ 5 \end{pmatrix}$

---

12. The vector $\mathbf{p}$ has magnitude 12 in the direction $\theta°$ below the negative x-axis, where $\tan \theta = 0.2$. Find the two components of $\mathbf{p}$.

First find θ:
$$\tan \theta = 0.2$$
$$\theta = \tan^{-1}(0.2)$$
$$\theta = 11.3099°$$

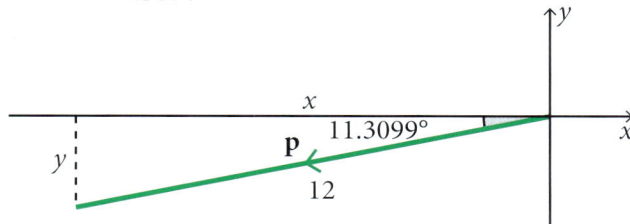

$$\cos 11.3099 = \frac{x}{12}$$
$$x = 12 \cos 11.3099$$
$$x = 11.8$$

$$\sin 11.3099 = \frac{y}{12}$$
$$y = 12 \sin 11.3099$$
$$y = 2.35$$

The two shorter sides of the triangle have been computed. Remember that both components of the vector are negative.

So: $\mathbf{p} = \begin{pmatrix} -11.8 \\ -2.35 \end{pmatrix}$ (3 s.f.)

> **Note:** Working with the angle to several decimal places ensures we do not lose accuracy when rounding our final values for x and y to 3 significant figures. Alternatively, use the ANS key on your calculator.

....

Exercise 13C

1. Find the magnitude and direction of the following vectors. Give an exact answer for each magnitude.
   (a) $\begin{pmatrix} 3 \\ 4 \end{pmatrix}$ (b) $\begin{pmatrix} -3 \\ 4 \end{pmatrix}$ (c) $\begin{pmatrix} 7 \\ 0 \end{pmatrix}$
   (d) $\begin{pmatrix} 6 \\ 4 \end{pmatrix}$ (e) $5\mathbf{i} + 12\mathbf{j}$ (f) $3\mathbf{i} + 10\mathbf{j}$

Exercise 13C...

2. Find the unit vector parallel to the following vectors.
   (a) $\begin{pmatrix} 6 \\ 8 \end{pmatrix}$ (b) $2\mathbf{i}$ (c) $\begin{pmatrix} -1 \\ 2 \end{pmatrix}$
   (d) $\mathbf{i} - \mathbf{j}$ (e) $\begin{pmatrix} -24 \\ -7 \end{pmatrix}$ (f) $-8\mathbf{i} - 4\mathbf{j}$
   (g) $\begin{pmatrix} -7 \\ 4 \end{pmatrix}$ (h) $-\mathbf{i} + 6\mathbf{j}$ (i) $\begin{pmatrix} 3 \\ -2 \end{pmatrix}$
   (j) $\begin{pmatrix} 0 \\ -6 \end{pmatrix}$

3. Calculate the following vectors in component form.
   (a) Vector $\mathbf{p}$ has magnitude 25, 40° above the positive x-axis.
   (b) Vector $\mathbf{q}$ has magnitude 14, 60° below the positive x-axis. Give an exact answer.
   (c) Vector $\mathbf{r}$ has magnitude 6 at an angle $\theta°$ above the negative x-axis, where $\tan \theta = 1$. Give an exact answer.

4. Vector $\mathbf{u} = \begin{pmatrix} 10 \\ 3 \end{pmatrix}$. Find a unit vector parallel to $\mathbf{u}$.

5. Vector $\mathbf{t} = \begin{pmatrix} 5 \\ -2 \end{pmatrix}$. Find a unit vector parallel to $\mathbf{t}$.

6. The vector $\mathbf{a} = \begin{pmatrix} -8 \\ q \end{pmatrix}$ has a magnitude of 17. Find:
   (a) The value of q, given that it is a positive integer.
   (b) A unit vector parallel to $\mathbf{a}$.

7. The vector $\mathbf{b} = \begin{pmatrix} m \\ 3m \end{pmatrix}$ has a magnitude of $5\sqrt{10}$.
   (a) Find the value of m, given that it is a negative integer.
   (b) A unit vector parallel to $\mathbf{b}$.

8. The vector $s\mathbf{i} - 7\mathbf{j}$ has a magnitude of 25. Find the value of s. Give your answer as a simplified surd.

9. The vector $\mathbf{p} = \begin{pmatrix} 4a \\ a - 1 \end{pmatrix}$ has a magnitude of 41.
   (a) Find the value of a, given that it is a positive integer.
   (b) Find the vector $\mathbf{p}$.

10. Vectors $\mathbf{p}$ and $\mathbf{q}$ are defined such that $\mathbf{p} = \begin{pmatrix} 2 \\ 4 \end{pmatrix}, \mathbf{q} = \begin{pmatrix} 3 \\ 1 \end{pmatrix}$.
    (a) Find the angle between vector $\mathbf{p}$ and the positive y-axis.
    (b) Find the angle between vector $\mathbf{q}$ and the positive x-axis.
    (c) Hence find the size of the acute angle between vectors $\mathbf{p}$ and $\mathbf{q}$.

13.5 Position Vectors

The **position vector** of a point A is the vector from the origin O to the point A.

The position vector of point A is written as **a**. (In your written work you should use an underline, i.e. a).

Consider two vectors **a** and **b**, which are the position vectors of points A and B, as shown in the diagram.

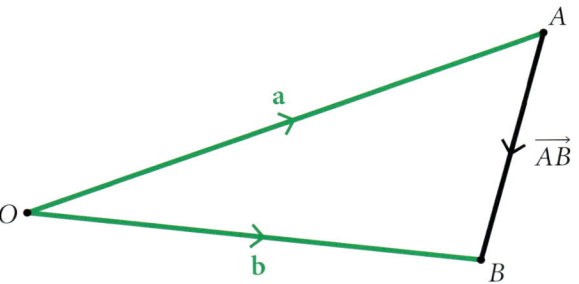

Using the triangle law of addition, $\mathbf{a} + \overrightarrow{AB} = \mathbf{b}$

$$\therefore \overrightarrow{AB} = \mathbf{b} - \mathbf{a}$$

This is an important result, which you will use frequently.

The position vector of point A can also be written as $\overrightarrow{OA}$. Using this notation, $\overrightarrow{OB} = \overrightarrow{OA} + \overrightarrow{AB}$ and so:

$$\overrightarrow{AB} = \overrightarrow{OB} - \overrightarrow{OA}$$

Worked Example

13. Vector $\overrightarrow{AB} = \begin{pmatrix} 2 \\ 7 \end{pmatrix}$. If the position vector of A is $\begin{pmatrix} 9 \\ 8 \end{pmatrix}$, find the position vector of the point B.

Draw a sketch to help visualise the problem. As always with a sketch, it does not have to be to scale.

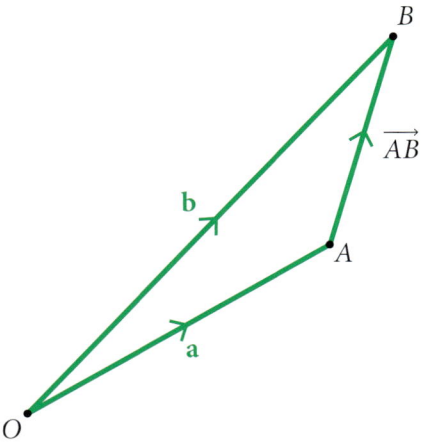

$\overrightarrow{AB} = \mathbf{b} - \mathbf{a}$

$\Rightarrow \mathbf{b} = \mathbf{a} + \overrightarrow{AB}$

$\qquad = \begin{pmatrix} 9 \\ 8 \end{pmatrix} + \begin{pmatrix} 2 \\ 7 \end{pmatrix}$

$\qquad = \begin{pmatrix} 11 \\ 15 \end{pmatrix}$

In section 13.3, we discussed multiplying a vector by a scalar to obtain another, parallel vector. Using this approach, it is possible to determine whether three points are collinear.

Worked Example

14. Show that the three points $A(-2, 1)$, $B(-1, 1.5)$ and $C(2, 3)$ are collinear.

Again, a sketch is helpful.

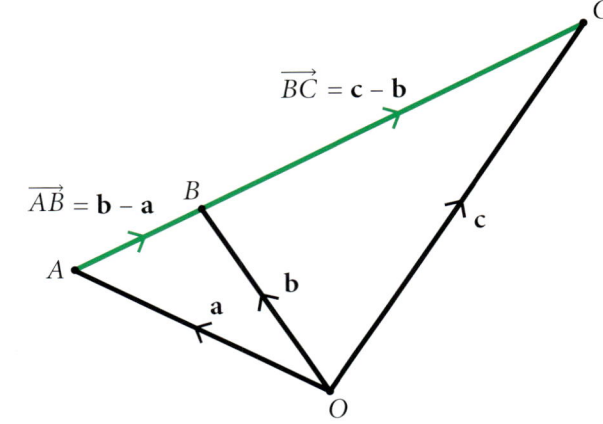

$\overrightarrow{AB} = \mathbf{b} - \mathbf{a}$

$\qquad = \begin{pmatrix} -1 \\ 1.5 \end{pmatrix} - \begin{pmatrix} -2 \\ 1 \end{pmatrix}$

$\qquad = \begin{pmatrix} 1 \\ 0.5 \end{pmatrix}$

$\overrightarrow{BC} = \mathbf{c} - \mathbf{b}$

$\qquad = \begin{pmatrix} 2 \\ 3 \end{pmatrix} - \begin{pmatrix} -1 \\ 1.5 \end{pmatrix}$

$\qquad = \begin{pmatrix} 3 \\ 1.5 \end{pmatrix}$

$\overrightarrow{BC} = 3\overrightarrow{AB}$

Hence the vectors $\overrightarrow{BC}$ and $\overrightarrow{AB}$ are parallel.
Hence the points A, B and C are collinear.

Position vectors can be combined, allowing you to find the position vectors of other points.

Worked Example

15. Point P has position vector **p** and point Q has position vector **q**. Find the position vector of the midpoint of line PQ in terms of **p** and **q**.

Let the midpoint of PQ be M. Draw a diagram with P, M and Q marked, as well as their position vectors.

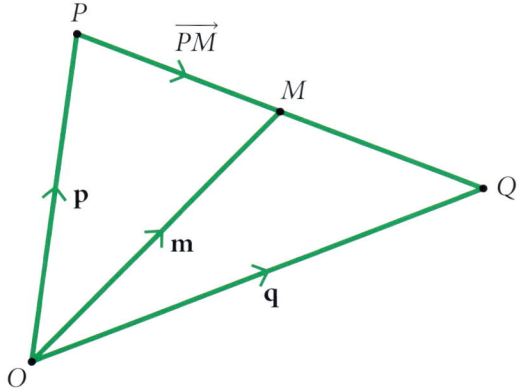

Using the triangle law of addition for triangle OPM:
$$\mathbf{m} = \mathbf{p} + \overrightarrow{PM} \quad (1)$$

We can also see that
$$\overrightarrow{PM} = \frac{1}{2}\overrightarrow{PQ}$$

Using the triangle law of addition for triangle OPQ:
$$\overrightarrow{PQ} = \mathbf{q} - \mathbf{p}$$

Hence:
$$\overrightarrow{PM} = \frac{1}{2}(\mathbf{q} - \mathbf{p})$$

Substitute this into (1) gives:
$$\mathbf{m} = \mathbf{p} + \frac{1}{2}(\mathbf{q} - \mathbf{p})$$
$$= \mathbf{p} + \frac{1}{2}\mathbf{q} - \frac{1}{2}\mathbf{p}$$
$$= \frac{1}{2}\mathbf{p} + \frac{1}{2}\mathbf{q}$$

Distance between two points

Consider two points A and B with position vectors $\begin{pmatrix} x_1 \\ y_1 \end{pmatrix}$ and $\begin{pmatrix} x_2 \\ y_2 \end{pmatrix}$, respectively. Then:

$$\overrightarrow{AB} = \mathbf{b} - \mathbf{a} = \begin{pmatrix} x_2 \\ y_2 \end{pmatrix} - \begin{pmatrix} x_1 \\ y_1 \end{pmatrix} = \begin{pmatrix} x_2 - x_1 \\ y_2 - y_1 \end{pmatrix}$$

The distance between points A and B is the length or magnitude of vector $\overrightarrow{AB}$. Hence:

$$\boxed{|\overrightarrow{AB}| = \sqrt{(x_2 - x_1)^2 + (y_2 - y_1)^2}}$$

Worked Example

16. Find the exact distance between the points A(2, –1) and B(4, 4).

$$|\overrightarrow{AB}| = \sqrt{(x_2 - x_1)^2 + (y_2 - y_1)^2}$$
$$= \sqrt{(4 - 2)^2 + (4 - (-1))^2}$$
$$= \sqrt{2^2 + 5^2}$$
$$= \sqrt{29}$$

You may be asked to find the magnitude of a vector in algebraic terms.

Worked Example

17. Two points A and B have position vectors $\begin{pmatrix} 1 \\ q \end{pmatrix}$ and $\begin{pmatrix} q \\ 1 \end{pmatrix}$ respectively.
   (a) Find, in terms of q, the magnitude of vector $\overrightarrow{AB}$.
   (b) If the distance between points A and B is $4\sqrt{2}$ units, find the two possible values of q.

(a) $|\overrightarrow{AB}| = \sqrt{(x_2 - x_1)^2 + (y_2 - y_1)^2}$
$$= \sqrt{(q - 1)^2 + (1 - q)^2}$$
$$= \sqrt{2(q - 1)^2}$$

(b) $\sqrt{2(q - 1)^2} = 4\sqrt{2}$
$$2(q - 1)^2 = 32$$
$$(q - 1)^2 = 16$$
$$q - 1 = \pm 4$$
$$q = 5 \text{ or } q = -3$$

Exercise 13D

1. Two points P and Q have position vectors such that $\mathbf{p} = \begin{pmatrix} 1 \\ 3 \end{pmatrix}$, $\mathbf{q} = \begin{pmatrix} 2 \\ -2 \end{pmatrix}$. Find $\overrightarrow{PQ}$.

2. Vector $\overrightarrow{AB} = \begin{pmatrix} -1 \\ -5 \end{pmatrix}$. If the position vector of point A is $\begin{pmatrix} 2 \\ 2 \end{pmatrix}$, find the position vector of point B.

3. In each case, show that the three points given are collinear.
   (a) $P(-3, -4)$, $Q(-1, 5)$ and $R(4, 27.5)$
   (b) $A(10, 13)$, $B(6, 7)$ and $C(-2, -5)$

Exercise 13D...

4. Find the distance between the points given. Give exact answers.
   - (a) $(-1, 0)$, $(1, 2)$
   - (b) $(-2, -3)$, $(1, 1)$
   - (c) $(5, 4)$, $(4, 3)$
   - (d) $(-5, -2)$, $(-4, 0)$

5. A vector connects the points $C(p, 15)$ and $D(7, p)$.
   - (a) Show that the magnitude of this vector is $\sqrt{2p^2 - 44p + 274}$.
   - (b) Given that the distance between points C and D is $\sqrt{82}$, find the two possible values of p.

6. Point A has position vector $\begin{pmatrix} 7 \\ 1 \end{pmatrix}$ and point B has position vector $\begin{pmatrix} -10 \\ -5 \end{pmatrix}$. Find the exact distance between points A and B.

7. The points C and D have position vectors $\mathbf{c}$ and $\mathbf{d}$. The point X divides the line CD into two parts such that the ratio $CX:XD = 2:1$. Find the position vector of the point X in terms of $\mathbf{c}$ and $\mathbf{d}$.

8. The shape $ABCDEF$ shown in the diagram is a regular hexagon.

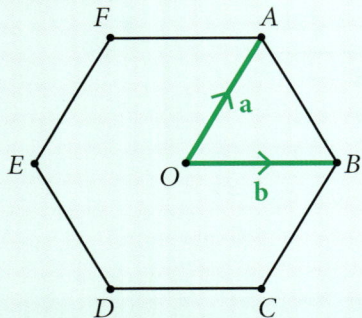

The position vector of point A is $\mathbf{a}$ and the position vector of point B is $\mathbf{b}$. Find the position vectors of each of the points C, D, E and F, giving your answers in terms of $\mathbf{a}$ and $\mathbf{b}$.

9. The points A, B, C, D and E have position vectors as follows:

$$\overrightarrow{OA} = \begin{pmatrix} p \\ 2p \end{pmatrix}, \overrightarrow{OB} = \begin{pmatrix} 0 \\ -10 \end{pmatrix}, \overrightarrow{OC} = \begin{pmatrix} 19 \\ -2 \end{pmatrix},$$

$$\overrightarrow{OD} = \begin{pmatrix} 13q \\ 3 \end{pmatrix}, \overrightarrow{OE} = \begin{pmatrix} 5r \\ -5 \end{pmatrix}$$

where p, q and r are positive integer constants less than 10. The distances AB, BC, CD and DE are all equal. Find the values of p, q and r.

Exercise 13D...

10. In triangle OAB, shown below, $\overrightarrow{OA} = \mathbf{a}$ and $\overrightarrow{OB} = \mathbf{b}$. The point M is the midpoint of AB.

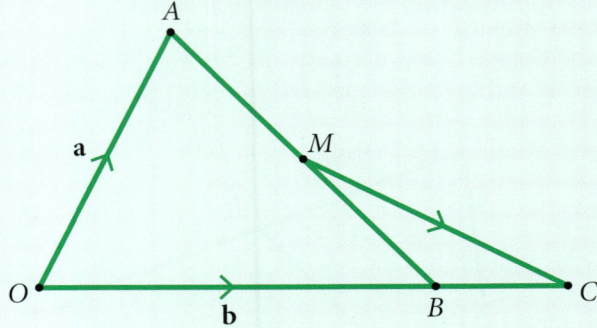

Point C is on OB projected. The lengths of OB and BC are in the ratio $OB:BC = k:1$
Given that $\overrightarrow{MC} = \tfrac{5}{6}\mathbf{b} - \tfrac{1}{2}\mathbf{a}$, find the value of k.

11. The diagram shows the logo of a bicycle hire company. It is made up of two triangles OBD and BCD. $\overrightarrow{OD} = \mathbf{d}$ and $\overrightarrow{OB} = \mathbf{b}$.

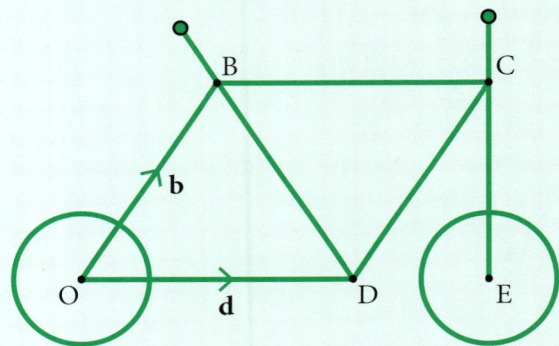

Given that $\overrightarrow{DE} = \tfrac{1}{2}\mathbf{d}$, and that $\overrightarrow{EC} = \mathbf{b} - \tfrac{1}{2}\mathbf{d}$, prove that the frame OBCD of the bicycle is a parallelogram.

12. In the diagram shown below, $\overrightarrow{OA} = \mathbf{a}$ and $\overrightarrow{OB} = \mathbf{b}$. M is the midpoint of OA and N is a point on OB. If $\overrightarrow{MN}$ and $\overrightarrow{AB}$ are parallel, prove that N is the midpoint of OB.

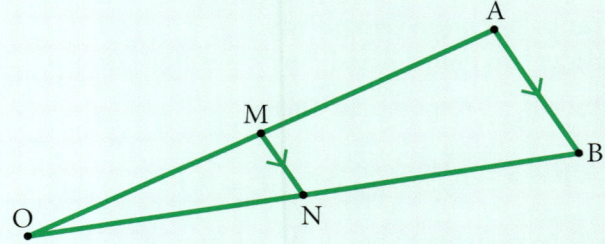

13.6 Summary

Two vectors are equal if they have the same **magnitude** and direction.

The sum of two vectors is called the **resultant**.

The **position vector** of a point is the vector from the origin to that point.

The difference between the position vectors of two points gives a vector between those two points, for example $\overrightarrow{PQ} = \mathbf{q} - \mathbf{p}$.

Multiplying a vector by a scalar λ gives a parallel vector which is λ times as long.

The magnitude of a vector can be found using Pythagoras' Theorem:
$$|\mathbf{a}| = \sqrt{x^2 + y^2}$$

If points A and B have position vectors $\begin{pmatrix} x_1 \\ y_1 \end{pmatrix}$ and $\begin{pmatrix} x_2 \\ y_2 \end{pmatrix}$ respectively, the distance between points A and B can also be found using Pythagoras' Theorem:
$$|\overrightarrow{AB}| = \sqrt{(x_2 - x_1)^2 + (y_2 - y_1)^2}$$

The angle between a vector and one of the coordinate axes can be found using trigonometry.

Chapter 14
Problem Solving

14.1 Introduction

The CCEA AS Mathematics specification now has an emphasis on **problem solving**.

This chapter contains worked examples of problem solving questions. There is also an exercise comprising exam-style problem solving questions. The questions may require techniques from any of the preceding chapters of the book, and often more than one. They may also require understanding of the mathematics you learnt at GCSE.

What does a problem-solving task look like?

A problem solving question typically involves several of the following features, but not necessarily all of them:

- Many steps may be required to reach the correct solution.
- The task may have little or no "scaffolding", i.e. it will often contain minimal wording.
- The information given may not be in mathematical form or in mathematical language.
- It is not always clear from the wording of the question which way the problem should be tackled. The mathematical processes required are often not given. The task may require more than one process, or it may require different parts of mathematics to be brought together to reach a solution. There may be a choice of valid approaches.
- The task may require "multiple representations", i.e. a sketch or diagram may be required as well as calculations.
- The task may relate to a real-world situation. Results should be interpreted in the context of the question.
- Understanding of the processes involved is required, rather than just the application of techniques.

In the real world...

- How fast must a rocket be launched to put a satellite into orbit?
- How many trees can be grown in a forest before it becomes over-crowded?
- What dimensions should be used for a beaker that will give it a capacity of 1 litre, while minimising

the amount of plastic used?

- How can we make sure the proportions of ingredients in a breakfast cereal are correct so that (a) the flavour is good, (b) the nutritional content is correct and (c) it does not become too expensive to manufacture?
- How many people should be questioned in an opinion poll?

All of these problems can be solved using mathematics. Often these problems need only mathematics you have learnt at GCSE and A-Level.

But which bits of mathematics should be used? Deciding on a valid approach is a large part of solving the problem. Real world problems do not have help telling you which way to start. The problem often doesn't appear to involve numbers. You may need to make some assumptions. People working in these fields are making decisions like this every day.

14.2 Examples of Problem-Solving Questions

The following examples and problems demonstrate the types of question that could be asked. As already noted, each question can be answered using the mathematical techniques and skills you have learnt at GCSE and AS.

....

Worked Examples

1. The diagram shows a circle with centre $C(-3, p)$. The points $A(2, 2)$ and $B(4, -2)$ both lie on the circle:

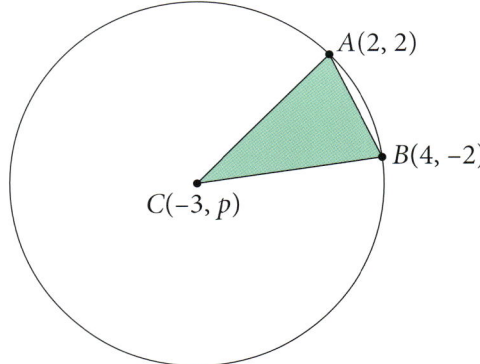

Show that the area of triangle ABC is 15 square units.

The midpoint of AB is $M(3, 0)$.

We can also calculate the gradient of chord AB:

Gradient AB $= \dfrac{2 - -2}{2 - 4} = -2$

To find p, note that the lines AB and MC are perpendicular. So he gradient of MC is the negative reciprocal of -2:

Gradient of $MC = \frac{1}{2}$

Gradient $= \dfrac{y_2 - y_1}{x_2 - x_1}$, so:

$\frac{1}{2} = \dfrac{p - 0}{-3 - 3}$

$p = -3$

To find the area of the triangle, use the formula:

Area = ½ base × perpendicular height

If AB is the base, then the perpendicular height will be the length of MC:

$MC = \sqrt{(3 - -3)^2 + (0 - 3)^2}$

$= \sqrt{45}$

And the length of AB will be:

$AB = \sqrt{(4 - 2)^2 + (-2 - 2)^2}$

$= \sqrt{20}$

Therefore we can calculate the area:

Area $= \dfrac{1}{2}\sqrt{45}\sqrt{20}$

$= 15$

Note: Alternative methods are available. For example, p could be calculated using the fact that AC and BC are equal in length.

2. $f(x) = ax^2 + bx + c$.

$f(x)$ has a factor of $x + 1$.

The graph of $y = f(x)$ has a turning point where $x = \frac{1}{3}$. Find one possible set of values for a, b and c, given that none of them are equal to zero.

This question requires the factor theorem.

It also requires either completing the square or differentiation.

$f(x)$ has a factor of $x + 1$. So $f(-1) = 0$, and thus:

$a(-1)^2 + b(-1) + c = 0$

$a - b + c = 0$ (1)

$f'(x) = 2ax + b$

There is a turning point where $x = \frac{1}{3}$, so:

$0 = 2a\left(\dfrac{1}{3}\right) + b$

$2a + 3b = 0$

$a = -\dfrac{3b}{2}$ (2)

There are two equations and three unknowns; this set of equations has more than one solution.

Choosing $b = 2$ gives $a = -3$ from equation (2). Then from (1):

$-3 - 2 + c = 0$

$c = 5$

Therefore $a = -3$, $b = 2$, $c = 5$

Note: Any non-zero multiple of these values would also satisfy the equations. For example $a = -6$, $b = 4$, $c = 10$.

Exercise 14A

1. Peter cuts a square out of a rectangular piece of metal, as shown in the diagram.

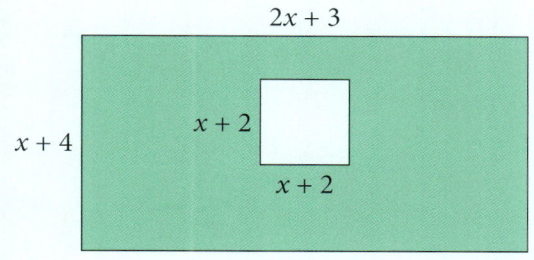

The length of the rectangle is $2x + 3$.
The width of the rectangle is $x + 4$.
The length of the side of the square is $x + 2$.
All measurements are in centimetres.

The shaded shape in the diagram shows the metal remaining. The area of the shaded shape is 20 cm². Find the perimeter of the square, giving an exact answer.

2. In the diagram that follows, AC is a diameter of the circle and O is its centre. B is a point on the circumference. The coordinates of O, A and B are shown. Find the three angles in triangle ABC.

Exercise 14A...

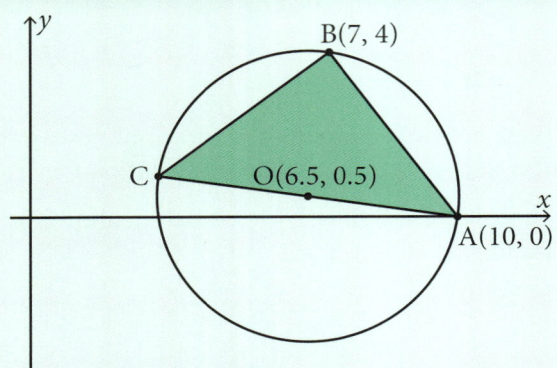

3. (a) What is the sum of all the integers from 1 to 1000?
   (b) What is the sum of all the integers from 1 to 1000 that are **not** multiples of 3?

4. Show using algebra that 9999×10001 must be 1 less than 10000^2.

5. The following diagram shows a rectangle with dimensions 20 cm by 10 cm. Find the exact area shaded.

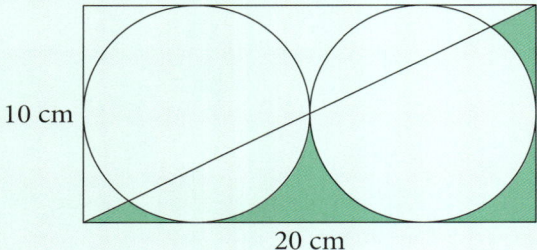

6. Two curves are given by the equations:
   $y = 2x^2 - (p + 1)x$
   $y = x^2 - p$
   (a) Show that the two curves intersect for all values of p.
   (b) Find the one value of p for which there is only one point of intersection.

7. (a) The graph of $y = 3\sin^2\theta$ is shown below. On a copy of the same diagram sketch $y = 2\cos\theta$. Mark clearly the points where the curve crosses the coordinate axes.

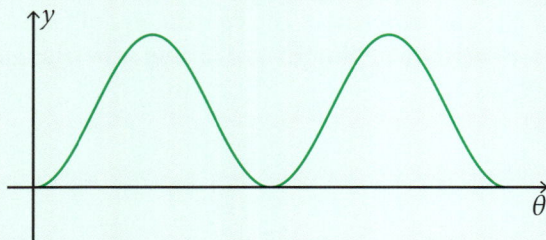

Exercise 14A...

(b) Solve $3\sin^2\theta = 2\cos\theta$ for $0° \leq \theta \leq 360°$.
(c) How does your sketch in part (a) help you to determine whether you have the correct answers in part (b)?

8. Find the equation of a cubic curve that touches the x-axis at $(4, 0)$ and passes through $(0, 2)$. Is it possible to find more than one such curve?

9. A circle has centre $C(1, 1)$ and touches both axes. Line AB is a tangent to the circle and intersects the x-axis at 30°, as shown in the diagram. Find the equation of line AB, giving an exact answer.

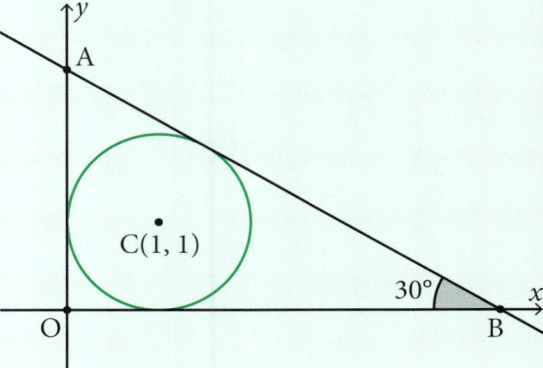

10. Consider the two shapes below. One is a square, the other a rhombus. Both shapes have all four sides of length x cm.

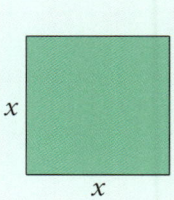 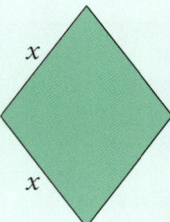

The square's area is 1 cm² greater than the rhombus's area. Show that the difference in the lengths of the two diagonals of the rhombus is 2 cm.

Answers

Exercise 1A

1. (a) 16, 144, 225, 400 (b) 27, 125, 1000 (c) 9, 10, 1.2, 13, 17.2 (d) 4, 2 (e) 4, 8, 64, 512
2. (a) $x^2 - 9 = (x - 3)(x + 3)$
   (b) $a^2 - b^2 = (a - b)(a + b)$
   (c) $1 - c^2 = (1 - c)(1 + c)$
   (d) $(d + 10)(d - 10) = d^2 - 100$
   (e) $e^2f^2 - (gh)^2 = (ef - gh)(ef + gh)$
3. (a) Rational (b) Irrational (c) Rational (d) Irrational

Exercise 1B

1. (a) 64 (b) 81 (c) 64 (d) 196 (e) 17 (f) 145 (g) 61 (h) 81 (i) $\frac{8}{27}$ (j) 0.04
2. (a) 7^2 (b) 10^2 (c) 10^{-2} (d) 11^2 (e) 10^{-3} (f) $\left(\frac{3}{7}\right)^2$ (g) $(0.3)^2$ (h) 10^{-5} (i) 0.4^2

Exercise 1C

1. (a) x^6 (b) $8x^{-1}$ (c) $3p$ (d) $12r$ (e) $4s^5$ (f) $27a^5$ (g) $9b^4$ (h) $12c^6$ (i) $12r^3$ (j) $32d^5$

Exercise 1D

1. (a) 5 (b) 16 (c) $\frac{1}{64}$ (d) 32 (e) $\frac{1}{81}$ (f) $\frac{1}{25}$ (g) $\frac{1}{1024}$ (h) 1 (i) $\frac{1}{4}$ (j) 8 (k) 16 (l) $\frac{125}{64}$ (m) $-\frac{1}{64}$
2. (a) g^{-6} (b) t^2 (c) 1 (d) f^3 (e) b (f) $\frac{1}{5}x^{1/5}$ (g) $8x$ (h) $2x^{3/2}$ (i) $\frac{2}{3}$ (j) $160x^4$ (k) $90x^{9/4}$ (l) $8x^{3/2}$ (m) $-\frac{1}{2x}$ (n) $3x^{1/3}$

Exercise 1E

1. (a) $g = \frac{9}{2}$ (b) $t = \frac{15}{2}$ (c) $f = -\frac{1}{4}$ (d) $y = \frac{21}{2}$ (e) $k = -\frac{11}{2}$ (f) $d = -\frac{7}{2}$ (g) $w = 12$ (h) $q = \frac{15}{8}$ (i) $z = \frac{7}{2}$ (j) $g = -\frac{12}{5}$

Exercise 1F

1. (a) $4\sqrt{2}$ (b) $\sqrt{3}$ (c) 2 (d) $\frac{11}{10}$

2. $15\sqrt{2}$
3. $6\sqrt{5}$
4. $27 - 10\sqrt{2}$
5. $41 - 12\sqrt{5}$
6. $3\sqrt{2}$
7. $7\sqrt{5}$
8. $9 + 6\sqrt{2}$
9. $7 + 3\sqrt{5}$
10. (a) $\frac{\sqrt{5}}{5}$ (b) $\frac{\sqrt{5}}{5}$ (c) $\frac{\sqrt{7} + \sqrt{35}}{7}$
11. (a) $44 - 24\sqrt{2}$ (b) $9 + 4\sqrt{2}$ (c) $\frac{5}{17} + \frac{2}{17}\sqrt{2}$ (d) $3 - 2\sqrt{2}$
12. (a) $76 - 42\sqrt{3}$ (b) $\frac{2}{3} + \frac{1}{3}\sqrt{3}$
13. (a) 14 (b) 47 (c) 13 (d) 33
14. (a) $6 - 2\sqrt{6}$ (b) $15 - 5\sqrt{5}$ (c) $12 - 6\sqrt{2}$ (d) $28 - 14\sqrt{2}$
15. (a) $6\sqrt{5}$ (b) $14\sqrt{3}$ (c) 4 (d) $\frac{\sqrt{21} - 5}{2}$

Exercise 2A

1. (a) $2\sqrt{5}$ (b) $4\sqrt{5}$ (c) $6\sqrt{2}$ (d) 4 (e) $\frac{-2 - \sqrt{6}}{2}$
2. (a) $x^2 - x - 2$ (b) $4x^2 - 4x - 3$ (c) $3x^2 - 4x + 1$ (d) $1 - x^2$ (e) $-10p^2 - 9p + 9$

Exercise 2B

1. (a) $x = -3$ or $x = -9$ (b) $x = -3$ or $x = -11$ (c) $x = -10$ or $x = -2$ (d) $x = -5$ (e) $x = -4$ or $x = -6$ (f) $x = 1$ or $x = -3$ (g) $x = 1$ or $x = -7$ (h) $x = 6$ or $x = -7$ (i) $x = 5$ or $x = 2$ (j) $x = -7$ or $x = -9$
2. (a) $x = 3, x = 4$ (b) $x = \frac{5}{2}, x = -\frac{5}{2}$ (c) $x = 0, x = 4$ (d) $x = 0, x = 1$ (e) $x = -6, x = 4$ (f) $x = 3$ (g) $x = 1, x = -1$ (h) $x = 1$ (i) $x = -\frac{1}{2}, x = \frac{7}{2}$ (j) $x = 0, x = 91$ (k) $x = -6, x = -8$ (l) $x = -1$ (m) $x = -1, x = 1$ (n) $x = -1$ (o) $x = \frac{1}{4}, x = -\frac{1}{8}$
3. (a) $x = 4$ (b) $x = 2, x = 9$ (c) $x = 6$ (d) $x = -2, x = 5$ (e) $x = 7, x = 8$ (f) $x = -6, x = 10$ (g) $x = 8, x = 10$ (h) $x = 1, x = 9$

(i) $x = -8, x = -9$
(j) $x = 3, x = 10$ (k) $x = 6$
(l) $x = 2$
4. (a) $x = -1, x = 2$ (b) $x = \frac{5}{2}, x = \frac{2}{3}$
   (c) $x = -2, x = 6$
   (d) $x = -\frac{4}{9}, x = -\frac{1}{2}$
   (e) $x = -\frac{8}{5}, x = -\frac{1}{2}$
   (f) $x = \frac{7}{3}, x = -\frac{3}{7}$
   (g) $x = -\frac{8}{3}, x = -5$
   (h) $x = \frac{4}{7}, x = 1$
   (i) $x = -\frac{3}{8}, x = \frac{5}{7}$
   (j) $x = 1, x = -\frac{1}{2}$
   (k) $x = 3, x = -\frac{9}{5}$
   (l) $x = \frac{1}{3}, x = \frac{7}{6}$ (m) $x = \frac{2}{3}, x = \frac{7}{5}$
   (n) $x = \frac{7}{2}, x = -\frac{6}{7}$
   (o) $x = \frac{3}{2}, x = \frac{3}{8}$
5. (a) $x = \frac{1}{2}, -3$ (b) $n = \frac{3}{2}, 4$ (c) $z = \frac{3}{2}, 8$ (d) $p = \frac{1}{3}, 1$
6. (a) $x = -7, 7$ (b) $y = -9, 9$ (c) $z = -\frac{7}{3}, \frac{7}{3}$ (d) $b = -\frac{3}{5}, \frac{3}{5}$ (e) $c = -\frac{4}{5}, \frac{4}{5}$ (f) $x = -\frac{1}{8}, \frac{1}{8}$ (g) $m = -\frac{7}{5}, \frac{7}{5}$ (h) $x = -6, 6$ (i) $y = -24, 24$ (j) $z = -30, 30$
7. 3, 4, 5 cm

Exercise 2C

1. (a) $-2, -3$ (b) $\frac{13}{5}, -\frac{7}{5}$ (c) $\frac{22}{7}, \frac{2}{7}$ (d) $-\frac{1}{8}, -\frac{15}{8}$ (e) $-\frac{8}{5}, -2$ (f) $\frac{17}{6}, \frac{3}{2}$ (g) 4, 20 (h) 50, 80 (i) $-12, -108$ (j) 0, 20 (k) 30, 36 (l) $-66, -78$ (m) 35, 55 (n) $-33, 15$ (o) 0, 72

2. (a) $-3 \pm \sqrt{13}$ (b) $-2 \pm \dfrac{\sqrt{13}}{2}$
(c) $-1 \pm \sqrt{5}$ (d) $-3 \pm \sqrt{10}$
(e) $2 \pm \sqrt{5}$ (f) $-5 \pm 2\sqrt{6}$ (g)
$-1 \pm \sqrt{3}$ (h) $2 \pm 2\sqrt{5}$ (i) $-2 \pm \sqrt{5}$

Exercise 2D

1. (a) (i) $(0, 20)$ (ii) none (iii) $(1, 19)$
(b) (i) $(0, 16)$ (ii) none (iii) $(2, 12)$
(c) (i) $(0, 12)$ (ii) $(5 \pm \sqrt{13}, 0)$
(iii) $(5, -13)$
(d) (i) $(0, 20)$ (ii) none (iii) $(4, 4)$
(e) (i) $(0, 16)$ (ii) none (iii) $(3, 7)$
(f) (i) $(0, 16)$ (ii) $(-8, 0)$, $(-2, 0)$
(iii) $(-5, -9)$
(g) (i) $(0, 16)$ (ii) $(9 \pm \sqrt{65}, 0)$
(iii) $(9, -65)$
(h) (i) $(0, 12)$ (ii) none (iii) $(-3, 3)$

2. (a) (i) $(0, 8)$ (ii) $(5 \pm \sqrt{33}, 0)$
(iii) $(5, 33)$
(b) (i) $(0, 16)$ (ii) $(2, 0)$, $(-8, 0)$
(iii) $(-3, 25)$
(c) (i) $(0, 16)$ (ii) $(-4 \pm \sqrt{2}, 0)$
(iii) $(-4, 32)$
(d) (i) $(0, 16)$ (ii) $(5 \pm \sqrt{41}, 0)$
(iii) $(5, 41)$
(e) (i) $(0, 8)$ (ii) $(6 \pm 2\sqrt{11}, 0)$
(iii) $(6, 44)$
(f) (i) $(0, 12)$ (ii) $(-7 \pm \sqrt{61}, 0)$
(iii) $(-7, 61)$
(g) (i) $(0, 20)$ (ii) $(-8 \pm 2\sqrt{21}, 0)$
(iii) $(-8, 84)$
(h) (i) $(0, 20)$ (ii) $(9 \pm \sqrt{101}, 0)$
(iii) $(9, 101)$

3. (a) (i) $(0, 20)$ (ii) $(7 \pm \sqrt{29}, 0)$
(iii) $(7, -29)$

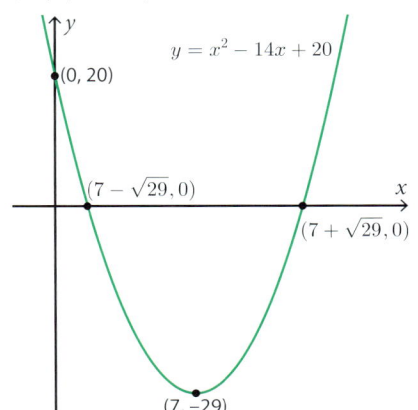

(b) (i) $(0, 16)$ (ii) $(-8 \pm 4\sqrt{3}, 0)$
(iii) $(-8, -48)$

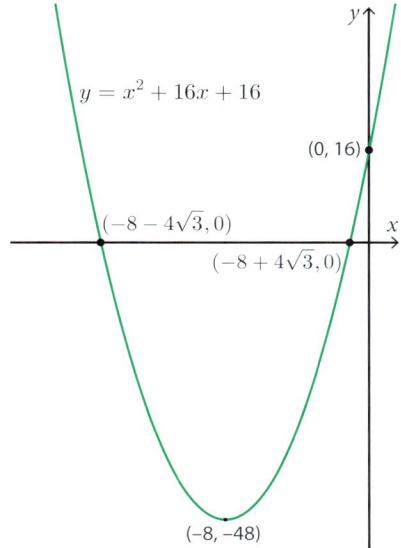

(c) (i) $(0, 16)$ (ii) $(-6 \pm 2\sqrt{5}, 0)$
(iii) $(-6, -20)$

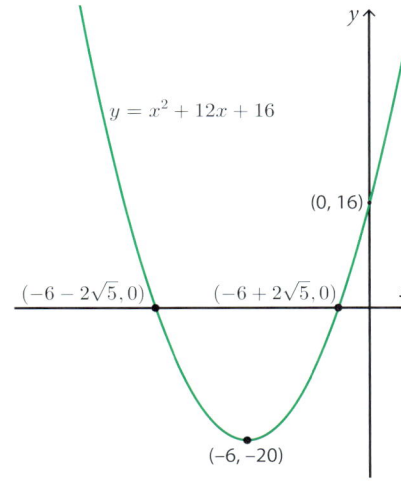

(d) (i) $(0, 6)$ (ii) $(-6 \pm \sqrt{42}, 0)$
(iii) $(-6, 42)$

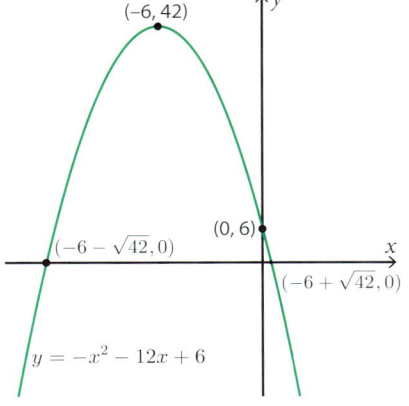

(e) (i) $(0, 8)$ (ii) $(7 \pm \sqrt{57}, 0)$
(iii) $(7, 57)$

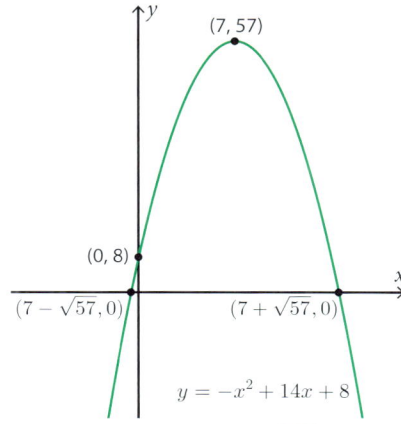

(f) (i) $(0, 14)$ (ii) $(8 \pm \sqrt{78}, 0)$
(iii) $(8, 78)$

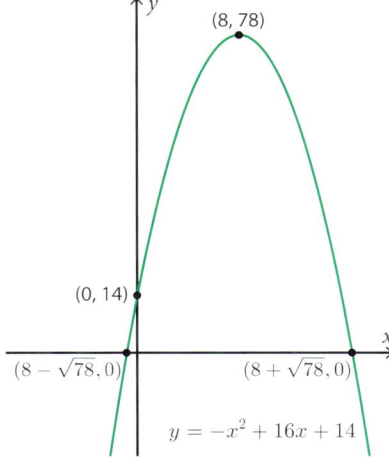

Exercise 2E

1. (a) $\dfrac{-1 + \sqrt{5}}{2}, \dfrac{-1 - \sqrt{5}}{2}$

(b) $\dfrac{-5 + 3\sqrt{5}}{2}, \dfrac{-5 - 3\sqrt{5}}{2}$

(c) $\dfrac{1 + 3\sqrt{5}}{2}, \dfrac{1 - 3\sqrt{5}}{2}$

(d) $\dfrac{-1 + 5\sqrt{5}}{2}, \dfrac{-1 - 5\sqrt{5}}{2}$

(e) $\dfrac{1 + \sqrt{5}}{2}, \dfrac{1 - \sqrt{5}}{2}$

(f) $\dfrac{2 + \sqrt{2}}{2}, \dfrac{2 - \sqrt{2}}{2}$

(g) $\dfrac{-3 + 3\sqrt{5}}{2}, \dfrac{-3 - 3\sqrt{5}}{2}$

(h) $\dfrac{-2 + \sqrt{7}}{3}, \dfrac{-2 - \sqrt{7}}{3}$

(i) $-1 + \sqrt{7}, -1 - \sqrt{7}$

(j) $\dfrac{-2 + \sqrt{2}}{2}, \dfrac{-2 - \sqrt{2}}{2}$

2. (a) $-2 + \sqrt{3}, -2 - \sqrt{3}$

(b) $\dfrac{-5 + \sqrt{33}}{4}, \dfrac{-5 - \sqrt{33}}{4}$

(c) $\dfrac{1 + \sqrt{13}}{6}, \dfrac{1 - \sqrt{13}}{6}$

(d) $\dfrac{-2 + \sqrt{14}}{2}, \dfrac{-2 - \sqrt{14}}{2}$

(e) $\dfrac{-1 + \sqrt{2}}{2}, \dfrac{-1 - \sqrt{2}}{2}$

(f) $\dfrac{-2 + \sqrt{10}}{3}, \dfrac{-2 - \sqrt{10}}{3}$

(g) $\dfrac{1 + \sqrt{3}}{2}, \dfrac{1 - \sqrt{3}}{2}$

(h) $\dfrac{3 + \sqrt{57}}{6}, \dfrac{3 - \sqrt{57}}{6}$

(i) $2 + 2\sqrt{2}, 2 - 2\sqrt{2}$

(j) $\dfrac{-2 + \sqrt{13}}{3}, \dfrac{-2 - \sqrt{13}}{3}$

Exercise 2F

1. (a) $-1 + \sqrt{3}, -1 - \sqrt{3}$

(b) No solutions

(c) $\dfrac{-1 + \sqrt{5}}{4}, \dfrac{-1 - \sqrt{5}}{4}$

(d) No solutions

(e) No solutions

(f) No solutions

(g) $\dfrac{-1 + \sqrt{33}}{8}, \dfrac{-1 - \sqrt{33}}{8}$

(h) No solutions

(i) 2

(j) $\dfrac{1 + \sqrt{5}}{2}, \dfrac{1 - \sqrt{5}}{2}$

(k) $-1 + \sqrt{5}, -1 - \sqrt{5}$

(l) No solutions

(m) No solutions

(n) $\dfrac{1 + \sqrt{6}}{5}, \dfrac{1 - \sqrt{6}}{5}$

2. Since two distinct roots, discriminant $b^2 - 4ac > 0$
    $\Rightarrow p^2 - 4(1)(p + 8) > 0$
    $\Rightarrow p^2 - 4p - 32 > 0$

3. $k = 4$

4. $q < -\dfrac{41}{16}$

5. Since at least one real root, discriminant $b^2 - 4ac \geq 0$
    $\Rightarrow (5t)^2 - 4(1)(2t) \geq 0$
    $\Rightarrow 25t^2 - 8t \geq 0$
    $\Rightarrow t(25t - 8) \geq 0$

Exercise 2G

1. (a) $x = \pm 1, \pm \sqrt{2}$ (b) $x = 1, \dfrac{25}{4}$

(c) $x = \dfrac{1}{2}, -2$ (d) $x = \dfrac{1}{3}, -2$

(e) $x = -5, 10$ (f) $x = 1, -2$

(g) $x = 1, -2$

2. $x = \pm \dfrac{2\sqrt{6}}{3}$

Exercise 3A

1. (a) $y = \dfrac{4x - 1}{2}$ (b) $y = 2x - 5$

(c) $y = \dfrac{3s - 4x}{12}$ (d) $y = \dfrac{2x - 7}{3}$

2. (a) $a = 0$ (b) $b = 5$ (c) $c = \dfrac{1}{2}$

(d) $d = -10$ (e) $e = -\dfrac{5}{4}$

3. (a) $(x + 2)(x + 9)$
    (b) $(x - 4)(x - 6)$
    (c) $(x - 1)(x - 5)$
    (d) $(x + 4)(x - 3)$
    (e) $(x - 7)(x + 6)$

4. (a) $x = 1, y = 0$ (b) $x = -3, y = 3$
    (c) $x = 7, y = 0$ (d) $x = 4, y = 5$

Exercise 3B

1. (a) $x = 11, y = -5; x = -3, y = 9$
    (b) $x = 8, y = -4; x = -4, y = 8$
    (c) $x = 9, y = -5; x = -3, y = 7$
    (d) $x = 7, y = -5; x = -3, y = 5$
    (e) $x = 8, y = -3; x = -2, y = 7$
    (f) $x = 6, y = -1; x = -2, y = 7$

2. (a) $x = 14, y = 5; x = -7, y = -2$
    (b) $x = 19, y = 5; x = -5, y = -1$
    (c) $x = 17, y = 6;$
    $x = -10, y = -3$
    (d) $x = 7, y = 4; x = -5, y = -2$
    (e) $x = 27, y = 7;$
    $x = -13, y = -3$
    (f) $x = 41, y = 7; x = -7, y = -1$

3. (a) $(2, -12); (-8, 48)$
    (b) $(1, -24); (-25, 600)$

4. (a) $x = -2 + 2\sqrt{3}, y = -6 + 2\sqrt{3}$
    $x = -2 - 2\sqrt{3}, y = -6 - 2\sqrt{3}$
    (b) $x = -4 + 3\sqrt{3}, y = -12 + 3\sqrt{3}$
    $x = -4 - 3\sqrt{3}, y = -12 - 3\sqrt{3}$

5. (a) $p = 3, q = 2$
    (b) $x = -5, y = 9$
    (c) $a = 5, b = 2$

(d) $x = -\dfrac{7}{10}, y = 8$

(e) $m = 3, n = 4$

Exercise 3C

1. (a) $x = 2, y = 4, z = 3$
    (b) $x = 2, y = -8, z = 1$
    (c) $x = 12, y = 0, z = -4$
    (d) $x = -1, y = -2, z = -2.5$

2. Apples 10p, bananas 25p, carrots 12p.

3. Ticket £5.50, popcorn £2, cola £1.50.

Exercise 3D

1. (a) $x \leq 7$ (b) $x \leq 21$ (c) $x < \dfrac{7}{3}$

(d) $x \geq -5$ (e) $x \geq \dfrac{2}{3}$ (f) $x < 11$

(g) $x > -1$ (h) $x < \dfrac{1}{5}$ (i) $x \geq 1$

(j) $x > -\dfrac{3}{2}$ (k) $x < -6$ (l) $x \geq \dfrac{60}{83}$

2. (a) $t \leq 3$ (b) $w > 2$ (c) $p \leq 0$

(d) $v < -10$ (e) $z < 1$ (f) $u \geq \dfrac{22}{5}$

3. (a) $x < -4$ or $x > 1$
    (b) $x < -5$ or $x > 4$
    (c) $-3 < x < 3$
    (d) $x < \dfrac{3}{2}$ or $x > 4$
    (e) $-5 < x < 2$
    (f) $x < -4$ or $x > 1$
    (g) $-5 < x < 2$
    (h) $x < -7$ or $x > 3$

4. (a) $x \geq 6$ or $x \leq -4$
    (b) $x > 5$ or $x < -2$
    (c) $-3 < x < 1$
    (d) $x > 8$ or $x < -3$
    (e) $-11 < x < 8$
    (f) $x < -11$ or $x > 9$
    (g) $x > 5$ or $x < -2$
    (h) $x \geq 8$ or $x \leq -2$
    (i) $-4 < x < 1$
    (j) $x < -4$ or $x > 2$
    (k) $x > 6$ or $x < -2$
    (l) $-8 < x < 2$
    (m) $-14 < x < 11$
    (n) $x \geq 9$ or $x \leq -4$

5. (a) $x \leq -4$ or $x \geq 1$
    (b) $-4 \leq x \leq 1$
    (c) $x < -7$ or $x > 5$
    (d) $x \leq -9$ or $x \geq 6$

(e) $-11 < x < 9$
(f) $x \leq -13$ or $x \geq 10$
(g) $x < -11$ or $x > 7$
(h) $-12 < x < 9$
(i) $-1 < x < 5$
(j) $x < 2$ or $x > 7$
(k) $-10 < x < 3$

6. (a) $1 < x < 3$ (b) $1 < x < \dfrac{7}{2}$

(c) $2 \leq x \leq \dfrac{13}{5}$ (d) $x > 5$ (e) $x > 5$

(f) $x \geq 4$ (g) $\dfrac{4}{3} < x \leq 6$ (h) $x > 5$

(i) $\dfrac{2}{3} \leq x \leq 5$ (j) $1 < x < \dfrac{11}{2}$

(k) $x > 5$ (l) $x \geq 7$

Exercise 4A

1. (a) $4a - 4b$ (b) $3c + d$ (c) $2e + ef$
(d) $a^2 + b^2 - 5a + 6b - 2ab$
(cannot be simplified)
(e) $2b - a$ (f) $6c - d$
(g) $7e + f + ef$
(h) $2g^2 + 3h^2 - 4g - 3h + 2gh$
(cannot be simplified)

2. (a) -4 (b) 0 (c) -6 (d) 0 (e) -8
(f) 16 (g) 10 (h) 6 (i) 0 (j) -2

3. (a) $2v + 2v^2$ (b) $-4w^2 + 8$
(c) $3y^2 + y$ (d) $16x^2 - 9$
(e) $8v + 12v^2$ (f) $-6w^2 + 3$
(g) $-2y^2 + 6y$ (h) $16x^2 - 16$

4. (a) $-5y(y + 5)$ (b) $6p(6 - p^2)$
(c) $13r(2q - 1)$ (d) $s^4(5 - 4s)$
(e) $-3y(3y + 8)$ (f) $p(6 - p)$
(g) $8q(2 - r)$ (h) $s^3(3s - 4)$

5. (a) $(x + 1)(x + 4)$
(b) $(x + 10)^2$
(c) $(x - 3)(x - 9)$
(d) $(x - 9)(x - 6)$
(e) $(x + 8)(x + 2)$
(f) $(x - 1)(x - 4)$
(g) $(x + 6)(x + 8)$
(h) $(x - 6)(x + 4)$

6. (a) $(x + 2)(x - 2)$
(b) $4x(2x + 3)(2x - 3)$
(c) $(x + 3)(x - 3)$
(d) $x(3x + 4)(3x - 4)$

7. (a) 52 (b) 101 (c) 65 remainder 8
(d) 41 remainder 9 (e) 96 (f) 25
(g) 84 remainder 6
(h) 45 remainder 15

Exercise 4B

1. (a) $x - 5$ (b) $x + 5$ (c) $x + 7$
(d) $x - 7$ (e) $x + 2$

2. (a) $\dfrac{x + 4}{x + 1}$ (b) $\dfrac{x - 2}{x - 1}$ (c) $\dfrac{x - 5}{x + 1}$

(d) $\dfrac{x - 2}{x + 3}$ (e) $\dfrac{x - 4}{x - 2}$

3. (a) $(x - 1)(x + 6)$
(b) $(x - 5)(x - 8)$
(c) $(x - 1)(x + 7)$
(d) $(x - 6)(x + 9)$
(e) $(x + 9)(x - 8)$

4. (a) $\dfrac{x^2 + 1}{(x + 1)(x - 1)}$

(b) $\dfrac{2 - 8x}{(3x - 2)(2x - 3)}$

(c) $\dfrac{-5 - 2x}{(x + 2)(x + 3)}$

(d) $\dfrac{1}{x - 1}$

Exercise 4C

1. (a) $x^2 - 2x$ (b) $x^2 - x + 3$
(c) $x^2 + 1$ (d) $x^2 - 2x + 1$

2. (a) $3x^2 + x + 3 - \dfrac{3}{x + 1}$

(b) $3x^2 - 6x + 10 - \dfrac{18}{x + 2}$

(c) $x^2 - 3 + \dfrac{7}{x + 2}$

(d) $2x^2 - 3x + 7 - \dfrac{20}{x + 3}$

(e) $x^2 - 3x + 9 - \dfrac{27}{x + 3}$

(f) $3x^2 - 12x + 35 - \dfrac{109}{x + 3}$

3. (a) $x^3 - x + 1$
(b) $x^3 + 3x + 1$
(c) $2x^3 + 2x^2 - 6x + 3$
(d) $x^3 - 2x^2 + x + 1$
(e) $2x^3 - x^2 - 2x + 1$
(f) $3x^3 + x^2 - 4x + 2$

4. (a) $x^3 - x^2 - 2x + 3 - \dfrac{5}{x + 2}$

(b) $x^3 + 3x - 7 + \dfrac{9}{x + 1}$

(c) $x^3 + 3x - 8 + \dfrac{26}{x + 3}$

(d) $2x^3 - 3x^2 + 3x - 6 + \dfrac{7}{x + 1}$

(e) $3x^3 - 7x^2 + 6x - 6 + \dfrac{8}{x + 1}$

Exercise 4D

1. (a) -4 (b) 22 (c) -3 (d) 9 (e) 0
(f) 4 (g) 3 (h) -24 (i) 34 (j) 60
(k) 18 (l) 5 (m) 1 (n) 10

2. -6

3. (a) -12 (b)
$f(x) = 4(x + 1)(x - 1)(x - 3)$

4. (a) 6 (b)
$f(x) = (x - 1)(3x - 2)(x + 3)$

(c) $\dfrac{7}{8}$

5. (a) -18 (b) 1

6. (a) $q = -8, p = -34$ (b)
$f(x) = 2(3x - 1)(2x + 1)(x - 3)$

7. (a) 222
(b) $f(x) = x(5x - 1)(x + 15)$

8. (a) $f(n)$ has remainder 5
when divided by $(n + 3)$. By
remainder theorem: $f(-3) = 5$
$\Rightarrow (-3)^3 + p(-3)^2 + 15(-3) + 14 = 5$
$\Rightarrow -27 + 9p - 45 + 14 = 5$
$\Rightarrow 9p = 63 \Rightarrow p = 7$ (b)
$f(n) = (n + 3)(n + 3)(n + 1) + 5$

Exercise 4E

1. (a) Not a factor; remainder -118
(b) A factor (c) Not a factor;
remainder -48 (d) Not a factor;
remainder -87 (e) A factor
(f) A factor (g) Not a factor;
remainder 26 (h) A factor
(i) Not a factor; remainder -19
(j) Not a factor; remainder 134
(k) A factor (l) Not a factor;
remainder -100

2. $f(x) = (x - 8)(x - 9)(x + 4)$

3. (a) $f(-3)$
$= (-3)^3 - 2(-3)^2 - 11(-3) + 12$
$= -27 - 18 + 33 + 12 = 0$
Hence by the factor theorem
$(x + 3)$ is a factor of $f(x)$.
(b) $f(x) = (x + 3)(x - 4)(x - 1)$

4. (a) $f(-10)$
$= 2(-10)^3 + (-10)^2 - 166(-10) + 240$
$= -2000 + 100 + 1660 + 240$
$= 0$. Hence by the factor theorem
$(x + 10)$ is a factor of $f(x)$. (b)
$f(x) = (x + 10)(2x - 3)(x - 8)$
(c) $x = -10, 1.5, 8$

5. $a = -5$

6. $p = -5$

7. (a) $f(x) = (x + 4)(x - 4)(x - 1)$

(b) $f(x) = (x + 2)(x - 3)^2$
(c) $f(x) = (x + 3)(x - 3)^2$
(d) $f(x) = (x + 3)(x - 3)(x - 2)$

Exercise 5A

1. (a) $x(x + 2)(x + 3)$
   (b) $x(3x + 4)(3x - 4)$
   (c) $x(3x + 5)(3x - 5)$
   (d) $x(x - 1)(x - 3)$
   (e) $x(x - 1)(x - 2)$

2. (a)

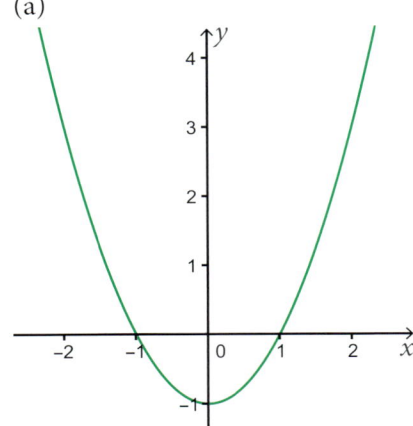

   (b)

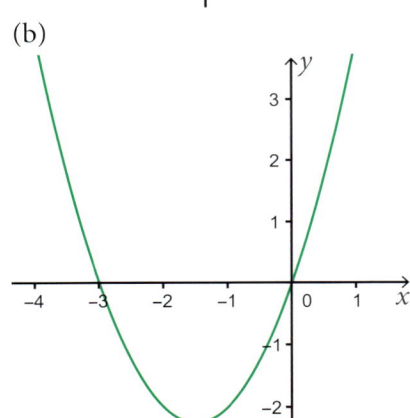

   (c)

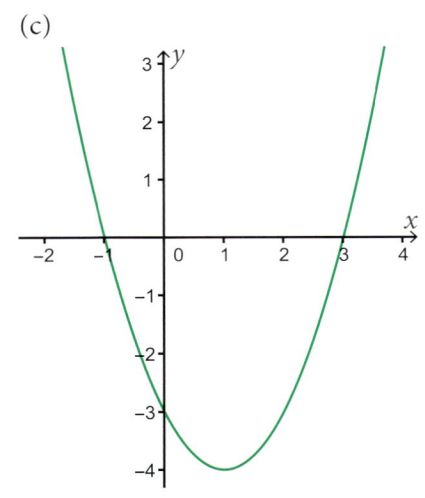

(d)

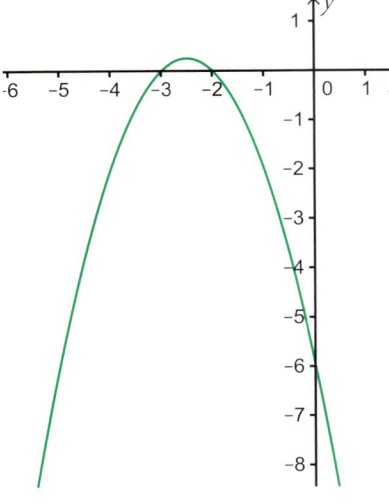

(e)

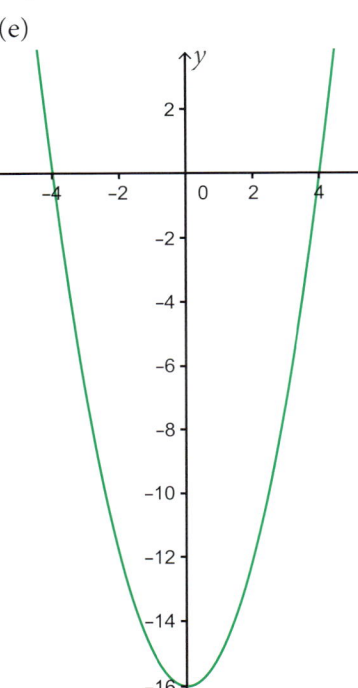

Exercise 5B

1. (a) $(0, -12)$; $(-4, 0), (3, 0), (-1, 0)$
   (b) $(0, -27)$; $(3, 0), (9, 0), (-1, 0)$
   (c) $(0, 0)$; $(0, 0), (3, 0), (-2, 0)$
   (d) $(0, 0)$; $(0, 0), (9, 0), (8, 0)$
   (e) $(0, -9)$; $(0.5, 0), (3, 0)$
   (f) $(0, 0)$; $(0, 0), (-0.5, 0)$
   (g) $(0, 0)$; $(0, 0), (5, 0), (-5, 0)$
   (h) $(0, 27)$; $(-3, 0)$
   (i) $(0, -1)$; $(0.5, 0)$
   (j) $(0, 0)$; $(0, 0), (6, 0)$

2. (a) $y = x(x - 9)^2$, $x = 0, 9$
   (repeated root)

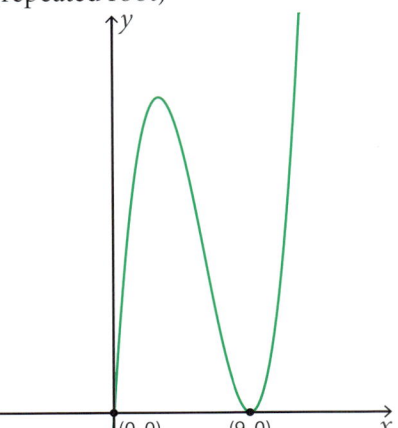

   (b) $y = x(x - 15)^2$, $x = 0, 15$
   (repeated root)

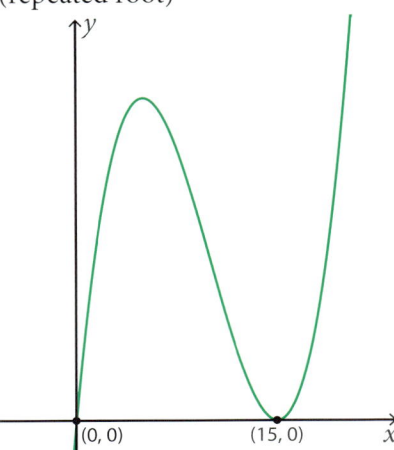

3. (a) $f(x) = x(x + 3)(x + 2)$,
   $x = 0, -3, -2$

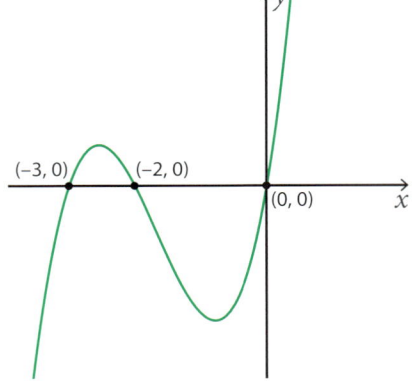

3. (b) $f(x) = x(x + 10)(x + 8)$,
$x = 0, -10, -8$

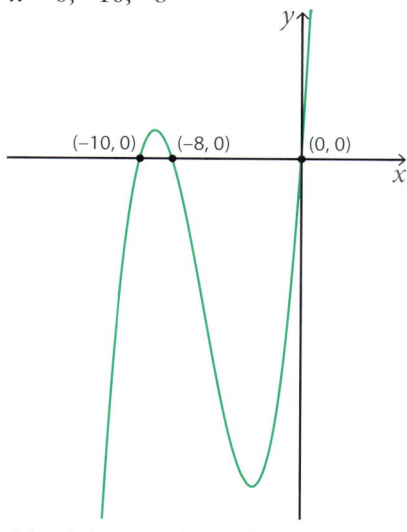

(c) $f(x) = -x(x + 1)(x + 10)$,
$x = 0, -1, -10$

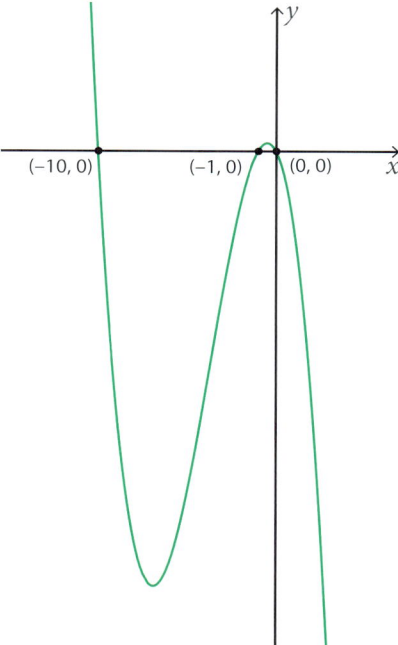

(d) $f(x) = x(x + 8)(x + 5)$,
$x = 0, -8, -5$

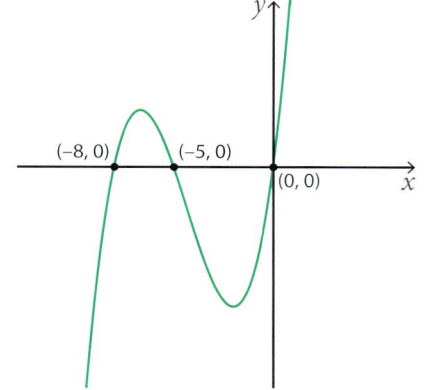

(e) $f(x) = x(x + 7)(x + 10)$,
$x = 0, -7, -10$

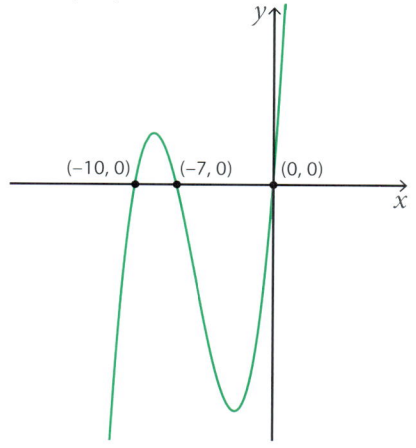

(f) $f(x) = x(4x + 5)(4x - 5)$,
$x = 0, -\dfrac{5}{4}, \dfrac{5}{4}$

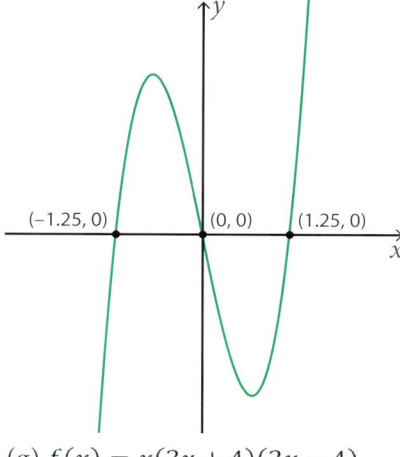

(g) $f(x) = x(3x + 4)(3x - 4)$,
$x = 0, -\dfrac{4}{3}, \dfrac{4}{3}$

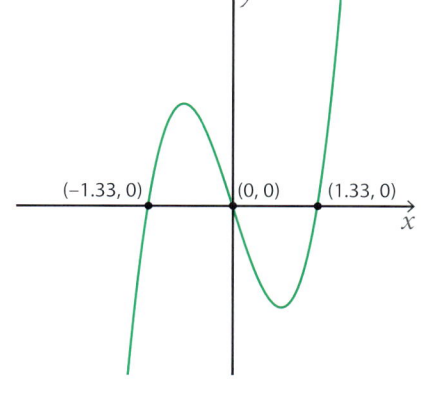

(h) $f(x) = -x(x - 1)(x - 2)$,
$x = 0, 1, 2$

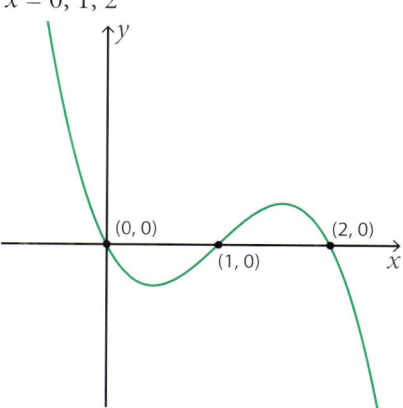

(i) $f(x) = x(x - 4)(x - 1)$,
$x = 0, 4, 1$

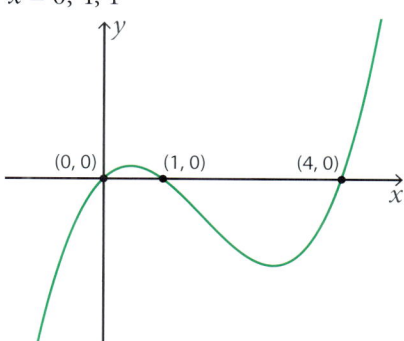

(j) $f(x) = -x(x - 5)(x - 7)$,
$x = 0, 5, 7$

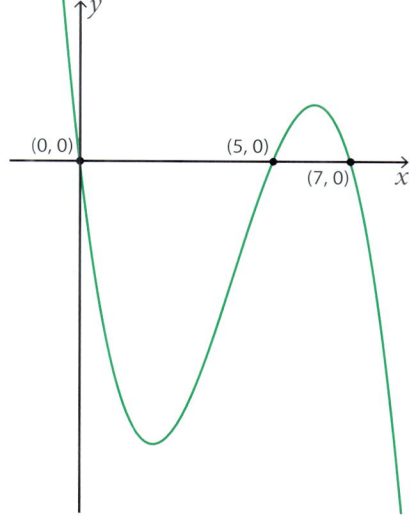

4. (a) $f(x) = x(x - 7)(x - 5)$,
$x = 0, 7, 5$

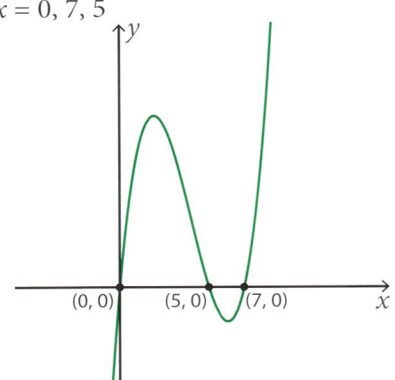

(b) $f(x) = x(x - 7)(x - 4)$,
$x = 0, 7, 4$

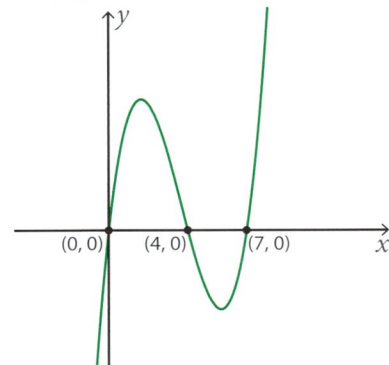

(c) $f(x) = -x(x - 8)(x - 6)$,
$x = 0, 8, 6$

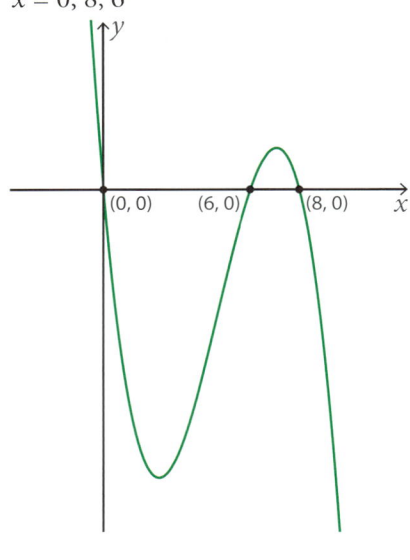

Exercise 5C

1. (a)

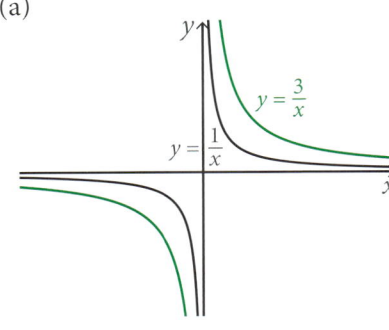

(b)

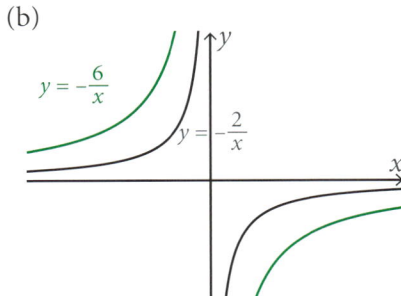

(c)

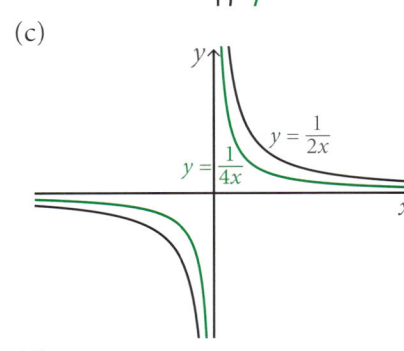

(d)

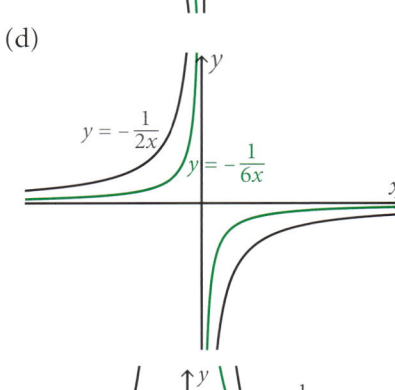

2.

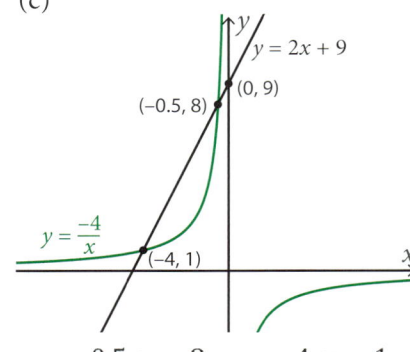

3. (a) 1; $x = 1$ (b) $(0, 0)$
(c) y approaches 1
(d)

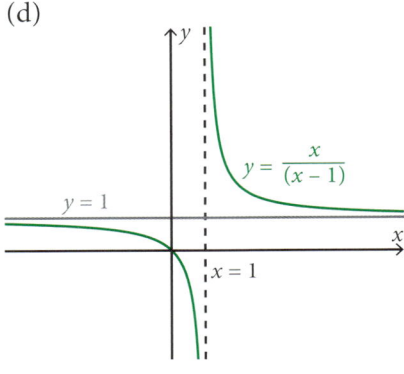

Exercise 5D

1. (a)

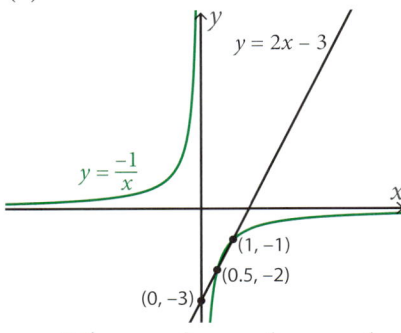

$x = 0.5, y = -2;\ x = 1, y = -1$
(b)

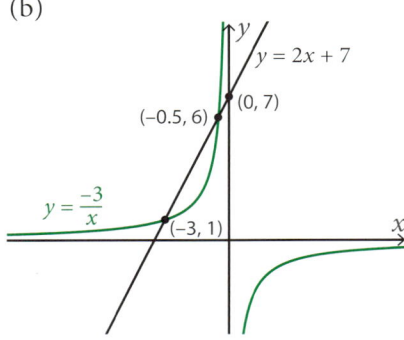

$x = -3, y = 1;\ x = -0.5, y = 6$
(c)

$y = 2x + 9$
$(-0.5, 8)$ $(0, 9)$
$y = \dfrac{-4}{x}$
$(-4, 1)$

$x = -0.5, y = 8;\ x = -4, y = 1$

1. (d)

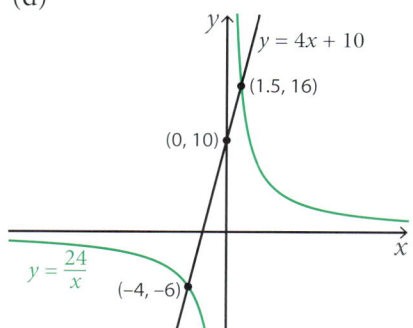

$x = 1.5, y = 16; \ x = -4, y = -6$

(e)

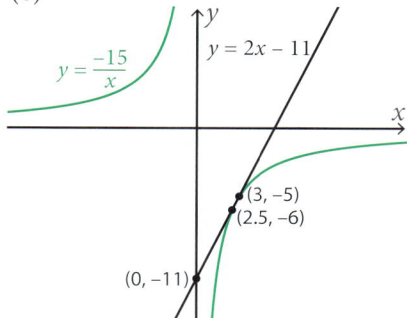

$x = 2.5, y = -6; \ x = 3, y = -5$

(f)

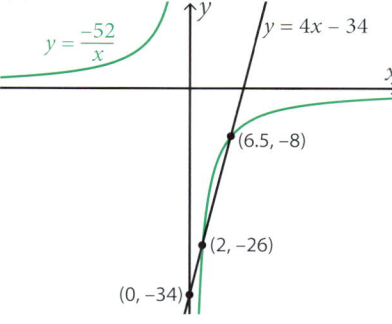

$x = 6.5, y = -8; \ x = 2, y = -26$

2. (a)

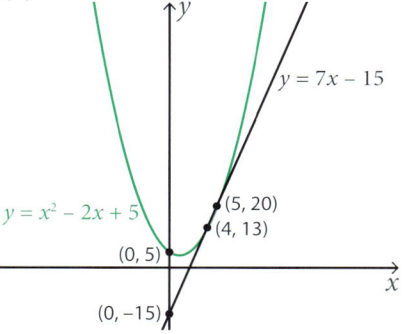

$x = 5, y = 20; \ x = 4, y = 13$

(b)

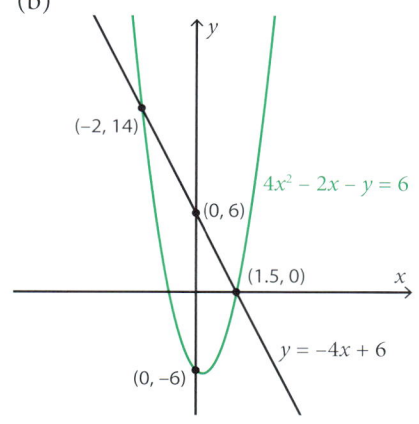

$x = 7, y = 29; \ x = 10, y = 68$

3. (a) $x = 1.5, y = 0; \ x = -2, y = 14$

(b)

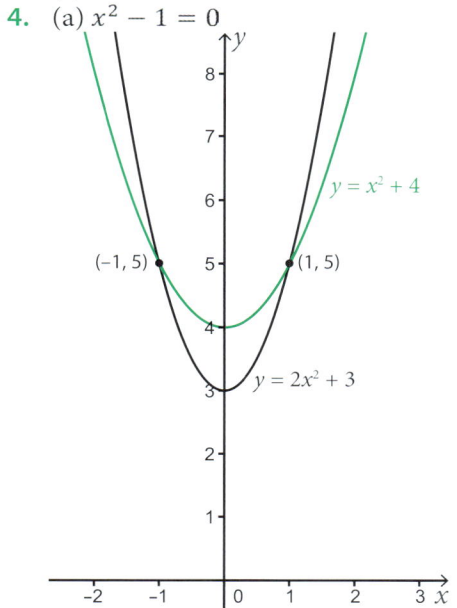

(c) $x > 1.5 \text{ or } x < -2$

4. (a) $x^2 - 1 = 0$

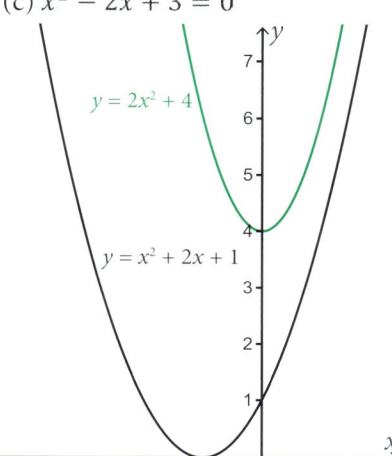

Two points of intersection
$(1, 5), (-1, 5)$.

(b) $x^2 + 2x + 1 = 0$

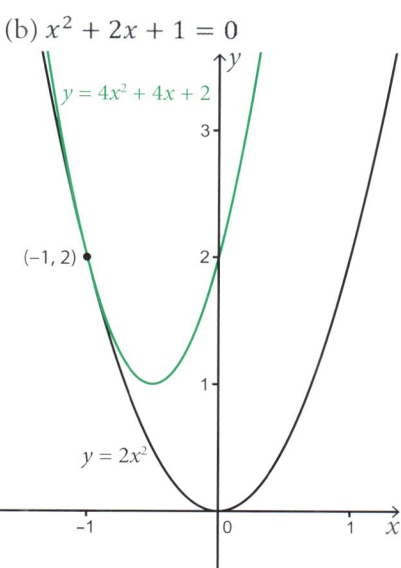

One point of intersection $(-1, 2)$.

(c) $x^2 - 2x + 3 = 0$

Zero points of intersection.

(d) $2x^2 + 5x + 2 = 0$

Two points of intersection
$(-0.5, -0.25), (-2, -4)$.

4. (e) $x^2 - 2x + 1 = 0$

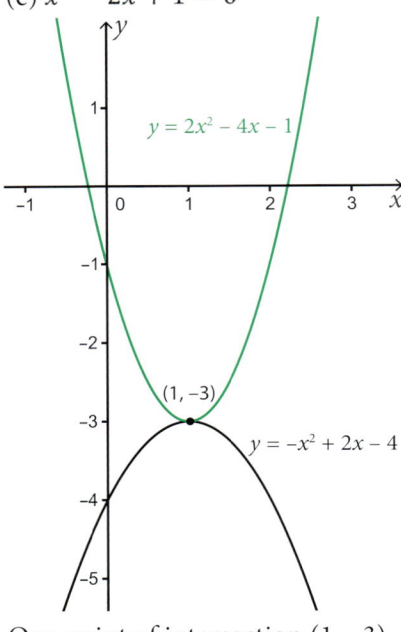

One point of intersection $(1, -3)$
(f) $5x^2 + 4x + 4 = 0$

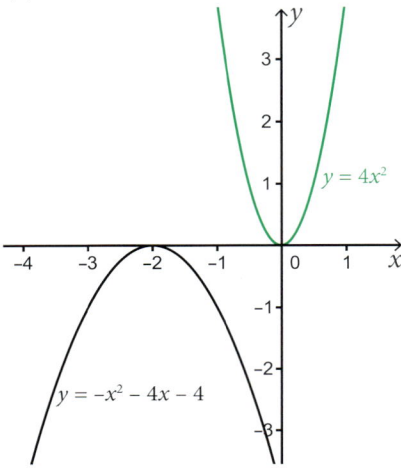

Zero points of intersection.

5. $x = 0$

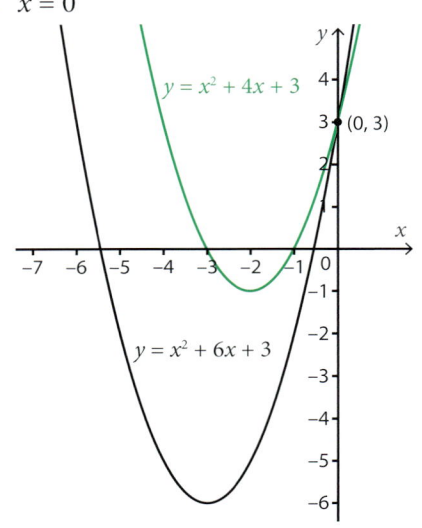

One point of intersection $(0, 3)$.

6. (a) $x = 0, 3$ (repeated root)
(b)

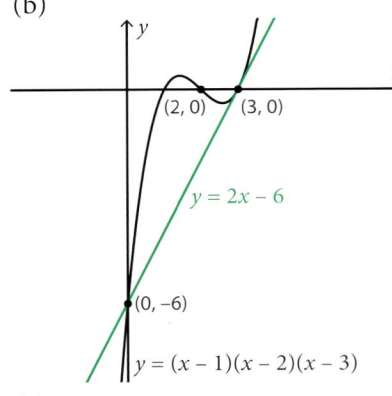

7. (a)

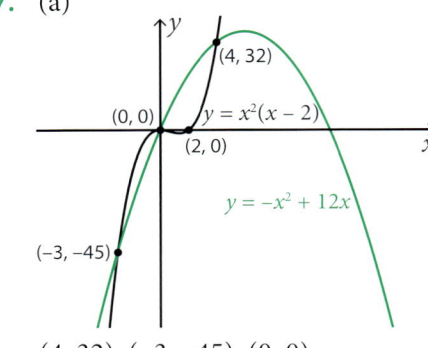

$(4, 32), (-3, -45), (0, 0)$
(b)

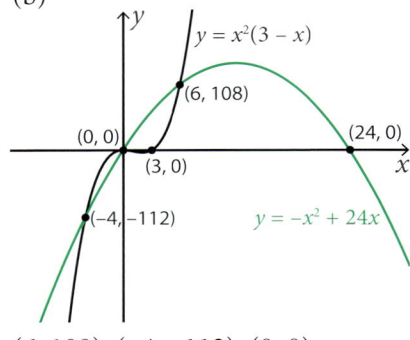

$(6, 108), (-4, -112), (0, 0)$

8. (a) (b)

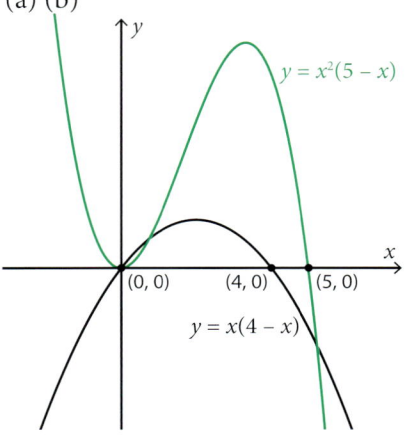

(c) 3 solutions. The third root occurs because $-x^3$ decreases at a faster rate than $-x^2$.

Exercise 5E

1. (a) Translation by 3 units in negative y-direction.
(b) Translation by 3 units in positive x-direction.

2. (a)

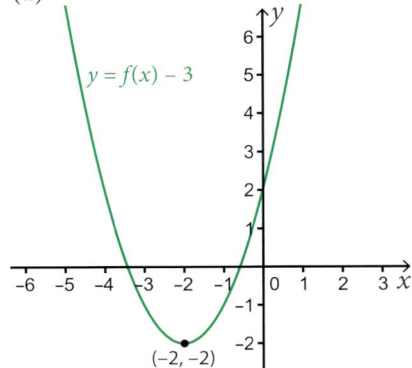

(b)

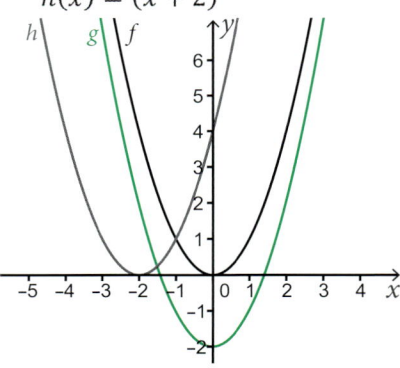

3. (a) 1 unit in negative x-direction.
(b) 20 units in negative y-direction. (c) 2 units in negative x-direction. (d) 10 units in negative y-direction.

4. (a) $f(x) + a = 3x + 2$
(b) $f(x) + a = x$
(c) $f(x) + a = x^2 - 2x - 2$
(d) $f(x) + a = x^3 - 1$

5. (a) $g(x) = x^2 - 2$
$h(x) = (x + 2)^2$

5. (b) $g(x) = 3x - 2$
$h(x) = 3(x + 2)$

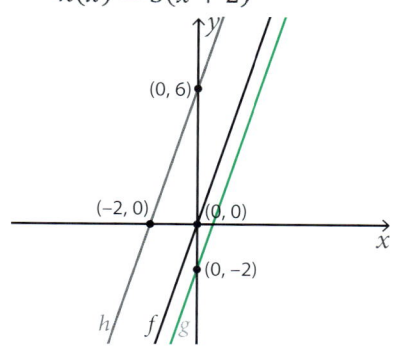

(c) $g(x) = \dfrac{1}{x} - 2$

$h(x) = \dfrac{1}{x + 2}$

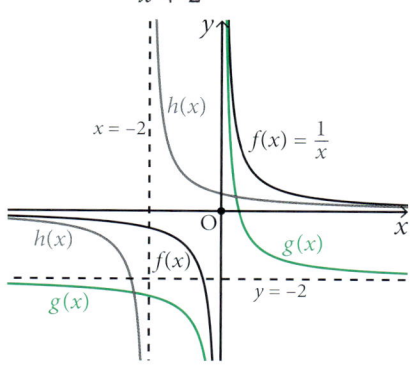

(d) $g(x) = (x - 2)^3 - 2$
$h(x) = x^3$

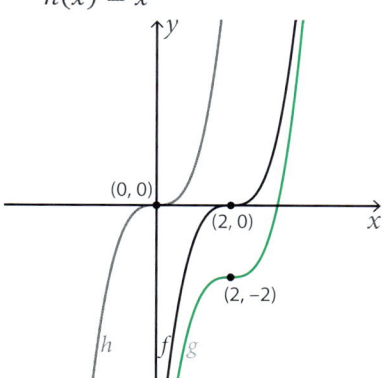

In each case, $g(x)$ is a translation two units in negative y-direction; $h(x)$ is a translation two units in negative x-direction.

6.

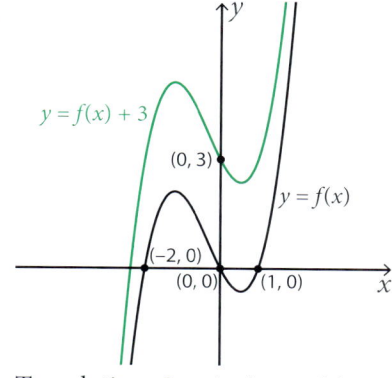

Translation, 3 units in positive y-direction.

7. (a)

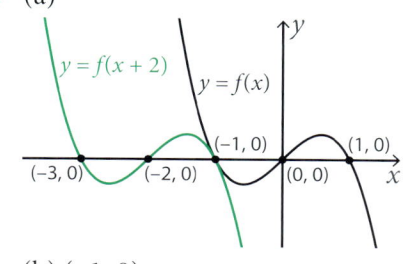

(b) $(-1, 0)$

Exercise 5F

1. (a) Reflection in x-axis.
(b) Stretch in y-direction, scale factor 2.
(c) Stretch in x-direction, scale factor ½. (d) Reflection in y-axis.

2. (a)

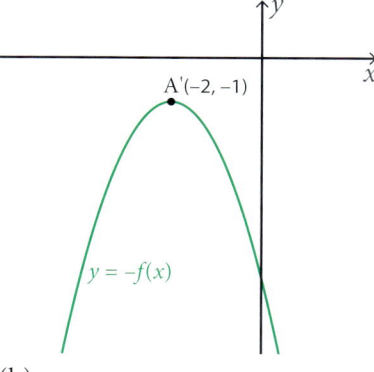

(b)

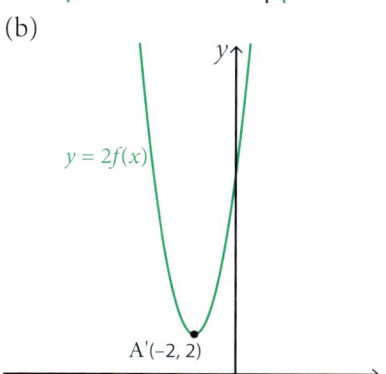

(c)

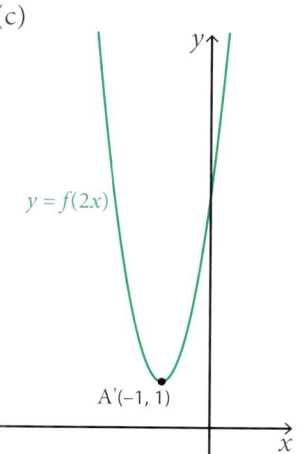

(d)

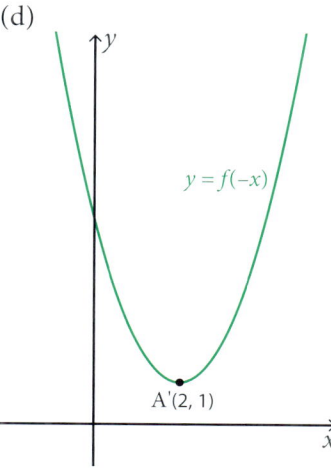

3. (a) $af(x) = 2x^2$; $f(ax) = 4x^2$
(b) $af(x) = 2x^3 + 2$;
$f(ax) = 8x^3 + 1$
(c) $af(x) = 6x$; $f(ax) = 6x$
(d) $af(x) = \dfrac{10}{x}$; $f(ax) = \dfrac{2}{5x}$
(e) $af(x) = -x^2$; $f(ax) = x^2$
(f) $af(x) = -\dfrac{1}{x^2}$; $f(ax) = \dfrac{1}{x^2}$
(g) $af(x) = -3x^3$; $f(ax) = -3x^3$
(h) $af(x) = 2(x - 1)$;
$f(ax) = 1 + 2x$
(i) $af(x) = 2x(x - 1)(x - 2)$;
$f(ax) = 4x(2x - 1)(x - 1)$
(j) $af(x) = -2x^2(x - 1)$;
$f(ax) = -4x^2(2x + 1)$

189

4. (a)

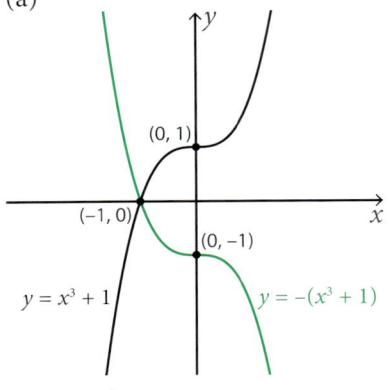

$y = x^3 + 1$ $y = -(x^3 + 1)$

(0, 1), (−1, 0), (0, −1)

$x = -1$

(b)

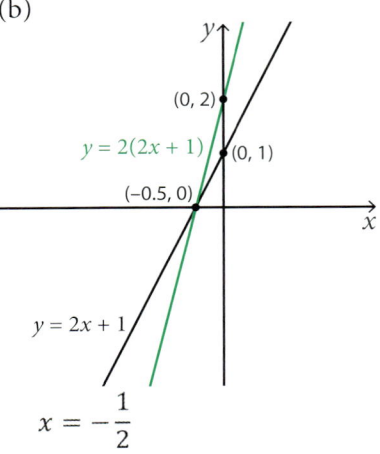

(0, 2), $y = 2(2x + 1)$, (0, 1), (−0.5, 0), $y = 2x + 1$

$x = -\dfrac{1}{2}$

(c)

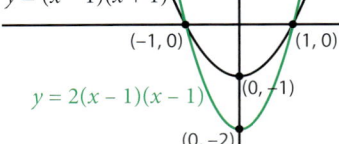

$y = (x - 1)(x + 1)$, (−1, 0), (1, 0), $y = 2(x - 1)(x - 1)$, (0, −1), (0, −2)

$x = -1, x = 1$

5. (a)

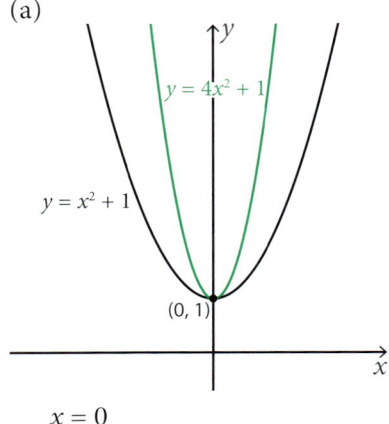

$y = 4x^2 + 1$, $y = x^2 + 1$, (0, 1)

$x = 0$

(b)

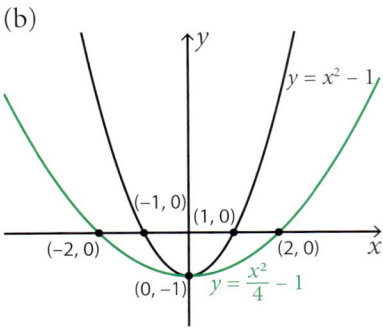

$y = x^2 - 1$, (−1, 0), (1, 0), (−2, 0), (2, 0), (0, −1), $y = \dfrac{x^2}{4} - 1$

$x = 0$

(c)

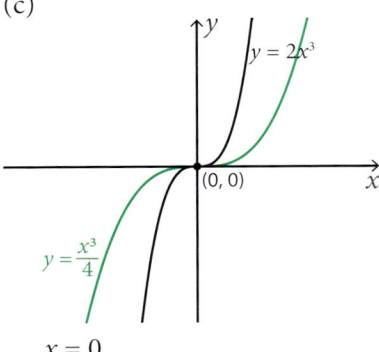

$y = 2x^3$, (0, 0), $y = \dfrac{x^3}{4}$

$x = 0$

(d)

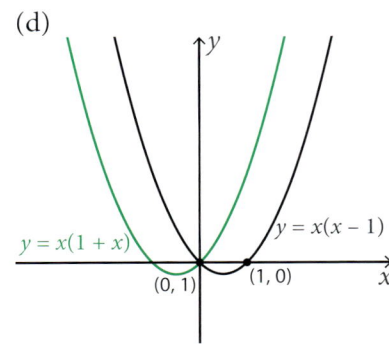

$y = x(1 + x)$, $y = x(x - 1)$, (0, 1), (1, 0)

$x = 0$

Exercise 5G

1. (a)

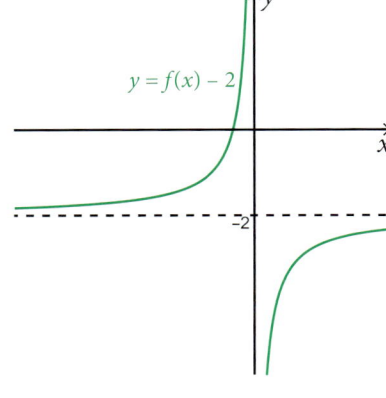

$y = f(x) - 2$, −2

(b)

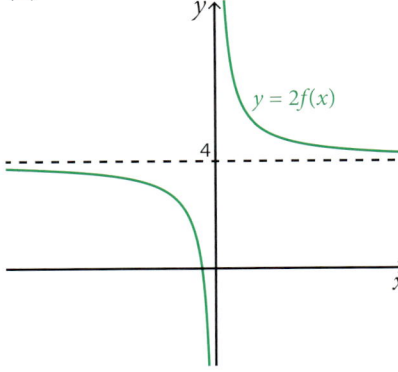

$y = 2f(x)$, 4

(c)

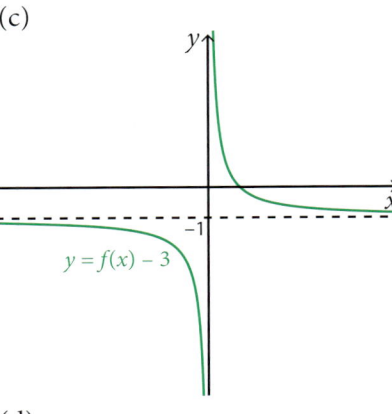

−1, $y = f(x) - 3$

(d)

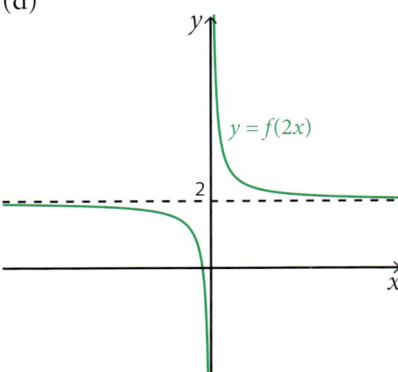

$y = f(2x)$, 2

(e)

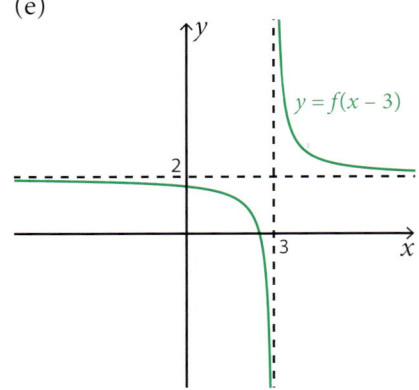

$y = f(x - 3)$, 2, 3

1. (f)

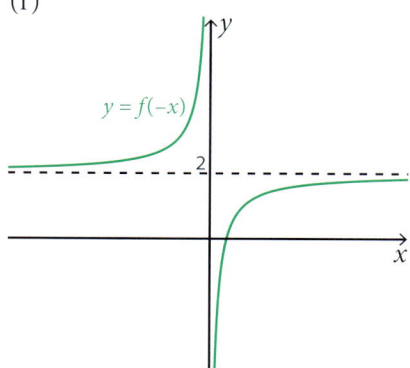

$y = f(-x)$

2. (a)

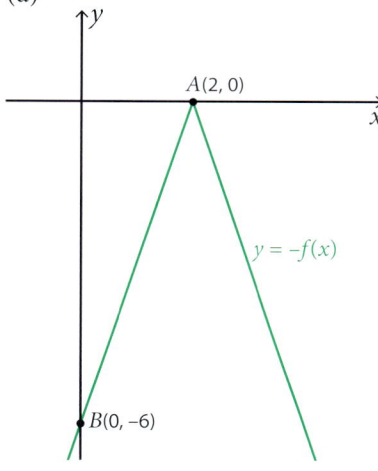

$A(2, 0)$
$y = -f(x)$
$B(0, -6)$

(b)

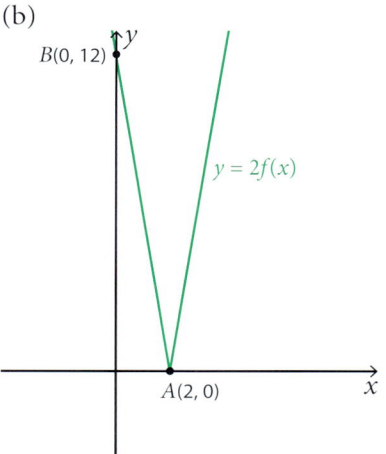

$B(0, 12)$
$y = 2f(x)$
$A(2, 0)$

(c)

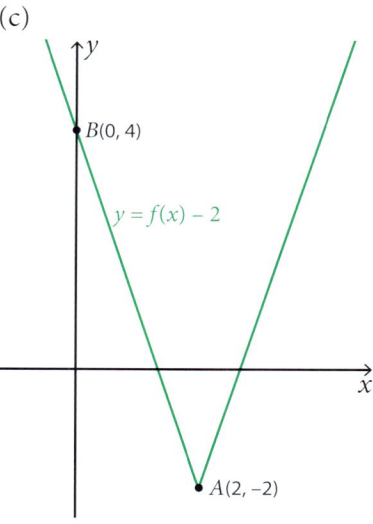

$B(0, 4)$
$y = f(x) - 2$
$A(2, -2)$

(d)

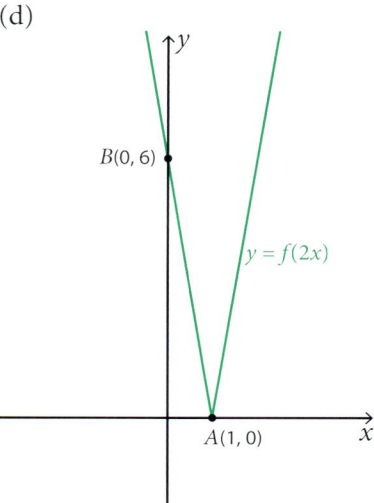

$B(0, 6)$
$y = f(2x)$
$A(1, 0)$

(e)

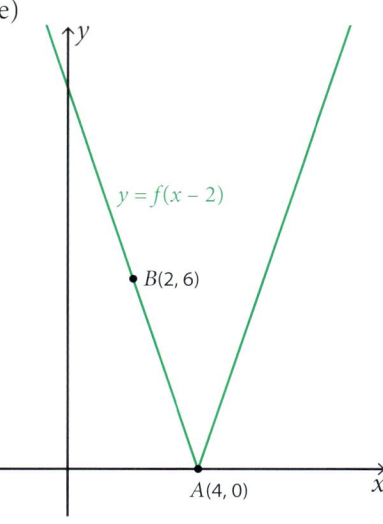

$y = f(x - 2)$
$B(2, 6)$
$A(4, 0)$

(f)

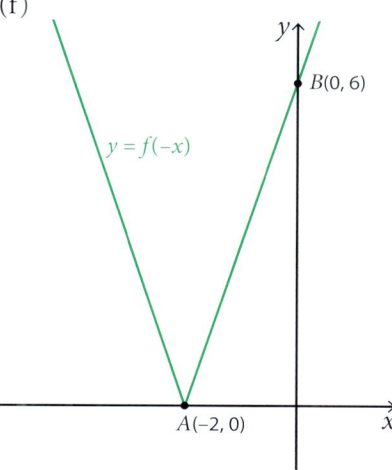

$B(0, 6)$
$y = f(-x)$
$A(-2, 0)$

3. (a)

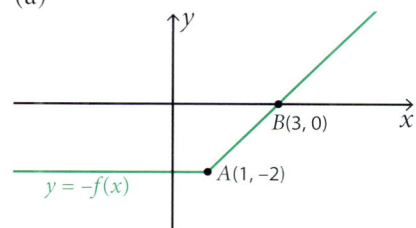

$B(3, 0)$
$y = -f(x)$
$A(1, -2)$

(b)

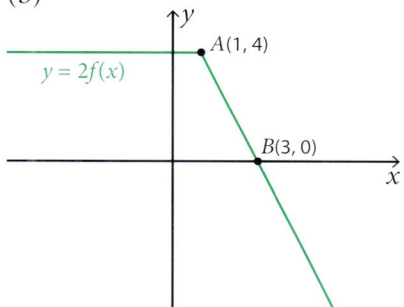

$A(1, 4)$
$y = 2f(x)$
$B(3, 0)$

(c)

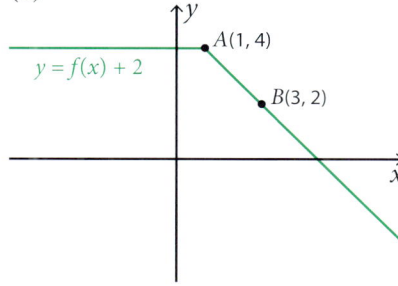

$A(1, 4)$
$y = f(x) + 2$
$B(3, 2)$

(d)

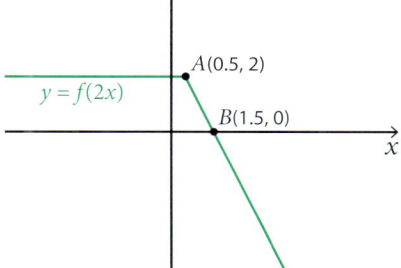

$A(0.5, 2)$
$y = f(2x)$
$B(1.5, 0)$

(e)

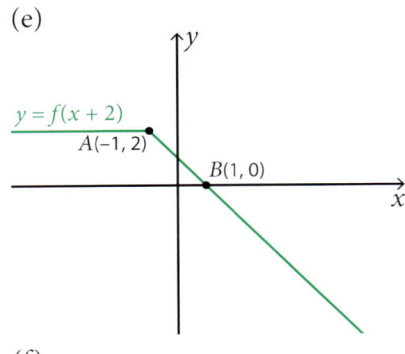

$y = f(x + 2)$
$A(-1, 2)$
$B(1, 0)$

(f)

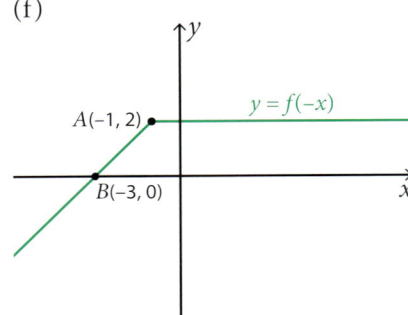

$A(-1, 2)$
$y = f(-x)$
$B(-3, 0)$

4. (a)

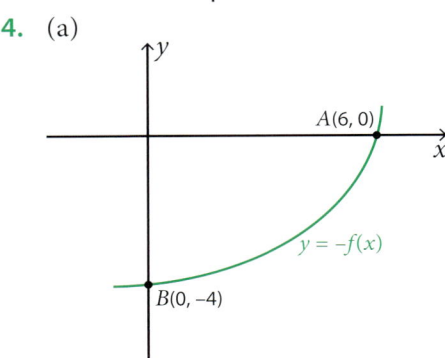

$A(6, 0)$
$y = -f(x)$
$B(0, -4)$

(b)

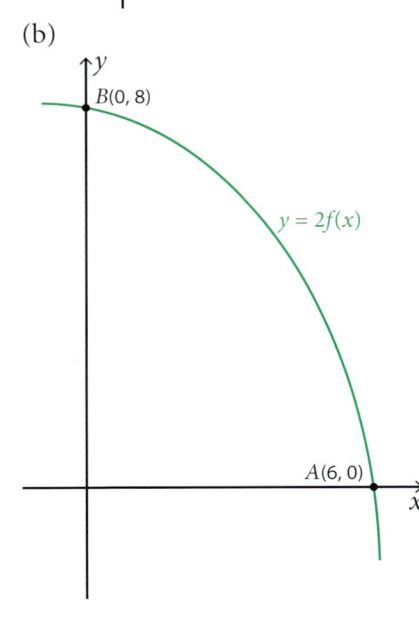

$B(0, 8)$
$y = 2f(x)$
$A(6, 0)$

(c)

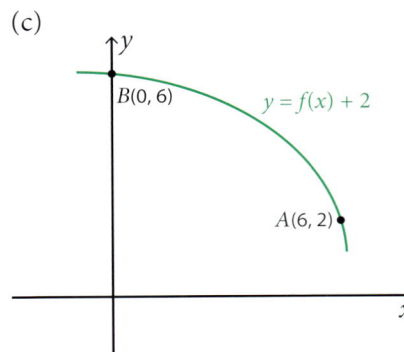

$B(0, 6)$
$y = f(x) + 2$
$A(6, 2)$

(d)

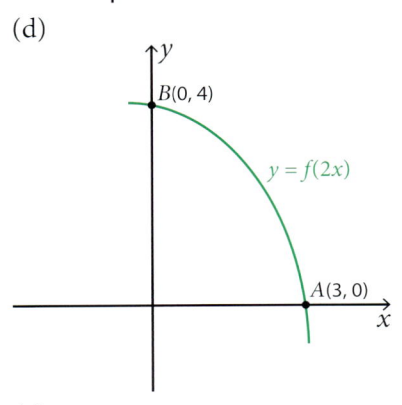

$B(0, 4)$
$y = f(2x)$
$A(3, 0)$

(e)

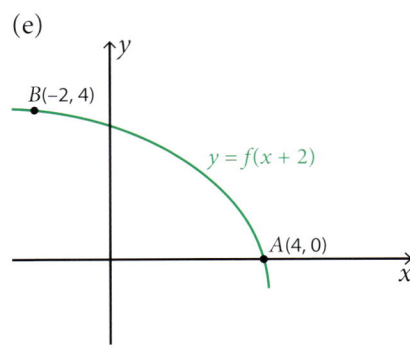

$B(-2, 4)$
$y = f(x + 2)$
$A(4, 0)$

(f)

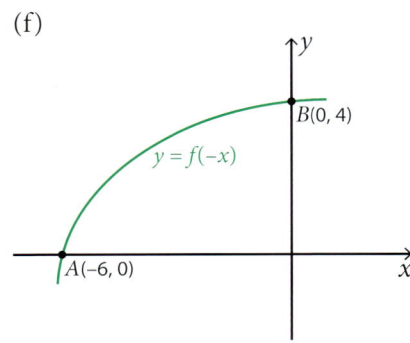

$B(0, 4)$
$y = f(-x)$
$A(-6, 0)$

Exercise 6A

1. (a) yes (b) no (c) yes (d) no
(e) yes (f) yes

2. (a)

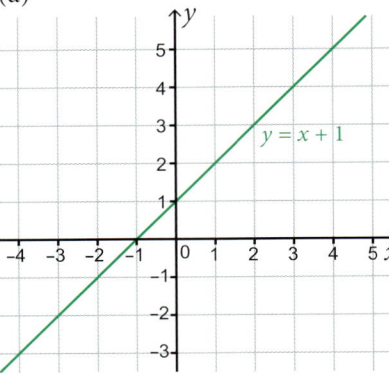

$y = x + 1$

Gradient 1, y-intercept 1.

(b)

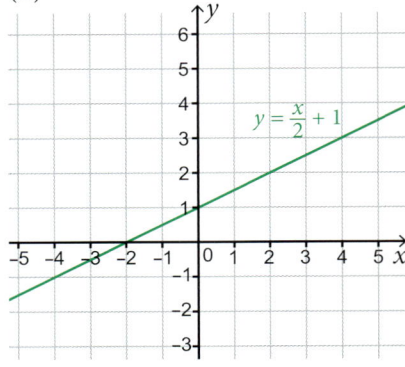

$y = \frac{x}{2} + 1$

Gradient ½, y-intercept 1.

(c)

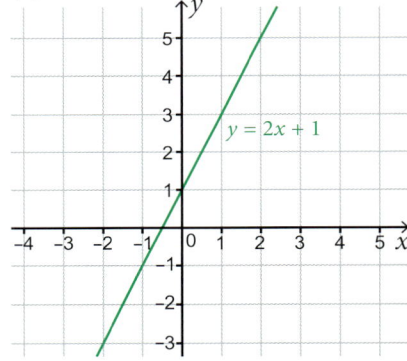

$y = 2x + 1$

Gradient 2, y-intercept 1.

(d)

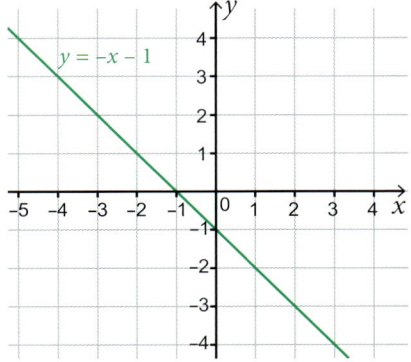

$y = -x - 1$

Gradient −1, y-intercept −1.

3. (a) Gradient 5, y-intercept 3
   (b) Gradient –2, y-intercept –3
   (c) Gradient 2, y-intercept ⁷⁄₂
   (d) Gradient 1, y-intercept –1

Exercise 6B

1. (a) 1 (b) $-\dfrac{1}{2}$ (c) $-\dfrac{4}{5}$ (d) $\dfrac{4}{3}$ (e) $\dfrac{1}{4}$
2. (a) $y = 2x - 3$ (b) $y = x + 4$
   (c) $y = 3x + 2$ (d) $y = \dfrac{1}{2}x - \dfrac{5}{2}$
   (e) $y = -2x$ (f) $y = -x - 2$
3. (a) $y = x$ (b) $y = 3x - 6$
   (c) $y = x + 2$ (d) $y = \dfrac{1}{2}x + 3$
   (e) $y = -3x$ (f) $y = -2x - 1$
4. $y = 9x - 33$
5. $y = 4x + 3$
6. $y = -x - 1$
7. $m = 1$
8. $y = 5x - 48$
9. $y = 7x - 53$
10. $y = 2x - 7$
11. $y = 3x + 13$
12. $x = 7$
13. $y = 5x - 14$
14. $C\left(\dfrac{1}{5}, 0\right), D(0, -1)$

Exercise 6C

1. (a) $3x - 2y + 3 = 0$
   (b) $3y - 5 = 0$
   (c) $x - 1 = 0$
   (d) $3x - 4y - 3 = 0$
   (e) $4x - 5y = 0$
   (f) $4x - 25y = 0$
   (g) $2x + 7y + 3 = 0$
   (h) $4x - 3y + 1 = 0$
   (i) $12x - 6y - 1 = 0$
   (j) $7x + 6y - 1 = 0$
2. (a) (3, 0) (b) (0, 4)
3. (a) (0, 0) (b) (0, 0)
4. $2x + y - 3 = 0$
5. $4x - 6y - 9 = 0$
6. $a = 3; b = 1; 3x + y - 6 = 0$
7. (a) A(2, 5)

(b)

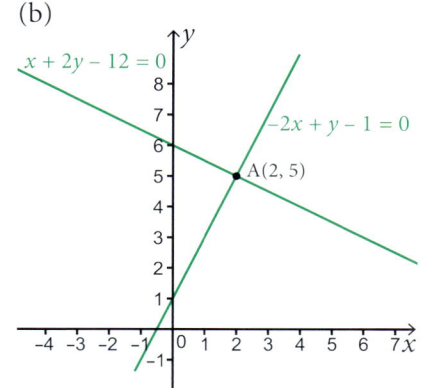

Exercise 6D

1. (a) (5, 5) (b) (5, 4) (c) (–1, –5)
   (d) (11.5, 4) (e) (2.5, –4.5)
   (f) (2, 1) (g) (0, 5)
2. (a) $\left(\dfrac{1 + \pi}{2}, 11\right)$ (b) $\left(\dfrac{5}{2}, 1 + \sqrt{2}\right)$
3. (a) B(–2, 6) (b) B(4, 7)
   (c) B(–26, 17) (d) B(–21, –24)
   (e) B(2, 3π)
4. (a) –3 (b) x-coordinate of
   midpoint: $\dfrac{(4k + 1) + (2k^2 + 1)}{2}$
   $= \dfrac{2k^2 + 4k + 2}{2} = k^2 + 2k + 1$
   $= (k + 1)^2$ (c) 1, –3

Exercise 6E

1. (a) parallel (b) neither (c) parallel
   (d) perpendicular (e) neither
   (f) parallel (g) neither
2. (a) and (c) perpendicular; (b) and
   (e) parallel; (d) and (f) neither.
3. $p = -7$
4. (a) $y = -\dfrac{7}{2}x - \dfrac{5}{2}$ (b) $\dfrac{2}{7}$
5. –3
6. 2
7. $2y + 3x - 9 = 0$
8. (a) –10 (b) $3x + 10y - 109 = 0$
9. $2x + 3y - 3 = 0$
10. (a) 1 (b) $y + x - 3a = 0$

Exercise 6F

1. (a) Gradient $m = 0.2$; y-intercept
   $= 73$. (b) For every increase of 1
   in t (an increase of one year), the
   value of y increases by 0.2.
   (c) Meaning of gradient: every
   year the average lifespan of British
   men increased by 0.2 years (2.4

months). Meaning of y-intercept:
in 1960 the average lifespan of a
British man was 73 years.
2. (a) 40 m s⁻¹
   (b)

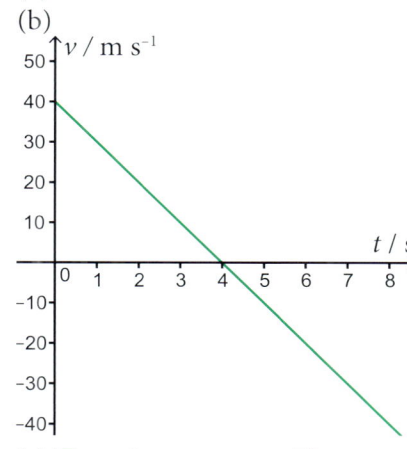

   (c) The y-intercept $c = 40$.
   (d) The gradient is –10, meaning
   that, every second, the velocity
   decreases by 10 m s⁻¹. (Eventually
   the velocity becomes zero when
   the ball reaches its peak, and
   then becomes negative as the
   ball falls back to the ground.)
   The y-intercept of 40 means
   that, when the ball was released
   at $t = 0$ seconds, it was thrown
   upwards at 40 m s⁻¹.
3. (a) Gradient $m = 5.6$. (b) For an
   increase in the pollution index
   of one unit, there are 5 or 6 more
   fish deaths during the year.
   (c) When $p = 0$, $D = 221.7$. This
   means that, even if the pollution
   index were zero (i.e. even if the
   water were completely clean),
   there would still be about 222 fish
   deaths per year.

Exercise 7A

1. (a) (i) $y = x$ (ii) (0, 0)
   (b) (i) $3x + 10y = 60$ (ii) (5, 4.5)
   (c) (i) $x - 3y = 1$ (ii) (1, 0)
   (d) (i) $x + 12y = 36$ (ii) (0, 3)
   (e) (i) $x - y = -1$ (ii) (-0.5, 0.5)
2. B(25, –8)
3. (a) $f(x) = (x + 2)^2 - 4$
   (b) $f(x) = (x + 4)^2 - 10$
   (c) $f(x) = -(x + 5)^2 + 31$
4. (a) $x = -2, -4$ (b) $x = 1, -5$
   (c) $x = 3\sqrt{2} - 1, -3\sqrt{2} - 1$
5. (a) 2 roots (b) 0 roots (c) 1 root

(d) 0 roots (e) 0 roots

Exercise 7B

1. (a) $4x - 3y + 4 = 0$
   (b) $3x + 5y - 12 = 0$
   (c) $x - y + 5 = 0$ (d) $x = 2$
   (e) $x - y = 0$
2. (a) yes (b) yes (c) no (d) yes (e) no
3. (a) $x + 2y - 7 = 0$
   (b) $x + 2y - 7 = 0$, and $y = 1$, so: $x + 2(1) - 7 = 0 \Rightarrow x = 5$
4. (a) $(13, 15)$ (b) $\sqrt{34}$
5. (a) $x + 4y - 12 = 0$
   (b) $x + 4y - 12 = 0$, and $x = 8$, so: $8 + 4y - 12 = 0 \Rightarrow y = 1$
6. (a) $-\sqrt{2}$ (b) $\dfrac{\sqrt{2}}{2}$ (c) -1
7. (a) $(19, 5)$ (b) $\dfrac{1}{5}$ (c) 0 (d) $(6, 5)$
   (e) East
8. (a) $60°$ (b) $120°$ (c) $3\sqrt{3}$ (d) $27\sqrt{3}$

Exercise 7C

1. (a) no (b) yes
2. (a) $p = 64, r = 8$, centre $(-4, -10)$
   (b) $p = 100, r = 10$, centre $(6, -2)$
3. (a) $(x - 8)^2 + (y - 7)^2 = 16$
   (b) $(x + 2)^2 + (y + 1)^2 = 100$
4. (a) $(x + 1)^2 + (y + 3)^2 = 2$
   (b) $(x - 8)^2 + (y + 3)^2 = 8$
5. (a) With $x = -9$ and $y = 7$, LHS $= (-9)^2 + 7^2 + 10(-9) - 20(7) + 100 = 0 = $ RHS
   (b) $(x + 5)^2 + (y - 10)^2 = 25$
   (c) Centre $(-5, 10)$, radius 5
6. $(x - 9)^2 + (y - 2)^2 = 4$
7. 4
8. (a) $(6, 4)$ (b) 10 (c) $6\sqrt{10}$
9. (a) $\left(-2 + \sqrt{6}, 0\right), \left(-2 - \sqrt{6}, 0\right)$
   (b) $\left(0, 2 + \sqrt{6}\right), \left(0, 2 - \sqrt{6}\right)$
10. $4\sqrt{5} - 7$
11. $(x - 8)^2 + (y + 4)^2 = 100$

Exercise 7D

1. (a) 2 (b) 2 (c) 0 (d) 1 (e) 0
2. (a) $(3, 10)$
   (b) $\left(\dfrac{1}{5}\left(-5 + \sqrt{10}\right), -\dfrac{1}{5}\left(25 + 2\sqrt{10}\right)\right),$ $\left(-\dfrac{1}{5}\left(5 + \sqrt{10}\right), \dfrac{1}{5}\left(-25 + 2\sqrt{10}\right)\right)$
   (c) $(6, -12)$

(d) $\left(\dfrac{1}{10}\left(-21 + \sqrt{191}\right), \dfrac{1}{10}\left(63 - 3\sqrt{191}\right)\right),$ $\left(-\dfrac{1}{10}\left(21 + \sqrt{191}\right), \dfrac{1}{10}\left(63 + 3\sqrt{191}\right)\right)$
   (e) No points of intersection
3. $a = 1, \dfrac{79}{47}$
4. (a) $A(-1, -3)$ (b) Centre of circle $(2, 0)$ from equation. Midpoint of AB is $\left(\dfrac{-1 + 5}{2}, \dfrac{-3 + 3}{2}\right) = (2, 0)$. Midpoint of AB is centre of circle, hence it is a diameter.

Exercise 7E

1. (a) -2 (b) -10 (c) -1 (d) $\dfrac{4}{3}$ (e) 0
2. $y = -x + 8$
3. (a) $A(x, y)$, $B(-11, 3)$, centre $(-7, 5)$. So $\dfrac{x - 11}{2} = -7 \Rightarrow x = -3$ and $\dfrac{y + 3}{2} = 5 \Rightarrow y = 7$
   (b) -2 (c) $2x + y - 1 = 0$ (d) $2\sqrt{5}$
4. (a) $(x - 5)^2 + (y - 13)^2 = 169$
   (b) $12y - 5x + 38 = 0$
5. $3y - 2x - 29 = 0$
6. (a) Centre $(2, 4)$, radius 4.
   (b) $y = -\dfrac{4}{3}x$ (c) $y = 0$

Exercise 8A

1. (a) 40 000 m s⁻¹ (b) 1.05 m³
   (c) -45
2. (a) $x = 10, y = 5$
   (b) $x = 10, y = -1$
   (c) $x = -9, y = -8$
   (d) $x = -2, y = -1$
   (e) $x = -5, y = -7$
   (f) $x = 2, y = -3, z = -2$

Exercise 8B

1. (a) 2 (b) 1680 (c) $\dfrac{1}{20}$ (d) 1440
   (e) 15 (f) 127
   (g) 2 (h) 1 (i) 100 (j) 48
2. (a) 8 (b) 10 (c) 45 (d) 56 (e) 35
   (f) 100 (g) 70 (h) 1 (i) 20 (j) 1

Exercise 8C

1. (a) $1 + 6x + 15x^2 + 20x^3 + \cdots$
   (b) $1 + 8x + 24x^2 + 32x^3 + \cdots$
   (c) $1 - 4x + 6x^2 - 4x^3 + \cdots$
   (d) $1 + \dfrac{3x}{2} + \dfrac{3x^2}{4} + \dfrac{x^3}{8}$
   (e) $1 - 10x + 40x^2 - 80x^3 + \cdots$
   (f) $1 + 10x + 45x^2 + 120x^3 + \cdots$
   (g) $1 + 15x + 75x^2 + 125x^3$
   (h) $1 - \dfrac{3x}{10} + \dfrac{3x^2}{100} - \dfrac{x^3}{1000}$
   (i) $1 + 40x + 600x^2 + 4000x^3 + \cdots$
   (j) $1 - 4.22x + 7.43x^2 - 6.97x^3 + \cdots$
2. (a) $128 + 448x + 672x^2 + \cdots$
   (b) $8 + 24x + 24x^2 + \cdots$
   (c) $1000 - 30x + \dfrac{3x^2}{10} + \cdots$
   (d) $1 - \dfrac{3}{x} + \dfrac{3}{x^2} - \cdots$
   (e) $256 + 768x + 864x^2 + \cdots$
   (f) $16 + 32x^2 + 24x^4 + \cdots$
   (g) $x^4 + 4x^2 + 6 + \cdots$
   (h) $4 + 8x + 6x^2 + \cdots$
   (i) $625 + 1000x + 600x^2 + \cdots$
   (j) $\dfrac{1}{a^3} + 3x + 3a^3x^2 + \cdots$
3. (a) $1 + 3x + 3.75x^2 + 2.5x^3$
   (b) 1.34
4. (a) $1 + nax + \dfrac{n(n - 1)a^2}{2}x^2 + \dfrac{n(n - 1)(n - 2)a^3}{6}x^3$
   (b) $n = 20, a = 0.7$ (c) 391.02
5. (a) $1 + 9px + 36p^2x^2$
   (b) $p = -1, q = 9$
6. $p = 0.125, A = 768$
7. 1280
8. $1 + 14x + 75x^2 + 180x^3$
9. (a) $1 - nx + \dfrac{n(n - 1)}{2}x^2 - \dfrac{n(n - 1)(n - 2)}{6}x^3$
   (b) $n = 3$
10. (a) $1 - 8x + 24x^2 - 32x^3$
    (b) 0.961

Exercise 9A

1. (a) $\dfrac{11}{4}, -\dfrac{1}{4}$ (b) $4 \pm \sqrt{17}$
   (c) $\dfrac{1 + \sqrt{5}}{4}, \dfrac{1 - \sqrt{5}}{4}$
   (d) $\dfrac{3 + 5\sqrt{5}}{2}, \dfrac{3 - 5\sqrt{5}}{2}$

2. (a) $x = \dfrac{1}{3}$ (b) $x = \dfrac{4p}{3p - 2}$

(c) $x = \pm\sqrt{\dfrac{2(1 + y)}{y}}$

(d) $x = \dfrac{2de - fc}{f - 2d}$

Exercise 9B

1. (a) 1.04 cm (b) 9.76 cm
   (c) 2.51 cm (d) 10.7 cm
2. (a) 4.8° (b) 47.2° (c) 31.4° (d) 6.0°
   (e) 29.4°
3. (a) $A = 49.9°, C = 98.1°$
   or $A = 130.1°, C = 17.9°$
   (b) $B = 48.5°, C = 109.5°$
   or $B = 131.5°, C = 26.5°$
   (c) $C = 53.6°, A = 88.4°$
   or $C = 126.4°, A = 15.6°$
   (d) $A = 78.1°, B = 44.9°$
   or $A = 101.9°, B = 21.1°$
   (e) $C = 59.9°, B = 67.1°$
   or $C = 120.1°, B = 6.9°$
4. (a) 0.444 (b) 26.3°, 153.7°
5. (a) 80° (b) 26.0 km
6. $AC = 6.29$ cm, $AD = 8.71$ cm
7. $CBF = 22.4°, BCF = 18.1°$

Exercise 9C

1. (a) $a = 6.12$ cm (b) $a = 7.48$ m
   (c) $b = 4.46$ km (d) $c = 11.4$ cm
   (e) $c = 7.09$ mm
2. (a) $A = 40.8°$ (b) $Y = 41.0°$
   (c) $P = 53.8°$ (d) $C = 82.8°$
   (e) $B = 69.1°$
3. (a) $A = 91.0°, B = 59.0°,$
   $C = 30.0°$ (b) $A = 29.0°,$
   $B = 104.5°, C = 46.6°$
   (c) $a = 9.9$ cm, $B = 63.1°,$
   $C = 73.9°$ (d) $b = 23.6$ feet,
   $C = 18.2°, A = 19.8°$
   (e) $b = 5.2$ km, $A = 68°,$
   $B = 44°$ (f) $c = 1.6$ cm, $B = 26°,$
   $C = 117°$
4. No. With three angles given, it is
   not possible to find the lengths of
   the sides.
5. No. The sum of the two shortest
   sides must be greater than the
   longest.
6. (a) 29.8 m (b) 55.1°
7. 10.9 m
8. 74 300 km

Exercise 9D

1. (a) 12.9 cm² (b) 120 000 m²
   (c) 1.17 km² (d) 1.44 cm²
   (e) 5.51 m² (f) 28.1 cm²
2. (a) $b = 3.78$ cm (b) $b = 14.5$ m
   (c) $b = 6.13$ mm (d) $b = 31.7$ km
3. (a) $C = 26.7°$ (b) $C = 67.8°$
   (c) $C = 80.2°$ (d) $C = 16.0°$
4. 5 cm²
5. 63.2°
6. $x = -1$
7. $\dfrac{100 + 25\sqrt{3}}{4}$ cm²
8. (a) $\dfrac{1}{2}pq\sin\theta$ (b) $\dfrac{1}{2}qr\sin\theta$

Exercise 9E

1.

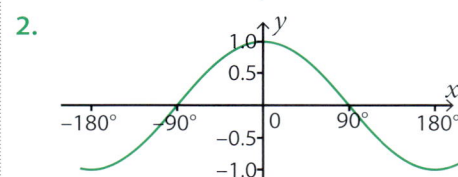

2.

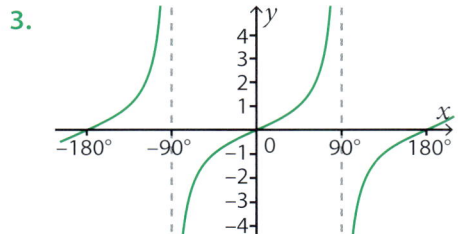

3.

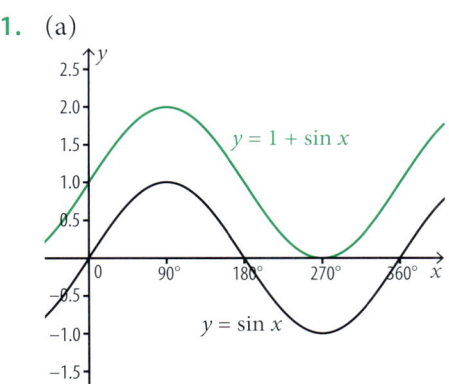

4. (a) 2 (b) 3 (c) 0 (d) 1
5. (a) 2 (b) 2 (c) 0 (d) 2
6. (a) 2 (b) 3 (c) 2 (d) 2

Exercise 9F

1. (a)

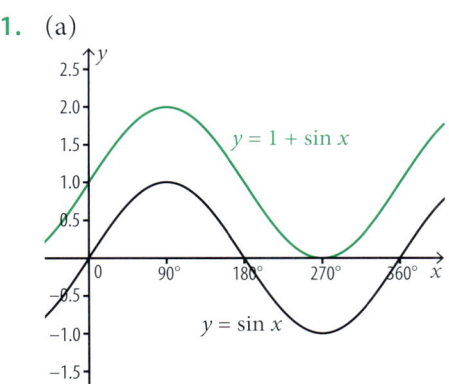

(b)

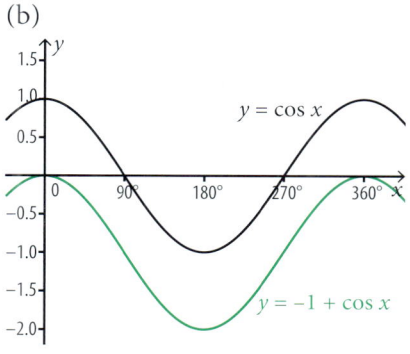

(c)

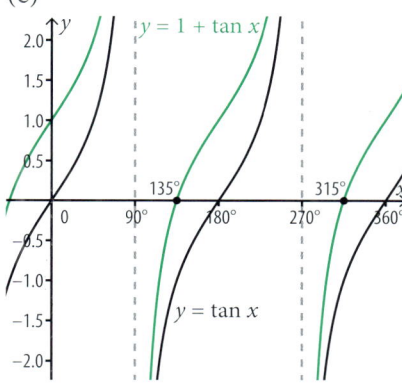

(d)

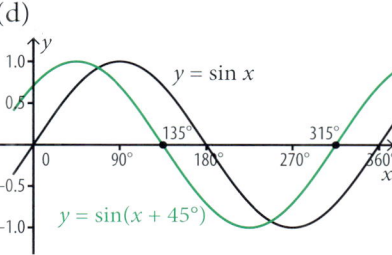

(e)

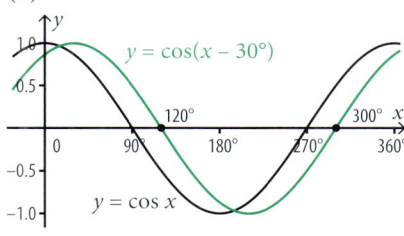

(f)

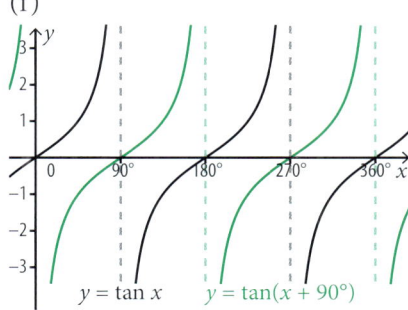

2. (a)

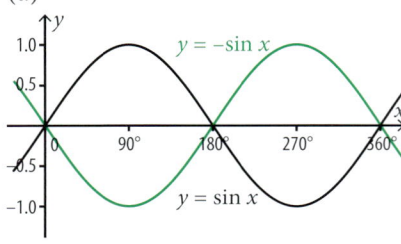

(b)

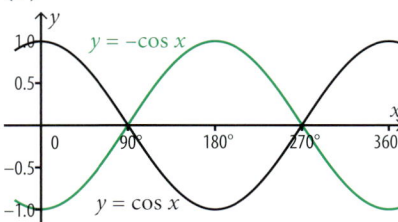

(c)

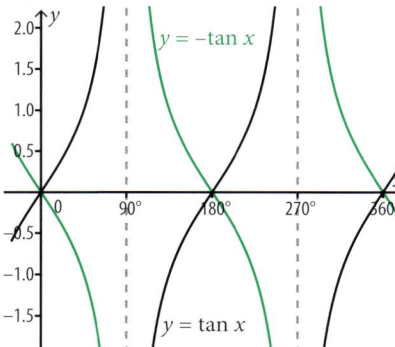

3. (a) $y = \cos x$ period 360°, $y = \cos 2x$ period 180°

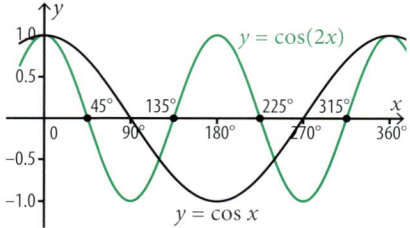

(b) $y = \sin x$ period 360°, $y = \sin \dfrac{x}{2}$ period 720°

(c) $y = \tan x$ period 180°, $y = \tan 2x$ period 90°

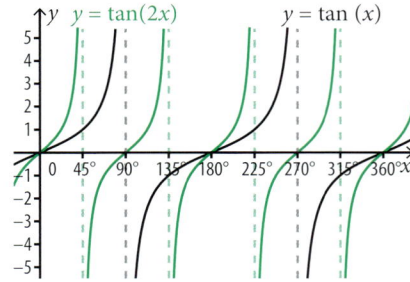

(d) $y = \cos x$ period 360°, $y = \cos 3x$ period 120°

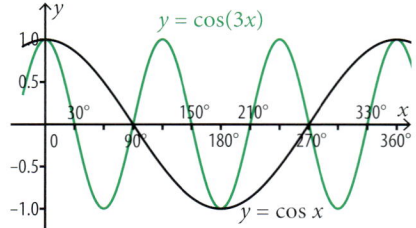

4. (a) $y = 1 + \cos x$

(b) $y = -\sin\left(\dfrac{x}{2}\right)$

(c) $y = 2 + \tan x$

5. (a) Max: 1 when $x = 180°$; min: –1 when $x = 0°$ (b) Max: 3 when $x = 90°$; min: 1 when $x = 270°$ (c) Max: 3 when $x = 90°$; min: –3 when $x = 270°$

6. They are the same functions:

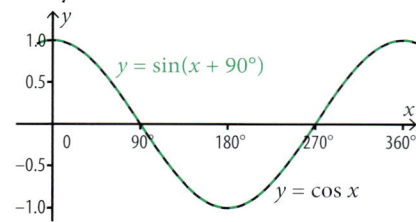

Exercise 9G

1.

Second Quadrant S	First Quadrant A
100°	45° 30°
180°	0° 360°
210°	320°
260°	
Third Quadrant T	Fourth Quadrant C
	270°

2.

	$\sin\theta$	$\cos\theta$	$\tan\theta$	Related acute angle
(a) 30°	+ve	+ve	+ve	30°
(b) 45°	+ve	+ve	+ve	45°
(c) 100°	+ve	–ve	–ve	80°
(d) 210°	–ve	–ve	+ve	30°
(e) 260°	–ve	–ve	+ve	80°
(f) 320°	–ve	+ve	–ve	40°

2.

		Related acute angle	Value
(a) $\sin 135°$	+ve	45°	$\dfrac{\sqrt{2}}{2}$
(b) $\cos(-45°)$	+ve	45°	$\dfrac{\sqrt{2}}{2}$
(c) $\tan 120°$	–ve	60°	$-\sqrt{3}$
(d) $\cos 150°$	–ve	30°	$-\dfrac{\sqrt{3}}{2}$
(e) $\sin(-120°)$	–ve	60°	$-\dfrac{\sqrt{3}}{2}$
(f) $\tan(-30°)$	–ve	30°	$-\dfrac{\sqrt{3}}{3}$
(g) $\cos(-135°)$	–ve	45°	$-\dfrac{\sqrt{2}}{2}$
(h) $\sin(-330°)$	+ve	30°	$\dfrac{1}{2}$

3. (a) $\dfrac{\sqrt{3}}{2}$ (b) $-\dfrac{\sqrt{2}}{2}$ (c) 1

4. (a) $\sin x = \dfrac{2\sqrt{10}}{7}$, $\tan x = \dfrac{2\sqrt{10}}{3}$

(b) $\cos x = \dfrac{\sqrt{57}}{19}$, $\sin x = \dfrac{4\sqrt{19}}{19}$

(c) $\cos x = \dfrac{\sqrt{21}}{11}$, $\tan x = \dfrac{10\sqrt{21}}{21}$

(d) $\sin x = \dfrac{2\sqrt{7}}{7}$, $\tan x = \dfrac{2\sqrt{3}}{3}$

(e) $\cos x = \dfrac{\sqrt{2}(\sqrt{3}-1)}{4}$, $\sin x = \dfrac{\sqrt{2}(\sqrt{3}+1)}{4}$

(f) $\sin x = \dfrac{2}{3}$, $\tan x = \dfrac{2\sqrt{5}}{5}$

(g) $\cos x = \dfrac{\sqrt{2}}{2}$, $\sin x = \dfrac{\sqrt{2}}{2}$

(h) $\sin x = \dfrac{2\sqrt{2}}{3}$, $\tan x = -2\sqrt{2}$

(i) $\cos x = -\dfrac{\sqrt{55}}{8}$,

$\tan x = -\dfrac{3\sqrt{55}}{55}$

(j) $\cos x = -\dfrac{6\sqrt{37}}{37}$, $\sin x = \dfrac{\sqrt{37}}{37}$

(k) $\cos x = -\dfrac{5\sqrt{29}}{29}$,

$\sin x = -\dfrac{2\sqrt{29}}{29}$

Exercise 9H

1. (a) $\dfrac{1}{\tan x}$ (b) 1 (c) $\sin x$ (d) 0
    (e) $1 + \cos^2 A$ (f) 2 (g) $\dfrac{1}{\sin^2 x}$
    (h) 1 (i) $\sin^2 x \cos^2 x$ (j) $\tan^2 \theta$
3. t

Exercise 9I

1. (a) $x = 60°, 240°$
    (b) $x = 150°, 210°$
    (c) $x = 30°, 150°$
    (d) $x = 45°, -135°$
    (e) $x = 135°, -135°$
2. (a) $x = 60°, 120°$
    (b) $x = 120°, 240°$
    (c) $\theta = 115°, 245°$
    (d) $\theta = 63.4°, 243°$
    (e) $A = 75.5°, 284°$
    (f) $y = 26.6°, 153°$
    (g) $x = 11.3°, 191°$
    (h) $A = 39.6°, 320°$
    (i) $x = 8.11°, 352°$
    (j) $t = 57.5°, 238°$
    (k) $\theta = 70.5°, 289°$
    (l) $z = 201°, 339°$
    (m) $y = 65.5°, 294°$
    (n) $\theta = 127°, 233°$
    (o) $x = 8.63°, 171°$
3. (a) $\theta = 31.7°, 122°$
    (b) $x = 26.6°, 63.4°$
    (c) $x = 60°, 120°$
    (d) $x = 15°, 45°, 135°, 165°$
    (e) $\theta = 29.4°, 89.4°, 149°$
    (f) $x = 97.2°$
    (g) No solutions in range
    (h) $15°, 75°, 105°, 165°$
    (i) No solutions in range
    (j) $A = 73.7°$

4. (a) $x = 105°, 285°$
    (b) $x = 45°, 135°$
    (c) $x = 0°, 240°, 360°$
    (d) $x = 15.3°, 195°$
    (e) $x = 22.5°, 113°, 203°, 293°$
    (f) $x = 20°, 60°, 140°, 180°,$
        $260°, 300°$
    (g) $x = 15°, 105°, 195°, 285°$
    (h) $x = 80°, 170°, 260°, 350°$
5. (a) $x = 45°, -135°$
    (b) $x = -104°, 76.0°$
    (c) $x = -170°, -110°, -50°, 10°,$
        $70°, 130°$
    (d) $x = -143°, -52.5°, 37.5°, 128°$
    (e) $x = -117°, 63.4°$
6. (a) $\theta = 30°, 150°, 210°, 330°$
    (b) $x = 19.5°, 161°, 199°, 341°$
    (c) $y = 60°, 120°, 240°, 300°$
7. (a) $x = 90°$
    (b) $\theta = 60°, 180°, 300°$
    (c) $t = 71.6°, 117°, 252°, 297°$
    (d) $x = 76.0°, 135°, 256°, 315°$
    (e) $y = 70.5°, 289°$
    (f) $x = 90°, 180°, 270°$
    (g) $\theta = 0°, 120°, 240°, 360°$
    (h) $x = 270°$
8. (a) $56.3°, 135°, 236°, 315°$
    (b) $202°, 338°$ (c) $31.7°, 328°$
    (d) $24.2°, 129°, 231°, 336°$
9. (a) $\theta = 47.1°, 132.9°$
    (b) $x = -74.5°, 74.5°$
    (c) $y = -119°, -39.5°, 61.3°, 140.5°$
    (d) $x = 51.3°, 128.7°$
    (e) $\theta = -120°, -30°, 60°, 150°$
10. $\theta = 5.65°, 95.65°, 185.65°, 275.65°$
11. $7 \sin^2 \theta + 6 \sin \theta - 1 = 0$;
    $\theta = 8.21°, 172°, 270°$
12. $\theta = 78.5°, 282°$

Exericse 10A

1. (a) x^5 (b) y^3 (c) z^{13} (d) p^{-3} (e) q^5
2. (a) 2.5 (b) 4 (c) –3
3. (a) $x = 0$ or $x = -3$
    (b) $x = 1$ or $x = -4$
    (c) $x = \frac{1}{2}$ or $x = -3$
    (d) $x = 0$ or $x = 2$ or $x = -3$
    (e) $x = \frac{1}{3}$ or $x = -2$

1. (a)

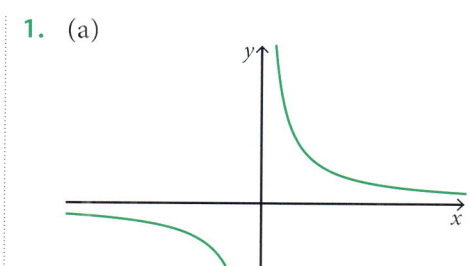

Asymptotes: $y = 0, x = 0$

(b)

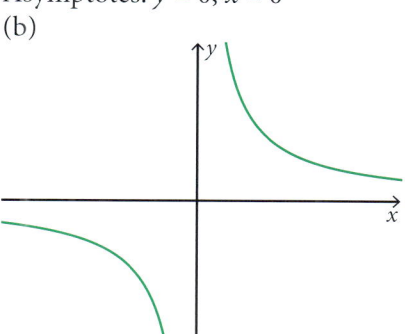

Asymptotes: $y = 0, x = 0$

(c)

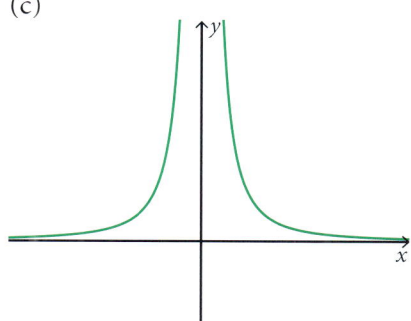

Asymptotes: $y = 0, x = 0$

(d)

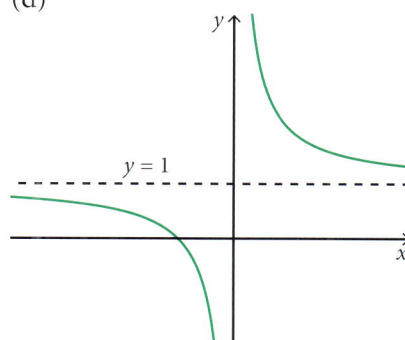

$y = 1$

Asymptotes: $y = 1, x = 0$

Exercise 10B

1.

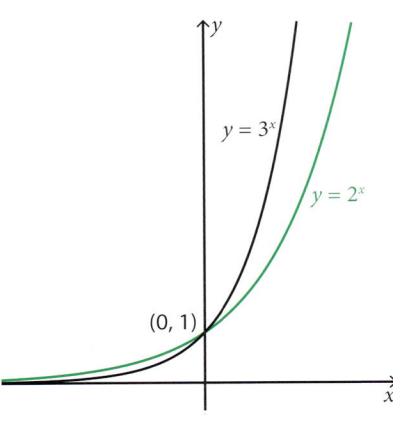

2. (a)

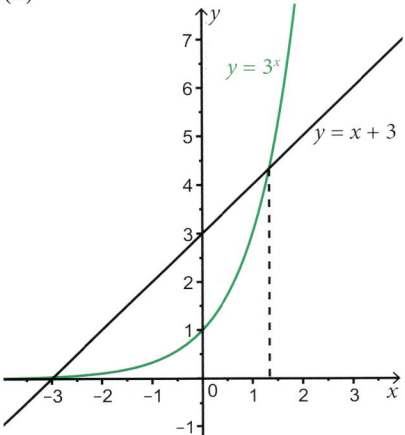

(b) $x \approx 1.3$ (c) $x \approx -2.9$

3. (a) $4^x = (2^2)^x = 2^{2x}$

(b)

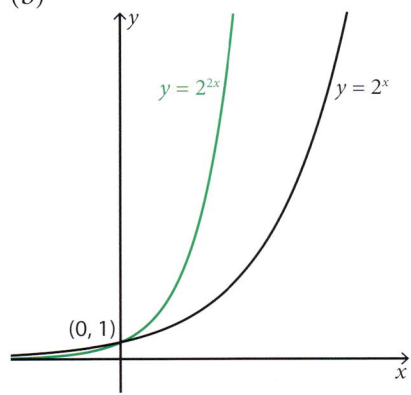

4. (a)

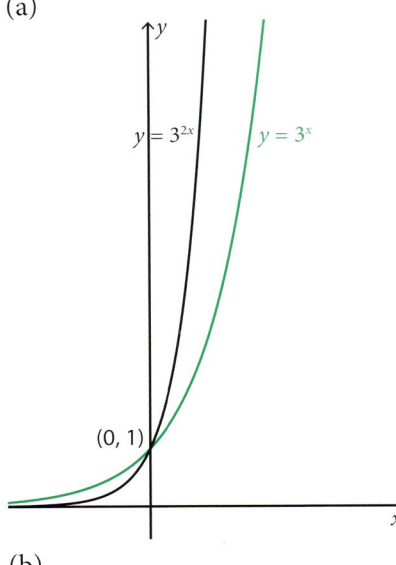

(b)

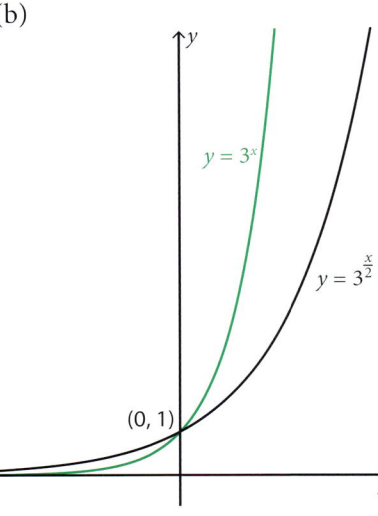

(c)

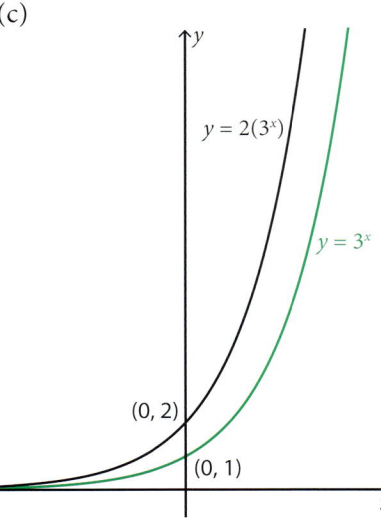

5. (a)

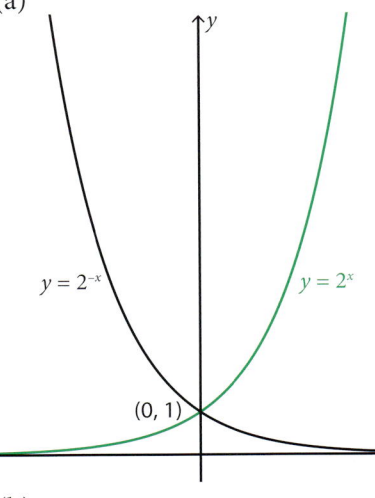

(b)

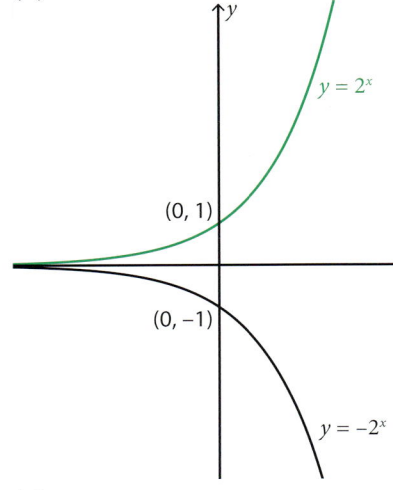

6. (a)

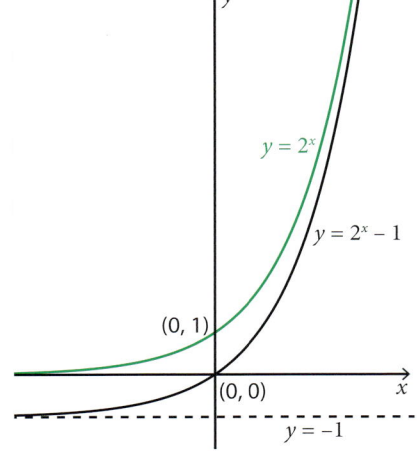

6. (b)

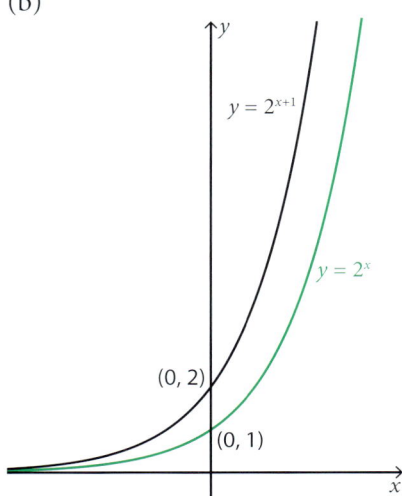

7. (a) $y = 3^x$ (b) $y = -3^x$

8. (a)

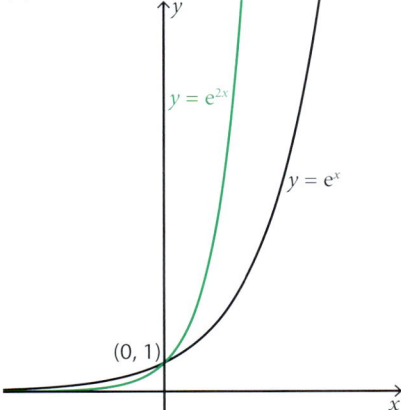

Stretch scale factor ½ parallel to the x-axis.

(b)

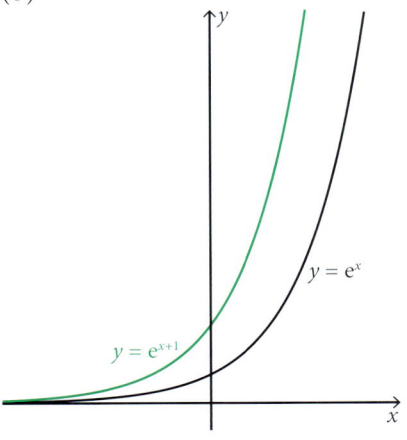

Translation by $\begin{pmatrix} -1 \\ 0 \end{pmatrix}$

(c)

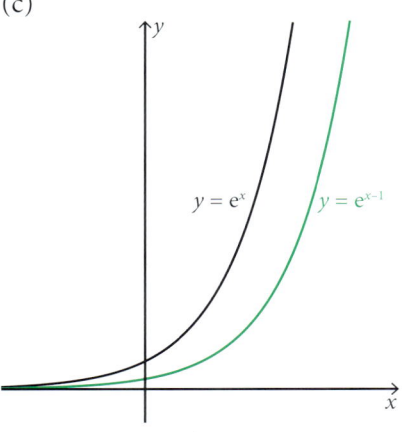

Translation by $\begin{pmatrix} 1 \\ 0 \end{pmatrix}$

(d)

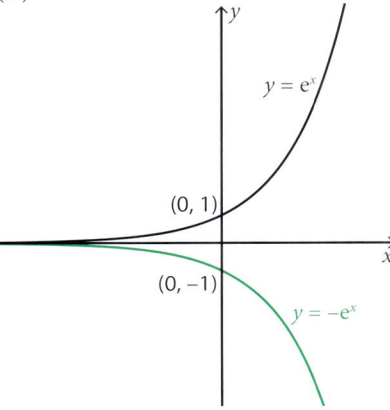

Reflection in x-axis.

(e)

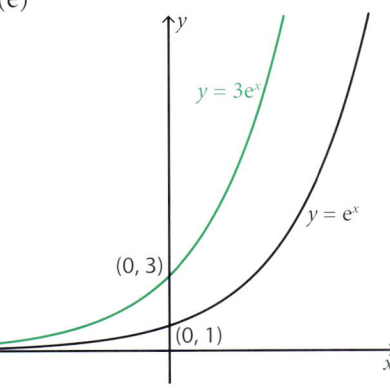

Stretch factor 3 parallel to y-axis.

(f)

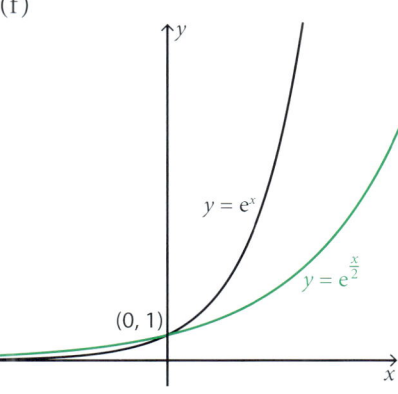

Stretch scale factor 2 parallel to the x-axis.

(g)

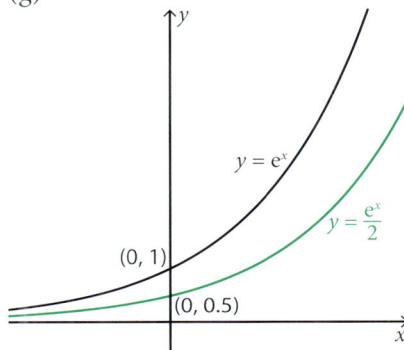

Stretch scale factor ½ parallel to the y-axis.

(h)

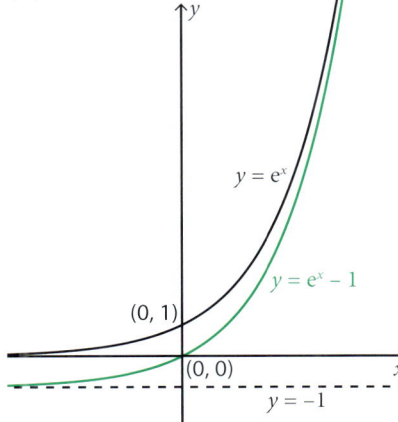

Translation by $\begin{pmatrix} 0 \\ -1 \end{pmatrix}$

9. (a) 2 (b) –1 (c) 3 (d) ½ (e) ½ (f) 1

10. (a)

x	−3	−2	−1	0	1	2	3
y	20.14	7.52	3.09	2.00	3.09	7.52	20.14

(b)

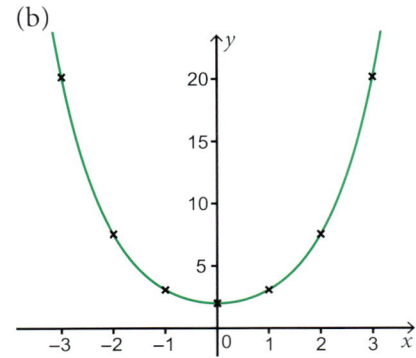

Exercise 10C

1. (a) 0 (b) 3 (c) 4 (d) 3 (e) 2 (f) –4
   (g) –2 (h) ½ (i) ⅓ (j) ½
2. (a) 2.65 (b) 2.01 (c) 0.431
   (d) 0.903 (e) 2.10 (f) 0.631
3. (a) $\log_{10} 100 = 2$
   (b) $\log_5 0.008 = -3$
   (c) $\log_4 \dfrac{1}{4} = -1$
   (d) $\log_9 1 = 0$
   (e) $\log_2 4 = 2$
   (f) $\log_8 8 = 1$
   (g) $\log_6 7776 = 5$
   (h) $\log_7 282475249 = 10$
   (i) $\log_{10} 10000000 = 7$
   (j) $\log_5 125 = 3$
4. (a) $7^1 = 7$ (b) $4^0 = 1$ (c) $2^7 = 128$
   (d) $2^{-4} = \dfrac{1}{16}$ (e) $6^{-1} = \dfrac{1}{6}$
   (f) $8^2 = 64$ (g) $4^3 = 64$
   (h) $7^4 = 2401$ (i) $5^4 = 625$
   (j) $3^{-10} = \dfrac{1}{59049}$ (k) $2^{7/2} = 8\sqrt{2}$
5. Makes no sense. Base 1 cannot
   be raised to a power to make the
   other number.
6.

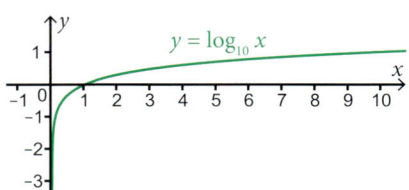

Asymptote at $x = 0$.
Possible observations:
- y is always increasing.
- Gradient of curve always
  positive, but always decreasing.
- Inverse of $y = 10^x$ (mirror image
  in line $y = x$).

Exercise 10D

1. (a) 2.30 (b) 0.993 (c) –2.30
2. 2.71828
3. (a) 1 (b) 2 (c) –1 (d) 2 (e) 8 (f) ½
4. (a) x (b) ab (c) $2x$ (d) x
5. (a)

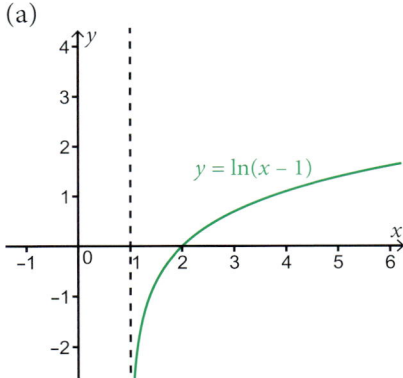

(b)

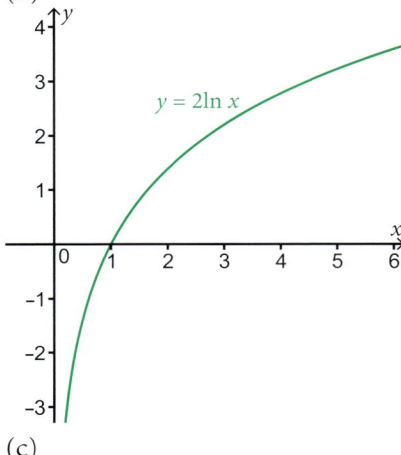

(c)

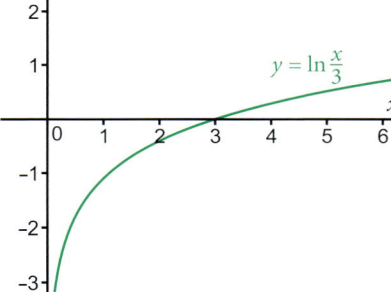

(d)

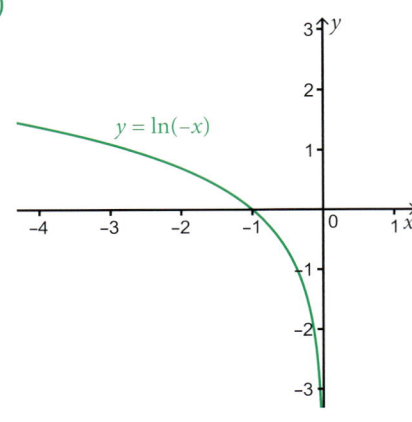

Exercise 10E

1. (a) $3\log_2 10$ (b) 5 (c) $4\log_3 2$
   (d) $3\log_7 3$ (e) –5 (f) $3\log 5$
   (g) $4\log_4 10$ (h) $16\log_2 3$
   (i) $-\log_4 10$ (j) $-3\log_{10} 2$
2. (a) $\log_a 60$ (b) Not possible
   (c) $\log_2 90$ (d) $\log_3 170$
   (e) Not possible (f) $\log_p 36$
   (g) 2 (h) 2
3. (a) $\log_a 15$ (b) Not possible
   (c) $\log_2 3$ (d) $\log_3 10$
   (e) Not possible (f) $\log_q 12$
   (g) $2\log 2$ (h) $\log_6 \left(\dfrac{11}{4}\right)$
4. (a) $\log_2 63$ (b) $\log_5 80$ (c) $\log\left(\dfrac{3}{2}\right)$
   (d) 1 (e) $\log_3 72$ (f) 2 (g) 3
   (h) $\log\left(\dfrac{a^5 b^2}{c^4}\right)$ (i) $\ln(a^6 b^4 c^2)$
   (j) $x^2 y^3$
5. (a) $\log a + \log b + \log c$
   (b) $\log a + \log b - \log c$
   (c) $2\log a + \log b + \log c$
   (d) $2\log a + \dfrac{1}{2}\log b + \dfrac{1}{2}\log c$
   (e) $\dfrac{1}{3}\log a - \dfrac{1}{2}\log b$
   (f) $1 + \log_5 a + \log_5 b$
   (g) $2\log_2 a - 2\log_2 c - 5$
   (h) $3 + 3\log_3 b$
6. (a) $\log(x^6 y^2)$
   (b) $\log\left(\dfrac{p^3}{q^3}\right)$ (c) $\log\left(\dfrac{a^7 b^6}{c^4}\right)$
7. (a) 3 (b) (i) $3 + a$ (ii) $2a - 1$
8. (a) $\dfrac{p}{4}$ (b) $\dfrac{3p}{4} + 1$
9. $\log_a 891$

Exercise 10F

1. (a) 3 (b) –1 (c) 9 (d) –½ (e) 0
   (f) 1.13 (g) 6.60 (h) 1.86 (i) 2.24
   (j) ⁵⁄₃
2. (a) 1.95 (b) 3.91 (c) 1.5 (d) 2.18
   (e) –1 (f) –0.232 (g) 1.46 (h) 1.83
   (i) 1 (j) 6.64
3. (a) 9.909 (b) 2.593 (c) –2.342
   (d) –1.390 (e) –0.513 (f) –0.818
   (g) –1.257 (h) 2.269 (i) –0.735
   (j) –0.192
4. (a) $x = 1.10$ (b) $x = 2.37$
   (c) $x = -1.39$ (d) $t = 0.916$
   (e) $x = 7.39$ (f) $x = 2$ (g) $y = 1$
   (Note: $y = -½$ is not a valid
   solution since $\ln(-½)$ is not
   defined.)
5. (a) $x = 0, 0.693$
   (b) $x = 1.10$ (c) $x = 1$
6. $x = \dfrac{2}{e^3 - 1}$
7. $(0, 1)$
8. (a) $4 + a$ (b) $4a - 1$ (c) $x = e^{3/2}$
9. (a) 3 (b) 9 (c) 2 (d) 4 (e) 4 (f) 2
   (g) 10 (h) 2 (i) 2 (j) 10
10. 1.5
11. (a) $5 + a$ (b) $2a - 1$ (c) $32\sqrt{2}$
12. $x = 2$; No, only if both bases can
   be written as a power of the same
   number (e.g. 8 and 2 are both
   powers of 2).
13. (b) 2.46
14. 12
15. $x = 1$
16. 36 years (rounded up)
17. 4

Exercise 10G

1. (a) $x < 4.91$ (b) $x > -2.51$
   (c) $x > 27.6$ (d) $x < -1.66$
   (e) $x \geq 3.11$ (f) $x < 11.4$
   (g) $x \leq 3$ (h) $x < 0$
   (i) $x \leq -1.58$ (j) $x < -3.42$
2. (a) $x \geq -11.425$ (b) $x > \dfrac{2}{3}$
   (c) $x < 0.580$ (d) $x \leq -6.17$
3. (a) $0.565 < x < 1.58$
   (b) $-0.860 < x < 0.140$
   (c) $1.26 < x < 2$
   (d) $-1 < x < 0$
4. 7

Exercise 10H

1. (a) £2063 (b) 11 years
2. (a) $t = 3, D = \dfrac{3}{4}D_0 \therefore \dfrac{3}{4}D_0 = D_0 e^{-3k}$

   $\Rightarrow \dfrac{3}{4} = e^{-3k} \Rightarrow \ln\dfrac{3}{4} = -3k$

   $\Rightarrow k = -\dfrac{1}{3}\ln\dfrac{3}{4} \approx 0.0959$

   (b) 7.23 hours (3 s.f.)
   (c) 10.0% (3 s.f.)
3. (a) 0.173 (b) 9 hours, 17 mins
   (c) 6.4×10^{10} m (d)

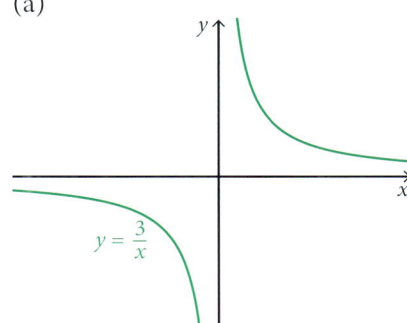

   (e) No, the expansion will slow
   down and stop before then.
4. (a) $D = D_0 e^{-at}$ (b) 0.035
   (c) 27.6 °C (d) 32 minutes (e)

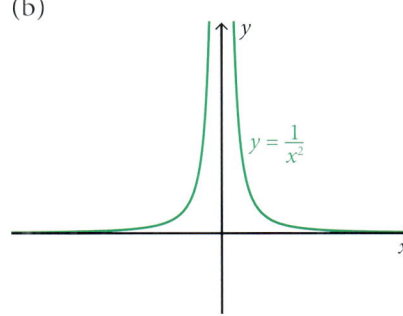

5. (b) 2200 (c) 7 days
6. (a)

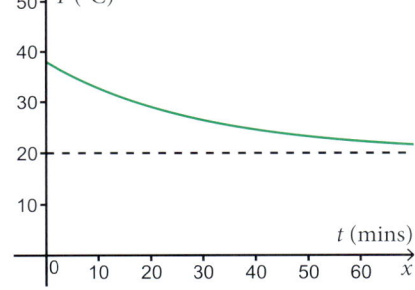

   (b) Initially, P_1 is 0 and P_2 is
   5000. However, in the long
   term P_1 approaches 2000 and P_2
   approaches 0, i.e. this species
   becomes extinct.
   (c) The model is unrealistic in
   that P_1 is initially 0. There must
   be a certain positive number of
   deer for them to breed and for the
   population to expand.
7. (a) 1.1407 (b) 8

Exercise 11A

1. (a) $-x$ (b) $x^2 + 2x - 4$ (c) $2x^2 + 2$
   (d) $-x^3 + x^2 - x + 1$
   (e) $4x^2 - 4x$ or $4x(x - 1)$
2. (a) x^3 (b) $x^{1/2}$ (c) $x^{-5/2}$ (d) x^{-1}
   (e) x^0 or 1
3. (a) $1 - x + x^2 - x^3$ (b) $x^{-4} + x^{-1}$
   (c) $4x^3 - 3x^2 - x$
   (d) $2x^{3/2} + 5x^{-5/2}$ (e) $x^{-2} - 1$
4. (a)

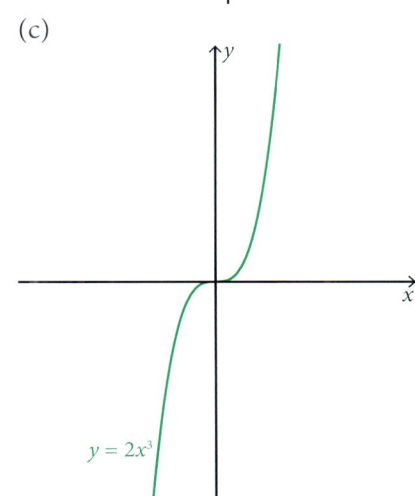

   (b)

   (c)

(d)

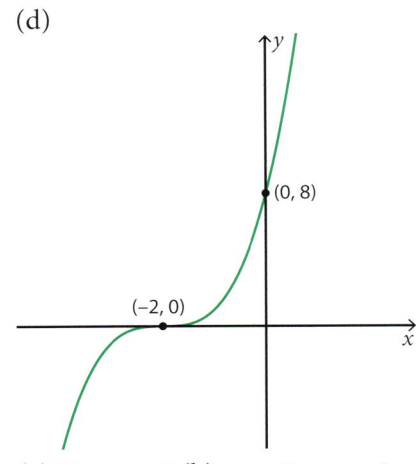

5. (a) $-1 < x < 3$ (b) $x < -9$ or $x > 0$
(c) $x < -1$ or $x > \frac{1}{2}$
(d) $-3 < x < 3$

Exercise 11B

1.

x_1	y_1	m
2	8	7
1.1	1.331	3.31
1.01	1.030301	3.0301
1.001	1.003003001	3.003001

Gradient = 3

2.

x_1	y_1	m
3	2	3
2.1	−0.79	2.1
2.01	−0.9799	2.01
2.001	−0.997999	2.001

Gradient = 2

Exercise 11C

1. (a) $\frac{dy}{dx} = 6x$ (b) $\frac{dy}{dx} = 2$
(c) $\frac{dy}{dx} = -7$ (d) $\frac{dy}{dx} = 10x^4$
(e) $\frac{dy}{dx} = 3x^6$ (f) $\frac{dy}{dx} = -6x^2$
(g) $\frac{dy}{dx} = -\frac{5}{4}$ (h) $\frac{dy}{dx} = -x^{-4}$

2. (a) $\frac{dy}{dx} = -x^{-2}$ (b) $\frac{dy}{dx} = \frac{1}{2}x^{-\frac{1}{2}}$
(c) $\frac{dy}{dx} = -\frac{1}{2}x^{-\frac{3}{2}}$ (d) $\frac{dy}{dx} = \frac{3}{2}x^{\frac{1}{2}}$
(e) $\frac{dy}{dx} = -\frac{3}{2}x^{-\frac{5}{2}}$ (f) $\frac{dy}{dx} = 4x^{-3}$
(g) $\frac{dy}{dx} = -x^{-\frac{5}{2}}$ (h) $\frac{dy}{dx} = x^{-\frac{4}{3}}$

3. (a) 3 (b) 4 (c) −0.25 (d) 0.25
(e) −0.25 (f) 1 (g) $-\frac{5}{64}$ (h) −0.5

4. (a) $\frac{dy}{dx} = 2x$ (b) $\frac{dy}{dx} \to \infty$
(c) $\frac{dy}{dx} \to -\infty$

5. (a) $\frac{dy}{dx} = 3x^2$ (b) $\frac{dy}{dx} \to \infty$
(c) $\frac{dy}{dx} \to \infty$
(d) The gradient of $y = x^2$ is negative when x is negative, whereas the gradient of $y = x^3$ is positive when x is negative.

Exercise 11D

1. (a) $\frac{dy}{dx} = 6x + 4$ (b) $\frac{dy}{dx} = 12x^3 - 1$
(c) $\frac{dy}{dx} = -x^{-2} - 8x^{-3}$
(d) $\frac{dy}{dx} = \frac{1}{3} + \frac{x}{2}$ (e) $\frac{dy}{dx} = 2x - 4$
(f) $\frac{dy}{dx} = 3x^2 + 6x$
(g) $\frac{dy}{dx} = 4x^3 - 3x^2 + 2x$
(h) $\frac{dy}{dx} = 4x^3$ (i) $\frac{dy}{dx} = \frac{1}{2}x^{-\frac{1}{2}} + 3$
(j) $\frac{dy}{dx} = -x^{-2} + \frac{1}{2}x^{-\frac{3}{2}}$
(k) $\frac{dy}{dx} = 3x^{\frac{1}{2}} - \frac{1}{2}x^{-\frac{1}{2}}$
(l) $\frac{dy}{dx} = -\frac{1}{2}x^{-\frac{3}{2}} - \frac{3}{2}x^{\frac{1}{2}}$

2. (a) $\frac{dy}{dt} = 8t + 3$
(b) $\frac{dP}{dv} = 2v + v^{-2}$ (c) $\frac{dv}{dt} = 10$
(d) $\frac{ds}{dt} = 1 + 10t$ (e) $\frac{dp}{dq} = q^{-2}$
(f) $\frac{dW}{dx} = \frac{5}{2}x^{\frac{3}{2}} - \frac{1}{2}x^{-\frac{1}{2}}$
(g) $\frac{dA}{ds} = -4s + 3$
(h) $\frac{dz}{d\theta} = 1 + \theta^{-2}$
(i) $\frac{dm}{dn} = 9n^2 - 4n + 3$
(j) $\frac{dA}{dr} = 2\pi r$

3. (a) $f'(x) = -4x$
(b) $f'(x) = -x^{-2}$
(c) $f'(x) = 8x - 1$
(d) $f'(x) = 1 - 2x^{-2}$

(e) $f'(x) = 1 - 4x^{-2}$
(f) $f'(x) = -\frac{1}{2}x^{-\frac{3}{2}}$
(g) $f'(x) = 4x - 5$
(h) $f'(x) = 6x^2 - 2x$
(i) $f'(x) = \frac{1}{2}x^{-\frac{1}{2}} + \frac{3}{2}x^{\frac{1}{2}} + 1$
(j) $f'(x) = \frac{2px + q}{r}$

4. (a) $f'(x) = 3$ (b) $g'(x) = 2x$
(c) $f'(x)g'(x) = 6x$
(d) $\frac{f'(x)}{g'(x)} = \frac{3}{2x}$
(e) $h(x) = 3x^3 + 2x^2$
(f) $h'(x) = 9x^2 + 4x$ (g) No
(h) $j(x) = 3x^{-1} + 2x^{-2}$
(i) $j'(x) = -3x^{-2} - 4x^{-3}$ (j) No

5. (a) x^2 (b) $2x - 1$ (c) $9x^2$ (d) $-\frac{10}{x^3}$
(e) $10x$

Exercise 11E

1. (a) $\frac{dy}{dx} = 4x$ (b) $\frac{dF}{dp} = 4p^3 - \frac{1}{p^2}$
(c) $\frac{dA}{dr} = 5r + \frac{7}{2}$
(d) $\frac{db}{dc} = -\frac{3}{2}c^{-\frac{5}{2}} - c^{-2}$
(e) $\frac{dx}{dy} = -10y^{-3}$

2. (a) $\frac{dy}{dx} = 2$ (b) $\frac{dy}{dx} = 12$ (c) $\frac{dy}{dx} = 9$
(d) $\frac{dy}{dx} = \frac{1}{2}$ (e) $\frac{dy}{dx} = -6$

3. $\frac{dV}{dp} = 6p - 4p^{-2}$.

When $p = 2$, $\frac{dV}{dp} = 11$.

4. (a) $A = 4\pi r^2$ (b) $\frac{dA}{dr} = 8\pi r$
(c) $\frac{dA}{dr} = 16\pi$

5. 124 m s^{-1}

6. (a) $\frac{dc}{ds} = 2 + \frac{1}{3}s^{-\frac{2}{3}}$ (b) $\frac{1}{8}$

7. 45 metres

8. (a) $\frac{db}{dq} = 3 + q^{-\frac{3}{2}}$ (b) $\frac{1}{4}$

Exercise 11F

1. (a) $\dfrac{dy}{dx} = 2x$ (b) 2 (c) $y = 2x - 1$
2. $y = 16x - 29$
3. $y = -8x - 11$
4. $16y + x - 66 = 0$
5. (a) Gradients at A and B are both -3 (b) $3y - x + 10 = 0$
6. (b) $y = 3x + 5$
7. 68
8. (a) $4, -4$
9. 23
10. (a) Gradients at A and B are both 8 (b) $8y + x - 34 = 0$

Exercise 11G

1. $(-1, 1)$
2. (a) $\dfrac{dy}{dx} = \dfrac{2}{x^3}$ (b) $(2, -\frac14)$
3. (a) $(4, 4)$ (b) $(9, 6)$
4. (a) $(1, 4)$ (b) $(0.25, 8)$
5. $-1, 5$
6. (a) $\dfrac{dy}{dx} = 6 + 6x^2$
   (b) $(1, 8), (-1, -8)$
7. 4 and -4
8. $(\frac12, 2), (-\frac12, -2)$
9. $(2, -^{34}\!/_3), (6, -70)$
10. (a) $\dfrac{dy}{dx} = 12x^2 - 84x + 125$ (b) 5
    (c) $y = 5x + 116$
11. (a) 45 cm² (b) 25 seconds
    (c) 81 seconds

Exercise 11H

1. (a) $(0, 2)$ (b) $(-2, -4)$ (c) $(4, 16)$
   (d) $(1, 1), (-1, 5)$ (e) $(-2.5, -6.25)$
   (f) $(5, -50)$ (g) $(2, -2)$ (h) $(5, 51)$
   (i) $(2, -63), (3, -64)$
   (j) $\left(\dfrac{\sqrt3}{3}, \dfrac{-2\sqrt3}{9}\right), \left(\dfrac{-\sqrt3}{3}, \dfrac{2\sqrt3}{9}\right)$
   (k) $(1, -1)$
2. $(6, -61), (2, 3)$
3. $(2, -16)$
4. (a) $\dfrac{dy}{dx} = 18x - 12x^2$
   (b) $(0, 2), (1.5, 8.75)$
5. (b) $f'(x) = 1 + 8x^{-2} - 48x^{-4}$
6. (a) $f'(x) = {}^{40}\!/_3x^{-\frac13} - \frac53x^{\frac23}$
   (b) $(8, 48)$
7. -18
8. (a) $\dfrac{dy}{dx} = 2px - q$ (b) $p = 3, q = 24$

9. $b = 3, c = 3$

Exercise 11I

1. (a) $f'(x) = 4x; f''(x) = 4$
   (b) $f'(x) = x^3 + x^2;$
   $f''(x) = 3x^2 + 2x$
   (c) $f'(x) = 1 - \dfrac{1}{x^2}; f''(x) = \dfrac{2}{x^3}$
   (d) $f'(x) = \dfrac12; f''(x) = 0$
   (e) $f'(x) = \dfrac{3}{2\sqrt{x}}; f''(x) = -\frac34 x^{-\frac32}$
   (f) $f'(x) = -\frac32 x^{-\frac12}; f''(x) = \frac94 x^{-\frac52}$
   (g) $f'(x) = 12x^5 + 12x^{-7};$
   $f''(x) = 60x^4 - 84x^{-8}$
   (h) $f'(x) = -4x + 1; f''(x) = -4$
   (i) $f'(x) = 1 - 3x^2; f''(x) = -6x$
   (j) $f'(x) = 1; f''(x) = 0$
2. (a) $\dfrac{dy}{dx} = -1; \dfrac{d^2y}{dx^2} = 1$
   (b) $\dfrac{dy}{dx} = 4; \dfrac{d^2y}{dx^2} = -12$
   (c) $\dfrac{dy}{dx} = 5; \dfrac{d^2y}{dx^2} = 0$
   (d) $\dfrac{dy}{dx} = -\dfrac12; \dfrac{d^2y}{dx^2} = -1$
   (e) $\dfrac{dy}{dx} = -7; \dfrac{d^2y}{dx^2} = 12$
3. (a) $\dfrac{dy}{dx} = 2; \dfrac{d^2y}{dx^2} = 4$
   (b) $\dfrac{dy}{dx} = \dfrac32; \dfrac{d^2y}{dx^2} = -\dfrac34$
   (c) $\dfrac{dy}{dx} = 0; \dfrac{d^2y}{dx^2} = \dfrac32$
   (d) $\dfrac{dy}{dx} = -2; \dfrac{d^2y}{dx^2} = 3$
   (e) $\dfrac{dy}{dx} = \dfrac52 c; \dfrac{d^2y}{dx^2} = 0$
4. Minimum $(6, -63);$ maximum $(2, 1)$
5. Minimum $(3, -36)$
6. $\dfrac{dy}{dx} = -8x + \dfrac{1}{x^2};$ maximum at $\left(\dfrac12, -3\right)$.
8. (a) $\dfrac{dy}{dx} = 6x^2 - 10x - 4$ (b) $-\dfrac13, 2$
   (c) $\dfrac{d^2y}{dx^2} = 12x - 10$
   (d) Maximum at $x = -\frac13;$ minimum at $x = 2$.
9. Minimum $(0, 3);$ maximum $(2, 15)$.

10. (a) 4 (b) Minimum at $x = 1;$ maximum at $x = -^4\!/_3$. (c) 4
11. (a) $f'(x) = 1 + 12x^{-2} - 108x^{-4}$
    (b) Minimum
12. Maximum at $(-0.775, 0.186);$ point of inflection at $(0, 0);$ minimum at $(0.775, -0.186)$.
13. (a) $\dfrac{dy}{dx} = 12x^3 - 24x^2$
    (b) Point of inflection at $(0, 0);$ minimum at $(2, -16)$.
14. (a) $k = 4$ (b) Minimum at $(1, -27)$, maximum at $\left(-\dfrac43, \dfrac{100}{9}\right)$.

Exercise 11J

1. (a) 3 s (b) 45 m
2. (a) 1 s (b) 3 m s⁻²
3. 2
4. (a) 50 km h⁻¹ (b) $\dfrac{d^2C}{dv^2} = 2000v^{-3}$
   (c) £40
5. (a) 5 m s⁻¹ (b) $\dfrac{d^2F}{dv^2} = 4v^{-3} + \dfrac{2}{125},$ always positive for $v > 0.5$.
   (c) 0.6 N
6. (a) $h = \dfrac{300}{\pi r^2}$ (b) $r = \sqrt[3]{\dfrac{100}{\pi}}$
7. (a) $l = 200 - \pi r$
   (b) $A = 400r - 2\pi r^2$
   (c) $r = \dfrac{100}{\pi}$ (d) $\dfrac{d^2A}{dr^2} = -4\pi$
   (e) $r = \dfrac{200}{\pi}; l = 0;$ circular
8. (a) $h = \dfrac{500}{x^2}$ (b) $x = 10; h = 5;$ cost $= £3000$
9. (b) $0 < x < 1$ cm (c) $x = \dfrac{5 - \sqrt7}{6}$
   (d) $\dfrac{d^2V}{dx^2} = -4\sqrt7$
10. (c) $\dfrac{d^2A}{dx^2} = -(100 + 25\pi)$
    (d) $A = \dfrac{200}{4 + \pi}$

Exercise 11K

1. (a) Gradient 12; Increasing
   (b) Gradient -12; Decreasing
   (c) Gradient 3; Increasing
   (d) Gradient -3; Decreasing
   (e) Gradient -2; Decreasing
   (f) Gradient 8; Increasing

(g) Gradient 3; Increasing
(h) Gradient 5; Increasing
(i) Gradient –½; Decreasing
(j) Gradient 1; Increasing
(k) Gradient ½; Increasing
(l) Gradient –⁵⁄₂; Decreasing

2. (a) Decreasing for $x < -1$;
Increasing for $x > -1$.
(b) Increasing for $x < -1$;
Decreasing for $-1 < x < 1$;
Increasing for $x > 1$
(c) Increasing for all values of x
(d) Decreasing for all values of x
(e) Decreasing for $x < -½$;
Increasing for $x > -½$
(f) Decreasing for $x < ½$;
Increasing for $x > ½$
(g) Decreasing for $0 < x < 4$;
Increasing for $x > 4$

5. Always decreasing.

6. $0 < x < ⁸⁄₃$

7. (a) $(1, -32)$, $(4, -59)$
(b) Decreasing for $1 < x < 4$

8. $x > 1$

9. (a) Minimum at $(0, 3)$, maximum
at $(⅔, ¹³⁄₃)$ (b) Increasing for
$0 < x < ⅔$

10. (a) $\dfrac{dy}{dx} = 8x^3 - 12x^2$ (b) $x > \dfrac{3}{2}$

Exercise 12A

1. (a) $x^2 + x$ (b) $x^4 + 2x^3 - x^2$
(c) $x^2 - 4x + 3$ (d) $6x^2 - x - 2$
(e) $x^4 - 1$ (f) $x^3 + 6x^2 + 12x + 8$

2. (a) a^5 (b) b^{-1} (c) c^6 (d) d^9

3. (a) $e^{\frac{3}{2}}$ (b) $f^{-\frac{1}{2}}$ (c) $g^{\frac{4}{3}}$ (d) h

4. (a) $\dfrac{dy}{dx} = 2x$

(b) $\dfrac{dy}{dx} = -3x^2 + 8x - 2$

(c) $\dfrac{dy}{dx} = -2x^{-3} + x^{-2}$

(d) $\dfrac{dy}{dx} = 5x^{\frac{3}{2}} - \dfrac{1}{2}x^{-\frac{1}{2}}$

(e) $\dfrac{dy}{dx} = 2x - 4$

Exercise 12B

1. (a) $y = 3x^2 + c$ (b) $y = \dfrac{1}{7}x^7 + c$

(c) $y = x^2 + c$ (d) $y = -\dfrac{1}{3}x^3 + c$

(e) $y = -x^4 + c$ (f) $y = x^6 + c$

(g) $y = x^3 + c$ (h) $y = \dfrac{1}{2}x^{100} + c$

(i) $y = \dfrac{5}{4}x^8 + c$ (j) $y = 3x^4 + c$

(k) $y = -3x^3 + c$

2. (a) $y = -x^{-3} + c$
(b) $y = 2x^{-1} + c$

(c) $y = -\dfrac{1}{9}x^{-3} + c$

(d) $y = x^{\frac{4}{3}} + c$
(e) $y = -ax^{-1} + c$

(f) $y = -\dfrac{1}{2}x^{-14} + c$

(g) $y = 2x^{\frac{7}{2}} + c$
(h) $y = x^{-1\frac{1}{5}} + c$
(i) $y = 72x^{-\frac{1}{8}} + c$

3. (a) $y = \dfrac{2}{3}x^{\frac{3}{2}} + c$

(b) $y = \dfrac{2}{5}x^{\frac{5}{2}} + c$

(c) $y = -\dfrac{1}{2}x^{-2} + c$

(d) $y = \dfrac{1}{3}x^3 + c$

(e) $y = \dfrac{1}{2}x^2 + c$

(f) $y = 2x^{\frac{1}{2}} + c$

(g) $y = \dfrac{16}{5}x^5 + c$

(h) $y = -x^{-1} + c$

(i) $y = \dfrac{1}{16}x + c$

(j) $y = -\dfrac{1}{6}x^{-6} + c$

4. Examples: (a) $y = x^2$
(b) $y = x^2 + 2$ (c) $y = x^2 - 2$

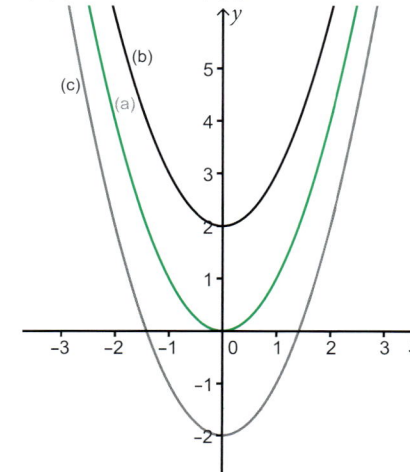

Exercise 12C

1. (a) $2x^2 + c$ (b) $\dfrac{1}{6}x^6 + c$

(c) $-\dfrac{1}{4}x^4 + c$ (d) $-x^3 + c$

(e) $5x + c$ (f) $\dfrac{3}{4}x^4 + c$

(g) $2x^{50} + c$ (h) $\dfrac{5}{3}x^6 + c$

(i) $-2x^6 + c$ (j) $\dfrac{3}{2}x^6 + c$

2. (a) $-x^{-4} + c$ (b) $4t^{-1} + c$

(c) $\dfrac{1}{16}x^{-4} + c$ (d) $\dfrac{1}{2}y^{\frac{5}{4}} + c$

(e) $-\dfrac{b}{2}x^{-2} + c$

3. (a) $y = z^{-\frac{9}{4}} + c$

(b) $y = \dfrac{1}{2}x^{-16} + c$

(c) $r = \dfrac{4}{3}\theta^{\frac{9}{2}} + c$

(d) $s = 10x^{-\frac{1}{10}} + c$

4. (a) $y = \dfrac{2}{3}y^{\frac{3}{2}} + c$ (b) $y = \dfrac{1}{2}x^{-2} + c$

(c) $y = \dfrac{1}{8}s + c$ (d) $y = \dfrac{1}{5}x^5 + c$

5. (a) $y = p + c$ (b) $z = \dfrac{2}{7}x^{\frac{7}{2}} + c$

(c) $p = -\dfrac{16}{3}z^{-3} + c$

(d) $y = 8x^{\frac{1}{2}} + c$ (e) $s = \dfrac{4}{3}t^3 + c$

(f) $I = -\dfrac{1}{6}x^{-6} + c$

Exercise 12D

1. (a) $3x + \dfrac{16}{7}x^{\frac{7}{4}} + c$

(b) $4x + 2x^{\frac{3}{2}} + c$

(c) $\dfrac{8}{3}x^3 + \dfrac{7}{2}x^2 + c$

(d) $\dfrac{2}{5}x^5 + \dfrac{3}{2}x^2 + c$

(e) $\dfrac{3}{2}x^4 + 2x^2 + c$

(f) $4x - 3x^{-1} + c$

(g) $2x^2 - \dfrac{1}{3}x^3 + c$

(h) $\dfrac{9}{2}x^2 - \dfrac{1}{3}x^3 + c$

(i) $-\dfrac{x^{-6}}{6} + \dfrac{8}{3}x^{\frac{3}{2}} + c$

(j) $-\dfrac{x^{-3}}{3} + 4x^{\frac{3}{2}} + c$